Lakotas, Black Robes, and Holy Women

Lakotas, Black Robes, and Holy Women

German Reports from the Indian Missions
in South Dakota, 1886–1900

Rothäute, Schwarzröcke und heilige Frauen

Deutsche Berichte aus den Indianer-Missionen
in South Dakota, 1886–1900

EDITED BY
Karl Markus Kreis

TRANSLATED BY
Corinna Dally-Starna

INTRODUCTION BY
Raymond A. Bucko

University of Nebraska Press
Lincoln & London

Library of Congress Cataloging-in-Publication Data
Kreis, Karl Markus.
[Rothäute, Schwarzröcke und heilige Frauen. English]
Lakotas, black robes, and holy women : German
reports from the Indian missions in South Dakota,
1886–1900 / [compiled and] edited by Karl Markus
Kreis ; translated by Corinna Dally-Starna ;
introduction by Raymond A. Bucko.
p. cm.
Includes bibliographical references and index.
ISBN 978-0-8032-2761-3 (cloth : alk. paper)
 1. Dakota Indians—Missions. 2. Dakota Indians—
History—Sources. 3. Jesuits—Missions—South
Dakota—History—Sources. 4. Sisters of St. Francis
of Penance and Christian Charity—Missions—South
Dakota—History—Sources. 5. South Dakota—
History—Sources. I. Title.
E99.D1K7413 2007
266′.2783089975243—dc22
2007010476

Contents

Illustrations

Preface

Encounter on the Prairie

25 March 1886. Toward evening on the prairie of the Dakota Territory. Among the tepees and huts of the Sioux village Owl Feather War Bonnet, a green, two-story building with three crosses on its roof. Outside, in the cold of late winter, a party of Indians is awaiting the wagon that is to bring the "Holy Women" from the train station a day's drive away. At last it arrives. Emerging from the wagon are seven persons, dressed in long black robes: four priests in soutanes and three nuns in black habits, with black and white head coverings tightly framing their faces. "Black Robes," like these four men, were a familiar sight to the Indians. The previous year two others had built the schoolhouse in front of which this encounter was now taking place; one of the arrivals had lived and worked in this building since the beginning of that year. Yet the sisters, as one of them later reports, attract curious looks with their peculiar dress, just as they, in turn, are fascinated by the "costuming of these children of the wilderness" [quote translated from the German]. The official welcoming occurs the next morning. About twenty Indians appear, the peace pipe is passed round, and three chiefs deliver welcoming speeches that an interpreter translates into English. Finally, and this is at the heart of the entire affair, it is agreed that on the very next day all of the Indians who desire to do so will be permitted to bring their children to this school, for whose founding these sisters had come to this faraway place (doc. 2.1).

This was the beginning of the St. Francis Mission school on the Rosebud Reservation of the Sioux (Lakota) Indians in South Dakota. Two years later the same religious orders, the Jesuits and the Franciscan sisters, established Holy Rosary Mission on the neighboring Pine Ridge Reservation of the Sioux. Soon after, the mission schools were directly affected by the last armed conflict between the Lakotas and the United States Army. Father Johann Jutz and Sister Kostka Schlaghecken, the founders of St. Francis and now superior and mother superior at Holy Rosary, held out at their mission post, even after the massacre at Wounded Knee Creek when the

fighting between the desperate Lakotas and the army moved to the immediate surroundings of the mission, and the Indians approached, "yet not to
kill us, but to get something to eat" (doc. 2.7, section 4).

The fathers and the sisters regularly reported on their experiences and
adventures to their fellow brothers and sisters, as well as to a wider readership. Given that both of these religious orders were at home in the German-speaking countries of Europe (see appendix for mission personnel
and their countries of origin), most of these accounts were written in German and then circulated throughout their homelands. Hence they continue to give German readers of today direct insight into how these people
from the Rhineland, Westfalia, Bavaria, Vorarlberg (Austria), and other
places labored to plant in the minds of the Lakotas their notions of Christian faith and life. However, for American readers and historians, these accounts are of much greater significance yet: they constitute unique sources
for the years of the founding and construction of the Catholic missions at
Rosebud and Pine Ridge, providing authentic testimony of the personal attitudes and first experiences of the missionaries in a way that was rarely expressed in later years. Of interest are not only the vivid descriptions of the
missionary efforts in and outside the mission schools, the goal of which
was to lead the "poor redskins" from out of the "darkness of paganism"
into the light of Christian faith and American civilization. The accounts of
the sisters and fathers, particularly in reference to the "Ghost Dance troubles," are also valuable testimonials of their assessment of the Lakotas'
situation on the reservations at the time, as well as critical commentaries
of the government's policies.

The Accounts

This work consists of German-language texts that were authored by the
Franciscan sisters and the Jesuits stationed at the missions, as well as contemporary church publications that were directly based on such firsthand
accounts. The selection presented here is limited to documents covering
the years from the founding of the first mission at Rosebud (1886) to the
end of the nineteenth century. There are several reasons for drawing a line
at this point: By this time the missions and their schools were firmly established on the reservations, and the initial phase of their founding, with

its particular circumstances and experiences, could be viewed as closed. Moreover, the political and legal framework underlying the missionary effort had undergone dramatic change by the year 1900. The status of "contract schools" (government-financed church-run schools), which had been applied during the early years, was forever terminated by the government. Not only did this require a shift in the financing of the schools, but it also prompted new political and public relations activities on the part of the Catholic Church in its administration of the missions. The founding of the journal *Indian Sentinel* in the year 1902, through the Bureau of Catholic Indian Missions in Washington DC, is one example of these efforts.

The journal began reporting on the Indian missions, including those among the Lakotas. It is considered to be the most important source on this subject. Thus it seemed appropriate to first make available the German texts for the period prior to the founding of the *Indian Sentinel*, given that there are no comparable American publications in existence. Here it is important to add, however, that the German-language Catholic press continued to report in detail, and on a regular basis, "firsthand" about the missions also after 1902.

The purpose of publishing this collection of documents is to create an awareness of the richness of German-language sources that exist for this period in American history. However, because the exploration of these archival materials is still in its early stages, only a representative selection could be included. The texts presented here are divided into two main groups:

1. The first group of documents is archived by the respective orders of the missions of St. Francis and Holy Rosary, that is, the Franciscan sisters and the Jesuits. It consists mostly of correspondence and reports created for internal use by the orders. This group of sources is represented here by Franciscan texts (section 1 of this collection), specifically, house chronicles and annual reports.

The chronicles of the two missions (documents 1.1–1.4) recount their development since their founding, one in 1886 and the other in 1888. They were, as was common practice with the order, penned by the respective mother superior in the form of house chronicles. Subsequently, they were also typewritten, copied, and apparently distributed in an irregular fashion within the order for the information and edification of fellow sisters in other parts of the world. Consistent with the regulations of the order, these chronicles were written in German and, during the first years, in German script. Later on they were at times brought up-to-date and copied, or entirely new versions were created, also to make them available to a small circle of friends and benefactors outside of the order. This is probably how the typed English translations of the early chronicles, housed in the mission archives of Marquette University, came into existence. Although these English versions occasionally have been used by researchers, they were often edited and are not completely free of copying and translation errors. Thus new translations of the German originals from the collections of the archives at Nonnenwerth/Rhine are presented here.

Distinct from these house chronicles are the extracts from the *Jahresberichte* (Annual Reports) (documents 1.5-1.10), of which printed versions became available starting in 1897. In these the work of the Franciscan sisters, in general, is presented, including their labors at the missions. This was done primarily by reprinting letters from the sisters and fathers at the mission places, and occasionally by using material from the house chronicles.

The archives for the German Jesuit province, to which these missions belonged, now located in Munich, has in its collection significant correspondence about the founding of St. Francis and Holy Rosary. *Mitteilungen aus der Deutschen Provinz* (Reports from the German Province) were printed beginning in 1897 for the order's consumption, regularly featuring the publication of letters from the order's different missions, comparable to the *Jahresberichte* of the Franciscan sisters. However, because of their large number, these sources can be referred to only here and there to complement the introductory chapters.

The images featured in the photo section of this volume are part of the information provided to the Franciscan sisters to be used inside the order. They are all from the archives of their German province in Nonnenwerth/ Rhine. Some of the photographs document the mission work and its successes from the perspective of the missionaries. Others are portraits by the well-known photographer John A. Anderson. Although the photographs and their makers are for the most part known, the comments that the sisters wrote on the images add some unique value.

2. The second, and relatively homogenous, group of texts exists in publications created for a wider audience, that is, for a generally interested pub-

lic outside the order. Examples of these—aside from some publications in newspapers and journals in the homelands of the Jesuits and Franciscan sisters—are primarily articles from the journal *Die katholischen Missionen*, which are found in the second part of this collection (documents 2.1– 2.24). This journal was published by the Jesuits until 1999, appeared every month with *Verlag Herder* (Freiburg/Breisgau), and reported on the Catholic missionizing efforts all over the world, not only of the Jesuits. As a source documenting the work of the Catholic mission orders on every continent, among Catholics as well as among the "pagans," this publication is an inexhaustible treasure trove. Yet these mission reports were also important for the development of the image of the "Indian" among the general public in German-speaking countries; the journal was well respected among educated Catholics and widely distributed.

For this collection of documents, all of the contributions from the years 1886 to 1900 that pertain directly to the missions in South Dakota were selected. Articles that deal with general questions of American school and Indian policy were not included, nor were those that discuss other Indian missions. The printed texts are mostly contributions from the category *Nachrichten* (News), in addition to lead articles that treat the Sioux missions in greater detail (documents 2.7, 2.11, 2.14, 2.23). In these reports from South Dakota, letters from the Franciscan sisters are printed as well, just as the Jesuit Fathers are given a voice in the annual reports of the Franciscans. In short, the reports in *Die katholischen Missionen* and the Franciscan texts supplement each other and must be read and analyzed together. Also, it appears that at times letters were used that were initially written for internal consumption. Given that the original manuscripts do not exist, it can no longer be determined to what extent these letters were edited prior to their publication. The small cross (†) that appears next to names of people in documents 2.21 and 2.23 indicates that these people are deceased.

Acknowledgments

This book would not have been possible without the generous and patient support of the archivists of the order of the Franciscan sisters, who not only made the texts available but also shared much valuable information with me: Ursula Ostermann, O.S.F. (Munster), Hildegardis Schäfer, O.S.F.

(Nonnenwerth/Rhine), and Mary Serbacki, O.S.F. (Stella Niagara NY). Mark Thiel, archivist at Marquette University (Milwaukee, Wisconsin), Dr. Clemens Brodkorb and Markus Pillat, S.J. (Archives of the German Jesuit Province, Munich, formerly Cologne) assisted me with their manifold advice and with the treasures in the collections under their care. Prof. Dr. Christian F. Feest (director, Museum of Ethnology, Vienna), the late John Garvey, S.J. (Canisius College, Buffalo NY), Prof. Dr. Klaus Schatz, S.J. (Graduate School of Philosophy and Theology St. Georgen, Frankfurt/Main) and Ludwig Wiedenmann, S.J. *(Die katholischen Missionen)* gave their valuable comments and assistance in obtaining and analyzing the sources. Finally, this American edition would not have come into being without the commitment and support of Gary Dunham of University of Nebraska Press, and without the encouragement of Dr. William A. Starna (professor emeritus, State University of New York, College at Oneonta). I am indebted to Dr. Raymond A. Bucko, S. J., professor of anthropology at Creighton University, whose excellent introduction places this collection of documents in its historical context. Last, but not least, the crucial part was contributed by Corinna Dally-Starna, who translated these texts from what in many ways is a distant past in such a careful and insightful manner. My own contributions to this volume benefited from her good eye as a reader and her skills as a translator. I thank them all.

Translator's Notes

Corinna Dally-Starna

Various measures have been applied to maintain the linguistic integrity as well as the texture—that is, the pace and "sound"—of the original German document.

Lengthy sentence structures have been largely retained, although in keeping with common rules of English grammar and syntax. Only a few unwieldy sentences have been silently separated to ensure intelligibility. Tense shifts have not been amended.

Personal names and tribal designations have been transcribed as they appear in the original. The exceptions are German versions of Indian personal names. These have been italicized and appear in the German nominative case regardless of that used by the authors. For example, *der kleine Tannenbaum*, or *dem kleinen Tannenbaum* (Little Pine Tree), are both rendered *Kleiner Tannenbaum* to ensure consistency throughout the text. An English translation of the name is furnished in brackets. The names of saints are rendered in their anglicized form.

Geographic references, including the names of the missions and agencies, have been standardized to reflect widely recognizable English language equivalents.

Words that in the original are written in a language other than German have been faithfully transcribed and italicized. However, capitalized English common nouns have been silently reduced to lowercase.

The German words *Wilde* or *Wilden*, and *Wilder*, often translated as "savages" and "savage," are frequently found in German language records of the period. "Savage" is generally applied to a person who is uncivilized, primitive, brutal, or fierce. *Wilder* carries similarly complex meanings that range from indicating a "cultureless" state to life in a state of nature in faraway places, more often than not connoting a brutal and dangerous character as well as lack of reason (Grimm and Grimm 1991, 30:16, 58). Also, *Wilder* many times points to the non-Christianized nature of an individual. Because the terms *Wilder* and "savage," and variations thereof, are

not wholly comparable in meaning, and to allow for more nuanced readings within the context of the Jesuit and Franciscan mission records, the
German has been retained throughout.

The appearance of a superscript *d* after a noun marks the use of the diminutive in the German text. This notation permits various interpretations
on the part of the reader given that it is difficult to ascertain whether an author meant to communicate size, youth, affection, familiarity, disdain, or
paternalism with respect to the person or object in question, or a combination of any these qualities. Moreover, where nouns cannot take the English
suffixes -let, -kin, or -et, only adjectives to signal fondness or smallness,
such as, for example, "dear" or "little" could be applied. These limited
choices would render most English translations of the German diminutive unsatisfactory. One example is the term *Rothäutchen*, the diminutive of
"redskin." On occasion, the missionaries refer to the Indian children in
this manner, implying smallness or youth, while at the same time demonstrating their mixed feelings of affection, disdain, and paternalism for
their charges.

Brackets have been used by the editor and translator, as well as by the
editors of the Catholic publications cited herein, to mark insertions in the
text. Those from the Catholic publications are footnoted. The remaining
insertions are by the editor or translator.

My utmost appreciation is due William A. Starna for patiently assisting
me in the preparation of this translation. I thank him for lending his broad
expertise to the translated manuscript in its various stages and proposing
critical changes. Charles T. Gehring, executive director, New Netherland
Institute, provided valuable technical advice and generously shared with
me his extensive experience with translation matters. Markus Kreis cooperated with me throughout the project, offering clarifications where they
were needed. I am sincerely grateful to all three for helping me make this
a better work.

Lakotas, Black Robes, and Holy Women

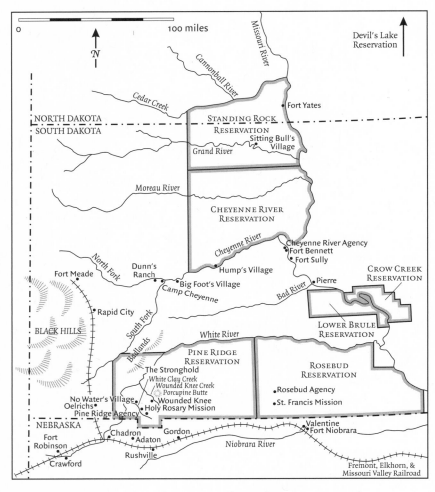

Sioux Reservations, 1890

Introduction

Raymond A. Bucko, S.J.

The Jesuit Relations and Allied Documents are a collection of Jesuit mission documents relating a wealth of information about the Native cultures of New France (northeastern North America) between 1610 and 1791. The documents were originally kept in Jesuit archives scattered in Canada, France, and Rome and were practically inaccessible to scholars in the United States until they were compiled, translated from the original French and Latin under the direction of historian Reuben Gold Thwaites, and published in English between 1896 and 1901 (Thwaites 1896).

The documents were clearly influenced by the cultural and religious assumptions of the missionaries and the Jesuit superiors in Europe who edited them; nevertheless, given our contemporary interest in understanding the cultural worlds of missionaries themselves, as well as the dynamics of cultural contact and transformation, the Relations' scholarly value has only increased since Thwaites's publication.

While Lakotas, Black Robes, and Holy Women: German Reports from the Indian Missions in South Dakota, 1886–1900 is not as ambitious as the Jesuit Relations in depth of time or breadth of documentation, it is equally important for understanding a later period of Catholic mission activity. Karl Markus Kreis's careful selection and Corinna Dally-Starna's fine English translation of a wide range of German documents from the first generation of Franciscan and Jesuit missionaries on the Pine Ridge and Rosebud Reservations in the Dakota Territories, along with Kreis's extensive scholarly introduction, provide a window on the world of these particular Catholic missionaries. Through that window, we glimpse late nineteenth- and early twentieth-century Lakota life as well. Neither the Jesuit Relations nor this collection of German documents were intended to exonerate or implicate the missionaries in the complex and often tragic histories that surrounded them and in which they took part nor to definitely solve many of the contemporary controversies over the missionization of North America. Each set of documents does, however, provide more information and greater nuances for more accurate interpretations of the past and understandings of the present.

Some comparison of the missions to New France and the Dakotas may be helpful. The Sisters of Saint Francis of Penance and Christian Charity, to give the group its full title, trace their inspiration and rules to the ideas of Saint Francis of Assisi in the 1200s; the order was founded in Europe in 1835 by Catherine Damen, primarily as a teaching order. The Society of Jesus, whose members are commonly known as Jesuits, was founded in 1540 by Ignatius of Loyola and his companions; this order of priests and brothers was initially charged with revitalizing Catholic life through missionary work, but within a few years education became its focus. The sisters and Jesuits worked together in Europe before coming to the North America, so each group was known to the other. Also, each of their North American administrative centers were located near each other, the sisters in Stella Niagara and the Jesuits in Buffalo, New York.

Beginning in 1871, many Catholic clerics and religious orders were exiled from Germany by the government of Otto von Bismarck due to political and social conflicts during a period known as the Kulturkampf. Bismarck sought to unify Germany and centralize his power partly through expelling these vocal Catholic opponents. The German Jesuits and Franciscan sisters consequently resettled in Holland. Later, representatives of both orders immigrated to the United States to minister to Roman Catholic German immigrants in New York State. When the Benedictine priest Martin Marty was elevated to the role of bishop and vicar apostolic of Dakota in 1879, he recruited the Jesuits and the Franciscan sisters to join his efforts to establish missions in the Dakota Territory.

In addition to being charged by Bishop Marty with spreading the Gospel to the peoples of the Dakotas, the German Jesuits were required by their general superior in Rome to write annual reports on the state of the missions, just as earlier Jesuits were required to send back reports from New France. The German Jesuits were well aware of the political impact of the New France *Relations*, which had been widely read as entertaining travel literature in Europe, where there was great interest in the customs and beliefs of the "exotic" peoples of the Americas. Focusing on what they judged to be the best and the worst of Indian behavior, seventeenth- and eighteenth-century European Jesuits also used the *Relations* to teach their flocks moral lessons, while refuting the arguments of ideological enemies of Jesuits in Europe—particularly the anti-clerical scholars of the Enlightenment. Thus, the *Relations* gained political and economic support for the Jesuit missions, while encouraging additional European settlement in New France (Library and Archives Canada 2001a, 2001b).

With the value of such documentation demonstrated, the Jesuits and Franciscans of the nineteenth- and early twentieth-century Dakota missions produced similar written works, which also made their way into popular publications in Germany and later in the United States. These stories fired the German imagination, which was already fueled by a very romantic view of Native peoples presented by the wildly popular writings of Karl May, who began publishing his tales in 1875.

The function of the documents generated by the Dakota missionaries closely parallels those of the Jesuits of New France. Each group highlighted the virtues of Native peoples to encourage greater piety and devotion in their own lands. The Jesuits in both eras were not above criticizing the actions of the government, advocating the fair treatment of the Native peoples, a role that was also taken up by the Indian Rights associations of the nineteenth and early twentieth centuries. Like these secular associations, the Dakota Jesuits were never able to step out of their own frame of reference to question the rightness or appropriateness of their own programs of "civilization and Christianization." Native peoples also struggled to establish and maintain their rights and social cohesion throughout this period both on their own and with outsiders as allies.

Neither the Jesuits of New France nor the German Jesuits and Franciscan sisters lived among "pure untouched Natives," but the seventeenth-century missionaries entered the field long before there was extensive contact with Europeans and when Native peoples held political, demographic, and military ascendancy. The Jesuits of that time often traveled with migratory bands of Natives or lived right in Native villages as with the sedentary Huron, whereas nineteenth-century Lakota lives had been more extensively disrupted, and despite their stunning military victory of the Little Big Horn, the larger military and governmental forces of the Americans compelled them to comply with a reservation system that circumscribed their movements and eventually severely limited their land base. The Jesuits of the Dakota Territory did visit Native encampments, but their ministry was highly centralized, with large individual mission stations and schools established north of Pine Ridge and at St. Francis. The Sisters of New France were restricted to the French towns while those of the Dakotas stayed by and large at the central mission itself, dealing primarily with the schoolchildren, their parents, and other Native people who visited the main mission stations. The sisters in the Dakotas did occasionally visit the Native camps as evidenced by their writings and photographs, but their main role was restricted to sustaining the schools and main missions.

The early Jesuit missionaries in New France contemplated and, in many cases, suffered painful deaths at the hands of Native Americans with equanimity because of the spirituality of St. Ignatius Loyola. The cosmological presupposition of Catholicism held that baptism was essential to eternal salvation. Except in danger of death, this ritual was supposed to be performed only for those who were educated in and accepting of the basic tenants of belief of Catholicism. This made the missionaries' efforts to educate Native Americans in Catholic doctrine a matter of supreme religious importance, even in the face of great personal danger. In contrast, the German Jesuits and sisters on Pine Ridge and Rosebud felt comparatively safe and secure, even during the period of the Ghost Dance and Wounded Knee massacre, when they determined not to flee the area.

While the Jesuit missionaries to New France were often among the first Europeans in contact with Native communities, it took a good deal longer to establish missionaries among the Plains Indians, where mobility, tribal warfare, and European rivalries complicated their efforts. As early as 1640 the Jesuits knew of the Dakota (Sioux) people, and Jesuit fathers Claude Allouez and Jacques Marquette unsuccessfully sought permanent contact with them from 1665 until 1674. The Recollect priest Louis Hennepin had more extensive contact with the eastern Dakotas beginning in 1680. The French Jesuits again attempted missions to the Dakotas in the 1720s but failed due to political instability and warfare. Then in 1763, the Society of Jesus was suppressed in the French territories of the New World and was not restored as an order of the Catholic Church until 1814 (Markowitz 2002: 134–77). So it happened that Catholic religious beliefs were initially brought to the Dakota Territory by French fur traders and by Natives from further east, who were migrating west.

The earliest significant effort at evangelization among the Dakotas was that of a French diocesan priest. Father Augustine Ravoux worked among the Minnesota Dakotas in the 1840s, learned their language, and wrote a catechism in the Dakota language. Father Pierre-Jean de Smet achieved more sporadic contact with them between 1839 and his death in 1872 (Markowitz 2002: 151–96). De Smet baptized widely but catechized sparingly. Nevertheless, he became the best known, if largely symbolic, founder of the Jesuit missions in the Dakota Territories.

Bishop Martin Marty had formalized the missions by sending three lay priests to the Lakotas, the western relatives of the Dakotas: Fathers Craft, Hospenthal, and Bushman. Father Craft became especially well known for his colorful—not to say contentious—personality and for his presence at the Wounded Knee massacre (Foley 2002). By 1885 Bishop Marty further consolidated the mission effort by recruiting German Jesuits and Franciscan sisters to the area (Duratschek 1947: 127). In this effort, he had the financial backing of a wealthy Catholic laywoman in Philadelphia. Katharine Drexel used her considerable resources to build and support both St. Francis and Holy Rosary Missions, as well as missions to other Native Americans and to African Americans. Drexel eventually joined the Sisters of Mercy in 1891 and two years later founded a religious order of women, the Sisters of the Blessed Sacrament for Indian and Colored People (127).

During this time, Protestant missionaries were locked in a bitter rivalry with Catholics and were equally active in the Dakota Territories. Congregationalists, led by Gideon and Samuel Pond, established a mission among the Santees in 1834. In 1875 the Episcopal Church, under the auspices of Bishop Hare, sent missionaries to the Lakotas who were being confined by the U.S. Army to the Pine Ridge and Rosebud reservations (Sneve 1977: 58). Interdenominational conflict and corrupt reservation administrative practices became so outrageous that President Ulysses S. Grant established a Peace Policy that sought to end the scandals by assigning each reservation to a specific Christian denomination. Under his policy, Pine Ridge and Rosebud were both assigned to the Episcopalians. The dissolution of the exclusivist provisions of the Grant Peace Policy in 1881 paved the way for the Jesuits and Franciscan sisters to come to Saint Francis and Pine Ridge.

The history of religious sisters' work among Native Americans is less familiar. While groups of religious sisters were involved in the missions of New France, they did not live among the nomadic hunting cultures, rather confining themselves to their own cloistered and carefully regulated way of life amid the growing French population of the region. When Jesuit fathers first attempted to impose a European model for the education of the Native children in New France, Indians resisted their efforts and refused to settle in villages as the Jesuits had wished. Similarly, Lakota children and parents resisted the early Jesuit and Franciscan sisters' efforts to impose restrictive and regulated ways of life on those attending missionary schools on the Lakota missions of Pine Ridge and Rosebud.

In an attempt to explain and illustrate their experiences, garner financial support, and attract other sisters to their work among the Lakotas, the Franciscan sisters wrote house histories, chronologies, and letters and sent photographs back to Germany. These documents—collected and translated and published in the present volume—are not only interesting for their observations of nineteenth-century Lakota life but also give voice to largely anonymous religious women whose lives were previously unknown to scholars outside their own religious order.

In contrast to their brothers in New France, the German Jesuits of Pine Ridge and Rosebud were not fastidious about recording local beliefs and customs. The Jesuits of New France did not closely observe and record Natives simply to enhance the historical record, publicize and raise funds for the mission effort, encourage new recruits and new settlers, or simply entertain curious European readers; the *Relations* were meant to expedite their own understanding of these people for the purpose of successful mission activities and also to serve as a guide for subsequent religious who would work in New France. In this effort, they presumed far greater cultural persistence among the Indians than did the Jesuits of South Dakota, who were far more interested in presenting the success of the missions to the reading public and securing their rights from what they felt was a largely hostile federal government in league with a variety of competing Protestant missions. By the late nineteenth century, cultural evolutionism and social Darwinism had become a dominant European-American ethos, and like most Europeans, the German Jesuits assumed that Native cultures would be eventually replaced by European-defined civilization through a natural and predictable evolutionary progress. The Jesuits in the Dakotas were as dedicated to advancing and accelerating the civilization process as they were to converting the Lakotas to Catholicism.

The first Jesuits began to learn the language and customs of the Lakotas both from their own contact with these Natives and also through the Benedictines who had earlier contact with the Lakota bands to the north. They also began to realize that they would have to adapt to the ways of their hosts to more effectively promulgate their religious and cultural message. In the next generation, Father Eugene Buechel excelled in these efforts and ultimately bemoaned the shift in the third generation away from learning the language and culture and toward an assimilationist agenda. Subsequent generations of Jesuits would again rethink this agenda, particularly in light of their experience that the Lakotas struggled to retain their culture and identity, and would move again toward the methods of their earliest predecessors and Father Buechel.

When reading these documents, it is essential to remember that Jesuits and sisters were and are not a homogeneous hive of identical members, but rather collections of individuals with a variety of habits, attitudes, and peculiarities. In the seventeenth century there were Fathers Jean de Brebeuf, Paul le Jeune, and Jerome Lalemant, each with a particular personality and disposition. In the early Dakota missions there were Fathers Johann Jutz and Emil Perrig, Brother Ursus Nunlist, Sister Rosalia Schulte, and Reverend Mothers Kostka Schlaghecken and Leopoldine Serries. Even today, many Lakotas tell stories—often hilarious—about long-gone Jesuits and sisters, remembering their personalities and the Lakota names given them. It may be difficult to detect the personalities that underlie published texts, but it is an important exercise, as is remembering that Lakota tribes also consist of individuals with a variety of viewpoints. A poem based on the experiences of a young Jesuit scholastic (in training to be ordained) stationed at St. Francis mission between 1966 and 1968 exemplifies this, in a tribute to the individuality of the sisters, foregrounding humor, German roots, and ambivalence on all sides:

Sister Fara Boarding School Cook

Got out of a car
which rolled three times
and ended upside down
in a ditch

the Sioux were obedient
in her kitchen and

ate her sauerkraut
slaws and kuchen

she'd make me sit down
to see her family photographs
from Germany
hollering over my head
at the girls
to peel the potatoes and
stop burning the meat

she could forgive God
for sending her here

and the Indians too
who brought her bittersweet and
yucca from the canyons

—(Janda 1978)

In his collection of poetry *Aboriginal Sin*, Tim Giago writes extensively and quite critically of the Jesuit educational effort but also expresses a fondness for Joseph F. Schlienger, S.J., a Swiss brother who served on the Pine Ridge reservation:

The Garden

Everybody loved Brother Schlienger,
He was called "Slinger" by most of us,
And he had a green, green thumb,
His garden was the mission's delight.

We all remember cabbage, carrots, watermelons,
Onions, turnips, tomatoes, and cucumbers,
Grown with love in "Slinger's garden!"
A temptation to the most righteous.

Everytime I eat a raw cabbage,

> Even today, I think of "Slinger",
> And the stolen treasures we shared,
> From Brother "Slinger's" garden.
>
> —(Giago 1978: 53)

In addition to the more personal and religious elements of *Lakotas, Black Robes, and Holy Women: German Reports from the Indian Missions in South Dakota, 1886–1900*, the documents contain important historical accounts—most dramatically of the Wounded Knee massacre but also of the ordinariness of life on the mission with glimpses, albeit rare, of Lakota customs of the time, as understood and interpreted by the religious. As Karl Markus Kreis mentions, the missionaries were not particularly self-reflective, nor did they struggle with issues of cultural or religious pluralism. They appear, at least in the written record, to have been quite secure in their own religious and cultural paradigms. The early mission documents say little of personal struggles, doubts, loneliness, conflict, or the anxiety of being a foreigner in a country where some groups were hostile to immigrants as well as to the indigenous population. A researcher cannot assume something did not happen simply because no known document mentions such an occurrence; private angst is simply not the stuff of early house histories or pious magazine articles and lay outside of the purposes for which these individuals wrote. The struggles presented in these documents are those of winning over the Lakotas to the faith, combating government funding policy that inhibited the growth of Catholic schools, advancing (in the minds of the missionaries) civilization, molding successful students, and competing with the local Protestant missions.

Nevertheless the missionaries adapted to the Lakotas as the Lakotas adapted to them, and this makes the mission documents of interest to contemporary Lakotas who, like all peoples, have a lively interest in their history and the world around them. When I was engaging in fieldwork on the Pine Ridge Reservation from 1988 to 1990, I taught an introduction to anthropology class at Oglala Lakota College. The unofficial title of the course was "How White People Think." I explained to my class—made up entirely of adult Lakotas—that although anthropologists have written extensively on "Natives" around the world, the value of studying anthropology lay in gaining insights about how white anthropologists understood reality by studying their analysis of other cultures at various times. That notion is equally true when reading *Lakotas, Black Robes, and Holy Women: German Reports from the Indian Missions in South Dakota, 1886–1900*, because these documents yield many insights into how the missionaries thought and can help make their actions among the Lakotas intelligible, if not always acceptable or even, in some cases, forgivable.

What I find most curious in these early documents is how rarely the priests and sisters speak of the personal relationships they develop with Lakotas. Given the all-encompassing focus of the Lakotas on kinship that extends to adopted relatives, to friends, and indeed to the cosmos itself, I suspect that friendship with missionaries was more important to conversion than the specific doctrines that any particular missionary espoused. The fact that the Catholic missionaries arrive with the titles of sister, brother, mother, and father must has struck a chord with some of the Lakotas. That they also came at the request of specific leaders such as Red Cloud and Spotted Tail must have made them acceptable to some and suspect by others. Missionaries spent long years and in some cases their lifetimes with the Lakotas, which would have promoted and solidified relationships. The decision to join a church was probably less about doctrinal clarity or theological nuance than it was about whose relatives belonged to which congregation and what their relationships were with the minister, sister, or pastor. At the same time, as is clear from the documents, some Lakotas kept themselves separate from both the missionaries and their beliefs.

Father Westropp, S.J., a later missionary on the Pine Ridge Reservation, recalls a conversation with Joseph Big Head in this cross-cultural comparison of mourning customs:

> Like the Irish of old, the Indians have a custom of wailing over the dead. One day he said to me: "Little Owl (my Indian name) when I die I want you to come to my grave and to cry, Ha hoo hoo hoo. Ha hoo hoo hoo, mi-ta-ko-la te-wa-hi-la qon, Ha hoo hoo hoo!" Like a good Irishman I of course promised. "And if you die before, I will do the same by you," he said (Westropp n.d.: 12).

In this passage the Lakota man is expressing far more than an acute sense of humor and knowledge of his own custom, a point Father Westropp

seems to miss. This also is a statement about a deep interpersonal relationship. The Lakota tells the priest to call him friend (*kola*—a term expressing a deep relationship) and to say "I am sad because of your death"
(literally "My Friend, the one I loved, ha hoo hoo hoo"). I myself have stood
and cried at the graves of many Lakota friends and hunka (adoptive) relatives. It is my hope that others will do the same for me.

Although in the nineteenth century there was a focus on what the government and interested American citizens who sought to transform the
Indians termed "the Indian problem," today one sees great concern about
"the mission problem." This current controversy over the Christian missions—often with the Jesuits at the center of the debate—dates back to the
seventeenth century as exemplified in such works as Lahontan's *A Conference or Dialogue between the Author and Adario, a Noted Man among the Savages.*
These controversies over the intent, methodology, and results of Jesuit
and Franciscan missionization both in New France and among the Lakotas continue to stir in public discourse and works such as those of James
Axtell, Daniel Richter, and Lakota mission critic Tim Giago and mission
apologist Charles Trimble (Axtell 1988; Giago 2006; Richter 1985; Trimble
2003). An effort that was understood by its proponents as morally good
and even necessary can be seen in retrospect as producing a spectrum of
results. Some consider boarding schools and the missions as wholly de-
structive of Native culture and family life; others believe the missions and
schools were essential to Natives in their struggle and survival; still others
insist that the missions had both positive and negative effects that must be
recognized as such. Charges of sexual and cultural abuse in mission operations make dispassionate evaluation even more difficult and heighten
the necessity of study and analysis, engagement, repentance, and reconciliation. As the superior general of the Society of Jesus said to a group of
Lakotas, Jesuits, and mission personnel on May 14, 1993:

> In my years as Superior General of the Society of Jesus, through many let-
> ters and conversations, I have been aware of the struggles you have gone
> through. I am aware of how much your life has dramatically and harshly
> been changed; of how you have struggled and suffered some of the worst
> effects of man's inhumanity to man. I am also aware of how your deep in-
> ner strength and your faith in your traditions, in God and in Jesus Christ

has kept you alive. I am happy that for the past century, members of this Society, the "Blackrobes", have walked with you in your struggles. We have desired to be with Christ crucified in your struggles and to experience with you Christ risen. I realize that we, as Jesuits, have at times been the source of some of that pain. For that we are deeply sorry.

This period also saw formal apologies to Native peoples voiced by a variety of Christian denominations in both the United States and Canada.

There are two works specifically on the Catholic mission to the Lakotas that serve as complements to the present volume. *The Jesuit Mission to the Lakota Sioux: Pastoral Theology and Ministry, 1886-1945* by Ross Enochs focuses primarily on the Jesuits and their work on the Pine Ridge and Rosebud Reservations. Enochs concludes:

> Even from its beginning, the Catholic Church took native feasts and transformed them into Christian celebrations. At Holy Rosary and St. Francis Missions, the Jesuits continued this tradition in the Congresses, baptisms, and several other ceremonies which incorporated elements of traditional Lakota dance, rituals, and councils. The Jesuits spoke their language, lived with them, participated in their ceremonies and became part of Lakota families. The Jesuits adapted to Lakota culture and became a part of it. Consequently, the Lakotas trusted them and many accepted the Catholic faith. (Enochs 1996: 154)

Harvey Markowitz, in a doctoral dissertation titled "Converting the Rosebud: A Culture History of Catholic Mission and the Sicangu Lakotas, 1886-1916," focuses on the cultural history of the Jesuits and Franciscan sisters at St. Francis from the mission's beginnings in 1886 until the mission fire of 1916. His assessment of the interaction between the Catholic mission and the Rosebud Lakotas is more ambivalent:

> Set within the context of the Sicangus' wider social and political struggles to come to grips with their new identity as reservation "Sioux," the first three decades of Catholic mission on the Rosebud were fraught with difficulties for both the missionaries and the Indians. However, both groups were able to draw upon the spiritual resources of their respective traditions and instill these difficulties with meaning and purpose. (Markowitz 2002: 448)

The fact remains that the Lakotas were and, in some ways, still are a colonized people. The Catholic mission system—although sometimes at odds with the government and, in the early days, always at odds with the Protestant mission systems—cooperated in the colonization of these people. Was the Catholic mission system part of the oppression? Did the missions mitigate that oppression? The Lakotas, though victimized, were not merely victims, and despite their sometimes dire circumstances, they managed not simply to survive but also to adapt, prevail, and maintain the core of their cultural and religious systems. Resistance was not only in rejection of outside influences, but also in selective cooperation, incorporation, and acculturation. Thus, certain Lakotas actively requested missions and schools as part of their own strategy for survival, a strategy that continues to be adjusted and negotiated to the present day.

The documents presented here often focused on the number of converts without analyzing the conversion process or understanding how the Lakotas understood and accepted, rejected, or accommodated Christianity and specifically Catholicism. One can swim in the lake of ink used to debate the nature of Black Elk's conversion to Christianity and ultimately learn more about the various authors' interests, agendas, and personal beliefs than about Black Elk himself.

Even so, the facts remain: there are contemporary Lakotas who count themselves Christian and Catholic; there are contemporary Lakotas who participate in both Christian and Lakota ritual practice; and there are contemporary Lakotas who vehemently reject the Christian infringement on the reservations. Modern missionaries are quite aware of this and have responded by moving away from religious and cultural certitude and imposition to a stance of reconciliation, without falling into complete religious relativism. As the documents in this volume demonstrate, the religious sisters and fathers of the nineteenth century had to continually readjust their practices and beliefs in relation to Lakota realties from the beginning of their mission, and this remains true today.

It is difficult to assess the range and depth of the influence of that first generation of missionaries. Were they "protected" from hostility during the Wounded Knee conflict, or did the Lakotas see them as quite peripheral and thus more to be ignored than protected? When reading mission documents there is a tendency to inflate the influence and effect of these

individuals and their beliefs, when in fact they were few in number, spoke
the Lakota language with rather limited facility, and covered vast territories with only horse and wagons. Today there is a temptation to polarized
evaluations made by both Natives and other observers of mission history:
either the missionaries forced all the Natives to be Christian, or they were
saviors of Native peoples. Neither "all glory" nor "all gory" can reveal the
genuine complexity of these encounters. Certainly the early missionaries'
government sponsorship, as well as their own acceptance of the "civilization" policies of the time, placed them in a position of privilege and domi-
nance. Just as clearly, some Lakotas chose not to convert to the new religion, or used baptism as a form of social alliance or—as is characteristic
of Lakota rituals—to address a specific spiritual need such as healing from
an illness. Although it impossible to be certain about how nineteenth-century Lakotas understood Christianity and their own conversions, the documents do demonstrate that the missionaries shared common ground with
the Lakotas: belief in spiritual reality beyond the physical world and in the
desire of humans to understand, access, and utilize sacred power.

The mission documents in this volume play up successes by portraying
adversity that is inevitably overcome and baptisms that are simply associated with true and total conversion to a belief system rather than a complex
nexus of social, political, historic, economic, and also spiritual realities.
Nevertheless, we find hints of complexities in the texts. Some of the documents speak broadly of illness and healing as an entrée to Lakota religious
life. While opposing the specific curing practices of Lakota medicine men,
the missionaries tried to replace them, or at least supplement their work,
by providing baptism and prayer that both the Lakotas and the missionaries believed to have miraculous healing effects. Healing rituals remain
important to Christian Lakotas today.

The relationships and structures established by the first missionaries
and illuminated in this collection echo among the Lakotas of Pine Ridge
and Rosebud, where Catholics continue to minister on the reservations.
For the most part, dialogue has replaced the adversarial and competitive
relationships among Catholicism, the Lakota religion, and Protestantism,
as can be seen in efforts at ritual adaptation and interreligious as well as
interdenominational dialogue and cooperation. In the nineteenth century,
missionaries told the Lakotas that they must practice only one belief sys-

tem and were so frustrated by the Lakotas' extravagantly ecumenical attitudes that the Lakotas had to keep such broadmindedness a secret, particularly if they continued to actively engage in Lakota ceremonial practice. Ironically, modern missionaries stress the harmony of beliefs and profess the ideology that one can be both Indian following traditional beliefs and Catholic, while other Lakotas insist that one should practice a single belief system, and that to be truly Lakota is to follow only traditional practices exclusively.

Other changes have been in motion. No longer are religious sisters confined to the educational and domestic sphere; they now labor as parish administrators and pastoral assistants. The St. Francis Mission turned its educational operation—the St. Francis grade and high school—over to local control in 1972. They continue to administer parishes, healing programs, and the Buechel Memorial Lakota Museum. The Jesuits on the Pine Ridge Reservation continue to operate a high school and grade school north of Pine Ridge, the Red Cloud Indian School, as well as a grade school in Porcupine, Our Lady of Lourdes. They also oversee the administration of reservation parishes and the Heritage Center Museum. The last Sister of St. Francis left the Rosebud Reservation in 2006. Today there are two Sisters of St. Francis working on the Pine Ridge Reservation, one of them a Lakota from Pine Ridge. Since the 1960s, the Jesuit presence on both reservations has diminished. Today it more resembles the centralized structure of the early missions more than it has since its inception. Three Jesuit priests minister on the St. Francis Mission, and one serves as superior. Seven priests and two brothers still serve at the Holy Rosary Mission. Of the priests, three are directly involved in pastoral ministry and four in administration and the schools. The brothers work at maintaining the physical plant. As with the founding of the mission, one of the priests is from outside the United States, from India. The legal name of the mission, Pine Ridge Educational Society, was changed to Red Cloud Indian School in 1969. The legal name of the Rosebud Educational Society was changed in 2005 to the St. Francis Mission.

Like their predecessors, the modern missionaries accommodate themselves to the Lakotas, but not in ways imagined by the founding mothers and fathers. Today it is not unusual to see the local parish priest at a Sun Dance or participating in a sweat lodge. Traditional prayer leaders regularly join priests at burial services. Catholic schools teach Lakota spirituality as well as Catholic doctrine. The Lakota language, once banned from the schoolyard, is now taught in the classroom. Even with such significant changes, tension and ambivalence about the past and present remain.

Like their spiritual ancestors in New France and the Dakota Territories, modern Jesuits and sisters continue to publicize their work among the Lakotas in print and now on the Internet. Their work, like that of their predecessors in New France and the early Dakota missions, continues to influence how Indian people are understood and imaged in the United States, albeit in competition with images produced by New Age beliefs, nongovernment organizations, scholars, the federal government, photographers, and the public print and electronic media. At the same time, Native people present their own images, using the same channels of communications—sometimes collaborating and sometimes colliding with non-Native observers and promoters. Holy Rosary publishes a newsletter, "Red Cloud Country" as well as an annual calendar depicting students in dance regalia. St. Francis also publishes a newsletter and annual calendar. Both institutions fund themselves through direct giving appeals to support their schools and pastoral work. Both missions can be found on the Web: http://www.redcloudschool.org/ and http://www.sfmission.org/.

The early missionaries to the Dakotas used a visual device for catechizing called the two roads. One road depicts the true path to heaven, which is the Catholic way. The other road, the wrong path, led to damnation. The image of the two roads is also used by Lakotas to represent the good red road and the black road of evil. The term two roads is also used today by the Lakotas to represent two distinct religious traditions: Lakota spirituality and Christianity. These two distinct spiritual roads first crossed when fur traders brought their beliefs along with their material goods and crossed again when the first missionaries arrived. Through the centuries, these two traditions continue to cross, run parallel, intermingle, diverge, and cross again. Whenever and wherever travelers on the two roads meet, there is a moral imperative today to seek dignity and equality during their time together.

None of us could or would do everything our ancestors did, but regardless of the road we walk, we can honor our ancestors, learn from their mistakes as well as their successes, and make our ongoing meetings better.

We live in a world where the meeting of faiths produces conflict as well as peace, oppression as well as liberation, division as well as community, and where the past remains vital in healing the present. The more we understand the complexity of the past, the more effectively we can work for justice.

Adding more voices to the discourse increases the complexity of the issues, but it also increases the possibility of a wiser interpretation. *Lakotas, Black Robes, and Holy Women: German Reports from the Indian Missions in South Dakota, 1886-1900* might be seen merely as tales of past encounters among persons long dead, but it truly speaks to a more hopeful present and points the way to a future of mutual understanding, healed relationships, equality, and cooperation.

Works Cited

Axtell, James. 1988. Were Indian Conversions Bona Fide? In *After Columbus: Essays in the Ethnohistory of Colonial North America*, ed. J. Axtell, pp. 100–121. New York: Oxford University Press.

Duratschek, Sister Mary Claudia. 1947. *Crusading along Sioux Trails: A History of the Catholic Indian Missions of South Dakota*. New York: Grail.

Enochs, Ross A. 1996. *The Jesuit Mission to the Lakota Sioux: Pastoral Theology and Ministry, 1886–1945*. Kansas City: Sheed and Ward.

Foley, Thomas W. 2002. *Father Francis M. Craft: Missionary to the Sioux*. Lincoln: University of Nebraska Press.

Giago, Tim. 2006. Debunking the Myth of Christianity. In *Lakota Country Times* (Martin SC), July 24, 2006.

Giago, Tim A., Jr. 1978. *The Aboriginal Sin: Reflections on the Holy Rosary Mission School (Red Cloud Indian School)*. San Francisco: Indian Historian Press.

Janda, James. 1978. Hanbleachia. Chapbook no. 6. Marvin SD: Blue Cloud Quarterly. http://www.sfmission.org/museum/documents/janda–hanbelachia.pdf (last accessed January 17, 2007).

Library and Archives Canada. 2001a. Accounts of a Missionary Offensive. In *The Jesuit Relations and History of New France*. http://www.collectionscanada.ca/jesuit-relations/h19-210-e.html (last accessed January 17, 2007).

———. 2001b. Edifying Narratives. In *The Jesuit Relations and History of New France*. http://www.collectionscanada.ca/jesuit-relations/h19-200-e.html (last accessed January 17, 2007).

Markowitz, Harvey. 2002. Converting the Rosebud: A Culture History of Catholic Mission and the Sicangu Lakotas, 1886–1916. PhD diss., University of Chicago.

Richter, Daniel K. 1985. Iroquois versus Iroquois: Jesuit Missions and Christianity in Village Politics, 1642–1686. *Ethnohistory* 32(1): 1–16.

Sneve, Virginia Driving Hawk. 1977. *That They May Have Life: The Episcopal Church in South Dakota: 1859–1976*. New York: Seabury Press.

Thwaites, Reuben Gold, ed. 1896. *The Jesuit Relations and Allied Documents*. 73 vols. Cleveland: Burrows Bros.

Trimble, Charles E. 2003. Trimble: Mission School Remembered. . . . *Indian Country Today*. Canastota NY. Posted September 2, 2003. http://indiancountry.com/content.cfm?id=1062509982 (last accessed January 17, 2007).

Westropp, Henry Ignatius, S.J. N.d. *In the Land of the Wigwam: Missionary Notes from the Pine Ridge Mission*. Pine Ridge SD: Student Apprentices in the Office of the Oglala Light.

PART ONE

*About the History of the Catholic Missions
among the Sioux*

1. The Founding of the Mission Schools and the Early Years, 1886–1890

The Lakotas and the "Black Robes"

There is probably not one historical self-portrait of the St. Francis and Holy Rosary Missions that does not trace their founding to the request for a mission made by the chiefs Spotted Tail for the Brulés (Sicangus) on the Rosebud Reservation and Red Cloud for the Oglalas on Pine Ridge. This "origin narrative" (Markowitz 1992) points to the desperate situation in which the Lakotas found themselves in the 1880s, which provided the basic conditions for the beginning of the mission work: military defeats, the decimation of the buffalo, a dramatically shrinking land base, the unchecked advance of white settlers, and the collapse of the cultural and social framework of their communities. Against this background appear the images of personalities such as Red Cloud, who after long and bitter experiences in wars and negotiations with whites saw in the missions an opportunity to lead tribal members out of misery and to learn enough from the white people to survive with dignity.

A certain amount of trust on the part of the Lakotas toward the "Black Robes," the Catholic priests, is in large part due to the mediating role played by the Belgian Jesuit Father Pierre-Jean de Smet. The last legendary figure of the Jesuit missionaries in North America, he assumed an important part in the negotiations of Fort Laramie in 1868. Because of the reputation that he enjoyed among the tribes, the U.S. government had sent him ahead to bring the Indians to the negotiating table (doc. 2.23, section 2), at first with success, as the realization of this important treaty seemed to prove (Utley 1963, 76–84). However, the government neither adhered to the treaty stipulations for the benefit of the Indians nor showed its appreciation toward the Catholic Church for the constructive role played by the missionary.

With the adoption of President Ulysses Grant's Peace Policy in 1870, which among other issues promoted the idea of civilizing the Indians through Christianity, the churches were to be given a central role: they were to pacify the Indians by means of their schools and churches. Each reservation was assigned only one religious denomination with the exclusive right to missionize. That way, the confessional rivalries, which could potentially undermine the acceptance of Christianity on the part of the Indians, could be controlled. The federal government intended to finance the Protestant and Catholic schools that were thus constructed. In the end, the greater number of areas was assigned to the Protestants, "thereby alienating the one group—the Catholics—with the most experience in the West" (Hoxie 2001, 3). For the Lakotas the distribution was as follows: the Catholics received the Standing Rock and Devil's Lake reservations; the Episcopalians, Rosebud and Pine Ridge. Having hoped for a larger sphere of influence given the many years of labor by Father de Smet, especially among the Sioux, the Catholic Church protested against this arrangement. In response to this unfavorable policy, the Catholic bishops founded the Bureau of Catholic Indian Missions (BCIM) in Washington DC. It was to represent the interests of the church in its dealings with the federal government and to serve as a charity organization throughout the country (Prucha 1979, 2–3).

But the Sioux protested as well. The Sicangus (Brulés) at Rosebud and the Oglalas at Pine Ridge did not want the "White Robes" (Episcopalians), who had been active there since 1875, but preferred the Black Robes, the Catholic clergy. At a number of meetings between 1875 and 1878, the chiefs presented their wishes to the Office of Indian Affairs and to the president in Washington—Red Cloud and Little Wound for the Oglalas, Spotted Tail for the Sicangus. To quote Red Cloud, the leader in earlier wars and negotiations: "I would like to have stock of all kinds to work with, and live like white people; I also desire to have farming implements of all kinds. I also want schools to enable my children to read and write, so they will be as wise as the white man's children [. . .] We would like to have Catholic priests and nuns, so that they could teach our people how to read and write."[1]

At the end of Father de Smet's labors (he died in 1873) the Swiss Benedictine abbot Martin Marty started to play an important role. Like the other Black Robe before him, he tried to mediate between the irreconcilable camps of the U.S. government and its branches, on the one hand, and the Lakotas, fighting for their existence, on the other. He too maintained personal contacts with some of the chiefs and sought to convert them to

Christianity: Sitting Bull of the Hunkpapas (without success), and Red Cloud of the Oglalas and Spotted Tail of the Sicangus (with more success). Marty was especially active in establishing schools in the Dakota Territory, and he did so in response to the wishes of the chiefs. Spotted Tail, for example, declared at a meeting of the chiefs at Rosebud in the presence of Marty: "The Black Robe is the kind of teacher we want. We do not want other ones!" [quote translated from the German]. Marty reports similar sentiments expressed during one of his visits to Red Cloud and in his talks with the headmen: "In the morning the chiefs came to tell me how happy they were to see me. Would I please not leave them again, but open a school and return the following spring" [quote translated from the German]. Red Cloud also reminded the visitor to press the president on the delivery of the promised farming implements (doc. 2.23, section 3).

The principle of exclusive allocation of mission areas increasingly earned the criticism of the Protestants, who also wanted to engage in missionary work on the reservations that had been assigned to the competition, causing this provision of the Peace Policy to be suspended in 1881. Abbot Marty, having been appointed titular bishop and apostolic vicar of the Dakota Territory in 1880, was now building several missions in that area with the help of the Benedictines. Benedictine sisters from Switzerland provided the teaching staff for the new mission school on Standing Rock Reservation (Zens 1940, 320–25; Duratschek 1947, 60–120). Marty sent three secular priests (Francis Craft, Joseph Bushman, and Charles Hospenthal) to Pine Ridge and Rosebud. Between 1883 and 1885, these men baptized eight hundred Lakotas, among them Red Cloud and his family and five other Lakota chiefs. Spotted Tail desired to be baptized as well; he was refused, however, given that he did not want to give up his eight wives (Duratschek 1947, 126). At Rosebud, Bushman and Hospenthal built a boarding school for about fifty children, furnishing it with everything, including school benches and beds. The financial resources for this came from Katharine Drexel, a wealthy heiress from Philadelphia and an acquaintance of Bishop Marty. Soon after, she was to establish the Order of the Sisters of the Blessed Sacrament, which devoted itself to laboring among African Americans and American Indians (Jutz 1918–19, 67).

Yet the bishop was still lacking suitable personnel for the mission stations and schools that were planned for the two reservations. He thus made an appeal to the local superiors of the order of the Jesuits, as well as to the Franciscan Sisters of Penance and Christian Charity (often referred to as the Franciscan Sisters of Heythuizen, after their motherhouse) in Buffalo, New York, where both orders were mainly active among German immigrants. The administrative and decision-making centers of the German provinces of the orders, of which these branches were a part, were located in Europe. Both orders had been driven from the German Reich in the course of the Kulturkampf and had now moved their provincial administrations to the Netherlands. In the letters of the superior of the "Buffalo mission," Father Leßmann, to his German provincial, it becomes clear that the decision to send Jesuits to Dakota was largely based on political considerations on the part of the church. A determining factor was—as Marty presented it in his first appeal for personnel to Father Leßmann in November of 1884—that the prospective sphere of activity in the Dakota Territory involved a relatively large number of people (26,000 Indians and 25,000 whites), whereas in the area around Lander (Wyoming), initially favored by Father Leßmann, fewer than 1,000 Indians lived. Marty also pressed Leßmann by hinting at the Protestant competition: "What hurts the most is that the Protestants are founding academies and colleges everywhere, are given the best locations and lavish funds, while I have to refuse the few [pupils] who are offered me, or put them off pending an uncertain future" [quote translated from the German]. Thus the Buffalo superior quickly changed his plans and recalled Father Johann Jutz and Brother Ursus Nunlist from Wyoming, where they had gone twenty months prior, and assigned St. Francis on the Rosebud Reservation to them as a new field of operation. The Franciscan sisters from Buffalo had been intended initially as teaching staff for Wyoming, but now there was a change in course. In cooperation with the Buffalo mother superior, the joint planning for the St. Francis mission was finalized, and Father Jutz was the first missionary sent there in 1885.[2]

As a result of his later role in connection with the Ghost Dance and the Wounded Knee massacre, Father Jutz became one of the most well-known personalities associated with the missions. His curriculum vitae was rather unusual for a Jesuit. Born in 1838 in Frastanz, near Feldkirch (Austria), as the oldest of eight children, he wanted to become a priest after six years in school, which his father did not permit. Thus he learned the trade of molder, which he practiced for fifteen years, and supported his family after his father's death until his younger siblings had grown up. When his fiancée died shortly before the wedding, he taught the village youth for six months until he enrolled at the Jesuit college in Feldkirch on the advice of a Jesuit priest. After four years of college, while earning money for school fees by tutoring and working in his trade, he entered the order of the Jesuits. During the German-French war of 1870–1871, he cared for soldiers suffering from dysentery. Jutz himself fell ill with typhoid and smallpox but made a full recovery. Following the war, he, like other Jesuits, was expelled from the German Reich. He went to Holland and England to pursue the usual studies at the colleges of the order. In 1878, at long last, Jutz was ordained a priest at age forty. Although since his novitiate he had wished to join the Africa mission, the superiors in 1880 sent him to America, along with eleven other priests, first to Buffalo and then to Prairie du Chien in Wisconsin. In 1883 his career as a missionary finally began. Along with the lay brother Ursus Nunlist, he was sent to Wyoming, to the Shoshones and the Arapahoes.

Jutz appears to have been a man who was not easily discouraged. In Lander, then the capital of Wyoming, he was supposed to take over a boarding school for Indian children built by the government. However, on his arrival he discovered that the school had recently been given to an Episcopalian. Thus he and Nunlist set out with ponies and a tent and went to live among the Arapahoes and perform the work of day laborers. After twenty months and a great deal of effort (Leßmann praisingly commented: "No matter how dirty or difficult," there was no work that they did not perform), and with the money from Katharine Drexel, he was able to build a mission house near Lander. In December 1885 Father Jutz left Wyoming along with Brother Nunlist to take over the station at Rosebud and establish a school there. From all appearances, Jutz's direct manner soon earned him some disapproval in this new sphere of activity. In his recollections he notes that although at first sight the school building appeared perhaps adequate as a vacation home, it was "most impracticable and unsatisfactory" as a boarding school and residence for the fathers, brothers, and sisters. Moreover, the location was wrong, as it was without a water source. Jutz, who at the time was characterized by his superior Leßmann as someone who was "obedient in a child-like manner toward anyone who had authority over him," but who "was not easily dissuaded from something that he deemed to be right and good by someone who did not have that authority," immediately shared his criticism with Katharine Drexel[3] [quote translated from the German]. She passed his letter on to the head of the BCIM, who—as Jutz guessed—had himself determined the location for the house and approved the plans. He reacted to Jutz's criticism with a good deal of anger and rebuked him for being ungrateful. As a result of this disagreement, Jutz was removed from his position as superior in March 1886, but remained at St. Francis until the summer of 1887, performing the work of a lay brother, "working without change from morning to night." Drexel nonetheless procured additional funds, and in the summer of 1886 an addition was made to the building to allow for the housing of 100 children. Thus the boarding school could be opened on 15 September (Jutz 1918–1919, 144–45).

Father Jutz left the positions of superior at both missions in South Dakota at his own request and was transferred to Boston in 1896. There he was active in a German congregation for ten years. From Boston he went to Blackwell's Island, New York, where he spent four years as chaplain in a hospital and in a men's prison. Jutz lived out the last years of his life in Buffalo, New York, as father confessor to the German congregation. He died there in 1924 (Bunse 1924; Bunse and Jutz 1924–1926).

Brother Nunlist came only later to St. Francis. He arrived on 25 March 1886 along with Jutz's successor as superior, Father Emil Perrig, and three Franciscan sisters in the company of Father Stephan, the head of BCIM (docs. 2.1, 2.3). Father Perrig was a 40–year-old Swiss. The three sisters were Alcantara Fallon, 26, from Ohio, Rosalia Schulte, 28, from Westfalia, and M. Kostka Schlaghecken, 36, from the Rhineland region. Brother Ursus Nunlist, 39, was from Aargau (a canton in Switzerland). Father Perrig had been previously active as an educator and music instructor at Canisius College in Buffalo, and the sisters had been teachers in the same city. By August 1886 additional support arrived: Father Florentin Digmann and the lay brothers Karl Graß, August Pankau, Heinrich Surich, and Georg Ständer, as well as Sisters Walburga Hartmann, probably Elisabeth Preis, and Laurentia Fritz or Crescentia Witzel. In order to provide for a water source, the lack of which Jutz had recognized right away, the fathers and brothers had to dig a well 195 feet deep (doc. 2.3).

In the meantime, preparations for the establishment of a mission on neighboring Pine Ridge Reservation continued. Under the supervision of the indefatigable Father Jutz, who had moved from St. Francis to Pine Ridge, and Brother Heinrich Billing, construction of the future Holy Rosary Mission began in August 1887 on a tract of land along White Clay Creek, four and one-half miles north of Pine Ridge Agency. Father Jutz had chosen the site, and Bishop Marty had obtained the right of usufruct from the U.S. government, after Cow Killer, the Indian owner, had signed over this parcel of land in return for financial compensation provided with funds from Katharine Drexel. In addition to several brothers from St. Francis, a great number of Oglalas helped with the construction. Following the Indians' advice, Jutz erected the building on a somewhat more elevated spot than previously planned to avoid the danger of flooding. The wages that could be paid were low, so that many Lakotas—at the request of Red Cloud—volunteered (Galler 1994, 19–25). The official opening took place on the high festival of the Jesuits, the feast day of St. Ignatius, on 31 July 1888. The founding staff of the Drexel Mission, as it was called after its benefactress, consisted of Father Jutz as superior, Brothers Ständer and Nunlist, who had moved with him from St. Francis, and Sisters Kostka Schlaghecken as mother superior, Alcantara Fallon, Elisabeth Preis, and Walburga Hartmann (doc. 1.3).

Later on one of the sisters reported how Red Cloud, one of the first visitors, had appeared: dressed in a wrap and Indian leggings, with top hat and two long braids. He had welcomed them with much dignity and courtesy and had expressed his joy about their arrival. He had also promised to send them a fat calf every year, a pledge that he was unable to keep, of course, for "circumstances were ever hard on poor Red Cloud; he is one of the most pathetic figures in the history of the Mission," this witness observed.[4]

Mission Work in the Schools and Parishes

The staffing of the missions in the early years remained fairly steady. At Holy Rosary there labored two or three fathers, six lay brothers, and about ten sisters; at St. Francis, three fathers, about ten brothers, and the same number of sisters. Starting in the middle of the 1890s, a scholastic (a Jesuit in training) worked as prefect at the boarding school, also to learn the Lakota language. Personnel were frequently exchanged between the two missions. Thus the number of fathers was always significantly smaller than that of the other mission staff. Yet in the published sources, these "chiefs" of the Jesuits dominate as authors of reports and as persons in charge, whereas the lay brothers remain mostly in the background, only at a later point contributing more frequently to the *Mitteilungen*. The sisters, on the other hand, who had their own organization, with mothers superior and an obligation for reporting, have more of a voice, although often only anonymously, as is apparent from the published letters in *Die katholischen Missionen*.

The work at the missions was concentrated in two areas: the parishes and the schools. As for their organization, these realms of activity functioned for the most part separately and, despite overlapping leadership, were borne by different personnel. The Franciscan sisters and the Jesuit brothers taught in the schools; the Jesuit fathers led the schools. At the same time, the fathers acted as pastors in charge of the mission communities, holding services and administering the sacraments at the central places as well as in the outlying areas.

The dominating presence of the fathers in the documents, therefore, must not cloud the fact that it was the Franciscan sisters and the lay brothers who were responsible for the instruction and thus for the lasting influence on the Indian children. When the fathers, other than in their leadership function, worked in the early years as school personnel, they did so merely as prefects (for extracurricular instruction) and in a few special subjects (religion and, in the case of Father Perrig, music). During the 1890s the duties of the prefect were transferred to a Jesuit in training (scholastic), as was commonly done in Jesuit boarding schools. Within this context of duty assignments, the fathers, as heads of the mission, were also responsible for representing the mission in its dealings with government agencies and with the administration of the order, as well as in matters of public relations and especially for soliciting charitable contributions. Thus, to a great extent, they influenced the image that the missions were presenting to the outside. The Jesuits reported mainly on their practical experiences as missionaries and pastors, on the one hand, and on the problems and successes related to the superintendence of the schools, on the other. Given the responsibilities of the sisters, they more frequently reported their firsthand experiences and impressions about the children. On the whole, the accounts convey the impressions of these observers usually in a naive and unreflected way: the zeal for missionizing on the part of the relatively young sisters, as well as of the restless Jesuits; the sense of foreignness and lack of understanding; and, at the same time, the urge to bring to these "poor *Wilden*" (*armen Wilden*) the "blessings" (*Segnungen*) of Christianity and "civilization."

At the center of the mission work stood, also in a physical sense, the schools. The greater number of the mission personnel worked here, and wherever the schools were located, the main churches of the parishes were found as well. The work within the parishes, in which the few fathers invested most of their time and energy, took place in a greatly diffused fashion, given the vast reservation area. The missionaries traveled about by horse and wagon for days at a time, visiting the sick, giving baptismal instruction, and saying a Sunday mass where possible (docs. 2.13, 2.14). For this aspect of the missionaries' work no precepts applied other than those issued by their church and order, that is, to save souls from paganism and Protestant heresy.

The work in the schools, by contrast, was subject mostly to requirements set by the government. Within the framework of the pedagogic function exercised by the Jesuit order, the primary schools with their vocational orientation were rather the exception. Although they had always existed throughout the history of the order, they did not represent the main goal of its pedagogical pursuits, which was in general higher education. Once the administration of a primary school was transferred to the Jesuits, they started to employ non-Jesuit teaching personnel, as they did in South Dakota. Although the Jesuits were not familiar with girls' classes in their own schools (of higher education), the training of the Franciscan sisters and their school experience was aimed at employment in schools of just this nature. Prior to having been sent to the missions, they had enjoyed thorough pedagogical training, and not only in academic subjects such as arithmetic, reading/writing, and language, but also in those relating to home economics. Moreover, the sisters who had been sent to the United States from Europe had also been taught English.[5]

The Jesuit fathers had pursued all the usual and wide-ranging studies in philosophy, theology, and humanistic subjects but had no special preparation as pedagogues. The two to three years as prefects during the course of their study provided them merely practical experiences. The Jesuit lay brothers, on the other hand, had only their training in a trade to offer, received either before entering the order in the form of an apprenticeship, as was common in their home countries, or afterward through instruction by an older brother. Thus their teaching activities were limited to such vocational areas.[6]

In dealing with the American bureaucracy, especially with the commissioner of Indian affairs and his agents, the school principals continuously emphasized the good training of their teaching staffs and, when applicable with respect to the sisters, their experience as teachers in American schools in the East (Buffalo). There was to be no doubt that the schools of the Jesuits and Franciscan sisters were good American schools, regardless of the foreign origin of many of their teachers.

The typical career of a missionary is that of Father Perrig. Having finished his studies, he spent six years as an educator at Canisius College in Buffalo. In 1886 he went from there to St. Francis, as superior, and in 1889, moved to the school of Holy Rosary Mission to serve there as prefect and music instructor, while at the same time assuming the duties of missionary in the parish. In 1895 he was transferred back to St. Francis to work as pastor in the outlying parishes. In 1908 his superiors sent him once again to Holy Rosary, where he died the following year. Perrig took great pains to learn the Lakota language and developed a dictionary to that end. He was known as the director of a band, with which he is frequently depicted in early photographs. His grim countenance and his nickname, Dr. Resolutissimus, are misleading, considering that as a teacher he must have been rather lenient. His superior in Buffalo offered the following critique: "Fr. Perrig is a much too good-natured soul, hence he does not know how to duly push and drill the pupils"[7] [quote translated from the German].

One difficulty with respect to school operations appears to have been grounded in the special way of life of the female and male teachers. The daily interaction of the celibate members of the orders with the opposite sex in a jointly operated school was as unusual as the coeducational boarding school. The admonition to observe a "strict separation" when interacting with the sisters can almost always be found in the first years of the confidential instructions that were left behind by the provincial of the Jesuits on the occasion of the annual official "visitations." Specifically, it was ordered that the living quarters of the opposite sex were not to be entered, and that all necessary communication had to take place in designated public rooms, and this only with the special permission of the superior. Moreover, it was emphasized several times that those brothers and sisters who were employed in teaching were only permitted to discuss matters with one another through their respective superiors, a rule that also applied to the day-to-day questions regarding school operations.

An additional directive by the provincial, one concerning German, the mother tongue of the Jesuits, casts an interesting light on their everyday lives. They were directed to speak English among themselves, also during recreation, and the brothers were to learn this language.[8] With the sisters the situation was different. Their language of instruction and conversation in the schools was naturally English. However, German was the prescribed language to be used within the order for prayer, during recreation, and in formal communication, and here it made no difference that several of the sisters had been born in and had grown up in the United States.[9]

During the period covered by this collection of documents, 1886–1900, the mission schools were operated as contract schools. Consistent with Grant's Peace Policy, according to which the federal government put denominational schools in charge of "civilizing" the Indians because of the insufficiency of its own school system, the government entered into contracts with individual schools by which they received a certain sum per pupil per year, paid through the Office of Indian Affairs and the Bureau of Catholic Indian Missions. Thus the number of pupils is a recurrent theme in the correspondence between the school administrations, BCIM, and OIA. In the reports printed here, the stated number of pupils varies. The number of registrations was not always identical with the number of pupils actually arriving, and many children continued to run away, especially in the early years. According to an overview in one of the chronicles of the Franciscan sisters, for the first year at St. Francis (1886–1887) there were 50 pupils registered "before the holidays," and about 40 appeared (doc. 1.1), whereas the superior at the mission, Father Perrig, speaks of 60 children for the opening day on 15 September 1886, but that this number had increased to 78 later on (doc. 2.3).

At first, all the children were taught in one class. In 1889 three classes were formed based on age. By 1891 the number of children had grown to

108 (doc. 1.1). Holy Rosary already reported 100 children in its first year (an equal number of boys and girls), of whom 30–40 children had at the beginning moved there from a Protestant government boarding school. In the second year there were altogether 125–30 pupils (doc. 1.3).

What spoke in favor of the boarding schools, along with pedagogical considerations that were promoted at the time (the children were to be removed from the influence of their parents so as to be better assimilated), were practical concerns. Given that the distances to be traveled between families and schools were for most pupils unmanageable on a daily basis, housing them at the same place where they were to receive their education was seen as an advantage. However, there were, along with the boarding schools at Pine Ridge, one-class day schools set up for the youngest schoolchildren by other denominations or the government. These were generally supervised by a married couple and were attended by about 25 children (Peterson 1983, 253).

The schools saw themselves as "industrial schools." Because the children were to be raised to be self-reliant heads of families, as defined by the white "civilization," not only academic subjects were taught, but also practical skills. The curriculum for the earliest grades included English and arithmetic, biblical history, and prayers. The Jesuit fathers also taught hymns in English and Lakota. Performance in school was honored at St. Francis in 1888, for example, with awards for proper conduct, industry, spelling, reading, and arithmetic (doc. 2.4). From the beginning, in addition to school, household chores were part of the children's responsibilities: cooking, washing, and doing dishes for the girls; carrying wood and water, and so forth, for the boys (doc. 1.1). Later on in the upper grades, under the guidance of the brothers, instruction in trade-related subjects for the boys was added, such as carpentry, baking, joinery, and field or garden work. The sisters instructed the girls in the subjects of home economics. The skills that were learned could be directly employed at the mission under the supervision of the brothers and sisters. In the beginning there was no strict assignment of the boys to the male teaching staff, and of the girls to the sisters, as is demonstrated by this list of areas of responsibilities at Holy Rosary for 1889: Sister Alcantara, school for the older girls; Sister Crescentia, sewing and housework; Sister Salesia, older boys' class; Sister Walburga, children's sewing room; Sister Laurentia, kitchen; Sister Catharina, laundry room; and Sister Michaele, small mixed school. In 1888 Sister Cypriana was responsible for the boys' school at St. Francis (docs. 1.3, 1.1).

Relationship to the Language and Culture of the Lakotas

Consistent with the official mandate of the assimilation policy, the language of instruction in the schools was English. Since 1886 the Office of Indian Affairs had several times directed all the Indian schools to "exclusively" use the English language, that is, in class and during religious services (Spack 2002, 33–34). In 1888, however, as a result of heavy protests from Episcopalian missionaries, the reading of the Bible in the mother tongue was explicitly excluded from this directive, which therefore also excluded religious instruction and religious services. Yet the English-only rule for regular school operations applied from the start, although there were perhaps, at the most, a couple of children from mixed marriages who knew a little English. The report issued by inspector Elaine Goodale for St. Francis on 29 May 1890 thus concludes: "The school is not up to the standard in the matter of speaking only English. The children talk Dakota freely among themselves, on the school grounds." Father Digmann, in his position as superintendent, also admitted this to the Indian agent in a letter of 23 August 1890: "Another difficulty was to get the children [to] speak English among themselves. They never were allowed to talk freely Dakota among themselves, but as we could not grasp them as tight as one can outside the Reservation, they did much so anyway."[10] The accounts of the Franciscan sisters do not contain any clear indication of how the female teachers conducted their classes. Against the backdrop of widespread anti-German and anti-Catholic sentiments among the American public, the teaching staff could not permit itself any lack of enthusiasm for the English language (Spack 2002, 33). It seems, however, that the brothers did not adhere to a ban on Lakota in the most strict manner and perhaps were not able to in their instruction of handicrafts. Specific references on this matter are not contained in the sources covering the first years. Yet it is reported that Brother Billing had learned Lakota, and later also Brother Hinderhofer, who came to St. Francis in 1900, having heard it, along with English, from "his" shoemaker lads. "From them I learn many a word in Indian or American English that is pronounced very differently than in

England" (Hinderhofer 1900–1902, 225–26) [quote translated from the German].

For the sisters, therefore, there was no reason to learn the Lakota language in a systematic fashion. Their encounter with the Native culture and way of life took place mostly within the confines of the school. Nevertheless, or perhaps for that reason, the strangeness of the traditional Lakota appearance during the early years continued to have a fascinating and humorous effect on the newly arrived sisters (docs. 2.1, 2.2), but never a frightening one. They describe their civilizing measures applied to the Indians—washing, cutting of the hair, dressing in European clothing—the way they understood them: as a service done to the armen Rothäutchen, to the "poor redskins[d]." To the female and male missionaries "their" Indians were, on the whole, "a harmless, friendly people" (doc. 2.3). Frequently their social virtues are emphasized, especially those of their kleinen Wilden, their "little Wilden," who "do not [give] us a tenth of the trouble that white children cause in the schools of Europe" (doc. 2.4.). Their unwillingness to do (field)work is repeatedly bemoaned as a major failing on the part of the "Wilden." On the other hand, in an internal report from the order there is found one sister's expression of surprise, that "as far as morals were concerned, there were no difficulties among the children" [quotes translated from the German]. In other words, the boys and girls of the boarding school conducted themselves morally beyond reproach, according to the standards of their strict teacher, which was clearly surprising to her (doc. 1.1). Yet the reports contain hardly any indication of how the children perceived their situation, if one, for a moment, disregards the significant fact that there were always some who continued to run away and go back home. In those cases, as well as with other violations of the norms of discipline, the fathers exercised, apparently without scruple, the common forms of corporal punishment practiced at the time (Galler 1994, 41–42; Adams 1995, 121). To project today's views on pedagogy back in time doubtlessly would be of little value. If anything, one would have to compare the educational methods in the mission schools with those practiced in other American schools, particularly those in parishes of German immigrants, from where the missionaries came.

School inspector Elaine Goodale noted at the time that she had found at the mission schools "abundant evidence of personal devotion and sincere interest in the people," praising especially the achievements in handicrafts and home economics, whereas the academic subjects appeared "wooden and old-fashioned" (Goodale Eastman 1985, 130). She mentioned the superior several times, and did so always as "good Father Jutz." It seems that he was remembered so favorably by her because, during an inspection visit, he had "a solitary luncheon" served to her and her escort (and later husband) Dr. Charles Eastman, who had begun to impress her with his commitment to his patients, "in the course of which we became much better acquainted" (Goodale Eastman 1985, 169–70).

Unlike those employed in the schools, the missionaries who labored as pastors had to accomplish the important task of overcoming the language barrier, particularly in these early years when the Lakotas had not yet passed through the schools. For Provincial Leßmann, therefore, it was an obvious requirement when selecting personnel for the Indian missions that the future missionaries had to learn the language of the Native population. In a letter of 1879 he writes: "Practically speaking, as far as the language is concerned, these Indians can only be helped if a young father sets about learning it [the language], and then dedicates himself to staying with them for good"[11] [quote translated from the German]. Later he handled this requirement in a more flexible manner, in that he, for instance, let Father Jutz, whom he held in high esteem, work with an interpreter. The Benedictines, among others, assisted in the process of learning the Lakota language, especially Father Jerome (Hieronymus) Hunt, who had been laboring among the Sioux for ten years.

In 1886, at the end of October, still in its founding year, Father Hunt came to St. Francis Mission for about two weeks to teach Lakota to the Jesuits, also passing on to them a catechism he had translated. During this time Hunt delivered the sermons on Sundays and on the festival days in this language. After he left, the fathers made their own attempt to preach in Lakota by writing down their sermons with a great deal of effort (summo labore) and reading them to an audience after they had been corrected by an interpreter. In the afternoon the Jesuits rewarded all those who had listened to their sermons on Sunday morning by showing pictures of the biblical story using a laterna magica (magic lantern). The forty-eight-year-old Father Jutz tried especially hard to acquire a facility with the language. At the end of November, he went to Fort Totten on Devil's Lake for a period of almost four months to continue to take lessons with Father Hunt.[12] Later Father Jutz justified his request for a transfer from Holy Rosary by noting, as his superior expressed it, that he "was scarcely any longer [able] to put himself into the minds of the Indians." Entirely in the spirit of the then prevailing understanding of the demands made of a missionary, the very same superior offers himself "for the Indian mission:" "I am not yet too old to learn the language . . . and with God's grace I feel strong enough to spend my entire life in that field of work"[13] [quotes translated from the German].

In contrast to the situation in the schools, where Lakota was officially prohibited, the missionaries in their missionizing work and as pastors depended on being able to communicate with the adult Lakotas. Given that the Indians knew hardly any English, the fathers needed to learn the Indians' language if they did not want to be obliged to have an interpreter with them at all times (which, for example, was not possible during confession). Moreover, hymns and prayers in Lakota were quite common during religious services. Thus, it was for pragmatic reasons that the fathers of the founding generation learned and cultivated the Lakota language. However, an explicit appreciation of the language, or the intent to preserve it as part of maintaining the Lakota culture, is not reflected in the texts of these early years. At the same time, one will search in vain for expressions of a fundamental appreciation of the traditional culture. On the contrary, the missionaries were convinced that the culturally determined "offences" associated with paganism would have to be overcome, in particular "polygamy," "wastefulness" (giveaways), dances, burial practices, and curing ceremonies, but also the lax upbringing by which the children were "spoiled" rather than encouraged to engage in work. The cutting of hair was demanded just the same as the renunciation of traditional clothing at church festivals. In that regard, the missionaries shared in the "civilizing" for the purpose of supplanting the traditional culture. "The contract schools, whether Protestant or Catholic, saw it as their sacred duty to demolish the paganism of their charges and replace it with a 'pure' religion, that is, Christianity" (Prucha 1979, 161).

From a religious point of view, the completion of conversion lay in Catholic baptism. Thus, from the beginning there emerge from the reports figures on the numbers of baptisms administered; for example, in 1886 for

St. Francis, fourteen children and three adults "in deathly peril" (doc. 2.3). For 1887 there are 12 baptisms of children reported from here (doc. 1.1); for Holy Rosary it is approximately 60 children for 1888 (doc. 1.3). In the eyes of the missionaries, the main problem with the adults was polygamy, Vielweiberei, which had to be given up for baptism to be administered. Many accounts make references to this subject, yet without ever questioning the function of this institution in the context of Lakota tradition. Equally unquestioned remains, on the basis of the mission understanding at the time, the opposition toward the representatives of traditional religion, that is, the medicine men. In the end, they personified for the missionary the "devilish" element of paganism and were in this respect their pagan, principal rivals. However, in the accounts much attention is also given to differences with the Christian competition on the reservations, especially with the Episcopalians. This rivalry extended not only to education. Rather, it appears that a large part of the conversion activity focused on gaining souls from the other Christian camp.

From today's perspective, and a distance in time of one hundred years, another question poses itself when reading these testimonies of a cultural conquest: How was it possible that in the face of this massive indoctrination many Lakotas were nonetheless able to maintain an independent cultural consciousness? Was there a continuation of traditional lifeways operating in Catholic guise, an unconscious undermining of the missionary efforts?

First hints, which are more pronounced in later years, are, although surely unintentional, contained in the initial reports from the missions. That the children, to the joy of the sisters, liked using religious items, such as rosaries, "the longer, the better," medals with colorful ribbons, and so on, to adorn themselves is a minor example. On the other hand, the willingness with which seventeen- to eighteen-year-old Lakotas strove to learn the sign of the cross and Catholic prayers appears unbelievable to us, as we easily overlook that for the traditional Lakotas to adopt new religious practices was quite compatible with maintaining their own religion. Consistent with this is the image of the Indian policeman, who, as it is reported in the first year of the mission, supervises the proper way of kneeling between the church benches (doc. 2.2), especially when considering that the Indian policemen were frequently recruited from among the traditional warrior societies that, in turn, were customarily also in charge of the proper observance of rituals.[14] Another factor that rendered the Catholic mission message relative in nature was most likely the presence of the variety of confessions on the reservations, about which the missionaries frequently lamented when reporting on their theological discussions with Protestants.

On a political level, the Indians had to learn to differentiate between the "tribes" of the whites ("Black Robes" = Catholics, "White Robes" = Episcopalians, "Short Robes" = Presbyterians, "Long Knives" = U.S. troops), and, if possible, to play them off against one another, as is indicated by Red Cloud's and the other chiefs' decision in favor of the Black Robes. For the individual Lakotas, then, a pragmatic approach toward the religions of the powerful whites meant nothing more and nothing less than to test their benefits in exceedingly difficult times, materially as well as spiritually.

2. Ghost Dance, Wounded Knee, and the Aftermath, 1890–1891

A Missionary's Mediation Attempt

In several respects the year 1890 was to mark the low point in the history of the Sioux. Over the course of the fifteen years since the victory at Little Big-horn, they had "lost their freedom, their livelihood, and a large part of their land; white courts, white bureaucracy had become a reality—the pressure to give up the old culture was considerable" (Feest 1990, 4–5) [quote translated from the German]. In 1889 their reservation territory had once again been significantly reduced and divided into several smaller reservations. The U.S. government drastically decreased the beef deliveries stipulated by treaty, with the ration for the Oglalas cut from 8,125,000 pounds in 1886 to 4,000,000 pounds in 1889. And even these decreased rations were not distributed in full; instead of the 470,400 pounds due them they received only 205,000 pounds in April of 1890. The Lakotas were suffering from hunger. The few who had embarked on the venture of farming in this in-hospitable terrain did not enjoy any benefit from it, given that there was no harvest after three years of drought in South Dakota. Introduced diseases did their part at Pine Ridge. In 1888–1889 a measles epidemic struck, and in 1889–1890, influenza and whooping cough, whose victims were mainly children (doc. 2.7, section 1) (Mooney 1991, 826–27, 845).

In this desperate situation, the Lakotas, like other Indian groups, were receiving reports of a prophet, or messiah, by the name of Wovoka from among the Paiute of Nevada, to whom God had revealed a message of peace: they should cease all disputes among themselves and with the whites, they should work, they should not lie or steal, and they should re-nounce all their old customs that were reminiscent of war in order to be united with all of their kin in the other world. A regularly performed round dance was to accelerate this unification. This message was eagerly received and passed on, leading the Lakotas to send a delegation, with Short Bull and Kicking Bear as its most well-known members, to Wovoka to learn for themselves what, in particular, this prophesy meant for them. They returned with this version: In the spring of 1891, all of the deceased Indians would return, and with them the animals slain by the whites. The foreign invaders would either be devoured by the earth or be forced to return to their own land. In order to make this new world possible, every six weeks the Indians were to dance in a specific way for four nights and one day, and bathe at the dawn of the fifth. The special shirts of the Ghost Dancers, the name applied to the participants, were to make them invulnerable against the bullets of the whites (Mooney 1991, 816–24).

It is indisputable that the original message of the Ghost Dance movement was a peaceful one. To what extent it took a more combative turn with the Lakotas, or whether this was a (perhaps intentional) distortion among the American public, is debatable. Statements by the missionaries at the time, including those found in unpublished diaries, do not provide any indication that the Ghost Dance as such posed an immediate militant threat. To the missionaries the religious aspect was in the foreground. They saw in the Ghost Dance a threat to their work and a reverting to paganism, especially with the converted Indians who now suddenly stayed away from mass. "Not one Indian attended mass. They are dancing again," noted Father Perrig in his diary from Holy Rosary on 17 October 1890. The fathers were eager to find out more about it, and so Father Jutz went to a dance place accompanied by a sister (probably Sister Kostka Schlaghecken), who both wrote about the event (docs. 1.3; 2.7, section 2). Father Jutz, the ardent missionary, tried to convince the participants about the folly of their doings. The sister limited herself to simply observing, but then, for her part, recorded more details about the appearance of the dancers.

In his report Father Jutz points out that the dance was being understood as a preparation for the coming of the messiah and the deliverance of the Indians out of their misery. However, what he does not mention is a remarkable indication of a blending of traditional and Christian religiosity. In the descriptions of those Ghost Dancers who had seen the messiah in their dance visions, he is portrayed with five stigmata, like Jesus on the cross, at which point the dancers emphasize that the messiah forbade them to address him by the name of Jesus. For Father Perrig, who is noting this in his diary, this suggests that "It gets more and more the appearance of deviltry."[1] Black Elk, an eager participant of the Ghost Dance, discussed below, also described the messiah of his vision having the characteristic marks of Christ on his hands (DeMallie 1984, 263).

Meanwhile, events on the reservations in South Dakota came to a head, an outcome of the fear of a new Indian uprising that was spreading among the whites. At Rosebud, Indian agent James Wright attempted to suppress the dance by sending Short Bull, one of the Ghost Dance prophets, away to Pine Ridge. Unfortunately, a new and untested agent named Daniel F. Royer was residing there, a man without any experience in dealing with such charged situations. He had come to this position after the previous agent, Hugh D. Gallagher, had resigned from his post in protest against the impossible state of affairs with respect to the food supplies. Royer had absolutely no control of the situation and called in the U.S. Army to prevent the eruption of hostilities. Seized with panic as a result of the oppressive measures taken against the Ghost Dance, the Ghost Dancers of the Rosebud Reservation moved to Pine Ridge and from there (reinforced by Oglala Ghost Dancers) to a place of refuge (named "Stronghold") in the Badlands, a rocky, desolate, and difficult to access area northwest of Pine Ridge.

The diary of Father Perrig affords useful insight into the increasing gravity of the situation. The first 500 soldiers, under orders from Brigadier General John R. Brooke, marched into Pine Ridge on 19–20 November (according to Jutz, on the 18th), as well as into Rosebud (doc. 2.7, section 3). All of the day schools are being closed. The agency orders all white government employees and teachers to arm themselves, while the Indian agent, along with his family, made off to Rushville (Nebraska). Children run away from the schools or are collected by their parents; this is repeated in the days following. There are conflicting rumors circulating about the intentions of the Indians. Father Perrig reports on several Sioux City newspapers that are giving the impression that the troubles among the Indians had been exaggerated, and he is asking himself: "Who is responsible for this costly and unwarranted scare?"[2] On 24 November three more companies of soldiers arrive, and on the next day the Indian police are reinforced by 100 men; guards are posted all around the agency. An additional ten companies arrive on 27 November. There are now a total of 1,200 soldiers at Pine Ridge.

At this stage, Father Jutz, superior at Holy Rosary, came to the opinion that he should set aside his initial reticence and make an effort to mediate the situation "in order to bring these Indian troubles to an end faster and more easily" [quote translated from the German]. He describes the details later in a report for *Die katholischen Missionen*, which is reproduced here in its entirety for the first time (doc. 2.7, section 3). Jutz's vivid account of his adventurous journey into the Badlands, during which he and his fellow travelers lost their way in the bitter cold of the night, stands alone. However, of additional interest are two pieces of related information gleaned from Father Perrig's diary. The first concerns the size of the camp in the Badlands, which according to the Indian High Hawk consisted of about five hundred lodges of the Sicangus (from Rosebud) and twenty to thirty of the Oglalas (from Pine Ridge). The second piece of information is the characterization of Jack Red Cloud as "a notorious dance-chief" who, in the place of his father, old Red Cloud, accompanied Jutz on his mediation attempt. This indicates the spread of the Ghost Dance to the families of the most faithful followers of the missionaries, something not mentioned in Jutz's report.

Jutz managed to bring a large delegation of chiefs to General Brooke at Pine Ridge Agency. Perrig names Two Strike, Big Turkey, Turning Bear, Short Bull, Bull Dog, High Pipe, as well as 28 others.[3] They stayed overnight in the schoolroom of the mission. Jutz first had to dispel their suspicion that this was a trap, a rumor that had been spread by a white person. He gave the chiefs assurances by offering, "if one of them were to be harmed, the next man could shoot me dead" (doc. 2.7, section 3) [quote translated from the German].

Based on Jutz's report, a number of the hostiles (referred to also as "recusants" by the missionaries) were in fact prepared to leave the Badlands and return to the agency, a result of the negotiations at the beginning of December. Others, led by Short Bull and Kicking Bear, continued to stay there. Several attempts, also supported by the returnees, to persuade those who remained at the "Stronghold" to return along with them failed. The reason for this, Father Jutz supposed, was that the head of the agency had been made to understand by someone high up in government that the mediation of a Jesuit was not to succeed (doc. 2.7, section 4). Later, Father Digmann reported that General Brooke had received a telegram from his headquarters, reading: "It seems that the management of the war had gone over in other hands. One bad general is better than two good ones."

According to Father Perrig, Brooke had already sent a policeman after Jutz on 4 December to call him back from his mediation effort.[4]

Attempts to induce the remaining hostiles to move from the Badlands to the reservation continued for a while. On 14 December 1890, Father Perrig reported that some 145 lodges had arrived, while 107 continued to stay in the Badlands. Even the leader, Short Bull, it was said, was considering a move to the agency. Yet events were reaching a crisis point. One day later, while resisting arrest, Sitting Bull was killed at Standing Rock Reservation. Among the Lakotas, dissension regarding their future actions was intensifying. On 19 December 1890 three hundred Oglalas gathered at Holy Rosary with the intent to go and get the others from the Badlands; more came over the following two days. However, on 24 December three messengers arrived from the Badlands, bringing word that the recusants would not come. A new calamity was looming. On 25 December, Father Perrig noted in his diary that soldiers would be sent out to intercept a group of Miniconjous led by Chief Big Foot. They were coming from the Cheyenne River Reservation and were on their way to join with the recusants in the Badlands. He also heard the rumor that the hostiles would apparently surrender after all. Then, on 29 December 1890, an Indian arrives "in the greatest state of excitement," reporting to Father Jutz that Indians were fighting with policemen or soldiers at Wounded Knee Creek (doc. 2.6) [quote translated from the German].

Holy Rosary Mission between Two Fronts

The tragic events at Wounded Knee Creek have been portrayed many times, thus a brief summary shall suffice here. On 22 December 1890, the group of Miniconjous left their village on the Cheyenne River Reservation and were moving toward the Badlands of Pine Ridge, presumably in anticipation of a forcible removal to the agency. There were above 340 people; slightly more than 100 of them were warriors. They were armed only with light hunting rifles. The army followed the party, whose leader, Big Foot, was ill with pneumonia, intercepted them on 28 December, and forced their unconditional surrender. The camp that was assigned to them at Wounded Knee was completely surrounded by soldiers of the 7th Cavalry Regiment. Four Hotchkiss guns, positioned on a slight elevation, were pointed at the tents between which the Lakotas had raised a white flag. On

29 December 1890 they were to be finally disarmed, but the warriors, most of whom were wearing their supposedly bullet-proof Ghost Dance shirts, exercised passive resistance. A shot from the rifle of a Lakota—it remained disputed why it went off—gave the signal for the men at the canons, who immediately barraged the camp with a hail of cannon balls, while the soldiers, who had gotten out of control, shot at everything that moved. The accounts about the number of dead vary. Today about 300 Lakotas are assumed to have died, two-thirds of them women and children. General Nelson A. Miles some time afterward determined that a large number of the 25 dead U.S. soldiers had been killed by their own comrades in the crossfire (Utley 1963, 244). Years later one of the sisters at the mission remembers that in 1922 or 1923, two traveling government agents had stopped at the mission, one of whom declared that he had been a soldier in the regiment that had fought at Wounded Knee, reportedly adding: "We came up <u>with the intention of wiping out those Indians</u>, and . . . we <u>did</u> wipe them out"[5] [emphasis in the original].

Following the massacre at Wounded Knee, there was a great deal of commotion at the agency combined with fears of acts of revenge and attacks by the other Lakotas.[6] Having received word about the fighting, Father Jutz set out for the agency to get more details. He found the road full of Indians in war paint, driving their horses together. Two Indians stopped him and pressed him to return, accompanying him on his way back, for his own protection, as it turned out (docs. 2.6; 2.7, section 5). The various groups of Lakotas were filled with rage and indignation in light of the intelligence about Wounded Knee, and it was by no means clear how they would act toward the missionaries. With neighbors coming to seek protection at Holy Rosary, reports about burning houses reached the mission. At night the missionaries posted guards. On the following day (30 December 1890) the events shifted to the immediate surroundings of the mission. First, the news that on the previous day, following the massacre, angry Indians had shot at the tents of the soldiers at the agency, wounding several, had caused some unrest. Then, Father Perrig reports, now and then Indians passed by on the road near the mission. At about ten o'clock a schoolhouse (a log cabin used as a schoolroom for the day school of a Mrs. Wells, who herself had sought refuge at the mission) very close to the mission was seen in flames (doc. 2.7, section 5). It had been set ablaze by a party of Sicangus, who shortly thereafter stopped at the mission and spoke with Father Jutz. Because of the pillar of smoke seen rising from where the mission stood, at the agency it was falsely assumed that the mission itself was on fire. Some time after the Sicangus had moved on, a troop of scouts arrived, followed by three cavalry regiments, to come to the aid of the missionaries. This did not prove to be necessary, and the sisters instead provided the hungry soldiers with lunch. Soon after, however, ten or fifteen Indians fired at the soldiers from across the valley, sending bullets literally flying past two Jesuit brothers and two employees of the mission. After a short time the Indians moved on to White Bird's Camp, where the schoolhouse was on fire, while gun fighting continued on the road. Perrig observed: "We could see the Indians sneaking around the hills on which the soldiers were and shooting at them from behind, others trying to pass the soldiers by leading their ponies, using them as a cover against the bullet[s] of the soldiers, others mounting in full gallop with frentic [sic] yells on an unoccupied hilltop." At half past one the soldiers appeared to be pulling back, prompting Father Jutz to request additional troops from General Brooke for the protection of the mission. Before long a cavalry regiment arrived with a canon, and the Indians retreated. At three o'clock in the afternoon everything was over. Two soldiers had suffered slight injuries and were cared for at the mission; it was not known whether there were any dead on either side.

"It seems there was an enormous waste of powder for nothing, which is no credit to either party's courage," opined Father Perrig in his diary entry. Not everyone was able to assess the situation in such a matter-of-fact way. The Jesuits and Franciscan sisters at the mission were increasingly left to their own devices, now that practically all of the children had been collected from the mission by their parents, and that the neighbors, having initially fled to the mission, were relocating to the agency (Jutz in docs. 2.6; 2.7, section 4). Given the tumultuous and chaotic situation at Pine Ridge, a number of the mission residents had to confront their fears that individual groups of Lakotas would not even spare the mission. Accounts by the sisters provide insight into the residents' state of mind during those days (doc. 2.7, section 5). Writing to her fellow sisters outside the mission, Sister Kostka Schlaghecken, the mother superior, reveals: "What else can we do but flee under the protective mantle of the beloved Blessed Virgin and trust in God? . . . Praise be to her that all of the sisters are full of courage; not one shows even the least bit of faint-heartedness. Any moment a wild horde can come and assault us. At night the brothers keep watch outside, and we go to bed fully clothed. Our situation is awfully grave. . . . In their agitated state they are like enraged animals and just as cruel as they had been in times past. That a person is white is enough [reason] to finish him off"[7] [quote translated from the German]. Sister Hilaria Geuting remembers having gone into the mission's courtyard in order to hang up laundry after the gunfight on 30 December, when suddenly she heard Brother Ständer behind her, calling out to her from a window with a hoarse voice, "Sister, Sister, come in for God's sake; we shan't want any more clean clothes if this goes on." This was at the time when the two soldiers who had been wounded in the fighting were brought into the mission house to be given first aid. The same source reports that, to the surprise of the sisters, one of the men started venting his feelings about the Indians "in good German but in no measured language." The other soldier was Irish, but the accompanying doctor was German as well.[8]

After reports about the massacre at Wounded Knee Creek were published, a false rumor was spread in Buffalo, the home of both orders, as well as among the American public in general, that the mission had fallen victim to the Indians' revenge. On New Year's Eve 1890, the evening papers in Buffalo appeared with the headline: "Holy Rosary Mission in South Dakota Burned to the Ground—All the Inmates Massacred!" For several hours both orders were numbed by the horror, until at ten o'clock in the evening the Buffalo Jesuit superior Father Behrens approached with haste, carrying a telegram from Father Jutz: "All safe at Holy Rosary Mission" (Mason 1935, 368–69; Brady 1969, 119).

On New Year's Day 1891, Father Stephan, the head of BCIM, appeared on the scene at Holy Rosary, on the order of Katharine Drexel, to remove the sisters from this presumably highly dangerous situation. However, the sisters refused this demand (doc. 2.7, section 5). Father Jutz does not appear to have been at all enthusiastic about Stephan's idea. His counterproposal was that at least a couple of the sisters should stay to look after a blind Sioux woman named Clara, who was living at the mission and required much care. When Sister Kostka informed him that none of the sisters wanted to leave, he was very pleased, because—according to S. Mason's mission history of the Franciscan sisters—the staying on of the sisters would be of considerable assistance to his efforts to move the Indians again to a peaceful settlement. Father Stephan was unable to change the sisters' minds.[9]

In the meantime Jutz made an attempt to assist with the care of the wounded survivors of the massacre. Having learned that about thirty injured women and children had been brought to the church of the Episcopalian pastor Father Cook, he asked General Miles to permit him to bring several of the wounded, especially the children, to Holy Rosary in order to care for them. Initially he was promised several times that he could do so.[10] A few days later it emerged that the general had changed his mind and did not want to turn over any of the wounded children to the Catholic missionaries. The fathers assumed that the reason for this refusal lay in a visit to the agency by the Episcopalian bishop W. H. Hare.[11] Father Jutz did not relent, and on 9 January he made another request to General Miles for the wounded children, which he also did in writing, as was demanded of him. But the general did not yield. Father Perrig noted that the wounded children were bedded on hay in the school of Mrs. Arnold, hardly covered, and appeared "uncared for, dirty as little pigs in a pigsty." On the following day these children were handed over to the Indians who were encamped near the agency, with Perrig commenting: "So we are cheated out of our expectations once more."[12]

Although the mission was not able to actively participate in overcoming the grave consequences of the massacre, the situation with regard to the relationship with the Lakotas gradually eased. Thus, eight days after the letter quoted above, Sister Kostka wrote: "The dear God, completely unexpectedly, appears to be responding to the prayers for peace. Many *Wilde* are coming from their camps to the mission of their own accord, strongly armed, to speak with the Black Robe Fr. Superior about peace and surrender. It is also now becoming apparent that they had absolutely no intention to do harm to the mission or its residents, and that they are our friends. . . . They all shook hands with us and said they felt joy in their hearts, for there was going to be peace now. We then gave them food" (quoted from Paula 1911, 133) [quote translated from the German]. This understanding is also related in other reports with a great deal of relief, for example, in the quoted Franciscan mission history, which contains an additional detail: unbeknown to the residents at the time, there is said to have been an old medicine man by the name of Cold Nose who had guarded and protected the mission house, "though he was still a heathen."[13]

Yet the situation remained unsettled for a while. The hostiles were to come to the agency now and surrender their weapons, which was, of course, difficult for them, especially after the massacre. Here, a survey of the visitors passing through Holy Rosary during these weeks in January shows that the mission, under the leadership of Father Jutz, was accepted and used by both sides as if it were, in a way, a neutral place.[14] The meal for the hungry soldiers on 30 December 1890 was already mentioned, which was followed by the gunfight between them and a party of Lakotas. This, however, did not represent a siding with the army, as became apparent on the following day when General Brooke called on Father Jutz to summon Red Cloud and several other chiefs to him and to the newly arrived General Miles. General Miles, Brooke's superior, had come to Pine Ridge on 31 December to assume command. At the time, Red Cloud was with the hostile Sicangus, who had carried him and a group of Oglalas off to their camp (Utley 1963, 233–34). In response to the general's unreasonable request, Jutz "quietly" replied that he would pass this information on to Red Cloud, if the opportunity presented itself. Perrig's comments on this restrained reply capture Jutz's sentiment: "We are not going on the useless errand of summoning somebody to the agency to whom we can not make explicit promises of impunity etc." Other visitors mentioned in Perrig's diary included, on 3 January 1891, two Indians who had come to the mission to ask for a white flag in order to bring a letter from General Miles to the Oglala camp four miles distant. In the evening two wagons full of women and children were fed when they stopped at the mission before continuing on to the agency. The following day, two messengers appeared, bringing word from Red Cloud and the abducted Oglalas that they intended to return secretly and on their way spend the night at the mission: "We willingly will receive them." Although there is no explicit entry found in Perrig's diary about the arrival of this party at the mission over the days that followed, there continued to arrive other groups of hostiles. At first, women and children to spend the night and to get something to eat, but also, as with Chief Turning Bear, to ask Father Jutz to intervene with General Miles regarding their return to Rosebud. In addition, a party of scouts took up quarters for the night in the boys' playroom.

At this point, the last hostiles had to realize that they had no choice but to yield to the superior force of the U.S. Army. Just prior to reaching the agency, they encamped near the mission at a place "as near as is consistent with safety to us and themselves," as one observer at the agency remarked (Green 1996, 62). On the following day, 12 January 1891, they began moving toward the agency, with many stopping at Holy Rosary. Perrig notes: "Whole crowds came into the house to get a cup of coffee and a piece of bread, tobacco, matches—some also begged for things which we could not give them as shoes, coats, blankets etc." Over the noon hour an almost unbroken train of men, women, and children moved past the mission, on foot, on horseback, and in wagons. Perrig reports that they counted 734 armed warriors. There were without doubt about 1,000 women and children, and more than 2,000 horses. The last Indians passed the mission around two o'clock, followed closely by the wagons of General Brooke's soldiers, who came and purchased bread and vegetables (doc. 2.7, section 5). One Indian told Father Jutz that several young warriors would rather fight than surrender their weapons, and Father Jutz tried to discourage them from doing so. On his way to the agency with Turning Bear, he witnessed how the young Lakotas were arguing vehemently with the old about whether there should be any negotiations conducted with the general. In the evening, two reporters requested to stay overnight because, due to the late hour, they were not able to make it to the agency (doc. 2.7, section 4). In the meantime more and more of the hostiles came to the agency and surrendered their weapons, if only reluctantly. On 15 January 1891, everyone was impressed by the large train moving to the agency, which included the Ghost Dance leaders and the hostiles; with that, the military struggles had ceased (Utley 1963, 260–61). Finally, a large parade of all the military forces was announced for 22 January, after which the soldiers were to begin their withdrawal from the reservation.

Also at this time, discussions about the massacre and the events that had led up to it surfaced among the American public. For our purpose, two issues are worth noting. On the one hand, it became increasingly apparent that the mission had been excluded from attacks by the hostile parties, albeit against strong opposition on the part of a group of Cheyennes at Pine Ridge who wanted to burn it down. To them old Red Cloud had declared that he would not tolerate that any harm be done to either the missionaries or their possessions.[15] Considering that Red Cloud's authority was by this time somewhat contested, there must have been others as well who advocated that the missionaries be protected. On the other hand, there were assertions made by the American press that the missionaries had instigated the unrest. Perrig notes a charge made by a Sioux City newspaper that the Catholic missionaries in general, and Francis Craft in particular, had fanned, or caused, the present discontentment among the Indians. An anonymous letter to the editor of the newspaper *Daily Inter Ocean*, dated 23 January 1891, which was reprinted several times, also accuses the Jesuits and Father Craft of condoning atrocities such as those committed by the Indians, in that they would afterward grant them absolution during confession. Father Jutz categorically rejected these accusations, as did Craft.[16]

Mentioning Father Craft in this context, and also because he is referred to in the accounts published here, requires elaboration. As noted above, Francis M. Craft had been one of the first missionaries at Pine Ridge and Rosebud, and a predecessor of the Jesuit missionaries. His relationship with the Indian converts was unusual. In 1884 Craft, who was part Mohawk and had previously been an Episcopalian, started a school for Lakota children on the Rosebud Reservation. After only two months of running the school, Craft had already converted a large number of Indians to Catholicism and had gained a great deal of influence with them, primarily due to his charismatic personality and his perfect facility with the Lakota language. According to Craft, when Chief Spotted Tail was on his deathbed, he had expressed his wish that a Black Robe become his successor, and given that Craft was the first to arrive after Spotted Tail's death, he was appointed chief and received the name "Hovering Eagle." Although as a Catholic priest Craft could not accept the title of chief, he was nonetheless adopted by Spotted Tail's family and thus became a member of the Sicangus. He made an attempt to adapt to the way of life of the Lakotas. They honored this by presenting him with an eagle feather, which he wore on his hat. Craft was of the opinion that the Lakotas needed to conform to the customs of the whites, if they did not want to go to ruin. Yet, as he noted in his diary, the church should not condemn what was "good or indifferent" about their way of life. His siding with the Lakotas necessarily brought him into conflict with government agencies, and when the Sicangus refused to send their children to a government school in Nebraska, he was accused of having incited them to that end. In 1885 Craft was banished from the Rosebud Reservation. From there he first went to Standing Rock. He paid frequent visits to both reservations, and the Jesuits knew of his intimate relationship with the Indians. At the beginning of December 1890, Father Craft appeared at Pine Ridge, asserting that the BCIM had sent him, yet refusing to show the Jesuits written authorization for this mission.[17] Father Jutz's questioning of the matter made him "quite mad." Only Father Digmann (superior at St. Francis) was able to appease Craft enough so that he presented the letter from Father Stephan in which his mission was explained. Among other things, Craft was to find out how many pupils from the government schools, Protestant as well as Catholic, had joined with the hostiles and were participating in the Ghost Dance. He refused the apologies that Father Jutz subsequently offered him. Instead Craft wanted to return to Washington, prompting the superiors Jutz and Digmann to immediately write to Stephan reporting their version of the incident. In the end, Father Digmann was able to move the ruffled Craft to stay on. On one of the following days, Craft observed the Ghost Dance at the camp of the Rosebud Indians. "He found it to be all right, quite catholic and even edifying," noted Perrig. On 24 December 1890 a letter arrived from Father Stephan, explaining Craft's mission, which, according to Perrig, was based on a serendipitous encounter between Craft and Stephan in Chicago. Due to illness, Stephan had been forced to postpone his planned trip to the reservations. He sent Craft in his place so that Craft could inform him about the sources of the unrest. On that fateful day, 29 December 1890, Craft had linked up with the army at the agency, where he had moved several days earlier to mediate between the opposing forces and to calm the agitated minds. When the gunfight at Wounded Knee began, and everyone was frantically running about, he was stabbed in the lungs by one of the warriors; on that day he was wearing a soldier's coat and hat. Despite his severe injury he continued to care for the wounded soldiers until he collapsed (doc. 2.6).

At first glance it might appear that by identifying with his Indian kin, Father Craft was much ahead of his time and of the cautiously deliberate Jesuits, such as Father Jutz. However, a closer look reveals more commonalities than the two priests might have been aware of in their quarrel. Both were deeply concerned about the survival of the Indians; both regarded government politics as one of the principal evils facing the Indians; and both sought to mediate in that extremely tense situation of December 1890: Craft during the battle, at the risk of life and limb, and Jutz through his attempts to make peace between the two sides, along with his and his community's perseverance in the turmoil following the battle. One recognizable dissimilarity, however, is the degree to which one of them was prepared to permit the Indians to retain elements of their traditional religion. No Jesuit would have assessed the Ghost Dance as "quite catholic [sic] and even edifying," given that they saw in it the work of the devil. Another difference surely lay in the political dimension of their work. Craft was an Indian lobbyist and a missionary who operated more like a lone warrior, whereas Jutz and the Jesuits were participants in a system of schools and government-run administrations of the reservations. For the future of the reservation Indians, this stage of missionary work—that is, the institutionalized reorganization of their lives after the catastrophe that culminated with Wounded Knee—was to take precedence.

3. Catholic Community Structures versus Government Policies, 1891–1900

Kulturkampf on the Prairie

As a result of successful lobbying in Washington and the efforts on the part of the missions, the Catholic schools received in total more financial government support in 1890 than all of the Protestant schools combined (Prucha 1979, 4–8). At the beginning of the 1890s only the government schools presented serious competition for the Catholic mission schools on the South Dakota reservations. There were seven government schools at Rosebud and nine at Pine Ridge, each with thirty to forty pupils. Of the remaining mission schools there existed only one small Episcopal boarding school at Rosebud with about fifty children.

The amount of federal funding for the mission schools had already been an issue during the 1892 presidential campaign, and in the end the U.S. Congress decided to successively cut these appropriations. Beginning with the 1896–1897 fiscal year, funding was to be reduced each year thereafter by 20 percent, leading to the termination of all financial assistance by the middle of 1900. Although Protestant mission schools were also affected by these measures, their losses were compensated for by the solid footing that the Protestants enjoyed in the state schools. Here their influence was in essence similar to that in the mission schools. In each of the state schools on the reservations, Protestant clergy conducted compulsory religious services, which were officially "non-denominational," but in actuality used Protestant Bibles and hymns.

Behind this policy of furtive Protestant indoctrination, instituted by the Office of Indian Affairs, was the fact that many of its employees were members of the anti-Catholic American Protective Association (APA). The APA accused Catholics of being subject to a foreign ruler (the pope) and, because of their un-American character, ill suited to Americanize the Indians as set out in the assimilation policy (Hoxie 2001, 67). The manifold complaints of the missionaries about discrimination on the part of the government, indeed, a Kulturkampf, are rooted in these experiences, and they present a direct parallel to the oppression that these orders and the Catholic Church as a whole suffered in the German Reich under Bismarck (docs. 2.17 to 2.20). Accordingly, the head of the Office of Indian Affairs, Indian Commissioner Thomas Morgan, who in the eyes of the missionaries was leading a "war of annihilation against the Catholic Indian schools" (doc. 2.23), attempted to remove Indian children from the Catholic schools and transfer them against their will to the government schools, which had difficulty recruiting pupils [quote translated from the German]. The official reason given was that, in accordance with an understanding of American law, Indians were wards of the U.S. government, which, therefore, felt justified in determining which school the children were to attend. After retiring as Indian commissioner, and in the position of spokesperson for the APA, Morgan declared: "The Roman Catholics have assumed an attitude on the Indian question that is un-American, unpatriotic, and a menace to our liberties. I challenge the course they have pursued, as that of a corrupt ecclesiastico-political machine masquerading as a church." In 1896 Morgan's successor, Daniel Browning, promulgated the regulation that Indians would be permitted to send their children to a mission school only after the government schools were filled. When the agent at Pine Ridge tried to implement this regulation by force, parents wanting to send their children to Holy Rosary sent letters of protest to the commissioner, who, however, bluntly replied that "Indian parents have no right to designate which school their children shall attend" (both quotes in Prucha 1979, 41).

Thus, by the second half of the 1890s, the question of the very existence of the mission schools became increasingly the focus of concern for the missionaries and the bishops. This concern, then, determined to a great extent how the schools presented themselves to the public, as is indicated, for example, by the resolution that was passed at the Catholic congress at St. Francis in 1896, "against the Kulturkampf, the way it has recently manifested itself in the Indian school system" (doc. 2.17). A revealing document is a resolution, whose text is reprinted here, that was presented to the U.S. Congress the next year, following a decision taken by this Catholic congress (doc. 2.19). Only in 1902, under President Roosevelt, was Browning's regulation against the mission schools rescinded.

The St. Joseph and St. Mary Societies

Against this backdrop of an increasingly more difficult political climate for the Catholic missions, the organizational steps taken by the missionaries now became imbued with social and political meaning beyond purely pastoral and missionizing considerations (Thiel 1998, 60–69). One of the most significant measures was the establishment of so-called sodalities, that is, societies of the church for adult Christians, segregated by gender. The sodalities that the Benedictines had begun at Devil's Lake in 1884 served as models for the societies to be established at Rosebud and Pine Ridge. To gain membership one had to be Catholic, had to have been married within the church, and had to have received first communion. Father Digmann counted on the societies to be the solution to the "Indian question," for the first rule of the societies was "that their members give up the old ways of Indian life, cut their long hair, dress like whites, engage in farming, make an honest living, and provide each other mutual support" (doc. 2.8). Members of the sodalities were known for their Christian conduct: They observed the Sabbath, converted their tribal members to the Catholic faith, had given up polygamy, did not curse, and did not get drunk. Their activities included religious worship, religious education, encouraging fellow members to lead a Christian life, and assisting them in times of sickness. However, structurally they resembled in some ways traditional men's or women's societies. In addition to the usual conventional officers, each society had special traditional positions such as doorkeeper, visitor of the sick, waiter, herald, hair cutter, and horse trader. According to Mark Thiel, who has presented the most extensive study on this topic, the sodalities gave especially men new, valued opportunities to gain status in their communities, in particular offering young adults moral role models similar to those found in traditional societies of former times.

This model of community work on the reservations was soon spread to other areas. In spring 1888 the missionaries of Standing Rock brought a delegation from the St. Joseph Society of Fort Totten (Devil's Lake) for a visit to their reservation. Together with interested Lakotas, the visitors founded four St. Joseph Societies and four St. Mary Societies, one pair for each local parish. After their official installation on the feast of St. Joseph in 1888, the parishes grew rapidly, and the members of the sodalities with their distinctive regalia (such as sashes), became the center of religious and social community life. Another reason for promoting the sodalities through the hierarchy of the Catholic Church was the substantial lack of priests and other religious. Training parish assistants from among the circle of sodality members was an attempt to mitigate this situation to a certain extent. The Catholic gatherings to take place nearly every year, referred to as Catholic Sioux congresses, also have their organizational starting point within these sodalities. The call for the first of these congresses at Standing Rock (1891) was explicitly directed at them.

The sodalities saw their greatest increase during the years following this first congress. Like the congresses, the sodalities can trace this success to the fact that in these years the social and cultural cohesion of the Lakota tribes was facing its greatest crisis, and offers to organize in some way were simply necessary means for survival. Thiel lists the activities and successes of these years: the establishment of additional sodalities in many communities; the evangelizing of relatives and neighbors; the lodging of itinerant clergy; and the building of chapels, also in the remote areas of the reservations. In the eyes of the missionaries, these were important steps for winning new Catholics in the face of the established competition, the Episcopalians. Furthermore, the missionaries tried to incorporate the male leadership of the individual camps, at whom the Protestants liked to direct their conversion efforts, by engaging them in the St. Joseph Societies, and to keep the women away from the Episcopalian sewing societies by involving them in the St. Mary Societies (Thiel 1998, 65–66).

Aside from the Christian competition, there were also other obstacles to the success of the Catholic mission. Many older Indians, especially the former Ghost Dancers, refused to be converted on principle. The younger people who were sent to boarding schools in the East, and thus removed from the influence of Catholic ministrations, became estranged from the church. With some of the younger generation, however, the Christian message did fall on fertile ground, resulting in a number of achievements that, in their spiritual quality, were to exceed by far what could have been imagined by either the missionaries or the older, tradition-minded Indians. One figure who stands out in today's spiritual exchange between the traditional Lakota religion and post–Vatican II Catholicism is Black Elk, who in those years had started on his path as mediator between the religions, keeping one foot in each camp. He had been a traditional healer since his youth, had traveled through Europe for a period of two years as a member of Buffalo Bill's Wild West Show, as well as on his own, subsequently became an enthusiastic Ghost Dancer, but now gradually drew closer to Catholicism. He married in 1892. His wife appears to have become Catholic in the ensuing years. Three sons, born in 1893, 1895, and 1899, were baptized, the first two in 1895 while Black Elk was active as a medicine man, which he continued to be until his baptism in 1904 (Neihardt 1988; DeMallie 1984, 14).

Sodality meetings typically took place each Sunday in conjunction with a prayer service or a mass, provided a priest was available. The religious services included hymns, prayers, gospel readings, and instruction in the faith as preparation for receiving the sacraments. The sodality meeting afterward was held jointly by the St. Joseph and St. Mary Societies. The president of the St. Joseph Society would open the meeting with an address on some aspect of the Christian faith. Then, two to four men appointed by him would speak on the same subject. The St. Mary Society continued the program by following the same pattern. Questions and a discussion followed, including mutual encouragements to lead a Christian life and confessions on past conduct. Thiel reports that in the middle of the 1890s, the membership figures for the Episcopalians at Rosebud showed a decline as a result of the work of the sodalists. The sodality members naturally were also reliable comrades-in-arms in the fight to preserve the Catholic mission schools. To that end they repeatedly circulated petitions on the reservations that frequently carried over one hundred signatures, and often several hundred (Thiel 1998, 66–68).

The "Congresses of the Catholic Sioux"

The most important public forum for articulating political demands such as the preservation of the mission schools were the gatherings, or congresses, of the Catholic Sioux, which started taking place in 1891. In the German reports they are presented in a particularly detailed fashion, and special attention is drawn to the fact that the congresses had their roots in German-speaking countries. This reference to what could be interpreted as another commonality with the Indians (like the popularity of the German church hymns, for example; docs. 2.11, 2.12), was not merely aimed at generating interest and sympathy among the German readership but had a background rooted in reality. In 1885 Bishop Marty had participated in the

Deutscher Katholikentag (German Catholic Congress) in Munster, reporting on his mission work and successfully collecting donations in its support (Fitzgerald 1940, 139–40; Barry 1953, 37–39). The first Katholikentag
to be held in the United States took place in Chicago two years later (September 1887), instituted by and for German or German-speaking Catholics. At the second congress, which took place in Cincinnati the following year, the expressed intention was to expand its base to include other
groups of Catholics, especially the Irish. With that, the idea of a political
demonstration of American Catholicism, following the model of the German-speaking Catholics, was established. At the same time, the African
American Catholics gathered for their first congress in Washington DC.
The fifth Catholic Congress took place in Buffalo, the home of the missionaries (Barry 1953, 105–6, 112–14, 169–74; Enochs 1995, 53).

In June 1891, only a few months after the end of the armed conflicts in
connection with the Ghost Dance movement, Bishop Marty invited the sodalities and all of the Catholic Sioux, of whom there were approximately
four thousand at the time, for a general congress. It was to take place at
Standing Rock Agency during the Fourth of July celebration, which had become a popular time for summer festivities also among the Sioux. The reason for having chosen this particular time was to provide an opportunity to
connect to traditional customs. In pre-reservation days the Sun Dance had
been the most important annual festival for the ritual renewal of the Lakotas. It was held on the day of the summer solstice, which is close in time to
the Fourth of July. In 1883, when the federal government banned the Sun
Dance, several of its accompanying activities were nonetheless continued
as part of the Independence Day festivities at the agencies. These harmless
and joyous events, lasting three to eight days, involved mock battles, giveaways, and the Omaha dance. The Catholic missionaries criticized these
agency festivals as representing a revival of old Indian customs rather than
being an exercise in American patriotism, and for this reason they supported the bishop's idea to introduce a competing event in the form of the
Indian congresses (Thiel 1998, 62–63).

Despite the great distances to be negotiated—travel by horse from some
of the reservations took several days—in 1891 a total of a thousand Lakotas
arrived for the first congress at Standing Rock. The circle formed by the
tents that were pitched measured a mile in diameter, with a shady place

in the center, created by a covering of pine boughs. The account of this event, which in mood and detail reflects the enthusiasm of the missionaries about the success of this first congress, emphasizes in particular the role of the societies (sodalities), and Die katholischen Missionen explicitly names the "German Catholic gatherings" as the model for this congress (doc. 2.8).

Concerning the report on the second congress (doc. 2.9), held on the Cheyenne River Reservation in 1892, it is to be noted that although a large delegation had come from Standing Rock and one from Rosebud (having increased in number from 20 to 150 wagons), none had arrived from Pine Ridge (Thiel 1998, 63–64). The largest of the reservations, measured by the number of its inhabitants, was still considered the stronghold of traditional customs. The content and the course of the events at this and subsequent congresses followed the pattern of the first: it commenced on the third of July and concluded on the fifth, with the president of the local St. Joseph Society heading the meeting. The sodalities assembled the participants for instruction and prayer, while the priests and the bishop said mass, administered sacraments, and, if necessary, consecrated a new church or chapel. Many participants waited for this special occasion to receive one-time sacraments. All of the local men's and women's sodalities reported on the activities of the previous year, including revenues and expenditures. The sodalities were, above all, in charge of the organization and the resolutions of the congresses, which ensured the preeminent position of the missionaries and a common objective.

An important resolution was always the one concerning the site for the next congress. At Cheyenne River, Rosebud was chosen for the following year (1893), also with the purpose in mind to set an example for the inhabitants of neighboring Pine Ridge, where the meager success of the missionary work gave reason for concern. After this matter had been decided, one participant spoke up, critically commenting on the fact that the women had not been given a chance to cast their vote; they could feel slighted if they were not heard. Bishop Marty dismissed this point with reprehension by stating that in the church it had been that way from the beginning, that the woman had to remain silent in public affairs, for the man had been appointed by God as head, and it was the woman's honor to govern the house and to raise and educate the men. At first Marty's rebuke was ill received, but in the end his explanation was accepted (Thiel 1998, 65). In light of this, the especially detailed account in *Die katholischen Missionen* about the subsequent congress at Rosebud is astonishing for its comprehensive reporting of the women's speeches (doc. 2.11).

Also at this congress, tensions arose between the bishop and the Indian delegates over the site for the next meeting. Marty wanted to move away from one large gathering and hereafter hold four separate regional events (doc. 2.11). At the root of this proposal were the sometimes two-week absences of the participants from their homesteads and fields and of the children from their schools, about which the agents complained. This time Marty was not able to prevail; opposition on the part of the Lakotas was too strong. They did not want to miss this opportunity for joint celebration and exchange, given that, at the time, this represented a rare opportunity to meet across reservation borders. At Devil's Lake the following year, 1894, there was again an overwhelming majority in favor of retaining the general congress. Only in 1896, when the congress was for the first time held at Holy Rosary on Pine Ridge, and with Marty making his last appearance, although no longer as bishop in charge, was he able to push through a resolution to the effect that in the course of the next year only regional congresses would take place (doc. 2.17). In his view, the large, general congresses had by then fulfilled their function of conveying mutual moral support to the young parishes. A new Catholic journal in Lakota, decided upon in 1895, was to serve as a means of communication among the Catholic Lakotas. It appeared for the first time in 1898. Still, in addition to the regional congresses, general congresses, one for North Dakota and one for South Dakota, started to be held at the turn of the century (Thiel 1998, 66, 75).

The establishment and maintenance of the Christian societies and their annual supra-regional congresses can be seen as examples of how the missionaries also seized on traditional social elements in an attempt to implement them for their own purposes (Deloria 1970, 110–11). To what extent, however, they were conscious of this interrelationship, and whether they saw it from the beginning as an explicit adaptation to the Lakota culture, cannot be deduced from the texts presented here. Other sources from these early days also do not contain any references to such a point of view, which is found in the North American missions only later on. Instead the idea of pastoral pragmatism predominated. The missionaries wanted to substitute Christian customs for former pagan customs and do so in forms that would be accepted. Accordingly, they initially saw the congresses more as substitutes for the pagan customs surrounding the American Independence Day celebration, that is, the remnants of the Sun Dance traditions with dances and giveaways. With respect to the sodalities (St. Mary and St. Joseph Societies) it is obvious that everything on the outside that was reminiscent of Lakota tradition (long hair, traditional dress, polygamy) was strictly excluded and replaced with Catholic forms. That traditional social elements nonetheless stayed alive in this new guise speaks for the vitality and adaptability of Lakota culture, but not necessarily for the missionaries' intention to preserve it, at least not on the part of the first generation. It is to be positively acknowledged, however, that the missionaries intuitively understood that what their "charges" required for their survival was a social basis as much as a material one.

4. Outlook into the Twentieth Century

The turbulent years surrounding the founding of St. Francis and Holy Rosary were followed in the 1890s by a first phase of consolidation and expansion of the missions into the social and political life of the Sioux. By 1900, the end date of the documents presented here, the Catholic Church had gained a strong footing among the Sioux. For the year 1898, one of the fathers reported to his fellow brothers at home that, of the inhabitants of both reservations, "more than half are said to be Catholic, hardly ¼ Protestant, the rest, more than ¼, pagans." Quantitatively speaking, this constitutes an astonishing success, considering the small number of years of systematic mission work. The Jesuits, however, saw the situation in a different light. They lamented that of the "minimally 1,541" Catholic children on both reservations, only 388 were able to attend the two Catholic schools, while the greatest number of pupils were taught at the "non-denominational state schools" (Eberschweiler 1900–1902) [quotes translated from the German]. Thus the issue that predominated in the mission reports around 1900, and at the beginning of the new century, was the financial security of the schools following the end of the contract school system. Only in the course of many years of negotiations, court actions, and public as well as personal polemics could a system for financing the schools be found: the tribal funds to which the Lakotas were entitled based on their treaties with the U.S. government (Prucha 1979, esp. 84–95).

It seems that this difficult process of negotiations and wrangling, played out in American politics and in public, promoted the Americanization of the missions in South Dakota. If nothing else, their stronger integration into American society was a parallel development, as is demonstrated by a number of issues. The BCIM increasingly sought the support of the American Federation of Catholic Societies by means of donations. In 1902 the BCIM founded the journal Indian Sentinel, yet in the second year it was pressed to issue a German edition (Indianerwache) for distribution among German-American Catholics. Two years later the Marquette League was founded to provide support for the missions. In addition, the internal structure of the mission work was consolidated. In 1907 the "Buffalo mission," which for decades had been the outpost of the German Jesuit province, including its affiliated Indian missions, was separated from the German province and newly organized in the United States. The Jesuits who had come from Europe were integrated into the American provinces and in time gained American citizenship; some of them also acquired property in the bordering regions of Nebraska as homesteaders. The ties to Germany, of course, survived this formal separation, given that personnel from German-speaking countries continued to be sent to the Indian missions, and by keeping the Catholic public in these countries thoroughly informed about the mission work, primarily through *Die katholischen Missionen*.

Just as the American Jesuit provinces underwent structural changes in the early part of the new century, so did the parish work in the missions. By this time the sodalities had begun functioning as the backbone of the mission effort by furnishing much needed personnel. The Jesuits were finally able to recruit catechists from among them—that is, lay missionaries similar to what the Protestant competition had been using for many years. In 1903 Father Lindebner still lamented that "until now not one could be found who could lay claim to this name"[1] [quote translated from the German]. However, it was precisely this priest who just one year later converted Black Elk, the former medicine man and Ghost Dancer, to Catholicism, baptizing him on 6 December 1904, St. Nicholas Day, with the name of this saint. Within a short period of time, Nicholas Black Elk became a model catechist. For several decades the catechists were a pillar of support for the mission work, in particular at Pine Ridge, where the traditionalist resistance was still greatest. Within a period of four years (1906–1910) their number increased from three to eight, the chapels from five to nine, and the community houses from five to ten. In addition, by 1910 there were eight part-time parish assistants. Some of the catechists, including Nicholas Black Elk, were even employed by the missionaries to missionize on other reservations (Thiel 1998, 77; DeMallie 1984, 18–22).

As the Jesuits and the Lakota catechists worked together so closely, it appears that some mutual respect had developed between a number of them, as is reported, for example, in the case of Father Lindebner and Black Elk (Steltenkamp 1993, 53–54). After the death of Lindebner in 1922, Black Elk requested his boots as something by which to remember the priest who had baptized him. Lindebner was famous for these carefully shined boots, into which he had changed every time he entered the Indian homes (Sialm 1921–23, 258).

One Jesuit, who today is often presented as a role model for his relationship with the catechists with whom he worked, is Eugene Buechel. Buechel, born 1874 in Schleid near Geisa (Thuringia), first came to St. Francis in 1902 as a scholastic and returned there after finishing his studies in 1908 in order to spend the rest of his life among the Lakotas. Throughout his life (he died in 1954 at St. Francis), and as clearly as other missionaries, Father Buechel saw himself as missionary and pastor. Yet there was something about the way he understood his calling that distinguished him from his fellow brothers. As is evident even from his first letters reprinted in *Mitteilungen*, he perceived Lakota cultural characteristics and traditions from the start in a less biased fashion. From his initial curiosity about and fascination with the Lakota culture, he developed a sincere interest and a great deal of respect for the people. It is almost symbolic in nature that it was he who in 1909 carried the old chief Red Cloud to his grave, the emblematic figure of the founding and development of the missions during the difficult times of the 1890s. Not only did Buechel work closely with Nicholas Black Elk, but he also did so with many others from whom he collected stories and words, as well as items of the changing material culture. From the beginning of his stay he took detailed notes on all aspects of their lives, becoming famous for his study of the Lakota language and his extensive photo documentation of reservation life.[2]

Buechel was not a theoretician of cultural evolution. In his few statements on such questions he ranks the Lakota culture as being at an early stage on the path to a higher Euro-American culture. Based on this understanding, then, he frames his demand that the Lakotas should be granted longer periods of time to pass through the stages toward "higher development" than they had been allowed by the first missionaries.[3] Yet behind such statements, which reflected the then prevailing view of the scientific community (Hoxie 2001, 144), are less abstract theoretical principles than his opposition to the impatient and intolerant representatives of a belief in progress who wanted to impose the Euro-American culture upon the Indians. His entire work, but especially his diary, reflects an attitude of unequivocal respect for the Lakotas as people and, necessarily corresponding with this, a fundamental respect for their social, cultural, and also religious practices. This attitude is hardly, or never, found with his contemporaries in the church. Thus Buechel is seen today, more so than during his lifetime, as a model with respect to his relationship with the Lakotas, especially among those who got to know him either in his role as pastor or as one who worked to preserve their culture. Compared to this "modern" attitude toward the Lakota culture, which in its approach already showed a willingness to engage in a dialogue, the crude anti-paganism of the founding generation of Jesuits appears barbaric, indeed, as having contributed to the "cultural genocide" to which the Lakotas fell victim (Tinker 1993). However, here one should differentiate between the reality of the Jesuits' everyday lives and their theological superstructure. Although the missionaries wished for nothing more than to replace the pagan religions as completely as possible with Christianity, they were neither successful nor persistent enough in their attempt to eradicate heathenism root and branch, which may to a certain extent speak in their favor. They acted in solidarity with their "charges" for whom they felt responsible in a paternalistic way, championed their physical survival, and in so doing accepted, at least in part, albeit initially probably for practical reasons, elements of the Lakota tradition, as the example of the sodalities shows. Although unintentional, the Jesuits thus contributed to the survival of the foundations necessary for the continuation of a Lakota religion and spirituality (Powers 1977, 125–28). Moreover, the willingness of Father Lindebner, a typical representative of the "old" missionaries, to transform the medicine man Black Elk, his radical pagan past notwithstanding, into a leading catechist within a short period of time, sending him with broad authority as a lay missionary to other tribes, is at the very least indicative of a great deal of appreciation and personal trust. An explicit formulation and application of the "accommodation principle," often described as being typically Jesuit, is rarely found in the statements of the first missionaries in South Dakota. This is not surprising, as it had been developed for mission work among "advanced civilizations," such as the Chinese, and not for "tribal cultures," in whose survival scarcely anyone in the nineteenth century believed. One must note, however, that the willingness for a pragmatic adaptation (accommodation) was never completely lacking.

Here it is necessary to call to mind the different administrative contexts in which the Jesuits labored; that is, within the framework of the parishes, on the one hand, and within the schools, on the other. This distinction is most apparent with respect to the Lakota language. The first missionaries were forced to study Lakota to make it possible for them to function effectively. In the process the fathers learned a great deal about the Lakota culture. This acquired understanding, then, prepared the foundation for the subsequently extensive work to preserve the Indians' language and culture. Later on, the Jesuits even depended on Lakota individuals to act as catechists in their parishes, having transferred to them parts of their duties on the basis of mutual trust. In the schools, however, other rules and goals applied: education with the aim to make industrious American citizens out of "little *Wilde*," while exercising control to stave off any factors that might act counter to this goal. Therefore, the Jesuits who were in charge of the schools were obliged to suppress the Lakota language in favor of English, and they did so, or ordered this done, with all the means that seemed effective to them, including corporeal punishment. The preservation of the Lakota language and culture had no place in that environment, with the exception of individual, decorative elements that could be fit into a set framework. Thus it is not atypical that Father Buechel's efforts in behalf of the preservation of Lakota culture had no influence on the workings of the schools during his lifetime. These contradictions marked nearly one century of mission work. Only in more recent times has this contrast between the different and, in part, opposing principles of the school and parish begun to dissolve, such as when Lakota language, culture, and spirituality are taught in the Red Cloud Indian School of the Holy Rosary Mission.

Today there are extremely divergent positions taken in assessing the coercion that was exercised in Catholic guise to become "civilized." For the "converted" and their descendants, the judgment naturally depends very strongly on what attitudes they, as Lakotas who live today, hold toward traditional and Christian religiosity. For some years an intensive and often painful exchange on this subject has been taking place. On the Catholic side, it is marked by tendencies toward a new thinking since the Second Vatican Council; on the Lakota side, by the nearly synchronous growth of a new cultural and political self-confidence. Among the Jesuits one finds today self-reflection, and even insecurity, about the meaning of their work.

How far the currently discussed tendencies of—in the words of a mission priest—"accommodation, adaptation, and inculturation" ought to go, or should be permitted to go from a Catholic-theological perspective, is controversial (Hilbert 1987, 143–45) [quotes translated from the German]. Such self-examination was in part stimulated by the realization that, in spite of the early successes, the conversion of the Lakotas remained "unfinished" (Rostkowski 1998), in many cases having brought to the fore a parallel religiosity, that is, traditional views and practices coexisting with Christian ones. Here, too, Nicholas Black Elk, as coauthor of the "classic" of Lakota spirituality, Black Elk Speaks, is only the most famous example. At the same time, the mission schools are being subjected to severe criticism by former students, who are leveling accusations against them for having suppressed their culture, particularly their language, and for the physical abuse that they suffered at the hands of the missionaries and teachers, while other former students are grateful for the education that they received.[4]

For the Catholic clergy, as well as for the representatives of a Lakota religiosity, the decisive questions concerning future development occupy a theological-spiritual level.[5] In the understanding of both Catholics and Lakotas, this level includes ceremonial forms as characteristics of practiced spirituality. Thus approximations in the area of religious ceremonies are particularly important, in that, for example, representatives of both religions conduct them jointly, or Catholic religious services include Lakota symbolism. Joëlle Rostkowski and Christopher Vecsey have recently described and discussed these newer developments against the backdrop of the history of Indian missions. Two names that continue to be cited on the Catholic side are Paul Steinmetz and William F. Stolzman, who were among the first to have taken up the practical dialogue and have also published on this subject (Rostkowski 1998, 339–48; Vecsey 1999, 53–56, 287–308; Steinmetz 1998; Stolzman 1992). They are followed by other Jesuits, such as Carl F. Starkloff (Regis College, University of Toronto), Raymond A. Bucko (Creighton University, Omaha), and John E. Hatcher (Sioux Spiritual Center, Howes, South Dakota; now superior at St. Francis Mission), who, in cooperation with responsible bishops, are pushing interreligious dialogue and inculturation from the Catholic side. In this dialogue Nicholas Black Elk is continually referred to by traditionalist Lakotas, traditionalist Catholics, and syncretists alike, as Vecsey notes.[6] Vecsey's work provides extensive documentation on the large number of individuals with differ-ing religious backgrounds and experiences who are participating in this interreligious exchange, on the various encounters that are taking place, and on the broad range of topics, from a coming to terms with the his-tory of the missions, over ritualistic-liturgical and theological questions, to burning social problems such as alcoholism on the reservations. For the individuals involved there are two paths, the Indian and the Christian. In the end, as Vecsey concluded from one of his interviews, these can run parallel or they can diverge, but they can also meet (Vecsey 1999, 376–77). To the first missionaries this open-minded attitude would not have consti-tuted enough of a success. Yet after one hundred years of mission work and mission experience, this learning from one another and with one another is probably the greatest gain for everyone involved.

I would like to close with a powerful story, set in time about halfway between the founding years of the missions documented in this book and the present. Esther Black Elk DeSersa, a granddaughter of Nicholas Black Elk, tells of a meeting between her grandfather and one of the missionaries at Holy Rosary, Father Placidus Sialm, which occurred probably in the mid-1930s:

> I remember something that happened when I was about ten or twelve years old. It must have been in the springtime; it wasn't cold, anyway. I happened to be home, because my mother was sick, and I stayed home all week to help out. I was at my grandfather's house, and he was sitting down, getting his pipe ready early in the morning, and here was Father Sialm knocking on the door. They opened the door, and he came in, and he saw my grandfather with the pipe. Father Sialm grabbed the pipe and said, "This is the work of the devil!" And he took it and threw it out the door on the ground.
>
> My grandfather didn't say a word. He got up and took the priest's prayer book and threw it out on the ground. Then they both looked at each other, and nobody said one word that whole time.
>
> And then they both went out, and I saw Father Sialm pick up the prayer book, and Grandfather picked up his pipe. Each one picked up his own.
>
> Then they turned around, and they just smiled at each other and shook hands! Then they went back in the house (Black Elk DeSersa et al. 2000, 137).

PART TWO

German Reports from the Missions

From the Chronicles of the Missions and from the Annual Reports of the Sisters of St. Francis of Penance and Christian Charity

Document 1.1

Chronicle. St. Francis Mission. Rosebud Agency, South Dakota.[1]

1886.

It has been God's pleasure, also since their immigration to America, to visibly bless the Congregation of the Sisters of Penance and Christian Charity from the third order of Saint Francis, whose first motherhouse had been established in Holland after having been driven out by the German Kulturkampf.

After six houses had been built in the United States, there came the request from the most reverend bishop of Dakota, by way of the reverend Jesuits, for sisters [to serve] as missionaries among the yet wild Indian tribes in America's Northwest, where outside of missionaries and government officials no whites are permitted to go.

Following a lengthy period of hoping and praying, there finally came the longed-for permission from the motherhouse in Holland to accept this mission. It was decided that three sisters were to commence this important work. The specific task of the sisters was to instruct the children of the *Wilden* in reading, writing, needle- and housework in a so-called *Indian Industrious School*.

On March 22 in the year 1886, Sr. Kostka, Sr. Rosalia, and Sr. Alcantara departed for this new sphere of activity, accompanied by the Very Reverend Fr. Perrig, S.J., the future superior of the new mission, and by the Very Reverend Father Stephan, director of the Catholic Indian missions in Washington, arriving safely in Valentine, the last railroad station, following a nearly four-day journey.

The Very Reverend Fr. Jutz, S.J., who had been active in the mission since January, came to conduct the travelers across the prairie to their new sphere of activity. Thus following a day's drive through the prairie, the new mission was opened on the festival of the Annunciation (March 25), under the name St. Francis Mission. The poor redskins had appeared in great numbers for the arrival of the sisters, who are called holy women by them, and the bitter cold notwithstanding, had camped in long rows in front of the door, all clad in the brightest traditional garb, their faces colorfully tattooed. A friendly handshake, accompanied by a loud "Hau" from the Wilden, was the first mutual greeting. Given that it was already fairly late that day, the deputies of the Dakotas postponed their welcoming visit until the next day. Meanwhile the new arrivals settled themselves as best they could in the sanctuary, of which they had grown fond right away. The mission house, having been built and fully furnished by a wealthy lady from Philadelphia (Katharina Drexel), provided room for 75 children. It was a large building, 90 by 100 feet, but unfortunately very impractical in every respect, the drawbacks of which became more and more apparent with the passing of time.

Finally, after everything had been put pretty much in order, the school was opened on June 15 under the protection of the sacred heart of Jesus. But what surprise and disappointment when on the first day only three pupils, namely one girl of 8–9 years and two boys of the same age appeared, given that there were nearly 50 enrolled; well, the poor Wilden have neither calendar nor date, and so one must forgive them many things. Over time, there were new pupils joining daily, until their number had grown to about 40 before vacation.

1887.

The digging of a well to obtain drinking water for the mission residents presented the greatest difficulty in the beginning, which almost imperiled the founding of the mission, for one was at a loss, of course, when after 150 [feet] of depth not a trace of moisture, much less any water, could be discovered, and work could only be continued at the risk of life. Then, finally, on the last Saturday in April, it resounded happily through the house that there was water in the well. One can easily imagine how great a joy this was for everyone, and on the following day (Sunday) a small festival was celebrated as a way to give thanks to Our Lady of Lourdes to whom this matter had been faithfully entrusted from the start. However, it cost yet an extraordinary effort, work, and patience until finally a windmill was built that brought the water up from the bottom. Before the well was finished, the water had to be carried from out of the canyons, 4–5 miles distant. When the famous Dakota wind later broke the pump wheel, time and time again, we were glad to have a pile of snow nearby in order to get water. Since the tower has been raised above the roof, giving the wind free access all around, the pump works well and the water suffices for the considerable demand of the entire mission.

The average number of pupils during the first year amounted to 50–60, boys and girls combined, who were taught in one class. The day was structured by dividing it into school work and manual labor, with housework such as cooking, washing, doing the dishes, etc., alternately shared among the girls on a weekly basis; the boys had to carry wood, get water, etc.

In consideration of the painful homesickness experienced by some of the little Wilden, who therefore frequently gave in to the temptation of running away, they were given permission to go to their parents' huts on Sundays from after holy mass until the evening. However, this subsequently proved to be very vexing and unpleasant, as many did not return in the evening, with several at times staying at home for the entire week. Later on this unfortunate situation was somewhat remedied by ordering the police to bring back the missing children.

On Holy Saturday 12 of our Indian children were baptized.

To enhance the holy Christmas celebration, the aunt of the noble Miss Drexel from New York had made a present of a very beautiful crib[d], which gave the Wilden, big and small, a great deal of joy, pleasing them enormously. During the sermon, which was delivered in the native language every Sunday at the 9 o'clock mass by the reverend missionaries, the story of the birth of Jesus was told to them and demonstrated with the help of the figures. Something that is characteristic of our dear compatriots can be reported about this first Christmas celebration. All of them were invited for a small "entertainment" on the part of the children by the Christmas tree, and promised a supper in addition, which is the main thing for them. Never before was the chapel so filled with worshipers; about 100 venerable chiefs had come for the service. After its conclusion no one thought of going home, instead the entire feathered and painted company spread itself out on the floor in the children's refectory without ceremony, now waiting for the big supper. Around 4 o'clock, out of pity for them, it was decided to give them the food at this time, whereupon the children were to recite their small parts. Everyone savored this to the utmost and after a substantial portion of apples, meat, etc., had been finished off, not one person thought to now wait for the distribution of presents under the Christmas tree, but instead set out on their way home in a great hurry. Fortunately, several sisters managed to convey 4 old redskins back into the school as audience. At the end of the school year there was also a small examination, and considering their wildness, general satisfaction was conveyed to the children.

1888.

On 7 September 1888, Mother Matilda arrived here from Trier for a visitation, accompanied by Mother Cäcilia, Sr. Cypriana, and Sr. Ludgardis. The two mentioned last stayed here; Sr. Cypriana for the boys' school, and Sr. Ludgardis for the housework. With that there were 6 sisters employed at the mission, who were greatly overburdened with worrying and working, especially since there was not yet any help, but instead only resistance to working found among the children. However, in the course of the year the children gradually acquired joy and pleasure for working and for learning in school, so that by-and-by they at least finished work once begun. Yet having to be at the mission on a continuous basis still left a lot to be desired, even though the children were permitted to visit their huts every first Sunday of the month. The exam at the end of the school year demonstrated good progress in that the children were by then giving their answers in a loud and clear voice, and their whole conduct was exhibiting more politeness, whereas in the previous year hardly a loud answer could be obtained even after much effort to that end.

Pleasant results were also achieved with respect to cleanliness, and the children were gradually instructed in the use of the handkerchief. There were almost insurmountable obstacles to overcome, especially in the first year, given that the children at their arrival in the mission from the surrounding *camps* were completely wild, careless, and dirty, neither speaking nor understanding a word of English. In the latter half of the 2nd year, when sisters and children understood one another better, the obstacles also gradually disappeared, and the trust in the sisters was heightened significantly.

To the Indians' credit, it must be said here in passing that, with respect to morality, one did not meet with any difficulty among the children, which is admirable considering their circumstances.

1889.

On 22 August 1889, Sr. Leopoldine arrived here from Buffalo, having been appointed mother superior of St. Francis Mission by the mother general, Mother Camilla, given that in the previous year Mother Kostka had been transferred as mother superior to the newly constructed Holy Rosary Mission, Pine Ridge Agency, while Sr. Rosalia had taken her place here in the meantime. Two weeks before, Sr. Aquina, Sr. Raphaele, and Sr. Barbara had arrived at this place. The one mentioned first took charge of the singing. A small church choir consisting of several boys and girls was formed, which showed itself so zealous that the first High Mass could be sung already on October 17, the celebration of the name day of the Very Reverend Father Superior F. Digmann. On regular Sundays, praying and singing is done in the Indian language, as before; on weekdays, the rosary is said during holy mass.

This year the big were separated from the small and taught in three classes, which contributed much to progress.

The new agent, Georg Wright, was more devoted to the mission than his predecessor, as a result of which many difficulties were removed. He was present "at the *commencement*" and for the distribution of the awards, in the end expressing his amazement. White children, he said, would not have gotten farther during the same amount of time, and perhaps not even as far. This is surely true when one considers the circumstances, [that is,] that they have to learn everything in a foreign language against which they harbor a natural antipathy; that they live on the reservation, near their homes and their relatives; that we, therefore, cannot deal so harshly with them, and so forth. At the closing, the Indian agent called upon the parents to make sure to send their children [to the mission school], and then distributed the awards to the recipients.

1890.

In the year 1890 construction had to be undertaken to satisfy a number of needs; the church was the beginning. On the 3rd Sunday following Easter, the Feast of the Patronage of St. Joseph, the groundbreaking for the new church was ceremoniously performed by the Very Reverend Father Superior F. Digmann. The construction was begun by placing our trust solely in St. Joseph, and thanks to him, we already had a divine service in it on February 2. The church was solemnly consecrated by the Right Reverend Bishop Martin Marty, O.S.B., when His Grace visited our mission. On that occasion he bestowed holy baptism on a four-year-old little Indian girl in an especially solemn manner, giving her the name Frances. The dear God brought this little girl to us on the evening before the Feast of St. Francis. An Indian wagon had approached in a great hurry, you must know, and simply unloaded the child, Banhanpa by name, in front of the mission house, with the remark that it was to stay here for several days because the parents were going to the sacred dance. The little (dirty) redskin[d] was now first subjected to a thorough cleaning. This Indian[d] was so cheerful and lively, feeling so much at home at this place, that she soon became everyone's darling, and it was decided to keep her. However, after 8 days the Indian wagon returned, and the child vanished as quickly as it had appeared. Yet a sister running after the wagons [sic] brought the little girl back.

One of our biggest girls, who not long ago had been recalled from this world, and who was the first child received into the mission house, had carried the same name. About 3/4 of an hour before the blessed passing of this child, her father came in a farmer's wagon driven in the fastest gallop, having learned that his daughter was near death. Beside himself with anger, he flings open the door to the sickroom, pushes aside the sister who was present, and before anyone knew what was happening, grabs the deathly sick child and throws it onto the hard wagon. It is to be attributed to the energy and presence of mind of the Very Reverend Father Superior and to the help from the Indians who were present that Frances could be carried back to the sickroom. Having arrived there, a peaceful death soon put an end to the child's suffering. With Frances having died, the father conducted himself indeed much more calmly, although one had feared a scene similar to the one that Six Hands had created two years previous. The latter, in an absolute fury over the death of his seven-year-old grandchild Waste, who 8 days before his death had received the name Xaverius, tried with all his might to kill the sisters with his knife and afterward also the reverend fathers who came running to their aid. While all the children left the mission house in a hurry, terrified by the raving mad Indian, running across the prairie in all directions, the fathers and sisters were only able to save themselves through flight and by hiding. The scene ended with Six Hands tearing the flower wreath from the head of the deceased boy, throwing it on the ground, then putting the dead body on his back amid dreadful howling, and then rushing with it to his hut. In front of the mission house the madly wailing bearer was met by several family members in their mourning suits (naked except for the loincloth), joining in the loud mourning cries. The little body was placed on a nearby hill inside an old box without a lid, covered with a *schawl*. Six Hands was arrested on the orders of the agent, but reappeared after 2 days being obliged to extend his hand as a sign of peace to each sister in the presence of a policeman. On Holy Saturday the body of little Xaver was brought down from the hill and received a church burial.

1891.

There were 108 children at the school that year. On the holy Feast of Pentecost the celebration of the first Holy Communion took place, as usual. Twenty Indian children partook of this joy. The Indian dance, and the war that followed, with all its troubles and sufferings, have not put a stop to our labors. It is probably mostly thanks to the works and good counsel of the Very Reverend Fr. Digmann (superior) that our children kept so calm.

Document 1.2

St. Francis Mission.[2]

St. Francis Mission was founded in the year 1886 by the Right Reverend Bishop Martin Marty, O.S.B. The caring chief shepherd approached the fathers of the Society of Jesus in Buffalo, who at the time were headed by the Very Reverend Fr. Behrens as provincial, with the request to take over this mission. The request by the right reverend bishop for sisters from our congregation for this new sphere of activity was related through the reverend Jesuits. There was no shortage of difficulties all around. Many improprieties needed to be removed, for the White Robes (Protestants) had been in the field before the Black Robes (Catholic priests). Taking over this sphere of activity on the part of the sisters also resulted in much that was bitter: first, because the necessary human resources were still lacking in this country, and second, one could foresee the difficulties that such a mission, with [respect to] the way of life in such a wild area, as well as with wild people of such a [the text ends here, in the middle of the page.]

An Overview

The task of the sisters at St. Francis Mission is to instruct the Indian children in school-, needle-, and housework. Here an eye must be kept on the entire education and civilizing process. We have now progressed from a single class to up to four classes plus a small nursery. In the upper classes the children receive about 3 hours of instruction daily, and each day an equal amount of time is devoted to working. The work of the boys in the workshops and in the field or garden is subject to the supervision of the reverend Jesuits.

The number of pupils, counting from the beginning until now, amounts to 552—263 boys, 289 girls. Of these there are presently 96 boys and 135 girls at the mission.

1. Of the remaining 167 boys and 144 girls, [the following] have died in 11 years:

   a) At the mission   2 boys - 7 girls
   b) At home, while enrolled at school   9 "   13 "
   c) After they left school   9 "   11 "
      or 51 children in total.

Jules Scably Bull left the school in 1893 to join the Buffalo Bill Co. He drowned while he was gone.

John Lance, who was sentenced to life in prison for involvement in a murder, died there in the year 1895.

Rosa Bull Eye came too close to an open fire while at home on a visit, causing her dress to catch on fire. Running away out of fear, she fanned the fire to such an extent that she died shortly thereafter from the burns she suffered. This happened in the winter of 1889.

Rosa High Bear left school in the year 1889 after having been here for almost 2 years. She was 17 years old then. Shortly thereafter she married in the Dakota fashion. Her husband discarded her soon after, about which she was very unhappy. In 1894 she ended her life by hanging herself.

2. Approximately 60 of our former students are in other schools.

3. Of our former pupils 31 boys and 25 girls are married; of these, 18 boys and 14 girls were married in the church.

4. A number of our former pupils are at home and not married; of these many are getting on well and are an honor to our school, but there are also some among them who represent the opposite.

The number of baptisms since the beginning here is about 2000. The number of those who had their first communion at this place is 315, among whom are 176 children.

Approximately 237 Indians were confirmed, among these were 156 children.

One hundred and seventy-five marriages were performed in the church.

Now after 12 years there are 16 sisters employed at St. Francis Mission. The church was built in the year 1890. The construction was undertaken by placing our trust in St. Joseph, and thanks to him we already had a divine service in it on February 2 of the following year. The church was solemnly consecrated by the Right Reverend Bishop Martin Marty, O.S.B. On this occasion the right reverend bishop bestowed the holy sacrament of confirmation on 30 Indians. Two years later 65 Indians received holy confirmation. During this visit the right reverend bishop also consecrated the two bells of St. Francis Church; one weighing 1000 pounds, the other 800. The sad news of the death of the dear and loved Bishop Marty, which occurred in the year 1896, filled the hearts of the Indians, whom he had loved most tenderly and for whom he had worked for 20 years, with deep pain.

Because of a lack of space several years after the church was built, a large house was constructed for the fathers and boys, and several years later there also appeared a large wing for the girls. The latter was solemnly consecrated by the Very Reverend Fr. Van Rossum, S.J.

The first school opening at St. Francis took place on June 15 in the year 1886. Of the 50 students who were enrolled, three turned up on the first day; others appeared bit by bit, until their number amounted to about 40 before the vacation.

The first child who had been received into the mission house was Franziska Ring Bull. It [the child] died an edifying death several years later at the age of 14 under unusual circumstances. It was just before Corpus Christi Day, shortly before 10 o'clock mass. After holy mass the annual procession was to take place outside in the open. It was a beautiful day and many Indians had turned up. All of the sudden, the father of the dying child, having learned that his daughter was near death, approached in a farmer[']s wagon driven in the fastest gallop. Beside himself with agony, he flings open the door to the sickroom, pushes the sister aside who was present, hurriedly grabs the deathly sick child, and throws it onto the hard wagon. It was a pitiful sight! It is thanks to the energy and presence of mind of the Very Reverend Father Superior and the help from the Indians who were present that Franziska could be carried back to the sickroom. Having arrived there, a peaceful death soon put an end to the child's suffering. "Alles für Jesus," [Everything for Jesus] was the favorite prayer of this Indian child throughout her illness. To the sister who stood by her during her suffering, she said, "Sister, pray: Alles für Jesus!" After Francis had passed on, the father behaved calmly. Usually, the parents want to take the children home when they become seriously ill. Their love for the children is frequently akin to a so-called Affenliebe.[3] In many cases, it is the parents who obey the children; what the child wants, it must have, to the extent possible. Often it is quite difficult for the parents to give up control over their children so completely. Also, at times the children give in to the temptation to run away. In the beginning they were granted permission to go home every Sunday after holy mass, later, once a month, and now, after 12 years, only once per year and that for Christmas, with exceptions made in special cases. The parents are very glad when their young offspring learn something. Their needlework especially pleases them; at Christmas and when school is finished they also like seeing their children appear on stage. At the first Christmas celebration they did not yet appreciate the latter, which is evidenced by the following: All of them were invited for a small entertainment on the part of the children by the Christmas tree, and they were promised a supper in addition. About 100 venerable chiefs had appeared. After its conclusion, the entire feathered and painted company, without ceremony, spread itself out on the floor in the children's refectory, now waiting for the big supper. Around 4 o'clock, out of pity for them, it was decided to distribute the supper to them at this time, whereupon the children were to recite their small parts. The food having been devoured, no one thought to wait for the distribution of presents under the Christmas tree, but instead set out on their way home in a great hurry. Fortunately, several sisters managed to convey 4 old redskins back into the school. They have grown more sensible since then, but there are three principal enemies against which we still have to fight in our mission work, which are: ignorance, laziness, and superstition.—

In April of the year 1892 one of our neighbors, *Lukas Gelbes Pferd* [Lucas Yellow Horse] caught a cold. Soon he also experienced severe pains in his head, and to rid himself of them he asked a friend to make cuts in his head where the pain was so that these pains could leave [his head]; otherwise they would have no other way out. The compassionate friend reacts to the wish of his extremely wise neighbor by making two long, deep cuts in his head. When this did not help, Lukas desired that one of the holy women would come and bring him medicine. The poor Indian was restored to health after some time; in the future he will not use such a remedy again. The medicine of the sisters has always played an important role for the Indians, but generally they also expect alms along with it, such as, for example, a loaf of bread, coffee, tea, and things of this sort. Such alms have to be distributed almost daily.—

Our work of Christianizing the Indians is in vain as long as they are not delivered from their innate laziness. They do like cash, but have no sense for saving. They almost fight over freight *orders*; they also have made many a dollar in the trade with firewood. They would engage in stock breeding along with horticulture and some farming on their own, but this area, being almost entirely devoid of rain, is a great obstacle to that end.

Superstition is still ingrained in some Indians. They know full well that they have to let go of it if they want to be baptized. Several years ago a sick person replied: "If I let myself be baptized, I am no longer allowed to permit any sweat baths and conjurings, and then I will soon be done for."

For the sweat bath cure an extra tent, not even 3 feet high, is erected, around which woolen blankets are drawn. Then hot stones are carried inside over which water is poured. This then fills the little tent with clouds of steam, more or less, depending on how fast the water comes down, fast or slow. Suddenly the patient sweats like a racehorse. He allows himself to be in this sweat for ten to twenty minutes, then he rubs himself dry to avoid the danger of catching a cold. Some Indians are of the opinion that such a bath also has the effect of a mental cleansing.

Recently, an old woman of about 100 years was brought here. She was dead, but well wrapped in a woolen blanket and furnished with a knife, which stuck in her belt (probably to cut out turnips in the beautiful hunting grounds in the other world). Underneath the head of the old woman was a bundle and above it lay a dead dog; thus [she was] well prepared to start off at once with a feast on the other side.—

On the occasion of the recent Christmas celebration our Indians had for their feast pork and beef, yet dog meat nonetheless had to be served as a delicacy. Because their council building, wherein they were assembled, was too small to accommodate all of them, the women were obliged to sit on the ground outside, while the men were seated comfortably around the warm stove, enjoying their food. As the food was being prepared, the Indians held speeches about the joys of Christmas. The men also read passages from the Gospel or took texts from Holy Scripture that they applied to the dear Savior and the Catholic Church. The whole affair had as its aim to strengthen one another in faith, and to guide to the true light the heathens who still walked in darkness. These poor Indians were much more happy and content in their situation than many a white person living with plenty. It is true, the former pagan customs will only disappear little by little, but it is also true that in the course of the years many a pleasing result has been achieved, with the children as well as with the old. In the beginning there was almost nothing but resistance to work present among the children; gradually they have developed a will for it. Recently, an Indian child said: "Not even for a day can one keep the hands entirely still, they were simply made for working." These children have to be given so much the more credit for having a will to work, because by nature they are not used to working. Moreover, they do not come flocking by the hundreds; on the contrary, one has to make every possible effort to attract them.

On 2 February 1895 the Marian congregation was founded here. The Very Reverend Father Van Rossum, S.J., named St. Aloysius as the patron saint for the boys' sodality, and St. Rosa of Lima for the girls'. The admission is always quite festive. For the first admission one of our girls was on her deathbed. She was 15 years old, and before her passing desired to be admitted into the Marian sodality. Who would have been able to deny this? She died already the next day as a Marian child, having received Holy Communion several times. Her last words for her then still heathen mother were: "Let yourself be baptized, mother, and go to church." The poor, desperate mother gave her word. She had to contend with many difficulties on the part of her unlawful husband, from whom she had to separate, but she dealt with them victoriously. She kept the promise made to her dying child. Before long, she followed her child into eternity. After a short time, her husband, who had pursued her for so long, became ill, but he too had himself baptized before his death, and thus followed those who had gone before him well prepared.

Another one of our best girls, also at the age of 15, died of a death not less edifying than that of her companion, the above mentioned Marian child (both full bloods).

On the feast of Christ's ascension, Martha, that was her name, was given the holy sacraments of the dying (1893), which she received with touching devotion. Two sisters were present. After the priest told the dear child that she would now receive extreme unction, she asked her mother to wash her feet. When her schoolmates visited her the following Sunday, she offered her hand to them, one by one, by way of farewell into eternity. She then said that she once more wished to confess and receive Holy Communion. That very evening the Very Reverend Father Superior went to the hut more than one mile distant, received her confession, and promised to bring her the dear Savior the next morning. It was toward 9 o'clock the following morning. A sister sat next to the dying child, holding its pale hand in her hands. Suddenly, the dying person cries out: "Now I will soon die!" Shortly thereafter the priest entered. There was just enough time to fulfill the child's wish. After a brief preparation she was offered the holy viaticum in the truest sense of the word, for with this food of the angels she passed into eternity. She breathed out her soul about a quarter of an hour after having received Holy Communion. When departing this life she was most intimately united with her Creator. Who would not want to die like this Indian child!

Most of the Indians die of consumption, the disease which as a rule carries off 9 out of 10 Indians.—

In March 1896, the sick Sister Renata was sent here from Buffalo to recover, but it was too late. Several weeks after her arrival she was carried to her grave. She is the first sister to have died at St. Francis Mission, and until now the only one resting on the hill near the cross.

The beautiful large cemetery cross is a gift from dear Mother Laurentia in Linz. The solemn consecration of it made for a worthy closing festivity at last year's general Catholic Indian meeting, which was held at St. Francis Mission for the second time. Following the solemn High Mass on the third day of the congress, the Indians moved in a beautiful orderly procession toward the cemetery. The weather was magnificent and a divine silence reigned all around. It was a moving sight when the large multitude arrived at the top of the hill and lined up on both sides of the cross. Following a passion hymn the Very Reverend Father Superior gave a suitable address. Then everyone followed the ceremonies of the consecration most attentively. Surely many looked up at the image of their dying Redeemer with a compassionate, repenting glance, and we want to be hopeful that as a result of this many a soul will be drawn to the love of Him Crucified.

The visit of our dear, late Reverend Mother Camilla at St. Francis Mission will remain unforgettable. She was all love and benevolence toward our mission. How we like to remember the days when she was in our midst, although we only once had the good fortune to have her with us. Sister Ludmilla, now reverend mother, and Sr. Leonarda were her attendants.

Twice on the occasion of the Feast of St. Francis did our dear Mother Cäcilia delight us with her visit. Once she came accompanied by Sr. Clotilda, and the other time accompanied by Sr. Marcelina.

Our new Right Reverend Bishop Thos. O'Gorman visited our mission for the first time in May 1897. Our Indians moved toward our right reverend prelate in procession and led the very same into the festively decorated church amid the chanting of one of their Dakota songs. Once they arrived, there echoed from the Indian choir the *Ecce sacerdos*, whereupon the right reverend bishop expressed his gratitude for the warm reception in a heartfelt manner. On the evening of that day the mission residents assembled around the Grotto of the Blessed Virgin, lit up by many candles and torches, raising their voices in praise of the Queen of Heaven.

Our dear chief shepherd was deeply moved; he joined us outside and told us about his visit to Lourdes. He himself had observed three miracles there. Later, in our small refectory, His Right Reverend Lordship also conversed with the sisters in a most affable manner.

What is written here gives some insight into our mission life. May our dear fellow sisters be moved by this to assist us through prayer so that the light of the true religion may increasingly work to banish superstition and heresy, and the longed-for day may be nearing when there will be only one shepherd and one flock.

Document 1.3

Chronicle of Holy Rosary Mission
Founded on the Feast Day of St. Ignatius.[4]

1888.

In the second year after the founding of St. Francis Mission among the wild Sioux Indians of South Dakota, the very reverend provincial of the German province, *Rev.* Fr. Behrens, S.J., took on a 2nd mission 200 miles distant from the first, upon the express wish of His Lordship, the bishop of Dakota, *R. Rev.* M. Marty, O.S.B., with his zeal for souls. His Lordship turned to the reverend mother general of the motherhouse at Heithuizen, at that time the Reverend Mother Alphonsa, with a request for personnel to take over the education and the housekeeping, given that these sisters had also been employed in the same fashion at St. Francis Mission since its founding. The mission building at Pine Ridge Agency too had been constructed at the expense of the generous Miss Cath. Drexel from Philadelphia, the subsequent founder and first mother general of the Sisters of the Blessed Sacrament for Indians and Colored People, for $65,000. The construction was supervised by the Very Reverend Fr. Jutz, the first superior of the mission, and several brothers, S.J., who were already in place at this time.— For an entire year their dwelling was a poor *shanty,* [or] plank hut. The holy sacrifice of the mass was offered daily.—When the acceptance of the mission was approved by the general council in Germany—after the construction had been completed, and at the repeated requests from the *Rev.* Fr. Provincial, S.J.—there were 4 sisters from St. Francis Mission appointed to it. These were the superior of St. Francis at the time, Sr. Kostka, as mother superior, Sr. Alcantara, Sr. Elisabeth, and Sr. Walburga. Having previously taken their annual blessed retreat at St. Francis, led by the Very Reverend Fr. Jutz, the sisters named here, together with His Lordship, departed for the new mission on Sunday, 29 July, reaching it the following day, and on the next morning, the Feast day of St. Ignatius, the first holy mass was offered on a rather pitiful altar[d] inside the new mission building in the boys' refectory, and with that, the new mission was opened on 31 July 1888.

As at St. Francis, the sisters, or *"Wynjan wakan"* as the *Wilden* call us, were something new for them here as well—creatures never seen before. They came on the first day, very curious, and asked if we were the four wives of the "*Stina sapa*" (Black Robe). This question was vigorously replied to in the negative; they were shown the cross of the rosary with the explanation that the sisters were the servants of the Great Spirit [and that] they did not want any husbands, etc., whereupon they looked very surprised, accompanied by the weighty exclamation: *Oh Wynjan wakan!*, that is, then you are holy women!, which they were left to believe.

When several weeks later the Reverend Mother Mathilda was sent by the general chapter for a visitation to the convents in America, visiting also this mission along with the Reverend Mother Cäcilia, Sr. Laurentia and Sr. Crescentia were added, so that there were now six sisters in number [at Holy Rosary].

The agent of Pine Ridge Agency at the time, Col. Gallagher, a very good Catholic, gave permission for the children of the Protestant *government boarding school* to go to the mission school if they so chose and wished. As a result, there right away came 30 to 40 Indian children to us from that school, and the gentleman mentioned here is due the honor and gratitude for the rapid increase in pupils at the mission school.

The curriculum was arranged back then in the same way as now, that is, in accordance with the *government* regulations for Indian schools: for the older children a half day of instruction in reading, writing, and arithmetic, and a half day for learning different household tasks. The girls learn cooking, washing, ironing, sewing, knitting, and spinning.— These Catholic mission schools are called *contract* schools and are supported by the government in that it makes a small payment for each child so that necessary provisions and clothing can be procured. However, school supplies, bedding, and furniture, all have to be purchased and maintained at the expense of the mission.

With the mission—chapel, classes, and other rooms—having been furnished and prepared during the month of August for the admission of the pupils, the school could be opened on September 1, the usual start of the semester.—On August 15, the Feast of the Assumption, the chapel was set up so that the first holy sacrifice of the mass could be celebrated there, and has been used for the divine service ever since.—The number of pupils who appeared on the first day was between 15 and 20. Mary Jarois and her brother Mike were the first. This figure grew in the course of the first year to 100, with an equal number of boys and girls.—Sr. Alcantara was employed as the teacher in the class for the older girls, a Miss Swuney from Rushville, Nebr., taught in the small mixed school, and Rev. Fr. Digmann took over the class for the older boys. During a visitation of the Very Reverend Fr. Behrens, he [Digmann] asked for a sister for the last mentioned class, which was granted, and Mother Kostka took charge of it until the end of that school year.—At the end, a small *entertainment* was arranged with recitations and songs by the children, which was followed by a modest distribution of awards. Then, as every year until now, they went back to their huts for 2 months vacation. During the first year's vacation, 3 sisters came to assist: Sr. Salesia, Sr. Catharina, and Sr. Michaela.—The *retreat* for the sisters that year was led by Rev. Fr. Bosch of St. Francis. In the course of that same vacation, the first grotto in honor of the dear Blessed Virgin was erected in the interior court yard, for which the sisters themselves carried hither stones from the nearby little grove, and they also built it themselves.

In addition, it must be noted that in the first year, after a sufficient amount of instruction and preparation, about 60 children were baptized, and 30 received Holy Communion.

The number of pupils in the 2nd school year amounted to 125 to 130, of whom, however, 7 died in the course of the winter, mostly of pulmonary diseases that degenerated into consumption.—Except for one boy named "Black Face," who died at the mission, the remaining 6 were brought by their parents into their huts, where they died.—

At the beginning of October of that year, the Right Reverend Bishop Marty conferred the holy sacrament of confirmation on 30–40 children; they were also admitted to the prayer apostolate. From this year onward the First Communion Children attended the holy sacraments every first Sunday of the month, where they jointly said the usual prayers with a firm voice.—On the Feast of the Immaculate Conception 16 girls, dressed in white, were solemnly admitted as Marian children, and ever since say their prayers daily, and on Saturday [attend] the brief devotions in honor of the Immaculate Conception of the dear Mother of God.—The sisters were employed as follows: Sr. Alcantara, who was appointed assistant, in the school for the older girls; Sr. Crescentia for sewing and housework; Sr. Salesia in

the older boys' class; Sr. Walburga in the children's sewing room; Sr. Laurentia in the kitchen; Sr. Catharina in the laundry; and Sr. Michaele in the
small mixed school. Unfortunately, the one mentioned last was not to be
occupied at the mission for long. Carrying the germ of consumption in her
when she arrived, she was already after 3 months into the first semester
too weak and sickly to continue holding school. After lengthy and patiently
endured sufferings, she departed for a better life the following July, on the
Feast of St. Anna, to the heartfelt sorrow of all the sisters who were taking their blessed annual retreat at that time. This dear and still very young
sister had been an edifying influence on everyone in times of health as well
as in times of sickness; modest to the extreme, she was most obedient, loving, and passionate in every respect. She was employed at the mission for
not quite a full year. We are confident in our hope that she is enjoying an
extremely rich reward for her virtues, and [that she] is a faithful intercessor
for the Holy Rosary Mission before God's throne. She was born Rosa Haas,
from Buffalo, N.Y., from the parish of St. Anna. For her burial the heathen
women from the area had appeared in great numbers, falling into their
mourning songs in a heart-wrenching manner at the cemetery once the
priest left. After the grave was closed, and as the sisters who had stayed until then were preparing to return to the convent, these wailing women said
quietly to one another: "Now one more cry!" which they did, to be sure.
This pagan, painful wailing, without the shedding of one tear, is similar to
a rather wild caterwauling of several voices. May the dear, blessed departed
one also ask for the enlightenment and grace of these poor women. R.i.p.

Before the end of the vacation an additional two sisters arrived from the
motherhouse in Buffalo to provide assistance: Sr. Valencia for the mixed
school in place of the deceased Sr. Michaele, and Sr. Hilaria for the nursing
of the sick and for the housework. In November of this year the wretched,
devilish Ghost Dance, which had been going on at the other agencies for
some time, also had its start at Pine Ridge, not far from Clay Creek. To
fully see through the diabolical cunning of this deception and superstition
from the beginning, personified by the corruptor of mankind, one would
have to trace history back for several years. There one would find several
Indian subjects, infected by the Mormon culture, steeped in heathenism,
fanatical, and hostile to whites, and unfortunately influential among their
nation, who are the architects of this Messiah craze. Since this cannot be

related here in detail, it shall suffice to note what this writer saw of the Ghost Dance with her own eyes.

On a beautiful October morning in 1890, *Rev.* Fr. Jutz, superior of the mission, 2 girls, and my humble self drove from the mission to the Ghost Dance place, about 20 miles distant. We arrived there at midday, about 1 o'clock. It was a large open space; as far as the eye could see nothing but heaven and earth, and about 150 tents of the *Wilden* erected in a circle. Trees and bushes within an area of 5–8 miles had all been removed.— When we arrived, this wild assembly of heathens, numbering about 500 heads, was ready for fighting, or in our case, for dancing. *Rev.* Fr. Superior drove the wagon right up to the circle.—Now, first something about the costumes of these wretched Messiah dancers. All of them wore a jerkin made especially for this purpose, which they simply called a Ghost Dance shirt and, in their mad superstition, believed to be impenetrable against the bullets of the whites, which, however, proved to be a delusion right after their first encounter with the federal troops.[5]—These jerkins were painted in accordance with their view and belief, depicting the triumph of the new Messiah's kingdom of buffalo and oxen in a most symbolic fashion. There could be seen powerful sky blue eagles, white bulls' heads with goggle-eyes, giant blue and black snakes, large colorful buffalo, and a lot of other possible and impossible beasts and monsters, terrible to behold. Of course, the more terrifying to whites the better, for the entire Messiah story should, according to their prophesy, cause all the whites to be transformed into buffalo and stockfish, which the Great Spirit would then give to them [the Indians] to hunt, or rather, to shoot and harpoon, and in so doing [they] would be restored to being the lords and proprietors of the transatlantic continent. Indeed, the poor, deceived descendants of Israel, as one believes, executed their task, one could say, bravely [and] hero-like, and had they expended the same effort and struggle out of a love for God, in our view they would have attained a high place in heaven in return for this, and their Messiah must not have possessed either heart or power by resisting, or by not listening to such torturous petitioning.— As noted before, at our arrival everyone stood in rows; men, women, and children all intermingled in a large circle, holding hands.—Suddenly, several old chiefs in the center of the circle start howling in a special tone, in which everyone joins, turning to the east and calling out: "The father said so!"—Now the entire circle starts dancing, first slowly, then faster, and it continues this way in a circle until, in the end, several are dizzy and hot so that they fall to the ground unconscious, writhing and twisting due to the overwrought state of the nerves and blood like mindless animals. This unconscious state, during which they have died and are in heaven, as they believe, is the ultimate objective of this ghost story, and what they dream or have a vision of while lying there is reported to the highest medicine men and believed.—Most of them had been told that they all should be brave and continue dancing; he, the Messiah, would surely come to build a new kingdom wherein they would be the first. After about a half hour of uninterrupted dancing in a circle and howling, just about half of the dancers were lying outside the circle in all cardinal directions on the bare earth, amid terrible grimaces and contortions, in a state of blissful ecstasy, several striking out about themselves with might and main.—The others, who were too strong to become unconscious, seated themselves on the ground to rest until the others came to again. After a short while a signal was given, the poor stunned people raised themselves slowly like drunks, and, led by others, they staggered back to the dance circle, and, without having taken any refreshment or nourishment, the same procedure started over, and this happened every day in the course of several months, until several thousand armed federal troops came marching in.

Document 1.4

St. Francis Mission[6]

On leaving mass on October 7 (Sunday), the Very Reverend Father Superior informed us that Indian Commissioner Browning with his secretary, our agent, and another attendant, were going to pay us a visit, coming here directly from Valentine. At half past two, the entire *police force* assembled in front of our house and then went to meet the commissioner in order to give him an honorary escort. As soon as the wagon of the agent with its black horses was in sight, the children lined up in front of the house. The commissioner went through the lines of children greeting them; then he took a fine *dinner* with his people. Afterwards the children sang the beautiful song "*Come where the Silees bloom*"; [they] also played on the piano the trio "*The Musical Box,*" at the agent's request. The commissioner was very kind and promised to do his utmost for us in Washington. When he would go on his circular tour in the spring, St. Francis Mission would be the place where he would stay, he said.

1895.

From September until the end of the school year, excepting the Christmas vacation, the usual number of students was 170, the highest we had achieved so far. Due to the lack of space for girls, not all of the applicants of the previous year could be admitted. That is why a building is now to be erected to serve as a dormitory, playroom, and classroom for the girls. Then we will be able to admit a good 200 children. Aside from the abovementioned building, a bathhouse is in the process of being constructed.

There were rather satisfactory results achieved in the classroom. The Very Reverend Fr. Van Rossum, who thoroughly examined the schools in May, declared that our Indians were just as far along as white children of the same age, which the agent confirmed at the last *entertainment*, by stating that their performance was without doubt as good as that of whites at their age, and perhaps even better.—As was mentioned to us, it was apparent that the schoolmistresses had the absolute trust of the pupils. The children's handcrafts, especially the sewing and embroidery, were admired by everyone; the parents were rightfully proud of this. In the various sewing rooms there were no fewer than eleven sewing machines at work, at which the older girls took turns.—The boys are working industriously on the farm and in the garden. Several are employed as regular workers, and as such, receive their pay. Two of these, who had saved their money, purchased wagons and horses.

Our (field) garden consists of 3 acres of land, being scantily watered by means of a well that was drilled especially for this purpose. Two other wells supply water to satisfy the needs of the mission, as well as for the Indians who live close by, including their horses. As was recently noted by an inspector, nearly all of the children here eat salad, for which they formerly expressed their gratitude by shaking their heads. A grotto was built in honor of the dear Mother of God; the beautiful flowers in the new hot house are for decoration. On February 2 the Marian congregation was founded. A good number of boys and girls were admitted. Admission took place in a rather ceremonial fashion. One of our girls, "*Lucie Paints his*

[her] Ears White," that is, *Lucie Streicht sich die Ohren Weiß an*, who was on her deathbed, also desired to be a Marian child. This request was granted. On the following day, having once more received Holy Communion, she had already reached eternity. Her last words to her then still heathen mother were: "Mother, let yourself be baptized and go to church." The woman promised this and faithfully kept her word, notwithstanding the difficulties that her husband created, from whom she had to separate. She died a good death after a short time. Before long, her husband fell severely ill, had himself baptized, and followed those who went before him well prepared.

Among the reverend Jesuits at Holy Rosary Mission and here [at St. Francis], the following changes occurred: The Very Reverend Fr. Digmann, superior at Holy Rosary Mission for the past 3 years, was appointed superior of St. Francis Mission for the second time. The Very Reverend Fr. Jutz of this place was transferred to Holy Rosary Mission in the same capacity.

In August, Mother Cäcilia sent to this place a new assistant, Sr. Adelgonde. There were now altogether fourteen sisters employed at the mission. The new building was made from sheet metal (*corrugated iron*), 36 by 112.

The highest number of students this year was 180. Because of the many little children, a nursery school was started. The result was quite satisfactory, and the little children contributed much to the amusement and entertainment [of the mission residents].

In March, the sick Sister Renata was sent here from Buffalo to recover, but it was too late. Despite the good care that she was given, the young sister approached the grave at a brisk pace. Resigned to God's divine will, she died several weeks after her arrival, and was the first sister to be carried to the cemetery.

Toward the end of the month of May, Major Geo. Wright, who for 6 years had been agent on this reservation, paid his farewell visit, accompanied by his brother and several of his friends. The newly appointed agent, Major McChessney, who on June 1 was to take the place of the former agent, was also present. Major Wright was favorably disposed toward [St.] Francis Mission, for which reason we honored him highly in the end. A throne was set up for him in the boys' play hall; his friends sat on both sides, forming a half circle, and in front of him were our Indian children in long rows. He was bid farewell with verses and songs, and, as the one being celebrated received a rug as a gift, which the children had made. He was visibly moved and expressed his gratitude in warm and heartfelt words. After *dinner* the entire company walked about between the three classes. On departing, one of the gentlemen put $20 in the hands of one of the sisters, yet without leaving her any time to express her thanks. The next day the farewell was celebrated at the agency; our children went there as well. For the *entertainment* at the closing of the school year, which was attended in greater numbers than ever before, the Very Reverend Fr. Zahm, S.J., from Buffalo was present as well, who later led the annual retreat for us, and afterward went to Pine Ridge, Holy Rosary Mission, to attend the Catholic Indian congress. M. Leopoldine and several sisters were present as well.—At the end of September, dear Mother Cäcilia went on her second visitation to Dakota. Sr. Marcelline accompanied her. We once again enjoyed the good fortune of having dear Mother Cäcilia in our midst on the beautiful feast of St. Francis.

In November, the Very Reverend Fr. v. Rossum visited our mission, where he also celebrated his name day. While here, he consecrated the large, new, now finally finished building. The celebration was quite plain, yet uplifting. In the spacious play hall a statue of St. Joseph was placed on the stage as a way to give thanks for the manifest assistance he has repeatedly granted us in financial matters. When the Very Reverend Fr. Provincial entered along with Fr. Superior, a hymn in honor of dear St. Joseph was sung, whereupon the Very Reverend Fr. Provincial, in his usual engaging way, explained the consecration to be performed. This was followed by the consecration. In closing, a hymn in honor of holy Father Francis was sung.—The sad news about the passing on of the dear, popular Bishop Martin Marty, O.S.B., which occurred during this month, filled us and the hearts of the Indians, whom he had loved most tenderly and for whom he had labored for 20 years, with deep pain. Although the reverend prelate had been suffering for some time, it was nonetheless unexpected that he was brought home for his eternal reward. "His reward will be great."—We were awaiting the imminent visit of His Episcopal Grace, when this bitter death notice arrived instead.

1897.

Although a magnificently furnished *boarding school* for the Indians was erected this year on the Rosebud Reservation, not far from our mission, the number of our students did not diminish; on the contrary, it rose. We have more than 200 children in the house. After God, we owe much gratitude for this to the assistance of our agent, who, although not a Catholic, is a benevolent gentleman with a love of justice, as well as to the fiery speeches of our Indians at the congress last July. Our new Right Reverend Bishop Thom. Fr. Gorman [O'Gorman] visited our mission and his Indians for the first time in May. These were days of honor and joy for this place. On the 22nd the right reverend prelate was brought from Crookston. When the bishop's wagon could be seen from afar, several boys sped toward the right reverend prelate on their ponies, and having come near him, called out to him: "Welcome bishop!" In the meantime the large bells were rung, sounding a great distance across the plain that stretches beyond the reach of the eye. Our Indian societies, as well as the children, fathers, brothers, and sisters moved toward the right reverend bishop in procession. Our reddish brown women with their light-blue veils must have presented a curious sight. Our church was decked out most festively. When the right reverend bishop walked up through the middle aisle, the *Ecce sacerdos* by Rampert was sung by the choir in four voices. Thereupon His Lordship bestowed on us his blessing and expressed in a heartfelt manner his gratitude for the warm reception he had received. Then the right reverend bishop was welcomed in the hall by the children through song and verse. On the evening of this beautiful day the mission residents gathered at the Grotto of Our Lady, lit by a hundred candles and many torches. The *"Indian Boys' Music Band"* struck up *"Alle Tage sing u. sage,"*[7] and the voices rose to the Queen of Heaven, who doubtlessly looked down upon her flock with benignant eyes. Our dear, right reverend chief shepherd was deeply moved. He joined us outside and said: "This scene makes me recall my visit to Lourdes, where I myself was eyewitness to three miracles." One of these he then related. This moment will remain unforgettable to those who were present. The following day, Sunday, after the solemn High Mass, the holy sacrament of confirmation was administered to 80 children.

In the course of the congress of Catholic Indians, which in July was held at St. Francis Mission for the second time, 24 Indians received holy baptism. A worthy closing festivity of the congress was the solemn consecration of the beautiful large cemetery cross. Following the final solemn High Mass on the 3rd day, the Indians moved in a beautiful orderly procession toward the cemetery. The weather was magnificent and a divine silence reigned all around. It was a moving sight when the large multitude arrived at the top of the hill and lined up on both sides of the cross. Following a passion hymn the Very Reverend Father Superior gave a spirited and suitable address, after which everyone followed most attentively the ceremonies of the consecration. Surely many looked up at the image of their dying Redeemer with a compassionate, repenting glance.

At the beginning of October Sr. Hildegard and Sr. Ludgera arrived here as assistants; the former as music teacher, the latter as classroom teacher. The Very Reverend Fr. v. Rossum, in whose company the two sisters traveled, once again conducted his visitation at St. Francis Mission.

1898.

On the first Friday in February a fifth class was begun. Girls and boys were separated in all of the classes except for the lowest class, which was considered to be more of a "kindergarten." Because the number of children grew steadily, it was decided to settle on a particular number of girls to be admitted and not to exceed it. Thus, the crowded children's refectory was cleared of 2 tables in the course of the vacation. Then the Very Reverend Father Superior was notified that for good reasons we did not want to admit more than 160 children, which was not well received by Fr. Digmann, however, who has such compassion for his Indians. Indeed, how could he refuse the poor parents and in so doing surrender their children to the government school? And there were so many additional and prevailing reasons to the contrary that, in the end, we no longer paid attention to the number on which we had settled, and admitted as many as the house could hold. It was touching when an Indian brought two girls to Fr. Superior and asked him to please put in a good word with the holy woman so that the children would be admitted. Standing in front of Fr. Sup. and the mother, he alternately looked at one and then the other to receive their consent. Among other things he said that, after all, one of our children had died, another girl had married, and so these were already 2 openings for his two girls standing outside. When the consent was finally given, the good Indian took a couple of leaps through the door to get his children and introduce them. The agent gave permission that all of the children who had been with us could return; we were also permitted to admit new students, but not all of those who had applied, because the government school had to be taken care of as well. Of the older children we withdrew some ourselves, allowing them, for good reason, to attend the government school. One of our older girls requested on her own to go there [and] naturally received permission, but regretted it already on the way, turned back, and asked to stay here. She remained until the end of the school year, and married a fine man in the true Christian fashion. At the wedding dinner following the wedding mass, the Very Reverend Fr. Superior and Fr. Perrig came to dine with the newlyweds. We regarded it as great progress that already several of our children have entered into holy matrimony this way.

1899.

At the beginning of that year we were severely afflicted by illness. About half of our children were sick with the measles. One girl of 11 years and another of 15 years of age died of inflammation of the brain. At the death of the latter a touching scene took place. As her life was coming to an end, the parents and siblings stood around the deathbed of their darling. The father quickly went to get the priest so that he would administer extreme unction to his precious child. Two priests and several sisters were present. With the child having passed on peacefully, the father could no longer contain himself. Grieving openly, he cried out: "Oh my God, how do you punish me, I deserve it, I deserve more yet!" Wailing in this manner he staggered about, holding up his hands and pulling out his hair. Finally, a father guided him into the church; there, in front of the tabernacle, he prayed aloud to his comforting Savior, yes, there he found consolation. Late in the evening of his child's death (it was his only daughter), he made a general confession and received Holy Communion the following morning. The children right away collected one dollar from among themselves to have a holy mass said for the deceased.

In April, Mother Leopoldine, along with M. Pudentiana and M. Kostka, traveled to Europe to attend the General Chapter, returning to St. Francis on June 17. Sr. Martha came here in August to take Sr. Aquina's place. To our joy, the Reverend Mother Cäcilia of Buffalo and her attendant, Sr. Leonarda, again celebrated the Feast of St. Francis, patron saint of our mission, in the midst of her children. M. Cäcilia arrived here ill, but thanks to the dear God recovered during her stay and, this being not a minor comfort to her children in Buffalo, was able to set out on her return journey thither after some weeks, although not without great effort on the part of the mother.

Thanks to the kindness and generosity of Mother Katie Drexel, two new churches[d] were built, one at Oak Creek, 30 miles from here, the second on White River, more than 60 miles distant. Now the Indians there have the opportunity to attend the worship service and exercise their duties as Christians. Usually one of the reverend fathers visits the various little stations and camps once a month.

1900.

We began the 19th [sic] century filled with gratitude toward the dear God who until now has so visibly cared for our mission.

Fr. Eberschweiler, who recently came from Europe, set up his sphere of work here. His Lordship teaches religion in all of the classes; he also led the retreat for the children.—In May Bishop Fr. Gorman honored us with a visit. Eighty-nine children and a good number of the old received holy confirmation. The days that His Grace spent with us were again days of honor and joy for the entire mission.

Dear Sister Ida, who had long been suffering, died on May 18, at 3 o'clock in the afternoon. Surely every sister experienced a great deal of grief because the dear departed one had suffered a stroke during the night and was no longer able to receive Holy Communion. The holy anointment was still administered to her.

At the beginning of November all of our children had to be inoculated, because there was an outbreak of smallpox in Valentine, 40 miles from here, which caused us great concern given that the Indians are very susceptible to this. The dear God protected us against this epidemic; we were able to observe the most holy Christmas celebration in quite a festive manner with those committed to our care. The midnight celebration, as well as the one for the New Year, was twice as beautiful, being [that it took place] in the middle of a world of heathens.

Document 1.5

From: Annual Report 1897[8]
Dakota.

The school of our sisters [at Holy Rosary Mission] was attended by about 200 Indian children, who very much like staying with the former, and oftentimes also make pleasant progress. But what difficulties the work of the sisters has to overcome, here as well as at Rosebud Agency! The government is in the process of withdrawing from them all of the support previously granted for these poor children. Thus the sisters do not only have to provide the little ones with instruction and education, but also with food and clothing, if the latter are not to suffer a very sad lot. But where to get the resources? It indeed takes a great deal of faith in God not to grow disheartened in the face of the needs created by the large number of children, which often do not appear to get satisfied and bring about the fear of true want.

We are receiving quite joyous news from the small hospital that was opened at Pine Ridge some years ago. It has to fill us with great joy, to be sure, when God uses our sisters to help the poor *Wilden* to conclude their earthly life happily.

Amid his agonizing suffering, an old Indian subjected himself yet to a free operation offered him by the doctors. However, he did not survive it for long. A Catholic priest prepared him for death, and with his assistance, the poor *Wilde* died fully resigned to God's divine will.

At this time there is also a young girl staying with the sisters who is affected with sickness of the chest, and who is preparing herself for her hour of death, calmly and resigned. On the Feast of the Immaculate Conception the sick received the holy viaticum and extreme unction with touching devotion. It was moving when her father visited her a short while ago, warmly expressing his gratitude to the sisters with the solemn declaration that he would relinquish his child to them for life and death, for he knew that she was nowhere better cared for than under their protection.

Dakota. Rosebud.

On the occasion of the Feast of the Immaculate Conception a 99–year-old redskin was yet granted the good fortune of receiving holy baptism here.

Although there are indeed many happy results being achieved in the missions, there are nonetheless a number of relapses evident among the zealous Indians. One of the old ones, who could be counted among the best, for instance, went so far as to burn all of his pictures[d] of the saints, and behaved as if he was out of his mind. The ambition, the desire to assume first place in the meetings, possesses the old *Wilden*, frequently causing many to lose their way.

Dakota. Rosebud.

IMPORTANT VISIT AT ST. FRANCIS MISSION.

In May, following a long period of anticipation, we received confirmation of the visit of our most worthy Bishop Thos. O'Gorman. No effort was spared to receive the new chief shepherd, who was visiting his Indians for the first time, in a dignified manner, and to give all of St. Francis Mission a good appearance. On May 22, toward eleven o'clock, we spied our wagon in the vast and open prairie, bringing us the longed-for father. Several of our boys sped toward the approaching shepherd on their ponies, the bells were rung, and the mission residents, fathers, sisters, and children, moved toward the great prelate in procession. The reddish brown women with their light-blue veils would have surely made a strange impression on the European. The old Indians thought to especially honor this great visitor with a Dakota song, and soon the air was filled with high-flown sounds that were many a time out of tune. His Lordship warmly saluted his congregation, which had led him to the church that was decked out in its most festive decoration. From the elaborately trimmed high altar he, for the first time, solemnly pronounced the benediction over those of his flock who were assembled, and expressed his gratitude for the warm reception.

Toward evening the prairie residents gathered around their favorite spot, the Grotto of Lourdes, which made for a very beautiful sight, being illuminated by 100 candles and the torches of the Indian boys. Soon there sounded the sprightly voices of the boys praising the Queen of Heaven, who doubtlessly looked down upon her flock with benignant eyes. His Lordship showed himself more than only a little delighted at this surprise that his Indians had prepared for him.

The following day, after the solemn High Mass, he administered holy confirmation to 84 children. (The adults were confirmed in July, when His Lordship attended the Indian congress.)

In the afternoon, His Episcopal Grace observed a baseball game played by the skilled boys from a tent especially erected for him, and afterward attended a meeting of the old Indians.

On the following day the schools were visited, and in the afternoon the beloved shepherd departed from his flock, now no longer foreign to him, whose warmest good wishes followed him, and which will long remember with grateful joy his first visit to St. Francis Mission.

On the occasion of the visit of the right reverend bishop at the Francis Mission, our sisters had the special joy of seeing the great prelate in their midst and to lodge him in their house. He spoke with them in the most affable manner and filled them anew with enthusiasm about their beautiful calling, their work among the poor *Wilden.*

Document 1.6

From: Annual Report 1898[9]
A Letter from the Missions.
Rosebud, South Dakota, Feast of St. Francis 1898.

Reverend Mother Ludmilla!

It has long been my desire to write to you, but pressing and urgent business did not let it get to that point until today. The good and the bad, the young and the old, the healthy and the sick, yes, even the dead Indians continuously create work for us. Two hundred and fifteen pupils, 93 boys and 122 girls, celebrated the Feast of St. Francis here today. In July and August, Mother Leopoldine and Sr. Agatha already wanted to take precautions, asking me to admit only 160: the little whiners only created work, but were unable to help! I could not deny the justness of this wish, but it did cut me to the quick. We had closed in June with 220. The agent, who, while not a Catholic, is nonetheless kindly disposed toward us, had told me that I could have all the former ones back that I wanted and, in addition, I had close to 70 new applications. But as we all know, no soup is eaten as hot as it is cooked.[10] On the occasion of a general absolution, I advised the sisters, for wholesome penance, to pray to the dear Mother of God and to St. Joseph to help us, so that only those former pupils and such new ones would come who they themselves would like to have here. We for our part made a novena to St. Joseph in the same vein. The granting [of the request] was remarkable. Those [pupils] who we ourselves liked to do without, asked of their own accord for permission to be released; in return, we had a good selection among the new applications. But what is most comforting and joyous for me [is that] all of the sisters are themselves glad and delighted by the large number of children. That is the work of St. Joseph. [The principle] "the more a beard is shaven, the stronger it grows," is applied by St. Francis de Sales to the church in general. This also pertains to our mission. The government has for the last three or four years steadily reduced its contributions, and St. Joseph, as his name implies, has constantly "contributed." Since you, Reverend Mother, have seen the mission, there have been buildings added every year; it was not the D E S I R E to build, but the simple N E E D to build. And even today one would prefer if St. Francis were built in an elastic fashion. Our only concern shall be to be quite obedient and to faithfully serve the dear God; the remaining cares we leave up to Him. He Himself has taught us accordingly.

The sisters all work faithfully, joyfully, and in harmony, each one in her place: hence God's blessing cannot be long in coming. Sr. Aquina, and since last year Sr. Hildegard together with her, are functioning apostolically through their music. Just yesterday three Protestant girls, who the music had brought in, came and asked to become Catholic. At the government school where the children have all of the modern conveniences to be sure, [such as] steam heat, electric lighting, etc., they have the greatest difficulty to get girls. We have twice as many as they and could have more yet if we had the room.

And now something amusing. Our sisters have introduced a new saint at the mission, St. Expeditus. He is, of course, already a sanctified martyr from the first church at the time of Diocletian, but none of us has thought of him or prayed to him. His maxim is: "Today, not tomorrow." What one asks of him, he shall grant on the same day. He assisted me on two occasions. Last month I was returning from a trip in the evening, saw the mission before me, but lost the way, and got into the so-called cañons (Hügel) [hills]. I left my horse standing on top of a hill and went searching for the way. When I returned, the hack was no longer to be seen. I walked home on foot and sent someone out right away, but to no avail. Thus I promised St. Antonius and St. Expeditus each a devotional rosary if the horse and wagon were to return within 24 hours. I did not even have to wait 24 hours! The following forenoon a *policeman* brought both. My breviary still lay right where I had put it; nothing lost, nothing damaged, only a minor scratch on one of the spokes. The horse had been caught at a *camp* close to 20 miles (Engl.) from the mission.—

The day before yesterday a pocket watch was stolen from the bakery. The immediate investigation uncovered nothing certain. Thus I advised Br. Baker to promise a devotional rosary to St. Expeditus. It did not take half an hour and we had the evildoer. Seeing that he was being searched for, he, in his fear, wrapped the watch in a moccasin and threw it into an unspeakable place. He brought it up with the help of a long pole and hook, clean and intact.

Since it is never too late for good wishes, as they say, I wish you, Reverend Mother, and all of your dear sisters, a very blessed St. Francis month, and commend the spiritual and temporal affairs of the St. Francis mission to the devout prayers of all of you.

In the Sacred Heart of Jesus,

Your most humble and grateful
Fr. Flor. Digman, S.J.

Document 1.7

From: Annual Report 1899[11]
A Letter from the Missions.
St. Francis Mission, Rosebud, Dakota, February 7.

Dear Reverend Mother!

. . . Now something from St. Francis Mission, dear Reverend Mother. That there have been some changes during the six years since your kind visit, that several buildings have been added, of course all made from wood and corrugated iron, is easily understood. In the meantime, the number of children has increased to 227, and even today we are not lacking in work and worries in the far west. Little Ludmilla, who you were holding in your arms during baptism, is still not here; she is ailing somewhat, but is being well cared for by our dear mother, [and] also receives her Christmas presents[d].—But the cemetery too has filled up: more than 366 redskins are already awaiting the morning of resurrection there. In the cemetery on top of the hill there now rises a beautiful large cross made from corrugated iron. It is visible far and wide as a sign that here the belief in Christ has been victorious over heathenism. With very few exceptions, all the redskins[d] resting on our God's acre died in the innocence of baptism and are no doubt saved. Old Anna, Joachim's wife, both of whom you surely remember, is there as well, and the first thing that Joachim told me at our joyful reunion was that his Anna had died and was resting here in the cemetery. He still shed a tear in her honor, but then right away proceeded to report that he had again another Anna for a wife; she was good too. Three weeks later, this one also fell ill and died a good death. Joachim mourned, lamented, and wept over his seventh wife, visited the grave several times, chanted and wailed the usual mourning songs, and now it is *all right*. Will he receive the seventh sacrament another time and get himself another Anna? Most likely, for the 80–year-old man is dependent upon help. Joachim still looks the same as before, only his jet black, cascading hair is turning somewhat gray.

During advent *Grosser Truthahn* [Big Turkey] and his wife *Kleiner Tannenbaum* [Little Pine Tree] received the sacrament of matrimony in our church. *Rev.* Fr. Digmann and the bride and bridegroom were already standing at the communion bench for the marriage ceremony to proceed. At that moment the one mentioned first [realized that he] had no rings left in the little box, and some had to be gotten from our mother in a hurry. The chief Waglesiunk-tanka, *Grosser Truthahn*, it is true, had been baptized approximately 9½ years previous, having received the name Peter Jacob, but his other half became Catholic only last summer at the Indian congress; thus the seventh sacrament could be received only at this time. Waziyelan (*Kleiner Tannenbaum*) received the name Katharina through baptism.—As you probably know, the last Indian congress was blessed with a great deal of success. Just now I am recalling an incident that is surely of some interest to you. The Very Reverend Fathers Digmann and Lindebner, the latter from Pine Ridge, drove by wagon from here to the congress in Lower Brulé, which took about three days across the prairie. On the evening of the second day they passed a small house on the prairie, which appeared to be a smithy and a small store at the same time, for there were several tin plates standing in the window. At the sight of the tin plates Fr. Digmann thought that such a plate could serve them well for their light refreshments to be taken during the trip. Thus Fr. Digmann dismounted, entered the hut, and soon the bargain was concluded. Now the saleswoman, a neatly dressed, honest woman, asked him whether he was perhaps a Catholic priest. At the father's affirmative reply the fine woman pleaded with him that he offer her mother-in-law, who was in the next room ill and near her end, the consolations of the holy religion. Of course, the father agreed to this at once. As soon as he laid eyes on the sick woman, he saw that death was already hovering over the lips of the good old woman lying there motionless, and that she hardly showed any signs of life. She was nonetheless in possession of her mental faculties, made a good confession, and received the general absolution, scapular, etc. Then the prayers for the dying were recited; no one was happier and more blissful than the dying granny. The fathers now decided to spend the night with these fine people[d] and to say holy mass there the next morning. They learned that the good inhabitants of this house[d] had come from Luxemburg, and had always remained true to their Catholic faith. Once every year, when possible, a Catholic priest visited them, making his rounds to the various stations—that was it! Thus they appreciated so much the more the grace of the dear God, so noticeably showing mercy and rendering assistance to the grandmother before her death. The following morning the priests said holy mass. In the course of it, the pious good old woman, who was still alive against all expectations, received the holy viaticum with deep devotion and feeling, and was most happy. After Fr. Digmann had once more said the prayers for the dying and prepared the grandmother fully for her passing into eternity, the reverend fathers continued their journey. On their return trip they again visited the cabin and, to their surprise, found the old woman still alive. She lay there, scarcely part of this life, so peaceful and quiet as if she had already passed on to her eternal rest.

Here in the land of the heathens and in the wild west, the love and assistance of God is often more visible and tangible than in the more civilized world. Two Strike, the principal chief during the Indian war 9½ years ago, probably the most famous and influential Indian far and wide, one of our finest redskins, also had himself baptized on the Feast of Epiphany, and received the name Paul Balthasar. He is still quite nimble despite his seventy years. Six Hands, however, is yet a heathen, and also the eyes with which he was born are blind.[12] The time of grace and affliction will hopefully not be in vain for him. It is pleasing that the Indians now bring their small children for baptism right away, and have given up the errone-

ous idea that the POURING ON OF WATER kills the little ones. Consequently, we have only a few heathen children among our redskins[d] at the
mission house here. On the whole, Christianity is little by little gaining a
greater foothold. This could be seen especially on holy Christmas, "the
great day in the snow," as the Indians call it. Already on Tuesday several
Indians came with bag and baggage, pitching their tents very close to the
mission. Every day the number of tents increased, and on the evening before the high feast, the mission was surrounded by a whole Indian village.
That we were certainly not lacking for guests, I surely do not need to mention. The Indian feels at home here, simply sits down at the table, and sets
about it with hand and mouth as if he had to provide for an entire year.
However, on Wednesday we got off easily. A cow died on us. No sooner
had the Indians gotten wind of this than they dragged the animal to their
tents where many hands got busy. Very soon the meat was boiling in the
sooty kettles on the fire. Then there was a wonderful meal, and soon after there was not a trace of the cow to be seen. We heard this anecdote[d]
only the following day and had to wonder why the redskins had not also
asked for a calf to boot. One day, during one of his visits here, *Rev.* Fr. van
Rossum treated them to a cow. No sooner had they finished eating it on
Sunday afternoon than *Grosser Truthahn* came running, asking the father
if he would not also want to give them the calf; it went with the cow and
they wanted to eat it along with it. They are simply people in a state of
nature, just like children! Thus, they came here from the different camps
all throughout advent, and even before, to tell our dear Mother L.[13] their
big and small wishes. They also wanted to have a Christmas tree in their
camps, and a small gift giving like they had seen here. However, not every
heart's desire could be met, and not every large and small request could be
considered. Yet the good mother was able to satisfy everyone, and so, with
a joyous heart, they were awaiting "the great day in the snow."

   On the evening before the high feast, around 6 o'clock, the giving of
Christmas presents to our children took place here. What joy and jubilation this was! Old and young enjoyed themselves and were pleased in the
utmost. However, the greatest joy was expressed by the old at the wonderful music of their darlings. In addition to some baked goods, *candy*, an
apple, handkerchief, or some other small thing, every boy also received
a flute or a horn. It did not take long and the wind instrument was tried

out, and soon there was nothing but wonderful music to be heard, all in
a happy jumble, almost to the point of stunning, even though the large
children's refectory with its 18 long tables can withstand its fair amount of
noise. The old folks were delighted at such exemplary music and encouraged their offspring to make sure to give their best in the musical arts. This
happened faithfully for several minutes, to be sure, to everyone's *gaudium*
[delight]. In the meantime, the three reverend fathers were fully occupied
in the church, where the Indians gathered around the confessionals the
entire afternoon until late in the evening. Around half past eleven, during
our divine *offizium* [service], the two bells in the tower[d] were already calling the entire Indian world from all around to the crib of the divine child[d],
and soon men, women, and children came tramping hither. The men and
lads of the St. Joseph Society and the women and maidens of the St. Mary
Society appeared in their different sashes and badges, which made them
more than only a little proud. They came marching solemnly and nicely
in order, two by two. The dear Savior surely looked down upon His dear
poor redskins[d] with much affection and joy as they stood around the crib
so trueheartedly and in such great numbers, and during that holy night
one could truly feel that the Redeemer had descended from heaven for
the sake of EVERYONE in order to save all those who are willing, and to
draw them to Him. At the sight of the poor, simple, good-natured Indians
one could not help but think of the poor shepherds of Bethlehem. The
church was completely filled; not one rich person was among those present, but I may say that every one—[although] poor as for outward possessions—left the church rich in eternal and heavenly treasures. The faces,
radiating with joy, reflecting internal satisfaction and bliss, gave evidence
of this. At 12 o'clock a solemn High Mass commenced. The sisters and
children sang a beautiful mass in several voices. In the course of the second holy mass we received Holy Communion, and in the one following,
many Indians approached the Lord's table. It was truly an edifying and
touching sight to see these *Wilden* receive Holy Communion so devoutly,
collectedly, and with such reverence. The bending of the knee was still
somewhat awkward and rough for some, yet the knee touched the floor
with such force that one could see and HEAR it from afar; they were concerned with doing everything right and nicely. Even the small children on
the backs of their mothers were solemnly quiet, as if they knew that the

heavenly Friend of the Children was right near them. Sometimes the dear Mother L.[14] takes the little ones on her lap or in her arms until the women return from the communion bench and reassign their satellite its place[d] under the blanket or shawl on their backs. When going up and down the stairs, this precaution is no longer necessary. Before they had learned to climb the stairs, the women would simply take their child[d] off their backs, hand it to the sisters, and then crawl up the stairs while we carried the little red-skinned creature up behind them.

At 10 o'clock on holy Christmas, everyone again attended High Mass. After the noonday meal everyone joyfully hurried to the societies' meetinghouse, right near the mission, where the gift giving and feast for the Indians among themselves was to take place. At 3 o'clock our children treated everyone to a pleasant entertainment, consisting of singing, music, and recitations, for which the entire nobility of the agency and many Indians were present. The Indians looked upon their clever children with true pride and a great deal of joy, although they did not understand a word of it, given that everything was done in English.—Following their urgent invitation, we afterward visited the Indians at their meeting in the societies' meeting house, which pleased them to no end. The tree had already been despoiled, but the feast was still in full swing, and just at that moment delicious dog meat was being brought to the table.[15] Two long tables were occupied by Indians seated close together; the others were stretched out on the floor, thoroughly enjoying the food. No one was left unfed. There were several hundred present, outside and inside the hut, young and old, big and small, all in the most joyful and festive mood—in the greatest harmony. This was reminiscent of the mutual love of the first Christians, and as everyone rejoiced so warmly about our appearance, crowding around us, we recalled the words from the Holy Scripture: "Er war wie mitten unter den Seinen."[16] Fr. Digmann also visited the festively joyous gathering and rejoiced together with the joyful. There was a great deal of activity in and around the mission: men, women, children, horses, wagons, a great number of dogs, not to mention all of the sooty pots, kettles, and other cooking utensils. Our children were then allowed to visit their huts for several days, and on Monday, at noon, the entire tent city had disappeared from the prairie.

This way you, dear Reverend Mother, have a bit of an idea about our Christmas celebration. Fortunately, it was not that cold during those days. In the course of last week the cold has intensified significantly; it is 40° below zero. Horrible! Considering that the mission house, church, etc., are standing entirely free out on the open prairie, not protected from any side, and they are only built from wood at that, one will surely believe that the blood freezes in one's vein. Although the church is being heated well, the sacred blood in the chalice froze on the priest during holy mass. In addition, there are the horrible snow squalls and the Dakota storms. That the winter, therefore, usually also brings with it colds and illnesses, is surely not surprising. Thus 50–60 children got the measles after Christmas; afterward we sisters took turns with colds, [and] the fathers and brothers followed our example. Thank God, these illnesses did not claim any victims. However, one very good eleven-year-old girl died on us of inflammation of the brain. The mission was otherwise spared, while many died all around. Just now a nice five-year-old girl was buried. Her father, *Leo Tödtet Rückwärts* [Leo Kills Rearward] is a very good sort, and one of our finest Indians. Yesterday, when the child was still alive, the wife of *Eselskopf* [Donkey Head], the neighbor of this Leo, came and wanted a shroud[d] for the sick child, who would die soon. We replied, there was still time, it was not yet known whether it [the child] was in fact going to die. Likewise, once before, an Indian came to me and said: "Holy woman, here is a thread, have a coffin made of this length for that girl there, and also go ahead and have the grave prepared." I asked him whether Margaretha, one of our girls, had died! She was ill, you must know. "No, not that," was the reply, "but she will die soon, and then I will bring her at once." Several hours later the mother of the sick child came, requesting milk for Margaretha. The child lived yet for some time, and the coffin and grave were waited with until then. That's the way it goes here! As soon as the last breath is taken, the body is wrapped in blankets and brought here. If the coffin is made quickly, the burial takes place right away.

Soon there will be small wooden churches built in five *camps*, one in each; the brothers are already cutting the wood for that purpose. They will be dedicated to the following saints: to Our Lady of Perpetual Help; to the holy angels; to St. Joseph; and to Peter and Ignatius.—On Whitsunday,

God willing, 40 children of our mission will receive first communion.—
And now in closing, dear Reverend Mother . . .

with the love of the divine heart,
your grateful child.
Sr. M. N.[17]

Document 1.8

From: Annual Report 1900[18]
A Letter from the Missions.
St. Francis Mission, Dakota.

Esteemed Reverend Mother!

. . . Viewed from a purely human perspective, the prospect of our future
is rather dim. Thus we have to hold fast so much the more to the Savior's
word: "*Suchet zuerst das Reich Gottes und Seine Gerechtigkeit; alles Übrige wird
Euch dazu gegeben werden.*"[19]

Some time ago I wrote to our Very Reverend Fr. Superior that I had only
one fear: "that God's kingdom would be taken from these people and given
to another" due to their minds being obsessed with earthly matters and
their indifference toward the spiritual. And yet! If the dear God allows Himself to be dealt with like during Abraham's times, I believe that He will find
more than 50 among these Indians whose intentions toward Him are honest. There are increasing differences in opinion, among the whites as well
as the reds, and that is good; that way one knows where one stands.

Until last year our St. Francis Church was the only Catholic house of
God on this reservation. At that time I received from Mother Katharina
Drexel, who first built our mission, 1500 dollars for the construction of a
second church. As soon as this became known, half-blood Indians came
to me and said: "For that money you can build two churches." Fr. Perrig
and I thought about this and became convinced that this was possible,
provided the Indians brought logs to the mission sawmill and later would
take care of the freight at no charge. They agreed to this and this way we
received two new churches last summer: one on White River in honor of
our holy Father Ignatius, and one on Oak Creek in honor of St. Peter. Both
are located about 10 hours distant from the mission.

At the end of December I went to the church of St. Peter, accompanied
by a sister and an Indian. There more than 300 Indians had assembled,
not counting the children. Given the opportunity, many had the intention

to change from the Protestant-Anglican Church to the one founded on the man who is the rock. Those who had received instruction before were admitted. They came for confession and were baptized conditionally. In addition to these, others came, knelt down, and wanted to confess; however, I sent them back for the purpose of further instruction.

During the later meeting, one of these mentioned last stood up and said: "I recently dreamed that I saw the Black Robe standing in the water; I myself stood on the shore and wanted to get to him to have myself baptized. However, he hindered me by saying: 'You cannot be baptized yet.' Now my dream has come true." A half-blood Indian voiced later that it was only a matter of two to three years until all of OAK CREEK would become Catholic. May God grant it; pray for this and commend this concern to the prayers of your sisters. The Protestants are very angry. They told several converts [that] they should now also take with them their dead from the Protestant cemetery, and a number of them will do so.

On this occasion, many who had been baptized by our Fr. de Smet 40 years prior also came for confession, but there was nothing Catholic about them other than the baptism. One was suffering from the flying gout and thought he would have to die. In former times I had often admonished him to confess, but he continued to put it off. The gout had caused him to yield and he gave a good life's confession. When I came to him a month later, he came out of the house to unharness the horses for me himself, and admitted: "What you did for me last month has done me a world of good." The sweet, good conscience has had a healing effect even on his sick body.

In that way the dear God sometimes gives comfort. On the other hand, we fight a tough battle with the dying out, though resistant heathenism, and no less with the envious Protestants. For ten years now they have continuously pressured our converts to change sides; there would soon be an end to the Black Robes anyway. Our school would cease, and the president would chase us across the border. I only told our people: "Hollow barrels sound the loudest," the less these so-called catechists know, the more they shout. But they nonetheless do harm in that they confuse the minds through their old and continuously warmed-over lies: that we prayed to the Mother of God, the saints, the pictures, that we did not receive true Holy Communion because we did not receive any wine, that we were paid

5 dollars for each baptism and were therefore so keen on baptizing, etc. Well, our master has said: "*Freuet Euch, wenn viele Lügen gegen Euch ausstreuen um Meinetwegen.*"[20] As even a Protestant superior of the Indian schools told me, the Anglicans stirred up the whole incitement against our Catholic Indian schools. They thought to destroy them by a systematic reduction of support. They themselves gave up their schools, but the Catholic ones were continued, thanks to the Catholic charity. When they saw that there was no getting at us in this way, an executive *ordre* was issued that denies the Indians the right to choose the schools for their own children. They know and sense that as long as the parents have a choice, the Catholic schools will grow steadily fuller, while theirs will become steadily more empty. Thus this brutally drastic measure is nothing but a demonstration of their own incapacity. Now, the *ordre* has not been made a law, although the Indian missionary, a staunch Presbyterian, had tried it. It is at the discretion of the individual agent to put it into effect.

Thank God, our agent is fair and favorably disposed toward us. Still and all, financially he cannot do anything for us. According to this law, starting 1 July 1900, we do not receive a penny in contributions to provide for the children's keep. They are already obliged to give to us the meat and flour that they receive in their families. However, that would be just enough to keep the wolf from the door. In addition, we no longer receive one thread of cloth; we have to pay for that ourselves, so too for the maintenance of the sisters. So you see, esteemed Reverend Mother, that our prospects, humanly speaking, are fairly dim. Nonetheless, I do not doubt that this whole change, brought on by evil, will prove to be to the greater glory of God. If only our bishops would go ahead and rouse the 10 million Catholics in the United States.

All of your sisters are working faithfully and bravely; God bless their labors. Help us to be worthy through your prayers, and that we will remain so, that He bless and protect us until the end.

With deep gratitude for your motherly love, and commending our tested mission to your prayers, I remain

your grateful
Fr. F. Digmann, S.J.

Document 1.9

From: Annual Report 1900[21]

Dakota. Holy Rosary Mission.

Our dear sisters at Holy Rosary Mission are reporting the following:

We here in the wilderness are now entirely dependent upon charitable assistance. With the passing school year any support on the part of the government ceased. Due to the change in agents on our reservation, the parents of our children were again given the liberty, which had been partially taken from them, to send the latter to a Catholic school. With that, we received several new little ones and presently have eighty-two boys and seventy-two girls. Only when the children come to us small can success be expected, both with respect to religion and culture. If they come later, having grown up under the influence of their heathenish parents and relatives, it is much more difficult for them to relinquish their pagan traditions; one of these traditions being that the little ones are already taken along to the dances. The older the children are, the more difficult it is for us to instruct them. There is almost nothing to be accomplished with strictness; only with a great deal of love and all but enormous patience do we slowly achieve our aim. . . .

Throughout the summer the hills appeared as if scorched, given that during spring we experienced a horrendous heat instead of rain. There was only a little hay and it can only be gotten for large money; this want worries the Very Reverend Father Superior more than just a little. The vegetables, on the other hand, did well; we had cauliflower in such abundance that it needed to be used for fodder in order to use it up. They had less luck with the vegetables at St. Francis Mission, but there the wheat grew well, which suffered a great deal at this place as a result of whole swarms of blue birds as large as pigeons visiting it. Thus the missions helped each other out in a neighborly fashion. Unfortunately, there is nothing to be gained by this financially, given that the two-day drive across the prairie costs as much as the goods if they were available nearby. . . . Despite the numerous difficulties that confront our activities here, we put our faith firmly in the dear God that He may make matters turn out in the poor Indians' favor. . . .

Dakota. St. Francis Mission.

We are receiving interesting details about the visit to St. Francis Mission by His Lordship, the Bishop O'Gorman from Sioux, which at the same time offer pleasant insights into the activities of our dear sisters among the poor redskins:

The news that our right reverend bishop would honor our mission with his noble visit on May 5, stay here several days, and administer the holy sacrament of confirmation to our dear Indians, was welcomed by us with joy and jubilation. After thirty of our Indian children had received First Communion on Whitsunday, the instruction and preparation for the worthy reception of holy confirmation were begun. Many adult Indians eagerly attended the lessons as well. Our Indian children could hardly wait for the arrival of the head of the Black Robes. It was an exceedingly active life in and around St. Francis Mission. Wagons full of Indian families arrived from different directions nearly every hour, from *camps* 25, 40, 60, 75, or even 100 miles away. The tent was quickly pitched, and soon the rising smoke from the fire indicated that the weary travelers were in need of refreshment and invigoration. The Indian, by the way, always has a healthy appetite. And he never requires an invitation or coaxing; he simply sits down at the table in the mission house, or says: "I am hungry, give me something to eat." Bashfulness is not an issue. Well, after all, we are here on account of our dear redskins; that is why we also always meet their reasonable wishes when at all possible. They are at home here at the mission as much as in their own tent or log cabin[d]. At the same time, we are likewise welcome to them, and their tent or cabin is always open to us. Each one of us [sisters] is warmly greeted with a good-natured "How, How," and a friendly handshake. On Sunday we just for fun counted the tents that are pitched around our mission, but had to stop at 40, because with an I N D I A N   V I L L A G E of this sort streets and symmetry are lacking, and the jumble makes counting impossible.

On May 5—it was a beautiful spring morning—everyone was in the most cheerful mood and in a state of joyous excitement. The mission house gleamed in its festive decorations already early that morning. Joy and jubilation went like a jolt through everyone when from the tower[d] the agreed-upon signal of the bell resounded, announcing the arrival of the beloved bishop. Now it grew lively in the TENT CITY. Those Indians who were still there quickly crawled out of their tents and came running to join us. Others, probably mostly the heathens, lay down on the ground in groups right nearby, looking curious about what was going to happen next. In the meantime, the procession was forming quickly: the reverend missionaries in their rochets, acolytes with cross and banners, then our 227 Indian children accompanied by the sisters, and finally the adult Indians, among them the societies, or men and women with their banners and badges.

The ringing of the bells greeted His Lordship already from afar. Now the wagon appeared on the rise. Our two "Strawberries," a couple of splendid horses, came with him at full gallop; the procession started to move. Two of our old Indians raced on horseback to meet the precious chief shepherd, and before we knew what was happening, they had reached the wagon, jumped off, thrown themselves on the ground in front of this high dignitary of the church, and then, bowed down, received the bishop's blessing. It was a touching scene. But when soon after His Lordship had the wagon come to a halt, got off, gave everyone his blessing, and joined the procession on foot, the crowd was seized with true exaltation. Having reached the mission house, the high prelate dressed in his bishop's robes, and then marched at the end of the procession across the prairie toward the church, in full array, with staff and miter. It was an edifying sight, a triumphal march that proclaimed that the night of heathenism has faded and that the light of the only true faith has cut itself a path at this place.

After the usual ceremonies at the portal of the church, our church choir, made up of several sisters and about forty Indian children, boys and girls, began to sing the magnificent "*Ecce sacerdos*" by Singenberger, while the precious chief shepherd majestically strode through the spacious and festively decorated house of God and then, absorbed in devotions, greeted Jesus in the holy sacrament. Now followed the ritual orations, whereupon the bishop addressed those present with a warm and paternal speech. He closed with the words, that St. Francis Mission, being a rich oasis in the middle of the desert where so much good was being effected, will and must continue to exist despite the dim future. This he confidently wished, hoped for, and expected. After he once again pronounced his blessing as chief shepherd, he went to the mission house. In the course of the day, the church dignitary blessed many with his fatherly benevolence, was approachable to everyone, and showed interest in everything. The Indians used this opportunity to present the "good father" with their small and large concerns in a plain and childlike fashion. This proceeded in an altogether warm and unceremonious way. One of their interpreters came marching along every time another small group or individuals approached. . . . His Lordship observed the progress in the mission activity with true pleasure and praised it very highly. His Episcopal Grace also voiced special joy and great interest at viewing the individual rooms and works of the children in the afternoon, mentioning frequently that one could hardly find matters any better in the institutions for whites.

In the meantime, the three missionaries were engaged in the confessional nearly all of the afternoon until late in the evening, given that not only our children but also many adult Indians would be approaching the Lord's table the following day. On Sunday, after the solemn High mass was said by the bishop, with the Indian boys serving as usual, His Lordship administered holy confirmation, after he himself had addressed the believers with a magnificent speech, and the Fr. Superior had preached in the Indian language. Eighty of our children were confirmed, also many adult Indians. Among the latter there was also the famous principal chief and leader of the last Indian war, Two Strike. It gave the bishop special joy to be able to confirm this brave. He devoutly approached the communion bench in a splendid blanket and with the finest Indian dress, and his bearing indicated that he is not only an able warrior, but also a good Catholic Christian. . . .

At about half-past twelve the church celebration ended. Now it came to exercising the MATERIAL acts of compassion, since very many Indians and other guests had appeared. Given that we had invited the agent, the doctor, and all of the officials employed by the agency, along with their families, and they having accepted the invitation as usual with great pleasure, the number of strangers was surely not small. There also had appeared a number of non-Catholic women teachers from Valentine, forty miles from here, having learned that our children would present a musico-dramatic entertainment for His Lordship. At three o'clock the performance began and the lavish program was executed in the most beautiful fashion. It is difficult to determine how many hundred Indians were in fact present, looking up at their CLEVER offspring and tribal kin on stage with genuine pride. Everyone here is permitted free entry, to be sure, and it goes without saying that financial success is not an issue, given that the redskins themselves have nothing, yet are prepared to receive something any time.

At the end of the performance, His Lordship, with heartfelt words, expressed his gratitude to the children and especially also to the sisters for the great joy that they had given him with this pleasant entertainment. The high prelate voiced his utmost satisfaction and issued the greatest praise to the sisters and children. He thanked the former for their untiring, self-sacrificing, and unselfish love with which they overcame every difficulty in order to do complete justice to their noble task. He emphasized more than once that true civilization was impossible without religion, and that only religion dignified man and made him happy. A school without religion was not a fruitful one and would at no time be able to accomplish its high aim. . . .

At the same time, His Lordship used the excellent achievements of the Indian children to rouse and enliven the spirit and energy of the Indians. He told them that this so beautifully executed program was proof that they could and would achieve a great deal, if only they continued working undauntedly, [and] that God had given them talents, courage, and strength to accomplish their tasks, just as [He had] to the WHITE-MAN here on earth. They too belonged to the "*kingdom of heaven*," and everything here at the mission house was aimed at guiding them happily to this end, to the "*kingdom of heaven*," because it was a school where religion was not excluded, for without religion true education was impossible.—

Unfortunately, we were not granted the pleasure to have the precious chief shepherd in our midst for a few more days. The children very much regretted the, for them, much too early departure; they would have so much liked to have "the good Father" stay with them longer. Everyone felt that the days of our Lordship's stay had been days of happiness, salvation, and blessing for everyone, especially for the entire Rosebud Reservation. No wonder that the children took the last fatherly words of the departing chief shepherd deeply to heart, yes, one of the little girls awoke the next morning with the words: "*We belong also to the kingdom of heaven.*"

Document 1.10

From: Annual Report 1901[22]

Dakota.

In both missions the number of children has grown significantly since September. The old Indians would like it best to have their children be with the sisters and not at the reservation school, but frequently [they] are forced into the latter by the government. Unfortunately, since September the government has withdrawn everything from the poor Indian children who belong to the Catholic missions, and now the worthy fathers as well as the sisters are dependent only upon divine providence. Thus the bishops in the west have resolved that they want to have collections held. In addition, an association for all of the Catholics of North America is to be established under the name: Society for the Preservation of the Faith Among Indian Children. From **St. Francis Mission** it is being written to us:

> There have been more applications for children submitted to us than ever before. Small and big ones [children] come here happily and with joy, without a thought about homesickness. The old Indians, so it was said, are reportedly very angry about the fact that the rations are to be taken away from us, and they intend to meet in great council. These poor people! With their councils they will effect little or nothing. . . .
>
> Our children are doing quite well on the whole. They are numbering 221; boys and girls from ages 6–19. They are not only taught in the various subjects, but are also instructed in tasks commensurate with their respective ages. The sisters not only direct the schools for the boys and girls, but also teach the girls everything that is part of housekeeping: cooking, washing, sweeping, cleaning, sewing, fine needlework, and so on. It is a true delight to see how the older girls work so hard at the sewing machine, cutting out and finishing dresses for themselves. Every three weeks they take turns with the different tasks, so that each one has the opportunity to learn each occupation. Moreover, this change stimulates the zest for work and prevents that the Indian children, who from the very beginning are used to doing nothing, become tired of working, or that their will starts to slacken.—
>
> There is some pleasing and joyful cooperation at the mission, as in a well-ordered family, and the children are at home here just like in their own tents or log cabins. No wonder that also our older, already released children view the mission house as their second home, and not infrequently wish to

be brought here in times of sickness in order that they may set out from here on their journey to eternity. Much that is edifying could be reported about this, which is of great comfort to the male as well as to the female missionaries who are active there. "Oh, I too would like to die in the mission house," the boys were heard saying after having stood at the deathbed of 15–year-old Charlie, who was longing for heaven and passed into eternity without pain. The Indian girls thought and spoke in the same vein at the death of their companion Edith, who was torn out of their midst by a stroke. Along with the missionaries and sisters, they knelt at the deathbed of the child, who could yet be administered the holy sacraments of the dying as she expired gently and peacefully in the Lord. "From here we go to heaven more safely!" a number of our former pupils maintained, and had themselves brought to the mission at the approach of death.

"Take me to the holy house (mission house) so that I may enter the 'house of the Great Spirit' (heaven) from there," the dying Susanna, a fine 27–year-old Indian woman said to her husband, also a good Catholic. He was afraid that the dying woman would not survive the 25 mile drive across the prairie, but the fine Indian woman said that this would not matter, it would be good enough if she died on the way to the holy house. The dear God fulfilled her most ardent wish. In May, on the evening of the first Friday devotion to the Sacred Heart of Jesus, Anton happily arrived with his deathly ill wife, who once more received the holy sacraments, and in the morning toward 3 o'clock, she followed the calling of the GREAT SPIRIT, who undoubtedly was a merciful judge of her.

The Indians know and recognize very well that the Catholic missionaries spare neither pains nor effort in assisting their sheep[d]. "The White Robe" (Protestant minister) only takes care of himself and his family, having himself a wife and children. "He does nothing for us," an old Indian said recently. "If I had 100 children," another remarked, "I would send all 100 of them to the BLACK ROBE and to the HOLY WOMEN. THESE we wanted, THESE we wanted, THESE *Gefleckter Schwanz* [Spotted Tail] asked for in Washington. The WHITE ROBE was merely FORCED UPON us."
. . . One and one-half years ago two small churches were built, one in honor of St. Ignatius and one for St. Peter; there are actually three more churches[d] needed, but where to get the means? All costs must naturally be borne by the mission house; for SUCH purposes there is no bell bag[23] in

the WHITE HOUSE. *Uncle Sam* simply has no special liking for Catholic churches and schools, and if he could have his way altogether, there would be no longer any member of an order at St. Francis Mission. He looks at things through very dark tinted lenses, which makes the Black Robes and the habits of the Franciscan sisters appear just too dark for him, and it does not quite suit him that the poor Indians have strong affection for the Catholic missionaries and sisters based on love and respect. . . .

The government intended to build a nonconfessional school on the spot where our mission is now. The Indians, however, were not pleased with this, but that was of no concern to anybody in Washington, and one day [the government] had wood brought here for the construction. Thus our redskins made short work of it, simply unharnessed the horses, and pulled the wagon to the agency eight miles away. There they left it to its fate. . . .

News and Reports from the Journal
Die katholischen Missionen

Document 2.1
From: Volume 14 (1886)[1]
News from the missions. North America.

In **Dakota** a new Indian mission was opened this spring. One of the sisters (Franciscan nuns from Heythuisen) writes about this joyous occasion in the following letter to her mother general:

> A whole year of indecision with respect to this Indian mission has thus passed. At long last, the day for the departure from Buffalo was set for March 22, of the St. Joseph's month. That morning three holy masses were said by the reverend fathers of the Society of Jesus in supplication for God's blessing for this new undertaking. Toward 12 o'clock noon we left the Sacred Heart of Jesus convent that had become so precious to us. Departing for that place with us was the Very Reverend Fr. Perrig, superior of the new mission. In Chicago, where we arrived after a drive of a half day and a whole night, His Lordship Stephan, director and spiritual superior of the Indian missions, waited at the railway station to welcome us, and having introduced us to the very reverend vicar general of Dakota, who told us many beautiful things about the Rosebud (*Rosenknospe*) Agency, we had the honor of continuing our journey under the *protection* of this high lordship. His Lordship Stephan is off to Washington, the capital; [he is] the praeses and representative of the missions in the Senate, and has to report to the government on their status. Much is being done on the part of the United States government for the Indians, who are treated just like children. At the various agencies they receive all the necessaries in fixed installments: meat, clothing, and so on. However, in return for this, they—to whom after all this land in fact belonged—have been little by little pushed back by the whites into immense, endless prairies, called reservations, where except for the missionaries no whites are permitted to go. There they subsisted on hunting buffalo and game as long as this was

sufficient for maintaining themselves, and given that they do not know anything about working and farming, it is the task of the missionaries to somewhat civilize the poor people, depraved in body and soul. Now I have unintentionally gotten ahead of myself a bit.— In the course of the remaining journey the high lordship, mentioned previously, cared for us in a truly fatherly manner, ordering only the best of everything and carrying every burden. It continued this way by train for two full days and about three nights without interruption as far as Valentine, the last station, whence no further train departs. Around 12:30 o'clock at night we stopped here, having traveled through the states of Ohio, Illinois, Michigan, Iowa, Nebraska, and in the beginning, for a whole night, the territory of Queen Victoria, that is, Canada.—We spent the remainder of the night at Valentine Station, which counted only a few houses, and whereto His Lordship Stephan had by telegraph announced our arrival.

The next morning, on the beautiful Feast of the Annunciation, the journey toward our destination continued in an open wagon across plains so endless as to the point of overtaxing one's eyes, called prairies, where there is neither house nor tree. We indeed passed some beautiful areas at times, on rough roads. Finally, toward evening, the very reverend missionary of the Society of Jesus, who has been here for several months, and who picked us up from Valentine, pointed out to us the roof of our new home above the peaks of the hills. In the distance, about a quarter of an hour away from there, the tents and huts[2] of an Indian village became gradually visible, and we had finally reached our destination; the mission house, our new home, lay before us, destined for us by the dear God. It is a 100–foot-long, two-story house with framed walls, painted light green on the outside, with white shutters fitted with movable louvers. Three beautiful crosses adorn the roof. Encamped in front of the door [waiting] to see the *Wakan winonhinca*, the "holy women," were a great number of Indians with ear pendants half an ell long made up of thick strings of beads, and with large *shawls*. We responded to their astonished looks with a friendly greeting. Their Lordships brought the three of us into our section, a beautiful large room with six large windows, located on the south side of the house. In due time we will separate the cells with partition walls. After we had unpacked somewhat, we first knelt down together to commend our mission to heaven by jointly saying one "Lord's Prayer" in honor of the holy Father Francis, the patron saint of the mission; one "*Unter deinen Schutz*" [We fly to thy patronage] in honor of the dear Mother of God; and one "Lord's Prayer" in honor of St. Joseph.—To us it seems so far away from Buffalo, as if we were at the end of the world. This notwithstanding, we feel quite at home in this wasteland.—His Lordship Stephan then put us in complete charge of the mission household. Next His Lordship instructed me to note everything that was minimally necessary for housekeeping so that he could procure it from Chicago. We are not ever to lack anything at all; he was instructed to see to this. If you, dear Reverend Mother, could only see this heap of blankets, mattresses, and new things for the children! All of this, along with this large site and the new house, is a gift from a wealthy lady from Philadelphia, who wants to remain unnamed, however; thus far, she has spent 12,000 dollars on this mission. I will send you the catalogue of all the available items. There is also a new sewing machine, which we put to use right away, and an organ.—On the day after our arrival we were asked to come to the room of Their Lordships, where close to 20 long-haired Indians had congregated to welcome us. All of them were squatting in a row along the wall with their legs folded under them and wrapped in large shawls. They had brought with them a long peace pipe, the symbol of their most intimate friendship, which was passed from mouth to mouth, so that the room was literally filled up with smoke. With the help of an interpreter, who understands a little bit of English, there were now speeches given by the three chiefs present, which the others applauded by means of an incomprehensible grunt. In the end it was unanimously agreed that all who wanted to send their children to our school should come here with them on the next day.—By 10 o'clock the following morning the finely dressed Indians were already approaching in their gypsy wagons. If you, dear Reverend Mother, could only see the costuming of these children of the wilderness—it is indeed interesting. The women and girls mostly have very long and heavy strings of beads of finger-long, thick, beautiful, white beads, assembled like the German bellpulls, hanging in the ears at the top and bottom, so that on account of the weight of these valuables there is hardly the resemblance of an ear remaining; the same decorations at the neck, [and] bands of brass rings as wide as the breadth of a hand around the arms. Several have added to their jewelry various American copper and silver coins pierced with holes. Most of the time they are painted red. Several have painted yellow stripes across the forehead and cheeks, while the skin is so dark that it seems doubtful that they have ever washed themselves. Almost all of them wear light-green dresses and cherry-red shawls and shoes made of cloth almost up to the knees, which are trimmed with rich beadwork. The men generally have black shawls and all of them long hair; some also wear braids.—Their Lordships thought that because it was the first visit, we were obliged to give them something to eat. We quickly went about it; baked about 200 buns, cooked all the available meat together, then coffee and cheese and biscuit[3] along with it, and the meal was ready. The interpreter dished it out. The two children's refectories, which are about 70 feet long and 38 wide, served as dining room. Following the meal the girls and women themselves had to wash and put back all of the things, tin plates and glasses, that had been used. After everything had been arranged again in proper order, the entire company, more than 80 in number, lined up along the wall, having been directed to do so by Their Lordships, and His Lordship Stephan came to summon us so as to introduce us to the entire attendant gathering of Dakotas. We had to extend our hand to everyone, to which they responded with a friendly "*Hoa.*" Several looked very serious and reflective. There were 21 boys and 20 girls who wanted to come to school right away. However, the number of school-age children apparently amounts to 1,400. Putting our faith in the prayers of our fellow sisters, we are hoping to make rather many of them into good Catholic Christians, since, after all, all of them carry about them, along with us, the same image of God, were ransomed by the same precious blood of Jesus, and are destined for the same heaven.—After Their Lordships too had greeted the entire company, it was indicated to the interpreter that this matter was settled. He then said two words to his red-painted fellow citizens, whereupon the whole lot went out the door in a very nice and orderly fashion, setting out on their homeward journey on their gypsy wagons.

Many of our future pupils, who visit us every day now, lie about in the kitchen and everywhere, watching us. This morning several bigger girls helped Sister Rosalia very nicely with washing, grinding coffee, etc. The main thing in the Indian schools, you must know, is to introduce the children to work in order to get them accustomed to a productive life, given that by nature they are very idle and lie about almost all day long sunning themselves.—Today at noon, just as we had finished eating, for which for the time being we still use the kitchen with the doors closed, someone knocked. It was the interpreter asking whether the head chief (erster Häuptling) and his sister were permitted to come in. We replied in the affirmative, and so there first entered a lady of perhaps 20–22 years, dressed up rather formally. She wears a black dress with ruffle, a white collar[d], black boots[d], [a] colorful shawl, and [she] smells of musk. She has only O N E hole in each ear with short pendants, while all the others have large holes at the top and bottom of the ears. The "lady" mentioned is just as black as the others, but has somewhat better manners. Behind her came the head chief, a very tall, black, intelligent-looking Indian with white shirtsleeves (the first we have seen so far wearing such a piece of clothing) and black wrap-around shawl, in which also the men are fully enveloped. His name is Puddle Dog (Schlammhund). He is very friendly and expressed the desire to shake hands with all of us, which makes them very happy. Then the second chief entered, whose name is Big Turkey (Großer Truthahn). The latter came yesterday with a great letter of recommendation from the priest who was formerly stationed here, who is presently at Rosebud Agency, which stated: Big Turkey was a good friend of the whites and had good intentions. Every time we said or read "Big Turkey" he pointed to himself, [to indicate that] he was the one being referred to. He also had his daughter with him, a very nice girl of 15 years, all over covered and adorned with strings of beads. She also wants to come to us to school. We could hardly keep from laughing when we beheld the hair of this chief. He had combed the hair together on the back of his head like a sun and had parted it, and from the center hung a thin braid[d]. All of the lines where the hair is parted are densely sprinkled with dry red or yellow soil. At our invitation, the entire assembly of chiefs sat down on a pile of boards that are lying there for drying, and we asked the interpreter whether they wished to have something to eat, whereupon he replied that the principal chief liked eating cakes (Kuchen). We then put together a little meat, some cake and biscuit for each person, which they consumed with a healthy appetite without the help of knives and forks. The illustrious people drank a little warmed-up coffee along with it. I then gave to each one a colorful picture[d] of the Sacred Heart of Jesus, in which they greatly delighted, showing it to one another and taking it home wrapped up in paper. At our request the interpreter translated several words into their language, which we repeated, which pleased them so much that they laughed out loud. There have been a number of printed books published in the Dakota language, which are very expensive, however.

Now I still have, in brief, another visit to report about, dear Reverend Mother. When this past Sunday the Very Reverend Fr. Jutz, S.J., who has been here since New Year, returned from the Rosebud Agency, located a good two hours from here, having had to go there on account of business, he brought word that the inspector general of the Indian schools from Washington and the agent had invited themselves for a meal here on Monday. Both gentlemen showed themselves very sympathetic toward the new mission and promised to do their utmost to support it. The inspector, who is Catholic, indicated [that] should the Indians sow grain and such later on, he would make sure that they would be able to sell their crops to the soldiers in the forts and could secure a respectable existence that way.

April 7. Again a break of six to seven days. There is so much to do that each of us would very much like to work with four hands. Nothing is quite ready and furnished at this time, and yet the longing to take children into the house is one that is felt by everyone, although it is impossible to answer to it before the dormitory on the third floor is finished. Then the mattresses, beds, blankets, and so on, which are presently lying in the lower rooms, can be brought upstairs and arranged. What great joy [it would be], if we were to have the chapel with altar, organ, communion bench, and so on set up by Easter! Then there would be one more place[d] on God's great earth where the dear Savior would be honored and worshiped in the most holy sacrament. Given that the tabernacle is still missing, the Holy of Holies cannot be kept at this time. We have two holy masses each morning, however. So far we have maintained our usual order of the day; once the children come, we will have to see how it goes.— In closing I still want to communicate some sketches of the people and the customs of our new countrymen. Dakotas, or as they are called in their language, Lakotas, means something like confederates, allies. The whole nation consists of seven tribes and they like calling themselves "The council of the seven fires." The war prophet and the visionary play an important role among them. In their view, their dreams are revelations from the spirit world, something that they knew and saw once before at an early stage of their existence. They count using only their fingers, and if one asks someone how many things there are, without a word he holds up an equal number of fingers; one bent finger means ten, two bent fingers twenty, and so on. They have no word to express a higher number than one thousand. Likewise, there is in their language an expression for one-half, yet for smaller fractions there are no words. The Dakotas count by winters. Someone is this many winters old; since that event so many winters have passed. When someone sets out on a journey he does not say he will return after so many days, but instead after that many *sleeps* (*Nächte*) [nights]. They calculate distances in the same way, by the number of *sleeps*. They have no division of time by weeks. Their months are usually the moons. The fairly universal belief holds that when a moon is full a large number of little *Kitnykady* (*Mäuse*) [mice] would begin nibbling on the other side, and they would continue this until they finished eating it. The new moon that comes into existence shares the fate of its predecessor. They think, you must know, that the new moon is a wholly new *haypem-wi* (*Mond*) [moon] each time around. The different moons derive their names from more important natural phenomena occurring at that time. They count 5 moons for summer and five for winter, leaving only two for spring and autumn. However, not everyone exactly shares the views of the others, and they frequently have heated discussions in their huts, especially toward the end of winter, about what sort of moon the present one was. In order to have their moons be consistent with the seasons, it is necessary that they leave out one every couple of years. Their religion is dark, [and] of their Gods there are many. Their imagination has populated the visible world with mysterious spiritual beings who usually have a relationship to the human family, either for weal or woe. These spiritual beings dwell within each thing and therefore nearly every single thing is an object of worship. It is for this reason that a Dakota dances in honor of the sun and moon, spreads his hands in prayer before a colorfully painted stone, and finds it necessary to offer more sacrifices to the evil spirit than to the Great Spirit. He has his god of the north and of the south, the god of the air and of the water, the god of the woods and the prairie.

Document 2.2

From: Volume 15 (1887)[4]
News from the missions. North America

In the previous volume, p. 197ff. [doc. 2.1], we reported on the arrival of the Franciscan nuns from Heythuisen at the new St. Francis Mission among the Indians in Dakota. Since then, two new letters have reached us, recounting the joyous beginnings of the work and its continuation.

Dear Reverend Mother! It has long been my intention to once again tell you about our mission. The postal connection is a bit more difficult here, far away from the civilized world. Letters are only conveyed by the 2–3 hour distant Rosebud Agency, and this by courier, while packages and freight for the mission have to be retrieved from the nearest railway station, Valentine. With horses and wagon this distance takes two days' journeys each time. From this you can see that we live with our dear Indians in complete isolation and withdrawn from the whole world. Other than some scattered tents of the Dakotas, we see nothing except the clear deep blue sky and the vast rolling prairies, which, in a delicate green, afford a lovely sight (see the image on p. 21 [not reproduced here]). Up until the previous decades, these steppes were the stamping ground of wild buffalo and reindeer herds,[5] among which bears and snakes did their mischief. How many times do I wish that you, dear Reverend Mother, and all of the dear sisters were here, so that you could once, along with us, delight in the sight of this beautiful nature created by God. Here no factory, no train, no deafening noise of machinery disturbs the solemn tranquility. You will perhaps be surprised that the schools have not yet begun. Unfortunately, setting up the house still creates a lot of work for us so that we have been unable thus far to admit any children. Because if the *kleinen* [little] *Wilden* are not gotten used to order from the start, they do not see any difference between their "tepees" (*Zelte*) [tents] and the school. So far about 30 beds for the girls are done; also, beds, blankets, [and] pillows are already arranged for an additional 20, and we are busy sewing sheets, towels, [and] pillowcases for the boys, for whom there are the same number of beds available. The reverend fathers and the brothers provide for the teaching and instruction of the boys in suitable trades, while caring for the girls is the duty of us sisters. They are obliged to learn all of the domestic tasks, [such as] washing, cooking, gardening and needlework, reading, and writing. Because it is impossible for us to make completely new apparel for all of the children in so short a time, given the numerous tasks, the Very Reverend Fr. Superior ordered the clothing for 50 boys and 50 girls from the Sisters of the Good Shepherd. If the house is set up well enough by the time the clothing arrives, the school can be opened around Pentecost, that is, with the help of the Holy Spirit.—For the time being, our existence rests on God's grace and the charity of good people. If the poor Dakotas in their tents knew how the fathers were laboring all day long hammering and joining in order to fix up the house in which their children and they themselves are to get to know the dear God, and if they knew what it meant to be raised Catholic, they would take the tools out of the hands of the fathers instead of comfortably looking on—as they do now—while idly lying on the ground enveloped in their large wrap-around shawls. In view of the great idleness and unsteadiness of the *Wilden*, we always feel pressed to expect all of the assistance from the dear God, who governs each heart. It will be difficult for a people accustomed to idleness from childhood to submit to a regulated and industrious life. However, we are putting our hopes in the many collective prayers, without letting ourselves be discouraged in the slightest. They will surely call God's blessing upon our good will. You, dear Reverend Mother, as well as all of the dear fellow sisters, please pray for us and our mission. How many more interesting matters could I relate. Yet if I wanted to go into all the particulars, it would be a whole book[d]. For today only one thing: The second chief, *Großer Truthahn* [Big Turkey], about whom I wrote to you in the first letter, several weeks ago had a message addressed to the Very Reverend Fr. Superior in English. The ingenious content of this dispatch was the following: "I wish, *ich wünsche*, that you prepare a grand *diner* for all the Indians tomorrow, because—they love this so much." The next day, a Saturday, on account of this self-invitation, there came from all directions for this grand *diner* all sorts of horse-drawn wagons, pony and ox carts, with Dakotas tattooed in red and yellow; but nothing came of it [the dinner] that day, of course. The Very Reverend Fr. Superior had replied to his [Big Turkey's] letter [that] we had no time to arrange grand *diners*; the Indians should work. The *Wilden* were thus promised a feast for the beginning of the school year. After the whole gathering—adorned with plumes

of feathers and odd treasures [as well as with] the heirlooms of their fore-
fathers and ancestors—had patiently waited until about 2 o'clock in the
future children's refectory, having filled the entire room with the thick
clouds of smoke from their peace pipes, they all drove back home without
haste. We had not paid any attention to them the entire time and had them
leave with empty stomachs and the thought of the grand *diner*. This past
Sunday, *Großer Truthahn* [Big Turkey] showed us the letter from the Very
Reverend Fr. Superior. Although he could not read one syllable of it, he
nonetheless preserved it like a valuable treasure. The chief made us a present of a brown peace pipe and explained to us as best he could how to use
it. With a great deal of pride he introduced his daughter to us, a sprightly
and indeed very pleasing fifteen-year-old girl. She, too, is to attend our
school. On a necklace of white and yellow finger-long beads, the girl
wore, along with various precious objects, strange animal teeth. A black
leather sheath, which the father pointed out to us, was suspended from a
belt made of beads in the width of a hand. On opening it, we found a long,
sharp butcher knife, which our future pupil regarded with a sense of comfort. Several weeks ago a very old, genuine, redskinned Indian visited us,
who had on him a peace pipe of peculiar sorts. On a long striped shaft was
a large, sharp hatchet, polished like silver, whose hollowed head served
him as pipe. Now, should someone doubt his peaceful intentions, or refuse the pipe, he would make short work of him. But have no fear, dear
Reverend Mother, no one does us any harm, not in the least. On the contrary, the Indians are greatly in awe of us and one gesture is enough to remove a dozen or more of these redskinned *Wilden* from the kitchen. They
usually come there, you must know, to see and greet the holy women, as
they call us sisters. In other respects, I must admit to you in confidence
that I would regard it as great favor shown by the dear God if, at life's end,
there was the prospect of the martyr's crown for me. Upon my word, a
whole life of toilsome labor would not be too great a price for this.

Now briefly something about a burial by the *Wilden* here, if it even deserves this designation. One morning last week, at 3 o'clock, a wagon with
a two-horsed team arrived, on which mother and grandmother sat with
the body of their 8– to 9–year-old daughter[d], screaming at the top of their
voices. The vehicle, which made up the entire funeral procession, passed
the mission at a distance of about 100 paces, and went to a hill. Having

arrived there, both dismounted, took the body off the wagon, and laid it on the ground. The mother then exchanged the black death blanket with a red one, wrapped herself in a white shawl, and laid down on the ground beside the child. Toward 12 o'clock, when I brought in the dry laundry, she was still in the same position. The wagon had left in the meantime, and the body had again been wrapped in a black blanket. Finally, around 5 o'clock in the afternoon, the Very Reverend Fr. Jutz rode on horseback up the hill to check on things. He found the grieving mother and grandmother still in the same place. The Indians had not yet made a grave, because in their view the body wrapped in multiple covers is perfectly safe on the green grass until the Day of Judgment, although horses and cows are grazing all around. Until not too long ago, the Indians hung all of their dead in trees. On looking more closely, Fr. Jutz discovered that the body had been put between four boards and wrapped with four doubled, thick red blankets. The child itself was completely covered with beads, ear pendants, and other precious objects. The Very Reverend Father removed all of these items, also the blankets, and handed them to the mother, who he then brought to us. After we had offered her a small refreshment, she was handed a shovel and given to understand that she was to dig a pit for her child. These *Wilden* must be shown everything, just like small children, in order to get them accustomed to a little bit of work. When finally at about 8 o'clock everything was done, the mother, still a very young woman, returned to us. Accompanied by animated gesticulations she told us in her language a long story, of which we did not understand a word, however. When by chance an interpreter entered, he translated the woman's sorrow into English for us. The poor mother believed that someone wanted to steal the heart of her child, that is why she had stayed with the body the entire day. She was unable to eat anything out of sorrow, and thus motioned to us to wrap up the food for her. As a sign of mourning she had cut her hair very short and wore none of the usual precious objects. The only consolation we could give her was that we told her: "*Wineincala, Wakontanka,* the girl is with the Great Spirit." A pained smile was her sole reply. We then hung the miraculous medal of the Blessed Virgin Mary about her neck, for which she thanked us with a hearty shake of the hand. After this she returned home to her tent, two hours away.—We have discovered that our Indians here are very compassionate at heart and without being asked share with one another what they receive here in food. On average, all of our Indians are tall, strong men with long, coal-black hair, teeth as white as snow, and a reddish-brown skin color. At times they paint themselves so brightly with colorful paints that one thinks to be looking at the setting sun when such a face unexpectedly appears in the doorway. The children, too, are all taller than their comrades of the same age in Germany. It is really quite interesting how well 6- to 7-year-old boys are able to ride, skillfully staying in the saddle even at the fullest gallop. The little riders courageously set spurs to their ponies and then, cap in hand, speed across the prairie with long, flying hair, as fast as the wind. At times old men visit us, who, in addition to other ornaments, carry on their belts the pelt of a strange animal. The animal may be as large as a fox, yet its skin is prettier than that of the polecat.[6] The inside of the mentioned pelt is scraped clean; the paws are richly adorned with beads. The previous week there was also a small boy here who had a mirror the size of a hand attached on both sides of the knee on his new blue pants. Not long ago a woman came to pay a visit with her child on her back. The little thing wore as adornment on each arm[d] a white porcelain milk pot[d] attached to strings of beads[d]. It was really funny to behold. When we put several lumps of colored sugar into its milk pots[d], the mother, who tasted them, expressed great delight. Usually a number of these poor, good-natured heathens attend our May devotions every evening with blessing. Kneeling on the benches is still so foreign to every single one of them that usually the first service passes before they have learned enough, by watching and trying in every possible and impossible way, to at least be able to kneel halfway straight, all the while holding on so tightly, however, that one could think they were glued in place. Yet all of this takes place with the greatest earnestness, indeed, with a certain amount of anxiety. Several sit on the floor between the benches with their feet on the kneeler, so that one can hardly watch this and maintain a sense of seriousness in the holy place. And yet the dear God must delight in the good will of the poor *Wilden*. The Indian policeman, a tall Dakota by the name of *Hallow Ham Bull*, "*hohler Ochsenschinken*," as he pointed out to us in black and white in a book[d], makes sure that all the Indians kneel. If someone lapses in that regard, he issues him a reprimand in a low voice, which is always understood right away. This past Sunday Their Lordships administered in our chapel the holy sacrament of extreme unction to an about 20-year-old Indian by the name of Ignatius. The poor man suffers from consumption in the most advanced stage. His father brought him here many times so that we would give him milk to drink and something to eat. It was so touching to watch how the poor, weak *Wilde* tolerated everything so patiently. Because he could no longer walk on his own, the Very Reverend Fr. Superior carried him up and down the stairs.

Document 2.3
From: *Volume 15 (1887)*[7]
News from the missions. North America.

Indian mission in Dakota. We have repeatedly reported on letters from the sisters who have taken charge of the girls' school at the newly founded station at Rosebud Agency. Before we once again put before our readers one of these interesting letters, we would like to communicate several notes on the founding and location of it [the mission] from a letter by Fr. Emil Perrig, S.J., the superior of this mission. On 25 October 1886, he writes to a fellow brother:

Our Indians belong to the tribe of the Sioux. A mission had been established among them even when they were still living on the Missouri River. When they were relocated by the government from their former place of residence to the present reservation, an attempt was made to impose a Protestant missionary upon them, but Spotted Tail (*Gefleckter Schweif*), the chief of these Indians, opposed this and demanded a "Black Robe." His wish was granted, and a Mister Frederik was the first missionary to the so-called Brulé Indians on the Rosebud Reservation. The reservation has a breadth of 40 English miles and a length of 80. To the south it borders on the state of Nebraska, to the west, on the Pine Ridge Reservation, to the north, on the great White River and the Cheyenne Reservation, and to the east, on the lower Brulé Reservation. The apostolic vicar of Dakota, His Lordship Martin Marty, transferred this mission to the German Jesuits, and Fr. Jutz took charge of it on 1 January 1886.

A wealthy, charitable lady had a school building erected that was to lodge 100 children, yet it turned out that it is far from being spacious enough for so many. The location of the house is beautiful all right, but has its disadvantages: water had to be retrieved from a distance of 5 English miles. Thus we first had to dig a well, hitting water only at a depth of 195 feet, which is pumped to the surface by means of a windmill.

On March 25, I arrived with Brother Nunlist and three Franciscan nuns from Heidhuyzen. On August 6, I received additional assistance: Fr. Florian Digman, the two Brothers Graß and Pankan, and three new sisters arrived. A few days later there also came the Brothers Surich und Ständer. Now we could expand our buildings and open the school on September 15. About 60 children were registered; since then the number has increased to 78, which is as high as we can go, given our present situation. On the whole, one experiences less displeasure with the *kleinen* [little] *Wilden* than with many white children; their main bad habits are idleness, a disposition to lying, and a ravenous appetite, which causes them to lay claim to anything that is eatable and accessible to them, without any compunction. The dear Brother Gardener could say a great deal about that. All the vigilance notwithstanding, many a turnip, cucumber, and squash were filched from him. Sometimes they did it like this: they pretended to be playing "tag," running over the melons and crushing the most beautiful ones; then they would come looking all innocent, asking the brother to please let them eat the pieces, so that they would not rot in vain. The boys also are very much prone to running away, not because they did not like being with us, but because they love roving about. The so-called *beef-days* (*Fleisch-Tage*), the days on which the Indians receive their biweekly meat rations, pose the greatest risk for running away. The Indians, you must know, are maintained at government expense in return for having taken their land from them and having crowded them onto reservations, and every 14 days they receive (or at least should receive) their rations of meat, flour, coffee, sugar, beans, salt, and so on. Such *beef-days* are of course great days of celebration. That is when the Indians travel to the agency in full regalia, faces and hands painted red, yellow, and green. Then it comes to feasting, and when the drums and whistles from the village announce from over there that it is beef-day, and that there is gluttony, dancing, and singing going on, then a great longing to participate is stirred in our children. It is almost unbelievable what the Indians can accomplish on such days; often they are finished with everything in three days' time, although typically they have had nothing left to eat in the last 4 or 5 days prior to *beef-day*.

Otherwise our Indians are a harmless, friendly people, who hold the "Black Robes" in high regard. Among the adults we can begin missionary work only later with better knowledge of their language. So far we have baptized 14 children and 3 adults in deathly peril.

We now let the letter of the sister follow, which contains many additional details of interest:

Given that you, to our joy, are taking such great interest in our dear Dakotas, I want to try and report something about our experiences. We have been on vacation for one week, after having begun to admit and teach children starting in the middle of June. On their arrival the little redskins were right away taken into a special room[d], where they were subjected to a thorough washing and cleaning. Because they have no water in their camps, having to get it from miles away, they are on average much in need of such a procedure. Then they were dressed from head to toe in brand-new clothing, after which they looked like completely different children. The boys' long hair and braids were also cut, which was quite all right by them. The girls, most of whom came without any ornaments, wore except for the usual wrap-around shawl nothing more than a rag of calico with a couple of skimpy sleeves, held in place by a rope tied around their waists. Before the vacation we had altogether 40 children, boys and girls. For the beginning of the new school year many more are registered. Is this not a substantial number, and is this not a very noble, divine deed to teach these poor creatures—who with the exception of four or five who already have received holy baptism, are all genuine wild heathens—to know and love the dear God? If only we had the zeal for souls and the love of a holy Franz Xaver [Francis Xavier] to make quite a lasting impression on these good-natured hearts of children!

Although there has not been any lack of difficulties, we have nonetheless experienced mostly comfort and joy with our wild pupils during this short period of time, and we are anticipating the beginning of the new school year with a true sense of longing for them. Hopefully, it will bring us an increase in auxiliaries, which the dear Mother Cäcilia promised us. It is altogether touching to see how the older boys of 17–18 years of age, without averting an eye, are trying to learn to make the holy sign of the cross, when it is shown to them by example, and how they repeat word for word the "Lord's Prayer" and "*Gegrüßet seist du Maria*" [Hail Mary]. One makes them very happy with rosaries, the longer the better, which the oldest always wear around their necks, [and] with medals on very colorful ribbons, [as well as] with rings [and] beads. Most have no eyebrows, as they pluck them out with special tweezers that they wear on their braids. I do not need to tell you that we, there being only three of us, were practically overloaded with work. It is certainly no small matter to cook, bake, and wash for 40 children, to oversee the girls day and night, to manage the entire household, and so on. Given that work is a tough nut for them, we have very little help from the children for the time being, and they know only too well that one does not get tired from idleness. At the same time there prevailed for a while such terrible heat that the thermometer recorded 42–43° C in the shade. A blistering hot south wind blew across the arid prairie bringing to mind the Egyptian desert. To make the whole matter more meritorious yet, we were plagued by a water shortage. The reverend fathers and brothers had a great deal of endlessly difficult work with the 195–feet-deep well. Because of the tremendous depth of the well, bringing up the water by means of a windmill did not seem to want to work. Hopefully, Our Lady of Lourdes, to whom we have appealed in this matter, will help. Thank goodness, for several days everything has been all right, and very nice cold well water is coming up from the bottom, pumped by the wind.

In spite of all the mentioned great difficulties associated with true mission life, and others [not mentioned], the three of us are very happy and full of joy, indeed happier than we have ever been in our lives, in the living faith that this is the place where the dear God wants us to be and whereto He Himself called us under holy obedience. His love knows how to sublimely substitute all the temporal pleasures with greater goods, and we do not want to leave this mission field, which has become so dear to us, for anything in the world, except for God's divine will. The reverend missionaries do everything possible to make our work easier. For their part, they perform the most arduous tasks from early in the morning until late at night in order to arrange everything as best as possible for the functioning of the mission.

To now return to our dear countrymen—their trust is mostly gained by administering to them medicine or ointments during their illnesses. I believe I can say without exaggeration that so far we have provided more than 50 sick Dakotas with pills and ointments. Hardly two or three days pass during which not one two- or four-team rig arrives with sufferers who have sick eyes or open sores, or with parents who are bringing in their sick children. The open sores are widespread due to the great lack of hygiene among the *Wilden*. The dear God appears to be blessing our remedies; usually the Indians come back after some time and say: lila *waste* *pesuta*, "very good medicine." Several weeks ago a true Episcopalian Indian came, who first looked me over with some suspicion. Then he showed his leg. He had fallen onto a pair of scissors and had a deep gangrenous wound below the knee, so that he could only walk with a limp due to the pain. After the wound had been treated with an ointment and bandaged, I brought him some pills to take, which must have seemed strange to him. He first looked at the pills, then at me, with a doubting, questioning look, wondering whether these kernels[d] were indeed any good. When I then expressed to him very seriously: *Yuta wasta*, "for eating—are good"—he took them. After several days he returned to have the bandage changed, already able to walk better. On parting, he asked for *pesuta*, "medicine for eating," with the comment: "lila *waste*." This past Sunday he was back; his leg is now completely well. This time he brought his little daughter[d] with him, who he later intends to send to our school. Moreover, he stayed for holy mass, kneeling nearly the entire time. Oftentimes there even come couriers from the village of the heathens, asking for a sister to visit the sick. One of the reverend missionaries then goes there, to be sure, and frequently there is the opportunity to administer holy baptism to the dying. During these visits one sees the dirt, the disorder, and the idleness of these heathen nations up close—to the civilized world almost unbelievable. Their dwellings are exactly the way they are depicted on pictures. One has difficulty entering on all fours through the 2–3 foot opening on the bottom. A table and bed are usually unnecessary luxury items in this part of God's earth. Ordinarily, there is a thin blanket spread on the cold, naked ground, on which the sick, in their clothing, are bedded, half sitting, half kneeling. Near these "tepees" (*Zelte*) the setup for a sweat bath can be seen. At half a man's height there are a great many switches bent one over the other, going in all directions, and stuck into the ground at both ends. The whole thing looks very much like a large, circular doghouse. On the one side in the interior of this creation lies a heap of stones. The subsequent preparation for a bath consists of heating up the stones to the point of glowing, whereupon a blanket is stretched over the hoops. The sick now has to see how he or she can best find room beside the stones without getting burned. Next, water is continuously poured over the glowing stones. Their illnesses, then, are driven out by the power of the vigorous steam being generated. They not infrequently also resort to superstitious remedies.—The manner in which the Wilden smoke meat is also very interesting. Given that they get the latter delivered from the agency every 14 days, and they are unable to consume everything all at once, and have neither cellar nor other meat pantries, they cut the supply into thin strips, which they hang on old laths for drying in the sun, like clothing. At our last visit to the "Coarse voice camp" (Lager der rauhen Stimme) we saw a lath full of such coal-black, dried-out large strips of meat hanging near every single tent.

Document 2.4

From: Volume 16 (1888)[8]
News from the missions. North America.

Indian mission in Dakota. From a letter of the Right Reverend Fr. Emil Perrig, the superior of the mission among the Sioux in Dakota, we quote the following news:

Last year our school was attended by on average 71 Indian children; the highest number was 82, the lowest 60. Their conduct was significantly better than before, and once we had dismissed several of the older boys and girls, the ones who stayed gave us little trouble. Nearly all of the children in our school are baptized; some last year, others this year on Holy Saturday. All of those who are baptized went to their first Holy Confession and five received first Holy Communion before they left school. In addition, we baptized a good number of adults and children when they were deathly ill. Other than those, we baptized only three married couples and one unmarried man from among the adults. Given that most of the adult Indians unfortunately offer so little prospect of a change of life after baptism, we have set aside all those who desire baptism until they abandon their superstitious practices and lead a decent life. This is a severe demand, but we want, to the extent that it is within our power, no Christian heathens, but instead Christians who were formerly heathens. There is certainly no lack of the greatest promises, but an Indian promise is as good as an Indian marriage: both are declared dissolved for the slightest reasons. An Indian man or an Indian woman of 25 years of age who has not already been married three or four times is the great exception. To steal another man's wife in broad daylight counts for a heroic deed. But this happens rarely, for they are cowardly, deceitful fellows. That is why they conduct their theft at night and when the husband is absent, and if a feud results afterward, it is amicably resolved by means of several woolen blankets or a horse that the injured party receives. These breaches of trust, polygamy, dealings with the most depraved whites, and lastly their belief in the power of the foolish or devilish practices of their medicine men, are the greatest obstacles to their conversion. These medicine men are the most cunning fellows, although it does not really take very much to deceive an Indian. Some are clever conjurers. They come to a sick person, and although they usually do not know at all what is wrong with him, they start doctoring away without hesitation, prescribing tea, powder, broths made from roots, and so on. Of course, this helps the sick person little. Then they start their conjuring. [They] burn all sorts of trifles, put a whole string full of amulets to use,—teeth from all kinds of possible and impossible animals, horns from oxen, stones, and so on—dance all around the sick person, blow on the body part that hurts, position themselves as if they wanted to suck out the illness, suddenly showing a small stone, a snake, [or] a bird, insisting that it was the cause of the illness. They practice this nonsense and worse as long as the relatives are able and willing to pay. When horses, household items, and money, and the woolen blankets are in their hands, and the sick person still has not been restored to health, then they declare him incurable and take off, leaving the people who they have virtually plundered not even the essentials. That is when one usually comes to us, wanting to have our medicine. However, we do not give them anything until they send away the medicine men and renounce their conjuring.

Usually, the dying are most willing to receive baptism; of 60–70 cases there have been only three who staunchly refused. When an Indian is in the throes of death, then more often than not the entire dwelling is filled with men and women, wailing dreadfully and pretending to be weeping; tears rarely flow. In the meantime, the closest relatives paint the dying person red, green, or orange-yellow to cover the pallor of death. Having breathed his last, what he owned and had loved most during his life is thrown onto the body; everything else is stolen by the "mourners." They at once carry the body out of the hut and lay him onto a scaffold or bury him, and one hour after death has entered the dwelling, there is nothing more inside than the four naked walls and a beggar's family without any means. Of course, we bury those who die a Catholic, provided we are notified and there is a willingness to wait for the burial as long as a Christian burial requires. We usually even present them with decent coffins. Once the body is in the ground, all lamentations cease immediately; it is the exceptional case that a sign of mourning is noticeable.

Next Tuesday, Fr. Bosch will arrive at this place to take part in our mission work, while Fr. Digman will probably go to Pine Ridge to open a school and Indian mission also at that place. A spacious and well-furnished building was erected there and will be completed in a few weeks. A generous benefactress assumed the expenses for this facility.

Our children do not give us a tenth of the trouble that white children cause in the European schools, although they previously never knew anything about obedience, self-control, diligence, gratitude, and so on, all of which, after all, is already taught white children at home. Our children never quarrel [and] do not fight, yet they are very lively; they do not insult, do not disobey, are rarely discontented or bad-tempered, and are not at all spoiled as far as food is concerned, as long as there is enough, and even if they have too little, they content themselves with it.

As a curiosity, I will include the names of the boys who received the first prizes at the closing of the school year:

PROPER CONDUCT: Leo Präriehühnchen [Leo Little Prairie Chicken], son of Rostbraten [Roast]. INDUSTRY: 1. Oliver Citronenfalter [Oliver Brimstone Butterfly], son of Adler [Eagle]; 2. Haarhemd [Hair Shirt], son of Hohlerhornadler [Hollow Horn Eagle]. SPELLING: Joseph Hat-kein-schlechtes-Hemd [Joseph Has-No-Bad-Shirt], son of Hohlerhornstier [Hollow Horn Bull]. READING: Jakob Blaßgesicht [Jakob Paleface], son of Gehörnter Hund [Horned Dog]. ARITHMETIC: Jakob Weißholz [Jacob White Wood], son of Linkshändiger Stier [Left-Handed Bull], and so on. Among the girls there

were the following prize-winners: *Susanna Weißkuh* [Susanna White Cow],
daughter of *Gutes Wort* [Good Word]; *Therese Bringt-das-Maulthier-heim*
[Therese Brings-the-Mule-Home], daughter of *Wandelnder Adler* [Walking
Eagle]; *Röschen Windsbraut* [Rosette Raging Wind], daughter of *Ochsenauge*
[Bull's Eye], and so on.

Pray for our mission and the poor heathens!

Document 2.5
From: *Volume* 19 (1891)[9]
News from the missions. North America.

Indian mission in Dakota. The two Indian missions led by German Jesuits, serving Rosebud Agency and Pine Ridge, are in the middle of the
insurgency that broke out among the Sioux Indians. It started, as Fr. Digmann, superior of the Francis mission at Rosebud Agency, writes, with
the appearance of false prophets among the Indians, who are asserting
that the son of the Great Spirit (Christ) had appeared to them, showed
them the five wounds that had been delivered him by palefaces, and told
them that the clamor and the tears from the Indians oppressed by the
palefaces had reached him, and that when the new grass was once again
beginning to grow, he wanted to appear along with the ghosts of the slain
Indians, destroy this miserable earth along with the palefaces through
hail, flood, and fire, and create a new earth filled with buffalo, elk, and
pronghorns.[10] Heathenish and Protestant Indians by the hundreds and
thousands throng to one of these prophets, who preaches them this
message, seeking to move the son of the Great Spirit to an early arrival
through so-called Ghost Dances, smoking, steam baths, and other superstitious practices. They continue the dancing until they collapse out
of breath and as if dead. When half an hour later they come to again,
they assert having flown on the wings of an eagle to the sun and even farther, having met their deceased parents, brothers, and kin in the hunting
grounds of the dead, where there is game in abundance; they report to
have shaken hands with the deceased and have learned from them much
about the future. To one missionary, who went to these fanatical Indians
to perhaps convince them of this devilish deception, whose victims they
are, one of these ghost dancers said on touching the robe of the father:
"You are a Black Robe. *Gefleckter Schweif* (Spotted Tail), our deceased chief,

told me that you are the only good and true ones who have the words of the Great Spirit. That is also why we had demanded Black Robes. But we were sent White Robes (Protestant missionaries) and now the quarrel over who is telling the truth is great. We Dakota will now receive from the Great Spirit our own prayer and our own divine service," and so on. One Indian, who last year had received baptism while on the verge of death, also wanted to participate in the Ghost Dance to see his deceased father. They ordered him to take off the scapular and all other consecrated things, and then let him sweat, but he had no visions whatsoever.

The actual cause of this recent uprising by the Dakota Indians against the North American government is the disgraceful oppression to which they are subjected, even more so than before, under the present rule of the agents. They are unashamedly cutting the supplies to which the Indians are entitled as per treaty in exchange for the land taken from them, and the plight resulting from this continues to drive the half starving Indians to acts of desperation. The following letter from Fr. Digmann of 4 November 1890 from the Rosebud Agency, describes for us the situation at the start of winter:

> The present government commissioner for Indian affairs is a Baptist and a dogged enemy of the Catholics. In May he sent us an ardent Episcopalian woman as inspector for our Indian schools. This notwithstanding, she was unable to avoid submitting a positive report about our school. That is why I counted without fail on new government support for this school year. In former times I would have the respective confirmation already over the vacation; so far nothing has happened. The house is full of children, almost full to overflowing: I have admitted 51 boys and 57 girls. In addition, our Indians' rations for this year have been cut in an inhumane fashion: IN EXCESS OF ONE MILLION POUNDS OF MEAT LESS THAN BEFORE; only approximately 2 pounds of flour per head and week, [and] at the same time, a bad, indeed almost no harvest whatsoever. Our mission feels the consequences. Daily the hungry come in droves wanting to eat. In the beginning I gave to them without asking for any services in return, as before. But when I saw that it was getting to be too much, and [that] I was unable to defray the expenses, I demanded: "First you work some, then you will get something to eat." But now they overrun me with

requests for work, so that I am unable to find enough to do, but to send them home hungry is not in my nature either. Thus I butchered a number of our cows; they fight over the entrails, eating them raw with nothing remaining of the animal other than skin and bones.

Given this plight, is it any wonder that their false prophets are presently finding such a following, when they preach to them that Christ will come in the spring, bringing them many buffalo, elk, and other game? Our Christians and even most of the heathens at our camp have kept away from this movement, or have gone there only out of curiosity. Now the leaders have made 40 robes—our Christians call them devil's robes (*Wakantoca Taogli*)—and they distribute them among Indians who are to act in the various camps as apostles of the "new prayer" (of the new religion). Before, they all were gathered at a place on White River, at times 2,000–3,000 warriors. With the approach of winter they returned home to their camps continuing the Ghost Dances there. Two or three from our neighborhood, staunch heathens who never came to church, also have taken the devil's robe and now want to start this mischief near us. They threatened one of our Christians: "If I touch you with an eagle feather, you will die"; but the Christian responded undaunted: "Here are many feathers; go ahead and try it, I am not afraid!" One of our catechumens told them: "Jesus Christ gave the people who stood by Him food, and fed five thousand with five loaves of bread. Let your Tatanka Ptekelan (*Short Bull* = *der kurze Stier*, the chief prophet) do the same, and I will believe him." Many have already cooled down somewhat, for the prophecy does not appear to fulfill itself and the earth still is not burning. Yet there are many remaining who believe that it will start in the spring. Then, of course, the swindle has to become apparent, and we are hoping for a favorable rebound for the spreading of Christianity.

At the Holy Rosary Mission at Pine Ridge the situation is very similar. In the course of the year 130 boys and girls lived in the mission school. Almost all of them were seized by influenza; five boys and two girls died of this disease.

At the request of General Brooke, one of the missionaries, Fr. Johann Jutz, S.J., set out on December 5 [*sic*] to visit the Indians at their fortified camp on White River, and if possible to prevent a new bloody Indian war from breaking out, which would have the saddest consequences for the settlers. Given the alarming agitation of the *Wilden*, this mission was a life-threatening one; nonetheless, our countryman, full of courage and devotion, subjected himself to it. Let us hear the account of his experiences, as the American press relates it based on his report:

The missionary embarked on his dangerous commission last Wednesday, December 3, accompanied by Jack Red Cloud (*Rothe Wolke*), the widely respected son of the famous chief. They chose a path not frequently used, down the White River, and consequently had soon lost their way after having set across the river. They had to keep themselves moving the entire night of Thursday, so as not to freeze to death. With that came hunger, because they had not taken one bit of provisions with them. Ten miles distant from the camp of the hostile Indians they were stopped by the sentries of the latter, who pointed their guns at them and held them until they had sent an Indian to the camp to inquire whether the two were to be admitted. A favorable reply arrived and they continued on their journey, but between the muzzles of gun barrels. The following forenoon, at 11 o'clock, they arrived at the camp, and two hours later the chiefs met with Fr. Jutz in council, which was attended by Two Strike (*Zwei-Schlag*), the principal chief, Kicking Bear (*Stotternder Bär*) [Stuttering Bear], Eagle Pipe (*Adler-Pfeife*), Big Turkey (*Großer Truthahn*) and Big Pipe (*Große Pfeife*). The peace pipe was conspicuously absent.

Fr. Jutz opened the council by asking the chiefs to state the particular reason for their complaints that had prompted them to assume such a militant stance. The responses are essentially as follows:

"We are objecting to the latest census report by Mister Lee. According to the count, which he is doing now, we would not receive enough provisions on which to subsist. Lee is counting fewer, a lot fewer in each *tepee* (*Zelt*) than it contains. We are to receive provisions in accordance with this count. We will starve to death. We know we will starve to death if it pleases the Great Father (the President of the United States) to set a trap in order to defraud us. We will have at least one large meal before the famine. Then we will fight our last fight, and the whites shall see more blood and more dead killed by our guns than ever before. Then we will joyfully go to the happy hunting grounds. If the whites had not intended to cheat us out of provisions, the Great Father would have never sent soldiers. There is no need for soldiers if the Great Father intends to deal with us honestly. By the way in which the census man is now writing down the numbers, which lie, and according to which we are to be fed, we know that he intends to defraud us.

"The Great Father has committed another injustice. He has drawn a new border line between the Rosebud and Pine Ridge Agency. As a result of this many of us have to leave our homelands and leave them to others. We can no longer believe the Great Father. He says to us: 'Children, you shall no longer have to move from one place to the next, unless it is your will to do so.' We are done negotiating, and are now making the promise that we will fight, and the Great Father will find that we will not break our promise. We will now be very open with you, Christian Father, and tell you something else, something that you may have thought about already. It is this: We do not want to come to the agency now and will not lay down our weapons, because we are fearing the consequences. We have done wrong, we know that. If we stop now, we will be punished. The Great Father would send many of us into his big iron house for many months. We would die. No, we do not want to go to the agency and surrender. We know the Great Father better than he us or than he cares to know us. After a long while some of us may come, once the soldiers are withdrawn."

Fr. Jutz then cautioned them to remain peaceful. He explained to them that the soldiers had not come to do the Indians harm but to protect the agency; that the rations at the agency had been increased, and that if they came to the agency General Brooke would send a telegraph to Washington and obtain permission for them to stay in this agency as per their wishes. It would be better for them if they stopped the violence, for then they would be forgiven more readily. Finally, he greatly urged the chiefs to return with him in a body. These suggestions were responded to favorably by several of the older people, but the younger ones, who were clearly in the majority, said no. In the end, the older people agreed to come to the house of the missionary located about four miles northwest of the agency, in order to meet there with General Brooke, and to tell him themselves what they had just told Fr. Jutz. This was again met with opposition on the part of the majority, and it nearly came to a brawl. Finally, the young chiefs grew less heated, and Two Strike turned to Fr. Jutz with the following words:

"Raise your hands to the Great Spirit and tell us, just as if you were about to embark on the journey to the happy hunting grounds of the red man, if what you told us about General Brooke is true, and that no harm will be done to us if we come to the agency only for the purpose of speaking with General Brooke."

Fr. Jutz complied with this request, whereupon all of the Indians raised their hands toward heaven and promised very solemnly that they would come.

With that the council was concluded, and the missionary as well as Red Cloud withdrew, with the former saying to the chiefs that if they broke their word toward him, he would never again believe an Indian.

And the Indians did not break their word. On Saturday, five chiefs from among the hostile Indians came to the agency with a guard made up of forty armed warriors and a flag of truce. General Brooke promised them as many provisions as they wanted, if they were willing to cease the hostilities and move their camp closer to the agency. The deliberation lasted three hours, whereupon the Indians, not having made any promises, returned to the camp to report back.

One must give credit to the Anglo-American press for appreciating the heroic deed of the selfless missionary. Thus the *Express*, for example, otherwise very much ill-disposed toward Catholics, honors this with the following words:[11]

> The daring mission of the worthy servant of God, who put his life at stake to calm the brave *Wilden*, deserves that everlasting fame with which history has immortalized many an eminent predecessor of his. Were all of the Indian agents so noble-minded, then the Indian question would soon be resolved, for the redskin appears to have an animal-like instinct that allows him to make a distinction between an honorable person and an intriguer, even better than attaining such [distinction] through the trained art of reasoning.

The disastrous management of affairs by the present Indian Department, on the other hand, is briefly characterized by the same paper as follows:

> The report of the Very Reverend Fr. Jutz on what the hostile Indian chiefs had to tell him is in its simplicity nonetheless wonderfully eloquent. The redskin loves the fire water as much as he despises the truth, but there is

no doubt that the Indians firmly believe that the Great Father in Washington is out to deceive them. The choice of some of the agents on the part of
this Great Father was obviously not a good one; that much is certain.

The noble mission of Fr. Jutz brings to mind another mediation of peace
in the year 1868. Back then the Sioux were still a powerful nation. Montana and the vast plains of Dakota belonged to them. They even roamed
through western Nebraska. At that time they indeed threatened the neighboring settlers with war. Our federal government wanted to avert blood-
shed by requesting that Fr. de Smet, S.J., the missionary venerated in the
entire west, go into the heart of their land and calm the agitated Indians.
On 30 March 1868, Fr. de Smet set out from St. Louis with Generals Sherman, Harney, and Terry. In Platte City negotiations took place with Chief
Spotted Tail and his braves. From there the generals went to Fort Laramie,
but Fr. de Smet [went] to Fort Rice.

Thirty-three Dakotas at Fort Rice readied themselves to ride with the
fearless priest into the lion's den.

On June 16 the small troop encamped at the source of the Beaver River.
There they were met by an advance party of the furious Dakotas, who took
them, following an exhausting ride, to the main camp of Sitting Bull on
June 19, at the place where the Powder River mixes its rushing waters with
the torrents of the Yellowstone. But the venerated missionary was not met
with a hostile reception. Instead he was assigned a spacious hut in which,
fatigued, he fell into a slumber.

When he awoke, there were four high figures sitting at his bedstead: *Sitzender Stier* (Sitting Bull), *Vierhorn* [Four Horns], *Schwarzmond* [Black Moon],
and *Halslos* [No Neck].

> "Black Robe," began Sitting Bull, "I have shed the blood of many whites,
> but it is the whites who have caused all of this. Did not Shevington have
> 600 women and children murdered? That is when I, tomahawk in hand,
> rose up, and I have done the palefaces every harm in my power. Today you
> are in our midst, and my arms are hanging down to earth like those of a
> dead man. I am prepared to hear your words of peace."

In his quiet manner, Fr. de Smet now lay before him the purpose of his
coming, and when afterward a council was convened, he spoke so plainly

and convincingly that the hatchet was buried and the life of many settlers saved. The government's peace commission, consisting of three great generals, sent a lengthy letter to the selfless missionary on 3 July 1868, containing the following passage:

> [B]ut for your long and painful journey into the heart of the hostile country, and but for the influence over even the most hostile of the tribes which your years of labor among them have given to you, the results which we have reached here could not have been accomplished. We are well aware that our thanks can be but of little worth to you, and that you will find your true reward for your labors and for the dangers and privations which you have encountered in the consciousness that you have done much to promote peace on earth and good will to men; but we should do injustice to our own feelings were we not to render to you our thanks and express our deep sense of the obligations under which you have laid us.[12]

"Would it be up to the Catholic Church to solve the Indian question," notes the *Christliche Woche* of Buffalo, "it would have been long solved—without powder and lead. The same mysterious power that centuries ago involuntarily bent the wild tribes of the south and north under the sweet yoke of the cross, still dwells in her today."

Sadly, the telegraph is reporting bloody events that have destroyed the work for peace that was undertaken by Fr. Jutz with so much courage. At the end of December, the Union troops reportedly smote more than one hundred warriors and above two hundred Indian women and children on Porcupine Creek. Following this horrible slaughter the more peaceful tribes also rose up and partially destroyed the Catholic mission on Clay Creek by setting fire to the schoolhouse of the sisters. (It is unclear from the telegraph whether the house of the sisters of Pine Ridge or of Rosebud is meant, most likely the former.) Pine Ridge was surrounded by several thousand Indians. Powerful divisions of Union troops are now to surround the Indian camp there. With a great deal of uneasiness are we awaiting more detailed news, which will probably arrive for the next issue. May it not be too sad!

Document 2.6

From: Volume 19 (1891)[13]
News from the missions. North America.

The Indian wars in South Dakota. The expected letters from the missionaries from the Pine Ridge and Rosebud Agency have not yet arrived. In the midst of the bloody events that have been taking place all around them, the missionaries, understandably, have been unable to find the time to write. Thus, for the time being, we are putting together the main developments by drawing from other letters and the American papers.

The famous Indian chief Sitting Bull (*Sitzender Stier*), the leader in the last bloody war of the Sioux against the United States, had been invited to Pine Ridge by the hostile Indians. As soon as General Ruge received word of this, he, on December 12, commanded the Indian agent Mc Laughlin by telegraph to arrest the feared chief. While this order was being carried out, Sitting Bull was shot by Indians who were in government service.

Not without interest will one hear the Right Reverend Bishop Martin Marty's assessment of the famous Indian chief. Bishop Marty (Swiss by birth) is one of the most knowledgeable authorities on the Sioux. Having spent many years among them as Indian missionary, he learned their pleasant-sounding tongue, the Dakota language, also compiling a book of its grammar and a dictionary, and thus taught this difficult language to other missionaries, as well as to mission sisters. He met Sitting Bull in person while he was still defiantly living on Canadian soil. Back then the bishop had traveled at the request of the government to the camp of Sitting Bull to move him to surrender and return home. He also had frequent contacts with him later on. And now he writes, signed by him, the following [account] about the slain Sioux leader:

> Sitting Bull was a full-blood Indian, a "*Home-Ruler*," a friend of his people, and thus an enemy of the whites. He was of the opinion that the Great Spirit had created the land on the other side of the Atlantic ocean for the white man, and the land on this side for the Indian, and he was never able to understand why God now allowed the whites to take possession of it. Thus he could very well accept that the son of God, whom the whites had crucified, had now appeared to remove the whites from the Indians'

homelands and return to the Natives of America the peaceful possession of their hunting grounds.

He had yielded to the government of the white man only to the extent that necessity demanded it, and at all times sought to remain as independent as was possible under the circumstances.

The principles of the Christian revelation as once explained to him by Fr. de Smet, and later by me, appealed to him, and the "Black Robe" was in his eyes the only friend of the Indian. As late as last summer it had been his intention to establish a settlement of his own on the reservation, for himself and his loyal followers, and during my last conversation [with him] he described the area to me and requested that I build a church and a school there. I believe that it was his intention at the time to become a Christian himself, as had been the case with Spotted Tail. A premature death prevented both from executing their plans.

How accurately Bishop Martin had assessed Sitting Bull becomes apparent from the speech that Sitting Bull made last year to the United States commissioners at the negotiations about new land cessions, and which was back then translated from the Dakota language into English by an interpreter, sentence by sentence. In German, it reads:[14]

When had the red man ever broken a treaty with the whites, and when had the white man ever abided by a treaty with the red man? Never! Back then when I was still a boy, the Sioux were the masters of the world. The sun rose in their land and set in it. They sent ten thousand horsemen into battle. Where are our warriors today? Who has slain them? Where is our land and who has got it now? Which white man can say that I ever stole even a cent from him? And yet I am called a thief. Which white woman, no matter how weak and vulnerable, was ever in captivity offended by me? And yet it is said I am a wicked Indian. Which white man has ever seen me drunk? Who has ever come to me hungry and left hungry? Who has ever seen me beat my women or mistreat my children? When am I to have ever violated a law? Is it wickedness on my part that I love my people? Am I an outlaw because my skin is red, because I am Sioux, and because I was born in the land of my fathers, and because I am prepared to die for my people and my land?

Is it not shameful that a heathenish Indian is permitted to use such language toward people who call themselves Christians, and that one has to agree with him? For it indeed becomes ever more apparent that also this desperate fight of the Indians was brought on by the most vile breaking of treaties on the part of the present administration which has no lack of individuals seeking to bring about the total annihilation of the poor redskins.

The next sad event, which the American papers report under the head-line, "*Die Indianer in die Pfanne gehauen*" [The Indians destroyed], is the blood bath on Wounded Knee Creek (*Verwundetenknie-Bach*), about 30 English miles west of Pine Ridge. On December 28, Major Whiteside had caught up with the band of Big Foot (*Großfuß*), about 150 well-armed warriors and 250 women with many children. As soon as the troops approached, the Indians, 150 strong, drew up in a battle line. Major Whiteside did like-wise with his troops, and on having advanced to within shooting range of their rifles, an Indian (it was Big Foot, as was learned later), unarmed and on foot stepped out in front of the line, indicating that he wished to speak with the major. Major Whiteside got off his horse and walked toward the chief. When they met, Big Foot extended his hand to him as a sign of peace, and said: "I am sick, and my people wish peace—," whereupon Major Whiteside interrupted him with the words: "I am not interested in further negotiations; now it is either unconditional surrender or fight. What is the answer?"—"We surrender," replied the chief. "We would have done so sooner, but we were unable to find you." Thereupon the Indians waved a white flag and were surrounded by the troops. A courier went to summon from Pine Ridge Agency the other four squadrons of the 7th regi-ment and the scouts who were to assist in the disarming of the Indians. They arrived that very Sunday. On Monday, December 29, a square was formed around the Indians. In addition, there were four Hotchkiss guns set up on a hill nearby, keeping the camp of the Indians in check. Then the Indian scouts who were in government service entered the circle at the orders of Lieutenant Taylor and started to disarm the Indians. The fact that members of their own tribe had to execute the disarmament touched a raw point with the hostile Indians, and within a few minutes the first shot was fired, which started the bloody fight. Immediately after the battle began, the scouts threw themselves on the ground, and in doing so allowed the troops a clear shot at the enemy. Then the Hotchkiss guns began to join the battle, with a horrible outcome.

The battle lasted a full hour and a half. Many Indians fled into a canyon located to the south, from which they could only be driven with difficulty. The soldiers shot them down where they found them, giving no quarter. Many women and children were also slain. The Indian losses are reported to be 300 dead. The soldiers counted 25 dead and 35 wounded. The Catholic priest Crafts [Craft], who, defying death, threw himself between those fighting, so as to possibly call a halt to the slaughter, was seriously injured by a stab into his lungs.

About the missionary who was severely wounded while heroically performing the duties of his office, *Die Illinois-Staatszeitung* of December 31 states:

> Yet more tragic [than the lot of the fallen soldiers][15] is the fate of a noble man of peace, namely that of the Catholic missionary to the Indians, Francis Crafts, who received a shot through the lungs in the course of this attack. This mortally wounded man, only thirty-three years of age, was an Anglo-American by birth. Formerly a Protestant, he converted to Catholicism in his youth, advanced to priesthood, and over many years devoted himself to the task of Indian missionary among the Sioux. He is fluent in a number of Indian languages. Only a few days before his death he passed through Chicago on his journey to Pine Ridge Agency, where Father Stephan, head of the Bureau of Catholic Indian Missions in Washington, had sent him, initially for the purpose of reporting. Apparently, Crafts had joined the troops as peacemaker, with the best intentions. Father Stephan himself has now rushed to the place of conflict.

Fortunately, the wound of Father Crafts does not appear to be fatal; as per the most recent news from Pine Ridge, he is well on the road to recovery. The priest received the stab wound in the back from an Indian, while another Indian, in mortal fear, was holding on to his robe, asking to be saved. Despite his wound, the missionary did not want to leave his place, dragging himself from one dying person to another. A young soldier called out to him: "Father, I am dying; hear my confession!" He hurried to him, heard his confession, and gave him absolution. At that moment, the head of the dying man fell against his chest, and he himself collapsed unconscious over the dead body due to the loss of blood. On January 7, he wrote to the editor of the *Freeman's Journal:*[16] "I was wounded as I attempted to put a halt to the fighting. . . . As usual, the entire calamity was caused by malicious whites, who were eagerly going about sowing the seeds of discord and distrust everywhere."

Fr. Jutz writes to the *Milw. Columbia* about the subsequent events:

> On December 28 I was fully convinced that in a few days the entire matter would be resolved peacefully. The majority of the Indians who had come over to the Badlands from the Rosebud Agency had been at the agency at Pine Ridge for some time, with the rest being on the way, only about six more (Engl.) miles from our mission, which is located four miles northwest of the agency. On December 29, when the blood bath at Wounded Knee Creek occurred, they all had arrived at the agency, and the affair surely would have come to peaceful ends. How did it still come to the battle? About 120 families had come down from the Cheyenne River Agency, most likely to join those in the Badlands in order to support them; for the men were all dressed in full war regalia, also wearing the dance shirts which they customarily wore at this new "Messiah dance," and which, according to their "medicine men," would protect them from the bullets of the whites. No longer finding the other Indians in the Badlands, and being pursued by a regiment of soldiers, they took their path to the agency along Wounded Knee Creek. On Sunday evening, December 28, they were encamped about 14 miles from the agency. That is where another regiment went early on Monday morning to take the weapons from the warriors and to then accompany them to the agency, where there were already rations ready for them.
>
> The old Indians showed themselves willing to hand over the weapons, but the young warriors did not want to agree to this. A shot was fired by an Indian (that is, without apparent reason, so that the Indians were alone responsible for the consequences) and killed a soldier. Thereupon all the Indian warriors started firing and about 20 soldiers fell. Thus the fight began, and the soldiers, of course, did what they could, shooting down every person they could hit. That women and children were killed and wounded in this murderous battle should not surprise anyone, for the soldiers had entirely surrounded the Indian "camp" and within that circle were the women and children. I do not at all believe that any soldier killed or wounded a woman or child deliberately. And I am entirely convinced that

General Forsythe does not bear any responsibility whatever for the death of the women and children, and that the same would have happened under the authority of any other commander.

As soon as the other Indians heard about this incident, they all were in an upheaval at one go. When on December 29, at 11 o'clock, an Indian came to me in a state of great excitement, telling me of the incident, I did not even want to believe it and said, I would go to the agency right after the meal to see for myself. But he said I should not go, they would kill me as well, for they were fighting at the agency; he had seen it himself. I did not let myself be deterred, however, and drove to the agency. When I came to a hill half a mile distant from it, I saw how the Indians were running about in a headlong frenzy, chasing after their ponies. In an instant, two [Indians] rode over to me, motioning me to turn back quickly, which I did, for to have resisted probably would have been dangerous at that moment. Yet I learned later on from another Indian that they did not intend to do me any harm, but wanted to keep me from greater danger. That afternoon several Indians fired shots in the direction of the agency, wounding two soldiers in their tents. They also threatened to burn down the government school, and demanded that the children leave; but there were too many soldiers around the school, thus they were unable to effect anything. All of the Indians who were around the agency, [and] also those who until then had shown themselves to be peaceful, set out right away and went to the camp about twelve miles northwest of the agency and about eight miles from our mission, where the majority still is. On December 30 those who had remained until that time followed, setting fire to a government day school close to our mission along the way. In the course of that day they burned down another day school, a Protestant Church, and a number of houses owned by men who have Indian wives. When the nearby day school burned, it was believed at the agency that our school was on fire, and there right away came soldiers on horseback, but we had remained unmolested. While the soldiers were in front of our house, several cannon shots were heard coming from Wounded Knee, where a troop of Indians had attacked some soldiers [traveling] with wagons of ammunition, killing two of them. The soldiers immediately mounted their horses to ride to that area, but came upon Indians after a half mile. Soon the shooting began on both sides, lasting until 4:30 in the afternoon. One soldier was killed and three were wounded. Reportedly, none of the Indians was either killed or wounded. At 4:30 the soldiers withdrew to the agency. No fighting has taken place since.

Document 2.7

From: *Volume* 19 (1891)[17]

The most recent Indian troubles and their causes.

(Reported by Fr. Jutz S.J., Superior of the Pine Ridge Mission, Dakota.)[18]

[1. Causes]

You desire from me a detailed account for *Die katholischen Missionen* about the most recent events that took place at close quarters, and I am responding to your request with that much more pleasure, as it gives me the opportunity to express to your readers my gratitude for the support that they have rendered our mission.

Above all, it is necessary to be clear about the causes of these troubles. It is my conviction that these causes lie first and foremost in the TREATMENT OF THE INDIANS BY THE GOVERNMENT UP UNTIL NOW, AND BY WHITES IN GENERAL. It is an indisputable fact that the rations promised to the Indians by the government as per treaty continued to decrease. The government may have had the intention to force the Indians more and more into working and farming, which I do not want to doubt, but then the Indians should have received better instructions about farming and been provided with implements. The tools, however, were by no means sufficient. Moreover, the instructions about farming were inadequate. Some of the men who were hired as *farmer* knew nothing or only a little about it themselves, and I do not believe that I am stating too much when I say that only very few cared to truly teach and offer directions to the Indians, but instead only cared about receiving a good wage and having the least amount of work possible.

Matters were no better with many another person employed at the agency. Once in my presence, and in the presence of several officers, an agent stated that he had spent 300 days out of the year with *gambeln* [gambling] before he became an agent. Another had expressed, as I know from an ear witness, that he, once having served his time, would never have to work another day in his life. He held out for nearly twice the time, and his assertion has been fully confirmed. That such men do not concern themselves very much with the welfare of the Indians is clearly understood by every thinking person.

Under these circumstances the Indians, instead of advancing to some degree, grew poorer and more helpless from one year to the next, at least the vast majority. Added to this were unfortunately several very dry years, so that the poor Indians got almost nothing at all out of their already negligible agriculture.

A LARGE NUMBER WERE NOT IN AGREEMENT with the most recent sale of their land. And given that afterward, and until this very day, they have not seen any profit or compensation whatever for the land they sold, even those who were still favorably disposed became embittered as a result, losing their last bit of faith in the promises made by the government. Indeed not only do they not see any profit, but here at Pine Ridge Agency the meat rations were decreased by 1,000,000 pounds, despite all the remonstrances on the part of the agent, Col. Gallagher, and other law-abiding men.

The vast majority of whites who came into contact with the Indians, on and off the reservation, only sought to make money and become rich quick, cheating them in every possible way. It is for this reason that the Indians wished to be freed from all whites, and the dislike that they harbor even for those [whites] who are married to Indian women, must indeed derive from this. However, so far they have seen a good example set by only very few whites. That the Indians are not hostile toward those who truly mean well, cannot be entirely denied, I think. As evidence thereof I only want to pose this question: Why, then, have the Indians throughout these troubles, even when in a state of greatest upheaval, made no attempt whatever to do us harm; indeed, [they] have even given us to understand that they would not harm us in any way, although they burned down more than 20 buildings all around us and even houses of Indians?!

A further cause, especially at Pine Ridge, may perhaps also be this: In the most recent landbill, Chief Red Cloud finally received a legal promise for money in exchange for the horses that were taken from him and his people by federal troops 12 or 13 years ago. However, it has surely been more than one year since this legal promise was made, and yet not one cent of it has been paid! How, then, can the Indians any longer have faith in government treaties? What, I wonder, would whites do, or would have done, already a long time ago under such circumstances?

[2. Ghost Dance]

In addition to this overall dissatisfaction and not baseless aversion toward the government and all whites in general, there came as the next cause the so-called GHOST or MESSIAH DANCE. As far as I was able to learn, this dance originated near the Mormons. No sooner had I heard more about this dance and its associated ideas than I thought that this business about the "New Jerusalem," about which the Mormons or the so called "Latter-day Saints" dream, must be related, and the more I heard about it, the more I was supported in my belief. That the Indians listen to such fanatics with the greatest eagerness, and believe them, should not be surprising considering their miserable situation. What could be more desirable to them than the prophesy of a new order of things [and] the complete overthrow of this oppression as well as the destruction of all whites? What could be more desirable to them than a doctrine that would restore their former times, when they had buffalo and other game in abundance, and when they did not have to suffer cold and hunger and were able to live entirely in accordance with their own ideas? This can also explain how this dance, which after all was supposed to be a preparation for the coming Messiah or Redeemer, was met with such rapid and also such general acceptance and enthusiasm. This dance, then, was used by the medicine men, who in the course of it were always the leaders and persons in charge, to increase and consolidate their status and their influence even more, and to push the hatred of whites to the extreme. This dance defies any description; one must have seen it with his own eyes to be able to get an idea of it. For days and weeks it was performed about 10 (English) miles from our mission, at White Clay Creek, along which our school is built. Having heard so much about it, I also wanted to have seen it with my own eyes. On a beautiful morning in about the middle of October, I left the mission with an Indian policeman and drove to the dance grounds. We arrived there at about 10 o'clock, a good while before the dance started; thus I was able to observe everything closely.

First, you must imagine a level plain, about a half mile in each direction, all around surrounded by low hills. In the middle of the plain a "holy tree" is erected, which might have been 5 m high. Tied to and hung on this tree are all sorts of objects: pipes, bows, pieces of antelope hides, pieces of buffalo skin, buffalo horns, medicinal herbs, pieces of cloth of all kinds and colors, turtle shells, and a number of other objects which are either important or of use to the Indians. In a circle at the foot of the hills, the tents of the Indians are arranged in groups together with the different chiefs or medicine men, leaving a large, expansive area open in the middle, surrounding the holy tree. With the time for the dance approaching, the Indian dancers moved onto the dance grounds in diverse groups, young and old, men and women, about one hundred each, in rank and file, with flying colors in front, singing, everyone adorned for the dance, their faces completely painted with all sorts of different figures. There, they formed a circle around the holy tree. This time there were probably six to seven hundred dancers.

When I arrived at the dance grounds there were only three men near the holy tree, fully clad in war or dancing regalia. They were standing motionless before their sacred monument, their eyes cast to the ground. A fourth was dancing about 100 paces away, and was coming closer and closer. Having joined the others, he bent over toward the holy tree, with his hands resting on his knees, then lower and lower until his face touched the ground. He remained like this for a while, then raised himself up slowly, and remained standing with the others without moving until the ceremony of the ghost watching began, which was the introduction to the actual dance. When I asked about the leader of the dance, an Indian pointed out three men to me, who were huddled on the ground about 200 paces from the holy tree. I right away steered the horses toward these men, but as soon as we were coming a little closer, one got up and walked away with his blanket over his head. The policeman who was with me repeatedly called out to him to please wait, yet he paid no attention, instead fleeing into his tent upon reaching it. I stopped at his tent, dismounted, and walked in as well. I found the entire tent full of old Indians, some of whom I knew well. I asked where the dance chief was and they pointed him out to me right away. Yet he did not look at me, but instead continued smoking his pipe in silence.

I then tried to explain to these men that this dance was not good, that the dear God did not want this dance, and that I wanted to teach them how they had to pray to the Father in Heaven, or to the Great Spirit, if they wanted to please Him and go to Him some day; this dance was coming from the evil spirit and for that reason they should give it up and go home. They listened to me in silence, but showed no desire to accept my advice. While I was still speaking with the old Indians, immediate preparations for the dance were being made, and so I left the tent to see what was to follow. Preceding the actual dance was the ghost or death watching. This happened in the following manner: The three or four men of whom I had spoken above were still standing in front of the holy tree, completely motionless, with their eyes closed or fixed on the ground, letting their hair hang partially down over their faces and looking like the dead, which they are indeed supposed to represent or whose place they are to take. Now men and women came to join them, stroking the ghost men with both of their hands from the top of their heads down over their cheeks, shoulders, and hands; then [they] began to weep loudly and then walked away again. This they call the seeing of the dead or ghosts. Once this ceremony was over, the actual Messiah dance began.

The leader of the dance, an old medicine man, was in the center, near the holy tree, and with him were three young Indian women or girls, one of whom was holding in her hands the famous pipe (tobacco pipe), and the others [were holding] other objects that are especially precious to the Indians.

Now the dance was opened. The medicine man loudly spoke several words that were repeated by everyone. Thereupon all of the dancers turned their faces southward, raised both of their hands, probably toward the Great Spirit, and sang at the top of their voices: *Até eheyelo*, that means in German: *So hast du es, Vater, gesagt* [You have said thus, Father]. This singing lasted for about 2 or 3 minutes; then they all turned to face the holy tree and firmly interlocked their hands. They all stood shoulder to shoulder, so that no one could have passed through them. Now everyone was calm. Then several dancers began to push with their shoulders and to move in that way. Soon this movement was passed along the entire circle. Next the movement with their feet began, so that soon the entire circle moved around the holy tree. Now all of them had their eyes closed or fixed on the ground. As soon as the circle was set in motion, the singing resumed as well, and every one of the dancers, be he young or old, sang until he could no longer do so, then stopped for a while and started again.

Boys' School of Rosebud Agency. [. . .] Our 5 little ones are sitting on the small benches[d], the second, [one] such black one with the ball, will become a Leopold on Holy Saturday; he is the first I have taken in and cleansed; he is a dear little fellow, 6 years old. (Photograph by Fred O. Bloom, Fort Niobrara, Nebraska. Reproduced with the article by Fr. Jutz: "The most recent Indian troubles and their causes," *Die katholischen Missionen* 19 [1891], p. 188.)

Illustration note: Illustrations are from the Provincial Archives of the Franciscan Sisters of Penance and Christian Charity, Nonnenwerth/Rhine (Germany). The captions are the inscriptions used by the sisters in the St. Francis and Holy Rosary Missions and archivists at Nonnenwerth or by the photographers. German captions have been translated into English. Photographers' names are indicated where available.

No 8 FATHERS AND BROTHERS OF ST FRANCIS MISSION.
ROSEBUD AGENCY, S.D.

(*Opposite top*) Girls' School of Rosebud Agency. (Photograph by Fred O. Bloom, Fort Niobrara, Nebraska. Reproduced with the article by Fr. Jutz: "The most recent Indian troubles and their causes," *Die katholischen Missionen* 19 [1891], p. 189.)

(*Opposite bottom*) Fathers and Brothers of St. Francis Mission, Rosebud Agency, South Dakota. (Photograph by J. A. Anderson, Rosebud Agency, South Dakota.)

(*Above*) Sisters of St. Francis Mission, Rosebud Agency, South Dakota, 1896. (Photograph by J. A. Anderson, Rosebud Agency, South Dakota.)

(*Above*) St. Francis Mission, Rosebud Agency, South Dakota, West Side. (Photograph by J. A. Anderson, Rosebud Agency, South Dakota.)

(*Opposite top*) Holy Rosary Mission, Pine Ridge Agency, South Dakota.

(*Opposite bottom*) Temporary Prairie Church during Catholic India[n] Congress. 1896. Holy Rosary Mission.

(*Above*) Indians leaving the Mission after the Congress. [1896.]

(*Opposite top*) Needle-work Class. 1896.

(*Opposite bottom*) Indian Mission, South Dakota. Children's Dormitory.

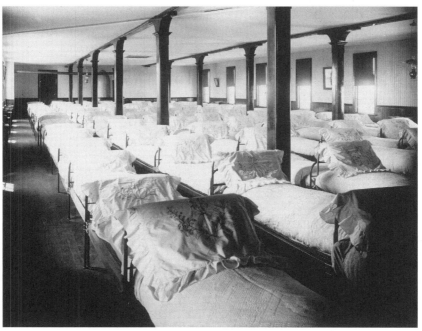

(*Above*) Indian Chiefs.

(*Left*) The old Roast (Joachim) together with wife Anna and daughter. Joachim and Anna were the first Indians baptized by Father Digmann. Both visit our chapel faithfully, but come even more faithfully for their bodily refreshment. Old fat Anna embraced me joyfully on learning that I intended to send this picture to you. (Photograph by Fred O. Bloom, Fort Niobrara, Nebraska.)

Kokipapi, Stampede and Family, *Alles fürchtet* ihn [Everyone fears him]. Still rather naturally wild. Recently, after having tried to kill a half-Indian, he had to be caught by means of a long rope, like the Indians catch horses on the prairie. He is the stepfather of our former pupil Charles Spotted Tail (*Gefleckter Schwanz*) and nephew of the old war chief and principal chief Two Strike (*Zweischlag*). St. Francis Mission, Rosebud. (Photograph by J. A. Anderson, 1900.)

Tasunka Waste, Good Horse, *Gutes Pferd*. A pleasant Indian woman; will hopefully become Catholic soon. Her sister is the wife of a wealthy white merchant at the agency. St. Francis Mission, Rosebud. (Photograph by J. A. Anderson, 1900.)

Hesapa, Black Horn, *Schwarzes Horn*. An able warrior, but still a staunch heathen. St. Francis Mission, Rosebud. (Photograph by J. A. Anderson, 1900.)

Cetan Wankantuya, High Hawk, *Hoher Habicht*. He is a chief; still a heathen. His daughter, 18 years of age, is at the new *boarding school* (the Indians' boarding school). She was forced to let herself be baptized by the Protestant preacher. Recently, she had the Very Reverend Father Digmann informed [that] she wanted to be baptized to pass into [Catholicism], and live and die a Catholic. St. Francis Mission, Rosebud. (Photograph by J. A. Anderson, 1900.)

Maza pankeska, Iron Shell, *Eiserne Muschel*. Our closest neighbor, only recently baptized along with his wife and afterward married in a Christian way, has already been to Europe. He is a brother of Hollow Horn Bear; his father was a chief. His children and grandchildren are here at the mission to be educated. St. Francis Mission, Rosebud. (Photograph by J. A. Anderson, 1900.)

Mato he hlogeca, Hollow Horn Bear, *Hohlhorn Bär*. A strong, proud Indian; still a heathen. He is an excellent orator. Two months ago [he] was still in Washington as delegate for the Indians to defend their rights—spoke with the Great Father (the president); was given many promises, but nothing has been received yet. He had the courage to tell the president right to his face: If you do not help us, we will start waging war. St. Francis Mission, Rosebud. (Photograph by J. A. Anderson, 1900.)

Wambli wicasa, Eagleman, *Adlermann*. This is, says the Very Reverend Father Digmann, a good and faithful soul. He is sincere in his intentions toward the dear God. He was baptized only recently. St. Francis Mission, Rosebud. (Photograph by J. A. Anderson, 1900.)

Mato kawinge, Turning Bear, which means, *sich drehender Bär.* He lives here in the village, is still a heathen, one of the best warriors, a famous orator, has killed 3–4 whites in former times. His children are here, also baptized. St. Francis Mission, Rosebud. (Photograph by J. A. Anderson, 1900.)

One of our Indian Families. (Photograph by Fred O. Bloom, Fort Niobrara, Nebraska.)

An Indian Family. (Photograph by Fred O. Bloom, Fort Niobrara, Nebraska.)

Nearest neighborhood of our Sisters on Pine Ridge. White Bird's Camp.

Sioux Indian Dance. (Photograph by Cross, Fort Niobrara, Nebraska.)

The movement became faster and wilder, not only with their feet, but also with their hands, as much as was somehow possible. After a quarter-of-an-hour or 20 minutes one could already see how several were beginning to stagger like complete drunks, but they were still held by their neighbors. Then they started to moan and groan loudly, rolling their eyes like crazy people, and finally could no longer be held. Let go by their fellow dancers, they staggered either into the circle or outside of the circle, flailing their arms around, falling to the ground, rolling in the dust, scraping the ground, raising themselves again, falling back down, now on their backs, then on their faces, until they remained lying down dead tired and completely exhausted.

I went near several of them, for during the entire time I had been inside the circle observing everything very closely. These poor creatures, men, women, and girls, were absolutely unconscious, covered with dust and sweat, and hardly able to breathe. After about half an hour most had recovered. There were probably more than 20 lying on the ground in this state.

The sight of these pitiful victims of superstition affected me so deeply that I would have been prepared to sacrifice my life right then and there had the dear God been willing to accept it and in exchange grant these poor people, still immersed so very greatly in the darkness of heathenism, the light of true faith. The dance had lasted for approximately one hour and a half, when they needed to sit down to rest in order to restart the same dance in about another two hours. They call this state dying, and the medicine men told them that in this state they would see the Messiah and their deceased parents and friends, and that those who died in this way would be especially sanctified.

And what these medicine men say is being believed, even when it is very clear to them [the Indians] that it is not true. Now to make it most evident to them that all of this was nothing but deceit, I said to a number of men standing by, of whom I knew many and who had only been observers at the dance, that they shall call over any one of those who had died in the course of the dance, and if that same person could tell me what he saw, I would give him one dollar. Since no one came forward, I offered 2, and finally, 5 dollars. Several of those present began to smile, but not one came to me to tell me anything. Thereupon I said to them how foolish they were to believe such things, when they themselves indeed knew and realized that everything they were told was only a lie. But this makes no difference to an Indian; once he has got something in his head, even the best reasoning will have no effect on it.

These confused people were so infatuated with this dance that they did not want to listen to any remonstrance or to anyone instructing them, as I experienced myself. Moreover, there is no doubt that this dance was a war dance, given that everyone was dressed in war regalia, and that the dance shirts, which had been made especially for this dance, were afterward to have the characteristic of providing protection against the soldiers' bullets. That this belief was wrong they will now surely understand, after so many of their warriors lost their lives at Wounded Knee, in spite of the dance shirt.

[3. Mediation Attempt]

This dance was in full bloom here as well as at Rosebud Agency, when on November 18 of the previous year the troops simultaneously moved into Pine Ridge and Rosebud. Here at Pine Ridge the Indians were perhaps somewhat surprised at the advance of the soldiers, but they did not appear to concern themselves with it to any great degree, and continued with their dance as before. The Indians at Rosebud, however, immediately set out with all of their belongings, came over to Pine Ridge Agency, and then withdrew to the Badlands, probably about 500 households or families. Along the way they of course took with them everything they found: cows and horses and anything else they came upon in the abandoned dwellings. They were naturally forced to do so once they had embarked on this wrong path, otherwise they would have had to starve. General Brooke now sent messengers to these hostile Indians, inviting them to come to the agency so that he could speak with them and hear what they desired, but they showed little inclination to comply with his wish.

When these unrests began, I had decided for myself to quietly observe the affair and not to get involved in any way, so as not to perhaps get caught up in difficulties and not give anyone reason for any kind of talk or suspicion, given that there are always people who see the evil in everything, especially concerning the Jesuits. Indeed, even here at the agency there are those who would very much like to have us be as far away as possible, and who are working against us, as I know only too well. However, I also know that we have many good and honest friends here, not just Catholics, but also those of different faiths, and especially these, our friends, do not belong to those who have no sense.

Now, on the 2nd of December, early in the morning, the thought instinctively occurred to me, and continued to prey on my mind, why I was so idle, when I too could do something to bring these Indian troubles to an end faster and more easily. I put these thoughts before Fr. Perrig, who is my loyal assistant, and when he agreed, I right away set out for the agency to introduce to General Brooke my plan to go to the camp of the hostiles in order to get the chiefs, or if possible everyone, to come to the agency, in accordance with his wish, so that they could settle their matters with him. The general was very kind, as he seems to be by nature, and gave his consent. Then he told me that he had just spoken with one chief, High Hawk, who along with two others had arrived from the camp of the hostiles yesterday, then pointing him out to me with the remark that I should please go to him myself and see what I could learn from him, and then advise him accordingly.

I went to the chief, greeted him, and then asked him first whether he had eaten anything—it was about 10 o'clock in the forenoon. He said: "No." Thus I led him to the *store* (*Laden*), bought him and his companions something to eat, and also coffee and sugar to take with them, and invited him to visit me at the mission on his way back. I was not able to learn much from him as he was very reserved in his remarks. Even before going to the general, I had gone to Chief Red Cloud and asked him if he would accompany me if I decided to go to the Indians in the Badlands. After giving it some thought, he said he would go with me if I so desired. Having reported everything to the general that I had been able to learn, I returned to the mission. At about 3 o'clock in the afternoon Chief High Hawk came to the mission, where we entertained him cordially and furnished him with plenty of provisions for the journey, and a little more. I told him that I would come down to them the next day along with Chief Red Cloud. He was very satisfied with that and departed from us in good spirits.

I right away sent a messenger to Chief Red Cloud to tell him to please come to the mission this very evening or tomorrow morning, so that we could set out early, for we had to cover at least 40 miles. The next morning, on [3 December,] the feast of holy Franz Xaver [St. Francis Xavier], I prepared everything for departure, but Chief Red Cloud was long in coming. Finally, at 11 o'clock, he arrived with his son Jack. Red Cloud apologized that he was unable to go with me; he had sore eyes and was already so old, and the way was so long and cold. His son would go with me in his stead; that would be just as well. I settled for that, and also took one of our farm hands along, who knew the area well having been a *cowboy* with the government herds for a number of years.

At about 4 o'clock we arrived at the *Hürd-Camp*[19] on White River, where we were served a cup of warm coffee which warmed us up a bit, for it was very cold out. Now we had another 16 miles to go. Because I wanted to return the next day, I had the horses hitched up again in order to continue the journey. Along the way, two more well-armed Indians had joined us, wanting to accompany the son of Red Cloud and surely me as well. Soon darkness set in and night began to fall so that I was no longer able to see the trail. I handed the reins to my farm hand who could still see better than I, and told our two escorts to ride ahead of us so that we could follow them more safely. We proceeded for a good distance in this manner. Suddenly the word was: "We have lost our way." We came to a halt. The two escorts rode to the one side, young Red Cloud and my farm hand went on foot to the other side, and I stayed with the conveyance. After a while those on foot returned, though without having found a trail; yet nothing more was seen of the riders. We tried very cautiously to continue on for a bit, but soon saw the impossibility of going any farther, and were thus forced to stop and patiently await the next morning. Given that there was not a tree or bush and therefore no wood anywhere close by, we also could not make a fire. Jack Red Cloud wrapped himself up in a blanket as best he could and laid down on the ground, where he was soon covered with a second blanket of snow. I laid down in the wagon box, as best I could, and my farm hand had to watch the horses, which were very restless in this large, cold "barn." Getting any sleep was out of the question, and it was a rather long night, but the morning came nonetheless and we were still alive. We set out a good while before daybreak to again look for the trail, leaving the horses tied to the wagon and Jack Cloud still resting under his white blanket. After little more than an hour the trail was found given that the moonlight had furnished us with some light. We returned to the horses, hitched up, and continued our march.

On approaching the Indian camp, we saw the guards that had been posted at the highest points, [at least] that is what we took these men for who were wrapped up in their blankets. I drove straight toward their camp, which was situated on an elevation between two hills, from where they could spy for probably a distance of 10 miles who was approaching them. Moreover, the people from Rosebud had encamped in a location whence they could within 2 hours withdraw into a natural fortress where, with little effort, they would have fought back troops that far outnumbered them. Anyone who has seen the area will agree with me. At this camp, then, I arrived on December 3 [December 4], at half-past eight in the morning. I right away inquired about the tent of Chief Two Strike, which was pointed out to me, and so we stopped there.

I found the chief inside the tent and a couple more Indians with him. I had brought with me a substantial quantity of smoking tobacco, which I gave to the chief as a present and of which he right away distributed some to the warriors who were seated around. I also had them share in the bread and meat—as long as it lasted—which we had with us in order to satisfy our own needs, [and] which they at once enjoyed with good appetite. Next, the old chief asked me why I had come to them. I replied, he knew very well that I and all Black Robes were his friends. He had, of course, already known me at Rosebud, and so had several others of his people here, who all knew that I have always been good toward them. He also knew that the Black Robes did not tell any lies and that we always had their best interests at heart. Because I also knew that they were my friends, I have come to them to help them, if they wanted to take my advice.

In the meantime the tent had filled up; as many as could find room sat inside, and a large number were outside. Now I asked them why they had come here to this rugged area, where it was so terribly cold, where soon they would have nothing more to eat, and where they in fact could not stay.

At this, they brought forth the following reasons:

1. "We were afraid of the soldiers."

2. "We were dissatisfied that the white men came to count us."

3. "We want to stay here at Pine Ridge Agency as we had been promised."

4. "We are afraid because we have killed cattle, but we are sorry that we
   did it."

Thereupon I answered them:

1. "You do not have to be afraid of the soldiers at all: they will not do you
   any harm if you want to be good. Just come with me to the agency,
   and you will see how friendly they all are. And the general is a very
   good and dear man, he will help you and do everything so that you
   will get more food; he already has got everything ready for you."

2. In response to my question of whether they were dissatisfied that the
   white men had counted them because they afterward received fewer
   rations, they said, yes, that was the reason. I comforted them by telling them that this would surely be put right again if only they wanted
   to go to the general and tell him this.

3. Whether or not they could stay here at Pine Ridge is something that
   the general first had to tell the "Great Father" (the president of the
   United States) and ask him about it, and whatever he would say, that
   is what they would have to do.

4. As far as the killing of the cattle was concerned, I told them it was
   very good of them that they regretted this now. "However," I continued, "do you not see that you will have to do again the very thing that
   you are regretting now if you do not abide by what I am telling you,
   for in a couple of days you will no doubt have nothing more to eat?
   So if you do not want to die, you will have to kill more cattle, and that
   is bad. You will not be punished for what you have done up to this
   point, if you now show good will and discuss your affairs with the
   general, and do as he tells you. The general is a good man, he will
   help you as much as he can, and speak with you kindly if you want
   to go to him."

Thereupon the old Chief Two Strike said: "Now as proof that everything that you have told us is true, raise both of your hands."

I did so at once, and along with me all the chiefs and warriors who were
present, three times.

At this point one of those present arose, thanked me and said: "Now our hearts are well again, after you have spoken such kind and such weighty words to us."

I thus replied that it pleased me greatly that they all had listened to my advice, but now I was asking them what they intended to do at this time: Did they all want to come with me right away, or did the chiefs want to come with me, or did they not want to come at all, for I needed to tell the general what they had told me because I had promised him that I would do so. To this Chief Turning Bear replied: "We cannot all come now; we have many old people here and many children, and it is presently too cold. But we chiefs want to come to you tomorrow, and then you can go with us to the general."

I agreed to this. I arose, [and] all of them shook hands with me and were very satisfied. Meanwhile it was almost 12 o'clock and with that high time to set out on our journey home. On our way home we once more stopped at the *Gouvernements-Hürd-Camp*[20] on White River, where we again warmed ourselves with a cup of coffee and then continued on our journey. We reached the mission at about 10 o'clock, chilled to the marrow, but recovered soon.

The following morning I went to General Brooke and reported to him on my success. He was very satisfied and invited me to come to him together with the chiefs, which I promised him. Then toward evening the chiefs and their escorts arrived at the mission, probably 40 in number. We received them in the kindest manner, fed all of them, including their horses, and kept them overnight. At first the warriors did not feel quite safe and right away set up guards. Then they had me summoned and asked me whether what they had heard was true: a white man along the way had told them they would all be taken prisoner as soon as they arrived at the agency. I told them this was a big lie; they should not trouble themselves about that; after all, I would be going with them, and if one of them were to be harmed, the next man could shoot me dead. That was enough for them and they were satisfied.

The following morning, after everyone had a good breakfast, we set out for the agency to [see] the general. This was an interesting procession, and a large number of curious people were expecting us at the agency. On approaching it, the warriors asked me where they could leave their weapons, as they feared that they would be taken from them. But I told them to just bring their weapons with them; I would make sure to tell them where they could leave them. On arriving at the general's quarters, I told them: "Now stand up your guns right here in front of the house, and when you come back out, you pick them up again." And so they did. General Brooke received the delegation with solemnity and dignity, yet with much kindness. After the chiefs had stated their concerns, the general told them they should now return and bring all of their people with them; he had everything here for them that they needed, [and] he would care for them for as long as they would have to stay at the agency and until they had all of their affairs put in order. The chiefs promised to do everything the general had told them, and left the room visibly satisfied.

With most of the present company having withdrawn, the general approached me, shook my hand with a smile on his face and with obvious satisfaction, and said: "Father, should I ever have any dealings with the Indians again, I will call on you first."

The Indians now went to Chief Red Cloud to also confer with him, but in the evening they returned to us, where they were treated the same way as the evening before. The next morning they went back to the camp in good spirits. That was on Sunday, the 7th of December.

[4. Before and After the Wounded Knee Massacre]

After the Indian chiefs along with their escorts had returned to their camp with honest intentions to right away come to the agency with all of their people, there were several among them who resisted. Heading these fanatical hostiles were Short Bull and Kicking Bear, two medicine men and leaders at the Ghost Dance described above. That is when the Indians separated into two parties. Those chiefs who had come to the agency indeed came with their people, as they had promised, and made camp close to the agency, as requested by General Brooke; the other group stayed behind.

Now there were new embassies, so-called *scouts* (*Kundschafter*) and other favorably disposed Indians, sent to the ones who had stayed behind, but for a long time without success. I, in turn, went to the general on a number of occasions, offering him my services, yet he declined them kindly, remarking that it would be of no use anyhow. I replied to him, in all modesty, that I did not believe so, given that my first visit certainly had not been fruitless.

However, at this point I must note that I do not believe that the general thought deep down inside that I would not have any success with a second attempt. Rather, I have every reason to believe that he was receiving his instructions from above. After all, it would have been a disgrace for the United States to call on the help of a Catholic priest, let alone a Jesuit, to bring these difficulties to an end more easily and rapidly! "*Uncle Sam*" has enough money, and what do a few human lives matter!—But until the last day of his presence here, General Brooke remained my truest friend, showing me the greatest trust and inviting me frequently to visit him, whenever I would have the time. He even honored us with a brief visit, but happened to come when I was not at home, which I regretted very much.

Finally, an embassy of 500–600 Indians was to be sent to the hostiles; yet all endeavors and attempts notwithstanding, no more than about 150 could be gathered. Hence, the affair continued to drag on. However, in the end the warriors could be successfully persuaded to be peacefully minded, and they set out for the agency. They already were near our mission and were supposed to arrive at the agency on December 29. Everyone had good reason to be hopeful that in a couple of days everything would be all right again and the peace secured. Yet it was precisely on the 29th of December when the unfortunate incident at Wounded Knee Creek occurred, which with one blow thwarted everything that had come to pass up to that point, putting all of the Indians, without exception, into a state of utmost agitation and anger, and with that made the situation more dangerous than at any time before.

The sad massacre at Wounded Knee Creek is well known to our readers. Fr. Jutz describes the fight that ensued in the immediate vicinity of the mission on the next day as follows:

We not only heard the thundering of the cannons and the crackling of the rifles, but we even saw the flashing of the guns. The Indians fought the soldiers hard and were on the verge of surrounding them. The soldiers retreated, coming ever closer to our house. That we no longer felt entirely comfortable in this situation can be easily imagined. "What shall we do? Where shall we go?" I was asked repeatedly; "When the Indians come, they will kill us all." I tried as much as I could to calm the fearful and to comfort them with the hope that they would not in fact come as far as the house. At about 1 o'clock I sent an express courier to General Brooke asking him to send more soldiers, if possible, because the fighting was very intense. Right away another black cavalry regiment came charging in support, and the Indians had to give way. At half past four the soldiers, for their part, retreated to the agency, each and every one of them, not leaving as much as one man behind for our protection. Thus we were completely defenseless against the wild warriors, without any human assistance. Had they wanted to destroy us, they could have done so without much difficulty. It was indeed a distressing situation! But he who dwells in the protection of the Highest is secure even in the greatest of dangers. All of us were convinced, and remain so until this day, that the Queen of the Holy Rosary, to whom our mission is after all dedicated, had spread her powerful mantle of protection over us. With the soldiers having retreated, a deadly silence settled over the entire valley, which, due to the smoke from the powder, appeared as if covered by a light cloud. The night passed quietly. We, of course, were on guard, for we certainly did not know what more there was in store. But not one Indian was to be seen. This is also the way it was for the next few days. From this day onward, from the 30th of December to the 12th of January, we were in the middle, between the camp of the Indians on the one side and the camp of the soldiers on the other. Some people, even soldiers, expressed their bewilderment at how we could be so calm and confident in this position, while most of the people at the agency, where there were after all 6,000–7,000 soldiers, were in a state of great fear.

One evening, two newspaper reporters came and asked for a night's lodging, which was granted them. The next morning they told me that the previous evening rather extraordinary feelings had overcome their souls when, sitting at the desk in their room, the sweet singing from the chapel along with the sounds of the organ had reached their ears, while on the one side of this heavenly peaceful house thousands of wild Indians were making their camp, and on the other, an army of soldiers.

Before long the one redskin or other could be again seen in our house, not to kill us, however, but instead to receive something to eat. These visits increased daily. Repeatedly, we had Indians here through the night, who were coming from the camp and were on their way to return to the agency, once probably 20 women and children. Of course, all came to the house hungry. It continued this way until the 12th of January. On that day, all of the Indians, probably 6,000 persons, went back to the agency. It was an enormous train [of people], on foot, by wagon, and on horseback, lasting more than three hours. From our windows we were able to observe them closely, for the road led past our mission at a distance of hardly 500 paces. That day we had so many visitors that the bread basket and the coffee kettle grew much too small.

On reaching the agency, negotiations with Commander in Chief Miles were held right away. Everything proceeded calmly. The majority of the Indians perhaps realized that they could not prevail against that many soldiers, and the few who probably would have liked to have struck once more, had to yield to the majority.

On the 24th of January, General Miles conducted a grand review of his troops, praising their courage and sacrifice for the sake of the fatherland, and on the following day the first soldiers withdrew. General Brooke left the agency on the 26th of January, and General Miles on the 27th. Presently, there is only one cavalry regiment at this place which is to stay here through the winter.

The Indians for the most part have moved back to their respective homes. Thus these troubles hopefully have come to an end. Once again everything is quiet, and I am convinced that if the Indians are treated in a decent and just manner, uprisings of this sort will never happen again, and that we are able to continue our work in the schools undisturbed, here as well as at the Rosebud Agency.

[5. Letter from a Franciscan Nun]

In closing, we add the letter from a German Franciscan nun, who also lived through these eventful days and hours at Pine Ridge, describing them quite vividly:

With a thousand thanks to God and His most holy mother, our protectress, we have remained mercifully spared thus far, and no one has attempted to do even the least amount of harm either to the mission or to its residents, though we have lived through horrible weeks.

On the day following the battle it was downright dreadful; in every direction there were bright flames touching the sky. Everything had been set on fire by the *Wilden*; around 10 o'clock the day school five minutes distant from us was ablaze. Oh, it was horrible, all of that and everything that followed! Thinking that the mission was burning, a short while later more than 1,000 soldiers practically came flying forth from the agency. One could not tell rider from horse, it was all one figure, that is how much they hurried, and [they] were already calling out from afar: "*All alive yet?*" (*Noch Alles am Leben?*). They pursued the arsonists who, however, along with the other Indians, were well defended in a thicket very close to the mission.—Then a fight ensued before our door, with bullets flying past the windows, but through which the Indians remained the victors. You should have heard the wild mocking cries of the Indians each time a soldier fell. Two wounded soldiers were brought to the mission. Around 4 o'clock the military moved back to the agency.

In the course of the following three to four days there was a deadly silence all around, not a soul to be seen, only the skies were clouded nearly every day with smoke from the fires that had been set. We retired only fully clothed, the brothers stood guard outside at night, the hoses were screwed to the faucets to extinguish fires, and each one of us knew what to rescue first; we did not know how the Indians were disposed toward us.—When one day the Reverend Fr. Superior (Jutz) wanted to drive to the agency, he was forced to turn back by two Indians carrying a loaded gun. As he was still deliberating the matter, they grabbed the wheels and rode alongside the wagon almost as far as the mission. As it turned out later, the two *Wilden* meant well by the "Black Robe," for just at that moment there was fighting going on at the agency and the Reverend Fr. Superior saw from a distance how fierce it was; he was unable to recognize the *Wilden*—they were painted horribly.

Throughout all of New Year's Day we exposed [the Eucharist] and worshiped the Holy of Holies for peace; meanwhile, prompted by the terrible news he had read, the Very Reverend Father Stephan came from Washington to fetch the sisters. In the morning, following Holy Communion, we all, in a body, had sacrificed our lives to God and entreated Him to accept this as proof of our undivided love. In the evening, during recreation, I said to the sisters, we will probably have to separate tomorrow, for the Very Reverend Father Stephan had come for us, yet my humble self intended to stay here along with one sister given that the superior did not want everyone to leave. This, however, was not met with agreement, and all resisted a separation so earnestly and fervently that I had to force myself to hold back the tears of emotion, and so it was agreed, unanimously and with ten voices, to stay together, provided the obedience would not decide differently.

When I informed the Very Reverend Father Stephan of this the following morning, he agreed to it, but because of his great worry, contacted our Right Reverend Bishop Marty by telegraph after his departure, who right away sent a dispatch here: in case of impending danger, to flee in obedience. A similar dispatch came the next day from Mother Cäcilia from Buffalo at the request of the good sister Katharina (M. Drexel). (The sisters stayed, however.)

We still heard the thundering of the cannons. Each morning we were face to face with death, and each evening it was reasonable to think: perhaps our mission will fall victim to the flames tonight. All of this is easily written and easily read, but one can have a sense of reality only by living through it.

About 700 *Wilde*, who had banded together from everywhere, were encamped in the thicket only a short hour from the mission. They were dreadful to behold, painted yellow with thick dots looking like drops of blood.

One day one of the young warriors came to us from the enemy camp, stating with a great deal of triumph and excitement: "*Me kill two Soldiers, me take guns, me take horses, fight is nice.*" (*Ich zwei Krieger töten, ich Flinten, ich Rosse erbeuten! Fechten ist schön!*) He then displayed the bullet-filled belt that he had taken from a dead soldier.

On the following Sunday there suddenly came a good number of *Wilden* on horseback galloping to the mission; they were armed to the teeth. Some had rifles, Winchesters, others axes, arrows, bows, and knives; they went to the superior and asked him what they should do to make peace. He advised them about what he saw was best, and then asked them why they were now so cruelly wild, frightening all the world, to which they replied, because the soldiers had shot women and children.

We then gave them something to eat, and although they looked dreadfully wild, we were not at all afraid. They shook hands with us and said they would be very glad if there were to be peace now, and they would send us many children for the school. They had already half washed off the war paint. The Very Reverend Fr. Superior right away informed General Miles, who replied that the chiefs should please come to the agency.

On the following day all 7,000 set out with hearth and home, wagons and horses, dogs and oxen. The whole train passed by the mission; it lasted from 9 o'clock in the morning until after 12 o'clock without interruption, and they marched not in single file but always took up the entire road. Many came to the mission, yet no one without weapons. They are now encamped at the agency and are completely surrounded by soldiers so that they will probably have to surrender.

Document 2.8

From: Volume 20 (1892)[21]
News from the missions. North America.

The first Congress of Catholic Sioux Indians. It is known that the great impulse that sprang from the German Catholic gatherings has also led to similar demonstrations in other countries, and to a stronger union of Catholics among themselves. It is probably less known that this powerful wave carried even to the Indian reservations of the far west, producing an emulation on a smaller scale.

On this year's Fourth of July, the first general congress of Catholic Indians of the Sioux Nation was opened. It was, of course, initiated by the Catholic missionaries, but the numerous representation of delegates from the different tribes amply proved that such a "family celebration" was entirely consistent with the wishes of the Indians. The preliminary purpose of this congress was to acquaint the Catholic Indians with one another as sons of one faith, bringing them closer to the one church, [acquaint them] with the progress of the Catholic religion among the individual tribes through reports by the respective delegates, and in doing so bring about a mutual spurring on and strengthening in the holy faith.

It was especially the effectiveness of the various Catholic societies, which had achieved entirely unexpected results particularly at Standing Rock and Fort Totten, that were to be made more generally known and to be properly honored on this occasion. "The first rule of these sodalities is," wrote Fr. Digmann, S.J., "that their members give up the old ways of Indian life, cut their long hair, dress like whites, engage in farming, make an honest living, and provide each other mutual support. Since I have attended this congress and have seen the unexpected results, I am convinced: THIS is the way to solve the Indian question."

The congress was opened with a solemn mass, which the Reverend Fr. Fintan, O.S.B., missionary at the Crow Creek Agency, celebrated. The delegation from Fort Totten, N.D., sang a choral mass, during which one could not stop wondering about the clear pronunciation of the Latin, as our source, Fr. Emil M. Perrig, S.J., tells us.

In the afternoon, around 2 o'clock, the men's and women's societies marched to the living quarters of the missionary, to escort in a festive procession the Right Reverend Bishop Martin Marty, O.S.B., along with the missionaries who had arrived, to the society's meeting hall. It took some time until one delegation after the other had lined up, with their colorful badges and flying colors. The oldest society, the St. Joseph's Men's Guild of Fort Totten, had been given precedence. The sturdy redskins looked quite stately with their plumes of red feathers and sashes, especially since there were also among them a considerable number of Catholic policemen in uniform. Next came the men's societies of Standing Rock, represented by no fewer than 232 members. In third place marched the delegates from Cheyenne River Agency, Crow Creek Agency, Yankton Agency, Rosebud Agency, and finally, the one from Fort Pierre, altogether about 170 men strong. Only a few of them wore the society's colors. The others, more recently converted Indians, had not yet formed a society among themselves.

The men were followed by the women in the same order, [wearing] around their necks the society's medal on a blue ribbon embroidered with silver [and] on their heads a blue veil. Three hundred and sixteen women wore the society's badges; about 200 followed without it [the badge]. Thus, in the end, there were nearly 1,000 Catholic Indian men and women lining the way, right and left, from the entrance to the mission house to the festival hall. Straight through their midst, on six richly decorated wagons, rode the Right Reverend Bishop Marty; the reverend missionaries Fr. Martin Kennel, Fr. Beda Marty, [and] Fr. Bernhard Straßmaier, O.S.B., of Standing Rock; Fr. Fintan, O.S.B., of Crow Creek; Fr. Florentin Digmann, S.J., of Rosebud; Fr. Emil M. Perrig, S.J., of Pine Ridge, Agent Mc Laughlin, Mrs. Mc Laughlin, and a host of Indian girls dressed in white. On arriving at the society's meeting hall it soon became apparent that it, while spacious, was nonetheless much too small for such a crowd of people. Thus the people were asked to take a seat on the large green field in front of the hall which had been transformed into an artificial grove. Fr. Martin, O.S.B., superior of the Benedictine missions at Standing Rock, director of the government school of agriculture, located 16 miles south of Fort Yates, as well as rector of the St. Benedictine Church there, warmly welcomed the guests to the festival and called the congress to order. Two Indians from Fort Totten and one from Standing Rock gave speeches of the kind that would have been met with well-deserved recognition by whites at any Catholic gathering. With truly touching ardency did these so-called *"Wilden"* speak about the love of the divine Savior, the blessings and comforts of the holy religion, [and] about the reward that could be expected by anyone who was enduring along with Jesus here on earth, poverty, contempt, and suffering. Given the fairly advanced hour, the Right Reverend Bishop Marty began to speak, telling his precious red children what inexpressible comfort it was to him to see how, after long years, God had blessed the efforts of the missionaries to such a high degree, and how the current congress was offering the most comforting hopes for a happy future for the Indians now and forever. By setting a good example, the right reverend bishop encouraged those present to emulate one another in demonstrating passion when receiving the holy sacraments and through charity toward all, Christians and non-Christians alike, and in doing so to help others to also come to know the truth. In closing, he submitted the three following resolutions, which he recommended to all for their earnest consideration:

1. We thank God with all our heart for revealing to us His only-begotten son Jesus Christ and for admitting us into the church established by Him. In her alone do we find true comfort and assurance during our lifetime, and an ever happy life in eternity.

2. We want to love and help one another as children of one Father who is in heaven. We want to firmly keep together in prayer and work, joy and misery, sickness and health, life and death.

3. We see as a great kindness of God the freedom and welfare of this republic, whose 115th anniversary we are celebrating today. Hand in hand with our white brothers we want to endeavor to become worthy citizens of this great commonwealth, and to contribute to the republic's greatness and prosperity to the extent of our abilities.

At 7 o'clock in the evening a large number of guests gathered around the right reverend bishop inside the great hall of the government school, where the Indian children gave not only surprising evidence of their skills in reciting English poems and dialogues, but also of their progress in singing and piano playing. Who in the world should expect to hear pieces for four and six hands, and indeed not of the easiest kind, performed on the piano by Indian children?

On the following day, Sunday, July 5, throughout the entire morning the missionaries heard the confessions of those to be confirmed who due to lack of time had not been able to arrive the previous evening; and during each holy mass, the communion bench was occupied by the devout. At 10 o'clock, after consecrating the enlarged and beautified St. Peter's Church, the Right Reverend Bishop Marty celebrated a solemn high mass. Six Indian boys served as acolytes, and Indian children sang the liturgical choral. The bishop himself delivered the feast day sermon. At 3 o'clock in the afternoon the church was again more than half full with children, men, and women, who were to be confirmed. Following a hymn to the Holy Spirit in the Sioux language, for which all the voices inside and outside the church united, Fr. Florentin Digmann once again explained to those to be confirmed, in easy-to-understand and heartfelt words, the effects of the holy sacrament and the means by which to preserve them lastingly. Thereupon the right reverend bishop administered the holy sacrament to 224 Indians, having confirmed in the same church between 80 and 90 less than one year ago. The conclusion of the celebration was once again an inspired hymn to the most blessed Virgin Mary in many hundreds of voices. In the evening the second gathering of the congress took place in the open field, in the midst of a large circle of pitched Indian tents. It was already late in the evening when it was learned that the Right Reverend Bishop John Shanley of Jamestown, N.D., and the very meritorious missionary Fr. Jerome Hunt, O.S.B., of Devil's Lake, had arrived. Hurriedly, a wagon was sent to Fort Yates to get the two venerated guests. The good redskins, to whom a "Black Robe" means everything, welcomed the arrivals with unfeigned joy, and listened with the greatest attention to the fatherly words of the right reverend bishop.

Early on Monday, July 6, the two right reverend bishops traveled to Cannon Ball, 26 miles from Fort Yates, accompanied by several missionaries and a number of Indians on horseback, to consecrate the new church there, the fourth Catholic church at Standing Rock Agency.

"When in the evening," continues Fr. E. M. Perrig, S.J., "we returned to the hut of our dear Indians, they had, after a long and peaceful contest between Rosebud and Cheyenne River, just reached the decision through voting to hold next year's gathering at the last mentioned agency. The convincing reason for this was, as Joseph Iron Owl (*Eiseneule*) from Fort Totten had already emphasized in his speech the previous day, the desire to spread the knowledge of the Catholic religion where until now only rarely a missionary had gone, and where there were neither Catholic churches nor schools. 'I now go home as a Christian,' *Eisenroß* [Iron Horse] of Cheyenne River had said, 'but I feel like an orphan, without a father, mother, or home, like a lonely fluttering bird, because we have no churches, no missionaries who gather us for prayer and continue to instruct us.' With that, the victory of the Cheyenne River Agency was decided. Once more the pious singing of the brave redskins echoed through the nightly stillness, then the marshals formed a giant circle of all those present. Having been given a signal, the Indians from Fort Totten began their round, ceremoniously shaking hands with everyone in the circle by way of farewell. They were followed by others, until not one person was left who had not taken leave from everyone individually with a brotherly handshake. With that, the first general congress of the Sioux Nation closed, of which it had been believed and asserted until now that, as far as Christianity was concerned, it was the least responsive of all Indian nations. That the congress took such a happy and generally satisfactory course was in great part also due to Major Mc Laughlin and his wife, both of whom showed themselves in the truest sense of the word to be a father and mother to the red children, and friends of the missionaries."

"The government," adds Fr. Digmann, "had shown itself noble with respect to the congress held, having provided the red participants with everything necessary for the journey; it will surely be to the benefit of the government if the movement thus initiated progresses in a positive way and speeds up the civilizing of the poor redskins. Big Turkey, *Großer Truthahn*, who I had taken with me to the congress along with 20 others from our agency, approached me and said that he too wanted to speak. 'Well then, what do you want to say?'—'I want to say that so far we have enjoyed a bad reputation due to Spotted Tail's (*Gefleckter Schwanz*) band, especially because of the most recent unrests. However, after seeing here how they are doing it, we want to follow that example and do likewise.' I, for my part, now have a good weapon in hand against the usual Indian excuse: 'Launkotapi ca unkohipi sni', that is, 'We are still Lakotas (heathens) and are not yet able to do it,' for example, marry for life in a Christian way, provide for ourselves, and so forth. 'THEY can do it,' I will now tell them, 'and you have heard it and seen it with your own eyes how happy they are in the process; why not YOU as well?'

"May God give His blessing for it and a joyous good progress! I returned in a sort of spring mood, but feel already what work is awaiting us."

Document 2.9
From: Volume 20 (1892)[22]
News from the missions. North America.

In the January edition (p. 16) [doc. 2.8] we reported in greater detail about the first congress of the Catholic Sioux Indians in Dakota. The second was celebrated on the last 4th and 5th of July at the Cheyenne River Agency. Altogether there were probably about 6,000 Sioux assembled from Fort Totten, Standing Rock, Sisseton, and the Brulé Agency, among them the most well known of the living chiefs, such as Hump Gall, *Kleiner Weißer Stier* [Little White Bull], *Richter Weißschwan* [Judge White Swan], Sam Campbell, and others. On the occasion of the gathering, the solemn dedication of the new church at Cheyenne Agency, endowed by the well-known Miß [Miss] Frances [Katherine] Drexel, was also undertaken. Following the church festivities, the first public gathering was held in an open field. There the meritorious Indian apostle Bishop Martin Marty, O.S.B., saw himself in the midst of at least 3,000 of his red children. The nearly 1,000–man-strong division of the notorious wild Cherry Creek Indians stood out especially with their picturesque national costumes. The scene presented an exceedingly interesting, colorful picture. The North American flag was flying on the tents pitched in a circle, and during the parade the flag of the St. Joseph's guild fluttered peacefully next to the Star-Spangled Banner of the great Republic. A *piquet* of 200 Indian policemen patrolled the camp under the leadership of Chief Straight Head, who had taken four scalps as recently as during the last Custer battle, and of *Kleiner Tomahawk* [Little Tomahawk]. In addition, 50 men of regular Indian troops and a division under Lieutenant Beacomb from Fort Sully had been moved in to keep order. Six thousand Indians participated in the final meeting. Inside the "great *wigwam*," the meeting hall, sat the president, Bishop Marty; at his side, the Benedictine Fathers Hieronymus (Hunt), Bernard, Franz, Fintan, Bedan [Beda], and the two German Jesuit Fathers Emil Perrig and Florentin Digmann. In the circle nearest them, the chiefs and the representatives of the various guilds and societies had taken a seat, and farther around, in four to five concentric circles, there were about 2,000 Indians squatting on the flat ground. Among them were many famous warriors who had distinguished themselves during the last Sioux war. Of course, also at this point, the stream of Indian verbosity flowed once again. Louis Lecomte, president of the St. Joseph's guild from Cheyenne Agency, held a short and energetic welcoming speech. *Eisenfeder* [Iron Feather] from Devil's Lake called on everyone as warriors of the cross to render mutual support. That same speaker also did not fail to remember the Columbus celebration. Christophorus, which means, carrier of Christ, had been the name of this great discoverer. Through him the joyous message had also reached them, and they issued a request to their white brothers to deal with them fairly, and to assist them so that their children would get their own schools so that they would learn something and be brought up to become good citizens. Finally, it was resolved that next year's congress would take place at Rosebud Agency, where German Jesuits are laboring.

Document 2.10

From: *Volume 21 (1893)*[23]
News from the missions. North America.

South Dakota. Education of the Indian boys. The German Jesuit Fr. Al. Bosch at St. Francis Mission, Rosebud Agency, in a letter of 15 January of this year, presents for us a rather delightful picture about the education of the Indian boys entrusted to him:

> The work of civilizing and Christianizing our Indians is hard, but it is not fruitless, and also has many attractive sides. First, there are our boys, who little by little are abandoning their natural wildness and their rough manners, assuming to an equal degree the habits of white children. When they first come, they look unclean and ragged, are stiff and timid, but submit themselves without difficulty to a thorough washing and cleaning, looking afterward altogether respectable and agreeable. Then the new cloth-

ing is distributed, and also in this respect the child of the wilderness is indeed not very spoiled. Coats of every conceivable shape, pants of every conceivable color are put on quickly and are worn with great satisfaction.

Today the boys have already grown more particular as far as clothing is concerned, and in that regard, I notice that they prefer the black suits over all others. Their black, thick hair, and their fiery, coal-black eyes will always give them away, of course, but aside from these racial characteristics no one would find a difference between our boys and those of the white settlers. Indeed, I would say that they appropriate the external education more readily, and are truly little masters with respect to singing and playing on the various instruments, such as drums, flutes, harmonicas, and others. With these instruments they create during their retreats a noise that can drive a nervous person mad and bring a wall clock to a standstill. Since the visit of Very Reverend Fr. van Rossum, our new mission superior, I have been getting the boys together for joint games, weather permitting, and here I admire again their adroitness and their fast learning and getting accustomed to the rules of the game. I have introduced the old Feldkirch "rounders ball" among them, the way we used to play it in my days. With the coming of spring we will try many more games, and the game with my three chariots will not be the least popular one. (Chariot, a light, small two-wheel wagon with a very low axle and a delicate double drawbar; during the race it is usually pulled by one boy while the guide stands free-handed on the foot-board, spurring on his horse[d] to increasingly greater speed by calling out [to it]. It is interesting to watch such a race by several chariots, how now here, then there the proud guide of the wagon loses his balance and tumbles into the dust, how now this one, then that one is gaining the advantage, and the victor of these Olympic games is finally greeted by the crowd's shouts of "hurrah.")

The greatest difficulty concerning our boys lies in overcoming their innate aversion to work. One must understand that these are children of natural beggars, who receive clothing and food from the government, and so they have never had the example of a hard-working father or brother to look to. However, as long as these boys are under one's watchful eyes and one works alongside them, they are very industrious. But as soon as they are left to their own devices, their Indian nature immediately comes to the fore. And yet we have to tell ourselves that if we are not successful in getting these boys and girls used to working, our mission work is built [merely] on sand. Thus we encourage, with all our might, our Indians, young and old, to work and work again, and in doing so provide for their own livelihood so as to make themselves independent from the meager assistance that they receive from the agency. And based on the judgment of those who look out for their benefit, they are, by and by, beginning to realize the necessity [of this]. They already take much better care to make improvements in farming and to the livestock allotted to them by the government, are producing more hay, [and] know how to build barns to provide shelter for their horned cattle and their horses. Since Fr. Digmann left our mission, I have assumed the leadership of the "St. Joseph's Sodality," and I convinced my young people with every possible argument to cut trees for their houses and barns, split wood, and things of this sort. They understood my advice, and at their first meeting, for which I was present, designated four young fellows to cut down the wood and transport it to the mission sawmill. First they wanted to build a council building, and then around it, with time, their dwellings. But I know my Indians! I am giving you the best idea of our old people when I say that they are BIG OLD CHILDREN WITH ALL THE EFFECTS OF THE ORIGINAL AND PERSONAL SINS WITHIN THEM, and only patience, over and over again, is the precious medicine that the missionary has to carry with him at all times. Oh, how many times do I have to avail myself of that medicine!

The most recent change in superiors showed the childlike and childish character of our Indians once again in its right light. When our new superior did not go about matters in exactly the same way as the former, they expressed all sorts of complaints and discord, and every little change was carefully scrutinized and used as evidence in support of his predecessor. But now the dissatisfaction is slowly subsiding, and they are beginning to realize that others also mean well by them and like to help them along toward a civilized and Christian life.

Next, Fr. Bosch happily welcomes the reelection of Grover Cleveland as president, given that, God willing, this means a change in the Indian policy.

Document 2.11

From: *Volume 21 (1893)*[24]

The Third Congress of Catholic Sioux Indians.

(Reported by Mr. Hillig, S.J.)

From the 4th until the 6th of July of this year the third Catholic gathering of Sioux Indians took place at the St. Francis Mission in South Dakota, cared for by German Jesuits. (Compare vol. [20] 1892, pp. 16, 256 [docs. 2.8, 2.9].)

An eyewitness shall describe this so important event for the Indian mission, which shows us, more concisely and more convincingly than many words, the successes of these still new missions. He reports:

> The iron horse carries us at lightning-speed through the vast open plain of the prairie, where here and there the last remnants of the once so numerous buffalo herds are grazing. (See picture [p.] 229 [not reproduced here].) In Crookston, way up in the north of Nebraska, the superior of St. Francis Mission, Fr. Jutz, S.J., receives us with his little wagon, and off it goes through a rolling high plain devoid of trees and bushes into Dakota, whose southwest corner, an area about the size of Belgium, has yet been left to the redskins. Finally, a white church[d] appears on the northern horizon and bids us welcome. This is the mission of Saint Francis, where the meeting will be held. Soon after us there arrived the first caravan of RED guests. Having given them time to pitch their tents, we, accompanied by one of the missionaries, went to their encampment. As soon as the Indians caught sight of the Black Robes, they came out from behind their tents and wagons, and lined up at the entrance, greeting us with a friendly: "*Hau kola, hau kola!*," that is, "good day, my friend," and extended to us the brown hand for pressing. Indeed, I have rarely shaken so many hands in one year as on this and on the following day.
>
> The next evening the large caravan from STANDING ROCK was expected. It was toward sundown when it became visible against the northern horizon. A cloud of dust was the first thing that could be seen. From this cloud there gradually emerged the upper part of the canvass covered wagons. With the wagons following each other so closely, these white arches, seen from the distance, merged into one single impression, and it looked like a giant white snake slowly winding its way through the dust.

Yet the closer the monster came, the more the rings dissolved into individual segments that ran on wheels and were drawn by Indian ponies. This was a long train, probably 70 wagons strong. And next to the caravan ran yet a whole herd of horses, foals, and dogs. On such travels, the Indian always takes all of his livestock along. "*Hau, hau!,*" it resounded out of each wagon as they drove by. "*Hau, hau!,*" was our reply. These Indian travel carts are strikingly reminiscent of our gypsy wagons. Also the passengers have some resemblance to this European nomadic nation with respect to skin color and facial features. He and she sit on the coach-box. He holds the reins. In the rear of the wagon, the actual moving tent, the rest of the family makes itself comfortable between all sorts of trunks, bundles, and pots. The poles for the tent to be pitched are fastened on both sides of the wagon. A horse running alongside carries the canvass. In less than half an hour all of the tents are pitched at the stopping place, and the coffee or meat kettle is already hanging over the cheerfully burning fire. All of this the careful housewife has done by herself. In the meantime, His Highness has unhitched the horses and is leading them to the watering place. Yet he asks himself now, whereto? And here we have touched on a sensitive issue: the question of water. The mission had a well dug, and this well is over 200 feet deep. A wind motor pumps the water up. This is the only well for one and one-half hour around. Now the question arose: Should one give this water to the horses,—in the course of these days there were half a thousand around the mission—or drive them to the creek an hour and a half away? Of course, a decision was made in favor of the latter, but the Indians were not content with that. They came again and again asking for permission to water their animals at the reservoir. One tried to make them understand that it really would be better to drive the horses a little farther than having to get cooking and drinking water for 1,000 people from the distant creek in the event of a calm. But all of this was of no use—the unreasonable request continued to be heard. It appears that some of them were not looking any farther than 3 feet into the future.

On the afternoon of the 3rd of July, preparations were made for the reception of the bishop. With an early signal from the bell, all the Indians came to church from their camp in the field. Toward 3 o'clock there was the lineup for the procession. First came the women and maidens, all adorned with a broad, blazing blue breast collar and a long head scarf of the same color; from a distance they could have been taken for blue nuns. The men, who followed in the lineup, wore wide, flame red sashes with embroidery and a red feather on top of the hat. Dakota costume was not tolerated. Most of the men also wore their hair cut short. Even that morning several had parted with their splendid and beautiful black head of hair. This means to break with the wildness, but it is a tough sacrifice for the Dakota man. Following the double row of men is the brass music [band], consisting of 15 young members, mostly Indian boys. The band is a creation of Fr. Perrig, S.J., who brought them over from Pine Ridge Reservation for the festival. Their performance was met with just approval by every music-loving listener. The missionaries, Benedictines and Jesuits, formed the end of the procession. Just like their flocks, so too did their shepherds come together here from all parts of Dakota, and now they went out to solemnly welcome the chief shepherd and founder of the Dakota missions, Bishop Martin Marty, O.S.B. Then the procession starts moving, everyone is following the cross, this radiant sign of redemption which is carried in front. Oh, let us hope that ALL of the Dakotas may join this crusade!, so I prayed in silence.

After half an hour the procession returned, this time with the chief shepherd in its midst. The bells rang, and in the church there followed the usual welcoming ceremonies. A forceful folk song, sung by several hundred Dakotas, made for the closing. What singing! [It was] a kind of war song, comparable to the autumnal tempest. Yes, deep down there still stirs the wild Indian nature of old. With the melody rising, it sounded as if the upward surging stream wanted to split the vaults. This must have been the way the old Teutons sang when Tacitus heard them for the first time.

The first of the three festival days was opened with a high mass *coram Episcopo*. What sight this was down from the gallery! On the right, on the epistle side, the women with the same sky-blue head scarfs that they wore yesterday; on the left, only men, one dressed like the next, one head as pitch black as the next. Now the holy mass commences, which the Very Reverend Fr. van Rossum, the superior of the German Jesuits in North America, celebrates. How devout they are acting, these sons of the prairie, who only 7–10 years ago knew nothing of our holy religion! One has to go far in countries that for more than a thousand years have been part of Christianity, to find SUPERIOR devotion and order than in this remote Indian church.

Fr. Digmann, known among the Indians only as "*Putinhin-sapa*," that is, Blackbeard, delivered in the Dakota language the feast day sermon on the two paths to eternity. All followed his words intently, and did not allow themselves to be fazed, even when, from time to time, an unruly infant began its high-pitched jeremiads and would not rest until its concerned mother left the church with it. At the end of the service the bishop conferred the blessing, whereupon everyone went in a nice and orderly fashion to their tent village, where shortly afterward thick clouds of smoke rose from numerous peace pipes.

At 3 o'clock in the afternoon the first open meeting of the festival began. The bishop was ceremonially led to the meeting place, and while he walked past the rows of Indians, they all fell devoutly to their knees to receive the blessing of the chief shepherd. Peter, *Großer Truthahn* [Big Turkey], had designed the hall for the celebration. A man-made arbor, winding along in an octagon shape, yet covered only with green bows on the top, harbors the seats for the active members. Inside the octagon stands a row of benches absent backs: these are the "reserved seats" for the missionaries. Centered in front of these benches stands a chair for the honorary president, the right reverend bishop, and another for the secretary. A table serves the one mentioned last as a writing desk and, at the same time, as a possible place of support for the upcoming speakers. Let us hurry now to get inside, for everyone has already taken his place, having uncovered his head for prayer; at present, the knights of the guard of honor are riding back and forth outside, eager to serve.

Following the brief inaugural prayer, Bishop Marty received permission to speak first. On his left stands the interpreter, in whose features the characteristics of the white and red races unite in a pleasant facial expression. Whenever the bishop paused at the end of a thought, there immediately followed the rendering of the same in the Dakota language, sounding almost as if the translation had been memorized, which was certainly not the case. From this beautiful speech we can only extract a few passages reflective of the Indians' situation. "We are very happy," thus began the chief shepherd, "to see you united here from all parts of Dakota, especially that those from Standing Rock have come in such great numbers, not shying away from the long journey in this summer heat (the poor people had been on the road for a full week); alone your love for the church has let you forget all the difficulties of the journey.—There was a time when it seemed that it was mutually incompatible to be both a Catholic and a Dakota, but today we see before us nothing but Catholic Dakotas, evidence that the church is founded for all nations. The ambassadors for Christ went all over the world converting the nations, and in these last days they also came to the Dakotas. Now, many of you have seen what advantage the whites have over the Dakotas with respect to a number of matters, yet they had been just like the Dakotas before the ambassadors for Christ settled with them. They owe their progress only to Christianity.

"The Christian doctrine determines that the practice of [one's] religion is to take place not only in church, but also at home within the family. This is God's will, that every human being who is born has a good father and a good mother, who teach him already at home to serve God, to please God. Moreover, the husband is to love the wife more than anyone else on earth."

This remark is exceedingly important with respect to the Indian, because in his view a wife is more the husband's maid than his companion. The Dakota heathen does not eat with his wife at the same table. The wife has to do all the work: get wood, cook, pitch the tent.

"Another of Christianity's advantages," the bishop continued, "was that husband and wife work, and do not procure their living through begging. You should expect your sustenance from your own endeavors and not from the Great Father (president). The Great Father bought from you a piece of your land and gives you your rations in return, but this will not continue in this way for much longer. That is why you must learn to earn your living with your manual labor. In former times, when the buffalo herds were abundant here in the prairie, this was different, but now it will be best if you use your prairie for stock raising. When I have the opportunity, I will speak with the Great Father, that he may support you in your endeavors. So work for yourselves and for others as Jesus and Joseph have worked.

"Thirdly, I wanted to appeal to you that you do everything that is necessary to raise your children for God. That is also the reason why I, when I came to preach the Gospel to the Dakotas, founded as many schools as I could. These missionaries here could have a much easier life; but God has inspired their hearts that they work for you for the sake of God and for His greater glory. That is why you must be eternally grateful to them," and so on.

Now it was decided that the following speakers should be called upon to speak about the progress of their respective parishes, but no one should speak for more than 10 minutes. However, there arose the difficulty that the good Indians have no real sense of a time frame of 10 minutes. This was resolved in that the speaker was given a sign when his time had expired. This circumstance, as well as the lack of preparation—except for the follow-up speaker no one had been told beforehand that he was to speak—had as a consequence that the true Indian eloquence did not fully come into play.

The first Indian speaker who came forward was *Wolkenstier* [Cloud Bull]. He was prepared. I myself was a witness when he recited his welcoming speech to a missionary, but, oh!, he in particular had a knack for getting stuck after the first two sentences, and again after the third, and once again after the fourth. The slight twitching of his mouth and the quivering of his hand when lifted for the first *gestus* [gesture] immediately revealed as he stepped forward that the eyes fixed on him from all around were hampering his courage and memory. Among other things, he said the following: "I have raised my heart up to God and want to encourage it to lead an honest life. I was a Dakota in former times, but I have been given prayer by the whites, and therein I want to walk.—You have come here to see the progress we have made in religion.—I hope you will hear much that is edifying."

Weiße Pfeife [White Pipe] said: "We very much want to work and reach God, but I want to tell you something: We are without church and without priests, so how can we make progress?"

Junges Feuerherz [Young Fire Heart] is called on and says, among other things: "I am from Standing Rock, where we have a school. I should like to inform you about the following: I have moved my people to cut their hair and support the school in that they all send their children there."

Großer Bär [Big Bear] exclaims: "Listen carefully! I have devoted myself to a great deed for God's cause: I say what I think. The Black Robe settled down there at Standing Rock. I have been with him for more than ten years. He is sending me to you. Now listen, you Sicangu! Pay heed to the words that were spoken to you. Take your children to school, to this school. Look at me, I mean well by you."

The next speaker is half Indian; Anton Claymorr is his name. Never have

I heard a voice that so resembled the sound of a trumpet as this speaker's. My ears were almost deaf after they had been blared at for about five minutes at close quarters. And with what conviction and captivating fire this speech came pouring out! One missionary told us that this man, by the power of his speech, had put an entire gathering into a state of real fear. He said: "Our Bishop is here, and we will have the pleasure of his presence for another two days. We understand his work and the words that he spoke to us. Let us abide by these words, even when he is not with us. After all, we must also follow God's commandments, and yet we do not see God. But let us follow his words with courage; as St. Paul says, we must fight for the kingdom of heaven. But it is not asking too much. Let us be sure to cleave to our faith and the rules of our sodality, thus we will be victorious. God, who is almighty, will extend His hand to us, if only we follow His commandments," and so on.

Einsamer Mann [Lonely Man] speaks: "I have embraced the faith and have convinced my children to do the same. God's work will not founder, so we have learned; thus let us take heart. In this country the devil attempts to draw the people into hell, but if we keep remembering our baptismal vows and send our children to the good school, we will go to heaven and there meet one another again.—I see assembled here a branch of the church of God, and my heart rejoices."

Gelbe Eule [Yellow Owl] could be heard saying: "Listen to me! I am extending my hand to you. We do not look back upon what we have thrown away, but move forward with courage. We go to the holy sacraments and listen to what the Black Robe says. I often think of both paths, the white and the black, and this causes me to be happy at all times."

Guter Schild [Good Shield]: "I extend my hand to you. We have sold our land and have nothing left, but we have found the true religion, and we want to keep it."

Now it was the women's turn, and here the lead was taken by:

Anna Schießt-die-Katze [Shoots-the-Cat]: "Our parish is small, but we toil and pray. Our nation is numerous, but it still walks in darkness, yet by and by it is converting. Let us simply trust in God; He will help us." Susanna Schönes-Haus [Beautiful House], a shy girl of about 20 years, is asked to speak as head of her sodality. A subdued laughter is heard all around. She speaks in similar fashion to the previous speaker. It is a great honor for these poor Indian women to be able to speak in public. In heathendom they would not have been permitted to do this. Perhaps someone would take offense that women are acting as speakers at all, but under the existing circumstances such a concession, which serves to inspire the men to have more respect for the women and the latter to have more self-confidence, should be perfectly in order. Several other Indian women, such as Magdalena *Springt-über-den-Hagel* [Jumps-over-the-Hail] *Gute Adlerin* [Good Eagle Woman], Luise *Fliegt-vorbei* [Flies By], [and] *Schöngesicht* [Beautiful Face] stepped forward and reported, in controlled language, the eyes modestly lowered, about the status of the sodalities that they were presiding over, or in several sentences touched upon matters already mentioned in other speeches. It was curious that while the men, on an average, accompanied, or rather illustrated, their words with a rich selection of the most descriptive hand motions, the women merely restricted themselves to pulling their head scarfs into shape from time to time. The last end of the women speakers was *Skeluta hinapewin*, or *Auftauchender rother Vogel* [Emerging Red Bird], a woman who was suffering greatly, as one could tell at first sight. "I extend my hand to you," she spoke. "I am ashamed to speak here, and I am also very ill. We are working hard. Seven months ago the seeds were sowed and one can see already how things are growing. We do not have a church yet, but we are moving ahead spiritedly."

While the speeches kept trickling along, a wagon with two large barrels approached the fenced-in meeting place. These contained refreshments of the best kind: crystal clear water for listeners and speakers. It was passed around in small vessels. The very same cup was passed around from the right reverend bishop and the other missionaries down to the dirty Indian baby crawling on the floor.

Now the right reverend bishop rises to deliver the closing remarks. He then announces the proceedings for the next day, and in the same way as the meeting was begun, by invoking the Most High, so it is closed in His name.

To all those who are somewhat interested in the mission work of the church, I wish they had been witnesses to today's meeting. Although I have tried in the above to assemble the main points from the various speeches, I do not see myself at all able to reproduce the deeper impression, or rather, the enthusiastic impression that seized us on this occasion. The old church is still alive. The nearly two-thousand-year-old trunk has once again added a new branch. It is feared that also the red race of North America will die out in a not all too distant future; let us hope that they will at least convert to the true God beforehand. We have the best reasons to hope so. May faith become for these poor Indians at least a radiant sunset masking their extinction, just as it had been the dawn of a new development for many European tribes.

It appears to be part of the plan of divine providence that the whites, who contribute so much to bringing these poor nations to the abyss of temporal misery, are destined to pull the same nations back from that eternal abyss. As we, occupied with these and similar thoughts, were preparing to leave the festival grounds, large metal kettles filled with chunks of meat were brought in. I guessed the plan: the intent was to secure the good mood and joy of the festival also by including the more materialistic side. Everyone who wanted to stay, stayed; however, for me it was impossible to attend the continuation of the festive gathering. The bill of fare for this Indian dinner probably read: meat, bread, black coffee. But meat is the main item. What rice is to the Chinese, [and] the potato to the person from the Westerwald, is meat to the Indian. It appears on his table morning, noon, and night, if he has got it. Once he has consumed his supply of beef, he butchers the loyal Phylax[25] and eats dog meat. He cannot at all comprehend why we whites, who otherwise have such good taste, cannot follow him in that. But he is indeed a strange character, the Indian. If he finds but one red fiber[d] in the meat, he declares that raw meat is good for whites, but not for the redskin. However, if you offer him a cow stomach or the liver, fresh and raw, the way it comes from the butcher, he takes it, goes to the next creek, runs it through the water once or twice, and then eats it with the healthiest appetite.

On the eve of the first day, beautiful fireworks were staged amidst the general admiration of the Dakotas.

The first day was now over. As we were about to retire, I once again looked over to the Indians' camp: it was a captivating sight. The white tents, illuminated from the inside, appeared like giant Chinese lanterns in the shape of pyramids. Flying about these was a swarm of sparkling fireflies, encircling them with gleaming silver threads. In the background, although far, far away, loomed a couple of deep, black thunder clouds that once in a while released their electrical charges, thus for a moment transforming themselves into mountains of fire. The fireworks that had just been touched off certainly could not compete with this in poetry and grandeur.

The second day required much hard work. At 8 o'clock the Very Reverend Fr. Jutz, S.J., celebrated a solemn high mass; the Very Reverend Fr. Bernard Straßmaier, O.S.B., delivered the sermon on the Catholic Church with enthusiastic words.

The next meeting was to take place immediately after mass. The right reverend bishop and the missionaries went to the society's meeting hall, but the ones who did not show up were the Indians. What had happened? When this morning the gathered Indians had been given six oxen for a present, the dear folks thought that they could not meet calmly until they had secured their just share [of the meat]. And so this had occurred within a short while, and now the meeting began.

In the course of this the annual rendering of accounts took place. The treasurers of the individual societies reported on membership numbers, how much money they had earned, how much and for what purpose they had spent it. Given that the Indians do not yet have a good grasp of our number system, they had noted some odd things on their lists; for example, 1,000 dollars instead of 10 cents. But when they read it aloud, they said it in the way they meant it. The goal that the right reverend bishop is pursuing with this simple rendering of accounts is to get these carefree children of the prairie used to order with respect to financial matters, about which they by nature know absolutely nothing. It was also edifying to hear about the donations of money and the support from which the houses of God and the sick benefited. One Indian, beaming with joy, put on the table before the bishop a purse containing about 500 marks; this was to be used for the building of a church. Anyone who is acquainted with the Indians, and knows how very little cash they own, must rightfully wonder about the splendid fruits of charity that Christian love has so quickly developed.

There was also another question settled: Where is the next congress to be held? The bishop proposed to the Indians to no longer hold one general congress in the future, but four separate gatherings of those stations located close to one another; he would then appear at each meeting every four years. The Indians listened to this speech silently and earnestly. Finally, a brawny Indian arose; one could tell by the blinking of his eyes that he was of a different opinion. Not a separation, but a closing of ranks, was the essence of the speech: "We must learn from one another. But how can this happen when we do not see one another? What is to become of our children, if you attend the confirmation only every four years?" No sooner had he finished, than a second speaker stood up: "Do you see the rope that holds the tent; it is strong and no one can tear it apart. But separate it, and you will see how easily the individual threads can be torn." Thus one speaker followed the next, all of them interceding in favor of a general Catholic conference. "All right," the bishop said with a smile, "if you do not mind enduring the exertions [of the journey], [then] I agree with you." This was now put to a vote. The victory of the Indians was complete. The location also was soon agreed upon, although each chief thought that his was the most beautiful.

The remaining part of the day was devoted to the preparations for receiving the holy sacraments. The entire mission breathed unity and inner peace. The confessionals were surrounded by and the middle aisle of the church filled with silently praying Indians giving thanks. The appreciation of this great grace and the joyful expectation of the even more valuable gifts of the holy sacraments of the altar and the confirmation, which tomorrow will bring, have wonderfully spread from the church, across the mission, and into the Indian camp. One feels exceedingly uplifted in this atmosphere.

The third and last day of the congress formed the religious high point of the whole. This day was set for the general Communion and the administration of holy confirmation. The church was once again closely packed. Once more the most exemplary order prevailed. Only the congregation's prayer seemed to stand out today even more than on the previous two days, with almost everyone having come, not only to be present at the holy sacrifice of the mass, like yesterday and the day before yesterday, but also to receive the Savior in Holy Communion, and many to partake of the offerings of the Holy Spirit. The longed-for moment had come. No sooner had the last "O Herr, ich bin nicht würdig!" [Lord, I am not worthy] left the lips of the priest, than they slowly arose from their benches, the dark figures, the descendants of the feared Sioux, stepping forward to the altar, solemnly and humbly, to receive the King of Peace and of True Love. One bench emptied after the next; first came the men, then the women. It touched me in a peculiar way when I saw how mothers with their children on their backs approached the Lord's table; should not the Savior, in entering the mother, also bless the little creature in a special way?

During confirmation, which was administered after holy mass, it was once again mostly adults who could be seen approaching the steps of the altar: men and women of all ages. They stand in need of the power of the Holy Spirit for the fight against the heathenism that dwells nearby, perhaps beside them under the very same roof.

Now the sacred act is over. A previously wild Indian horde has turned into an army of Christ. The bishop said the closing prayers, and like the expression of a long suppressed enthusiasm resounded in the august surroundings, carried by the sounds of trumpets and trombones, "*Großer Gott, wir loben dich, Herr, wir preisen deine Stärke!*" [Holy God, we praise thy name; Lord of all, we bow before Thee].

The congress of the Catholic Sioux Indians thus closed in a moving fashion.

Document 2.12

From: *Volume 22 (1894)* [26]
News from the missions. North America.

Indian mission in South Dakota. "Our Pine-Ridge Reservation," writes Fr. Florian Digmann, S.J., on 18 January 1894, "is about 50 x 100 Engl. miles square, and yet I am the only one who is able to attend to the Indians, for Fr. Perrig is tied to the school and also holds a service in the Church of the Sacred Heart of Jesus at the agency every Sunday. Since November we have a newly built church to care for as well. It is located about 25 English miles from here, on Bear Creek, and is dedicated to St. Joseph. In several camps the Indians have already asked me to please build a church[d] for them. The agent himself, although not a Catholic, likewise requested a couple of months ago that I build a church[d] on White River, in order to tame the wild Indians there. 'Carnal weapons do not have any effect there,' he said, 'there one has to use spiritual ones. Our success at Rosebud, and be it ever so modest, and the success especially of the CATHOLIC missionaries and Catholic schools on the reservations, is appreciated ungrudgingly by objective observers. However, there is no lack of envious people, and they are active. The Presbyterians came along with us to the reservation (1888) and already have five churches, the Episcopalians indeed six. The latter now

want to build one on Bear Creek as well. However, the Indians there con-
sulted with one another and SWORE not to allow any other 'prayer' but that
of the Black Robes. Thereupon they came to report to me. I built them the
church, trusting in God and St. Joseph. St. Joseph will have to help me re-
duce my debts; I have incurred them to please him. There are no benches at
this place yet, but that does not trouble my Indians; they are satisfied with
a couple of boards placed over sawhorses, or even with the floor. As soon
as the missionary arrives, someone jumps on his pony and summons those
who live scattered about. Meetings are held in the largest log house; those
who have applied for baptism are being instructed. Then we sing and pray
together. They greatly enjoy singing. And who would not like the heartfelt
melodies of our German sacrament hymns and those to the Blessed Virgin
Mary? Last June I went on an excursion to the upper White River, taking up
quarters with a Catholic half-blood Indian. It did not take long and a full
blood came in, who, judging by the offices he holds on the authority of
the government and his sect (Episcopalian), is one of the most intelligent
of his tribe. The first thing he said, addressing my host, was: 'I think I am
going to give up preaching and holding services on Sunday; there is hardly
anyone attending anyway.' Then he turned to me: 'Friend Blackbeard,' he
said, 'I actually came to see you and ask you about a number of things that
I do not like about your 'prayer' (church). 1. With you, the men of prayer
(priests) are not allowed to marry, and that does not please me. 2. You believe more than what is written in the holy book, and that does not please
me. 3. With you, the bishops wear a precious ring, have the people kneel
before them and kiss the ring, and that does not please me. 4. You never
come into our church, although we pray to the same Great Spirit, and that
does not please me.' I responded to him point by point, roughly and in
brief as follows: To the 1st. No one is forced to become a priest, but those
who have their calling from God and follow it solemnly swear by a promise
made to God to remain celibate and to live chastely. Why? Because according to the view of the church, the priest's heart is to belong fully to God and
His people. But if he is married, then he will certainly share [himself] between God and his family. 'That is true,' he added, 'Paulus says so as well.'
To the 2nd. We believe God's word, whether it is written or not, as soon as
it is certain that He has spoken [it]. Jesus said: go and TEACH, not: go and
WRITE. What would you say about your son, if he did not want to believe

you unless you gave it to him in writing? He: 'That would not be right.' To the 3rd. Through our bishops we honor the descendants of the apostles, that is, the ambassadors for Christ and the princes of His church, and the honor paid them reflects on the Savior. Here in America you never get to see anything of the ceremonies that are the custom at the princely courts in Europe.' He: 'Yes, I never thought about that.' To the 4th. We Catholics are convinced that Christ has founded only ONE church, ours, which alone teaches the WHOLE truth, and only the truth. With you, however, many things are denied, or taught differently than with us. If we now attended your church, we would thereby acknowledge that YOU have the truth, and only the truth, thereby disavowing our conviction and our faith, or making God double-tongued and contradictory of Himself. This position was new to my full blood, and he was honest enough to recognize the correctness of our action. Finally, I said: 'Suppose, my friend, on my way back to the mission, I came to a fork in the road; one going to the right, the other to the left. I take the latter, thinking that it will lead me home, but find out after some time that it is wrong. Should I keep driving nonetheless?'—He: 'No, you must turn back and take the right one.'—'This is YOUR case, when one day you will become fully convinced that the 'Black Robe Church' is the only way to heaven given us by Christ.' He promised to think it over, and to pray. Some time later he met me at the agency, extending his hand to me from afar, [and] of his own accord telling his brothers of the Indian court of justice, who were present, how he had tried to overcome me but had gotten beat on every point.

"On January 10, another 30–40 Indians, mostly heads of family, gave me their names, along with their request that I build a church[d] for them. The Episcopalians have already been long after it, but the people want to become Catholic. The same goes for two or three other camps. If only I could duplicate myself!" The missionary closes with a request for prayer and with the hope for speedy reinforcement.

Document 2.13

From: Volume 22 (1894)[27]
News from the missions. North America.

Indian reservation in South Dakota. Visit to a village of pagan reservation Indians. On the occasion of his stay at the Catholic St. Francis Mission, Mr. Hilligs, S.J., composes the following description of the state of the still heathen Indians of the reservation:

On an Indian carriage road, winding along odd bends, we reached a village that consisted of about 25 single story and single room gray log houses. The ground is gray, covered with half-dried, half-trampled-down prairie plants. Not a tree, not a bush is there to refresh with its greenery the monotonous, gloomy picture. Here and there in the shade of a low house squats the family on a spread-out mat. Let us approach one group. The woman, wrapped in an old, green calico dress, rubs a piece of half-dissolved soap between her brown hands; one can tell it is merely to pass the time. One of us had a photographic apparatus with him; she sees it and asks whether we had bread in it. Two children are crouching next to her; the one, its entire face covered with a rash, holds a green twig in its hand from which it picks grass green berries and brings them to its mouth. The missionary reprimands it for this. 'We have nothing to eat,' is the brief explanation by the mother. The other child gnaws on a bone which is most likely from no less an animal than the loyal dog of the house. And the husband? He sits at the end of the mat, his legs folded under him; from time to time he throws his pitch-black hair, tousled by the wind, back over his shoulder, his eyes passing over the hungry family seemingly unconcerned. He does not speak. These poor people probably have not had anything to eat for three to four days.

Other people have fixed up a tent or a hut of pine bows next to their log house; it is cooler inside this than in the house. Something is standing before us, it could be a sort of dog house, not a pointed, but a rounded, dome-shaped low tent. Next to it lies a pile of stones. What is this? It is a sweat bath, one of the Indians' principal remedies, as is well known. The patient whose sweating is to be induced goes into the tent wearing bathing dress. Meanwhile, the stones have been thoroughly heated on a wood fire. These are now carefully placed inside the tent, the patient is handed a bucket of water, and the tent is laced up as tightly as possible. The person inside pours the water over the red-hot stones, and the healing white steam rises with a sizzle. Yet instead of cooling themselves down with a cold dash of water, they run out of the sweat bath, half-naked as they are, letting themselves be dried off by the wind. Much good may it do you!

Approximately at the center of the village stands a spacious, round shack, made of crude beams and boards. Above the roof, which is open in the center, towers a flagpole. This is the dance hall of the heathen Indians. Had we passed by here on another day, we may have had the opportunity to see the redskins dancing, but there is surely nothing on for today. The entire group of able-bodied dancers of this place and surrounding area left for the agency the day before yesterday in order to celebrate the 4th of July there in the Indian way, that is, with some grand dancing. It is noticeable how especially on this day the opinions split into two sharply opposing camps here at the reservation. The one group, driven by pagan instinct, travels for miles to delight together with their tribal members in the laughable remnants of dying heathendom. The others, guided by grace, congregate in the shadow of the mission to kindle, through mutual edification and instruction, the Christian faith that is blooming in their hearts into a state of exaltation. For the dance, the one group has rid itself of all culture. Not one piece of clothing may be reminiscent of the civilization of whites; only pelts or feathers, bells or beads, and red ochre as paint are allowed. The others have even divested themselves of their magnificent head of hair and put on European Sunday clothing; with the exception of the darker skin and other racial characteristics, there is hardly anything that is suggestive of the wild Indian.

We had left the village filled with such reflections and were now stepping lively through the monotonous prairie. For a long time gray-green heather and blue sky were the only things we saw; heat and thirst, the only things we felt. Next to the path that we followed I noticed a wooden cross, one foot high, suspended from which were two dead birds. On my question about its significance, someone explained to me that this was most likely a mimicking of our sign of redemption, perhaps placed here by a medicine man to conjure certain evil spirits. Soon we were to encounter an even more disconsolate aspect of heathendom. Before us was an Indian burial ground. Yet this word is actually not applicable in this case, for the dead bodies are not buried here. They stand about openly in boxes and trunks. Several of these coffin boxes have split open due to the alternating effects of rain and heat, and through the wide cracks grins the decay. One coffin is particularly noteworthy. It sits on an iron bedstead and is covered with a colorful cloth. Tobacco and a pipe lie beside it. The deceased is to delight himself with that in the eternal hunting grounds, yet to this day he has not touched them; the tobacco pouch is already half disintegrated. Other dead bodies, wrapped in coarse cloth, had been covered with earth one foot deep, but rain and wind have exposed them to the wrapping. Oh, how wretchedly these bodies are decomposing here, and where is the soul of these poor creatures? Without faith, death is indeed a horrible matter.

After a deeply felt prayer for the enlightenment of the pagan Indians, we turned our backs on this desolate scene. From above, the rays of the midday sun burn down on us mercilessly; from below, the thoroughly heated ground liberally reflects the received warmth. The otherwise so hardy prairie grass appears to be on the verge of withering. Only the cactus is decked out in its freshly green dress of spines; one can tell that it feels comfortable in this tropical heat, and as if out of gratitude to the sun, it has donned its flower ornaments: these are delightful blossoms, created of the finest red and yellow silk. One would like to pick them and take them along, if only there were not so many pointy spines enveloping them. Another plant that would likewise make for a decoration for European parks grows in abundance in this hot, sandy soil: from a palm-like crown, one foot high, rises a stalk twice as long, whose upper half is covered with clusters of white bellflowers. Each perennial plant creates a splendid bouquet on its own. The closer we get to White River, the more numerous this flower becomes; the ground turns more hilly, and this appears to be to its liking. We are slowly moving downhill, and finally we once again come upon a few trees in the form of long-needled firs. Another few steps and in front of us opens a wide, dreary valley, through which meanders with wide bends a narrow strip of water. A double row of green leaf-bearing trees and brushwood has taken the creek into its midst and follows it along all of its turns. Farther away, up the two valley inclines, stands a scanty pine forest. This is [the] White River, the end of our three-hour march. No ruins crown these banks, no village, no house occupies this quiet valley bottom, no garden, no cornfield points to human activity. And yet, for the poor missionaries, this spot is the most romantic spot in their extended environs. How fortunate for them that they seek and find their happiness in higher matters; the bare land and the uneducated inhabitants, the summer with its tropical heat, the winter with its arctic cold and terrible snowstorms—these are the missionary's pleasures in these western prairies. Toward evening we arrived back at the mission.

Document 2.14

From: Volume 23 (1895)[28]

About Mission Life in South Dakota.[29]
(Reported by Fr. Alois Bosch, S.J.)

The Dakota winter is a rough, treacherous, and thus a dangerous fellow, who has no sense of humor, and because of that, one has to be extremely wary of it. Well then, let us make a quick tour through the Indian villages on the other side of the little White River before the enemy is upon us and the visit becomes an impossibility! So I thought on the eve of December 18, and the following morning found me busy packing my mission wagon. But far be it for me to take off like the great servants of God; I made sure that none of all the bits and pieces that were supposed to be taken along was forgotten. The trunk with the provisions rose high above the rest of the baggage. It also served as my seat. Anyone wanting to get to it had to have a word with me first. Next to it, rolled in an oilcloth cover, lies the [sleeping] bag made of buffalo hide. In it I dream at night of converting entire Indian villages. Farther in the back sits the portable altar with the *Bilderbibel* from Herder in Freiburg,[30] also in a box. Then there are two bags of oats and the little corn bin with the long lines inside it for tying up the horses on the prairie; also horse blankets, and some smaller items that are of no less importance, however. Who, for example, drives about for such a long time without wagon grease, or an ax, or spare ropes? Well, all of that is also packed in the back of the wagon. Now I go to Fr. Superior, for whose blessings I ask, quickly toss myself into my buffalo robe, walk once more around the wagon and the horses with a careful eye, and off it goes with an easy trot.

And with what emotions? Let us admit to our weaknesses! They will be revealed at the last judgment anyhow. Thus, with a certain natural repug-

nance and dread: the Indian is so terribly dirty. Also with a feeling of un-
certainty: where will my night quarters be? Thirdly, I feel like the prophet
Jonah in times past. Will the stiff-necked people heed my words and at
least let me baptize their dying children? Will I at least be able to move a
couple of ancient grannies and old-timers to accept baptism? And then
the weather? Will there be rain or a snowstorm? Huh, how sharply and
cold does the northwester howl, and will my two horses get safely across
the half-frozen White River? . . . But why these dark thoughts and brood-
ing? They do not come from above! We are in God's hand, so on then! Ho,
ho, ho, Prinz and Gray, away from these dark thoughts toward the bright
land of faith in God and apostolic courage! After a little more than an hour
we are already across the White River, which still has a bridge at this spot,
and it does not take much longer and I stand in front of a hut that I must
first look over.

Not so very long ago a school boy[d] had been lured away from us, you
must know. The poor boy was suffering from consumption, and the way
Indian parents are—incidentally, the parents of whites are often the same
way—they think their evocations and medicines could save the fleeting
life of their darling. That the poor child is fed much better when with us, is
much better dressed, and if at some point there is need for it, is cared for
much better, they do not see, or, the blind parental love acts only toward
the satisfaction of seeing their child with them and having it near them,
let it ever suffer so much as a result. But there are the few who concern
themselves with the religion from whose influence the child is thus withdrawn. And so I found my little Richard, a boy[d] of 12 years, as a perfect Dakota child, fully under the influence of the medicine man and a couple of
old witches. On seeing me, his whole face started laughing, and because I
wanted to take him to confession, this friendly reception already gave me
hopes for success. However, as soon as I only remotely intimated this, he
hung his head[d], and then there were tears, and in the end there came the
fateful, blank look from which a Dakota cannot be disengaged. It is truly
something peculiar with the patients of the medicine men and the humbug that they practice with them. Or is it not a settled affair with us missionaries that each child, even if it has been under our influence for 2, 3, 4
years, is lost to us and the receiving of holy sacraments, as long as it is being subjected to the treatment of these servants of the devil (this is not too

strong a term)? It was not very long ago that we, in order to put a stop to the carryings-on of these people, had to deny two of our school children a [Christian] burial, because they did not want to hear anything of extreme unction, partially on their own initiative, partially decided by their parents and the medicine men. Incidentally, here one could once again see that the devil is an arch-blusterer. This punishment created a great deal of bad blood, and the parents, who during the illness of the child wanted to hear nothing of God and His sacraments, suddenly wanted to have the body buried in the acre [cemetery] of the "great and mighty one." But that did not happen. We remained firm in our position: "You do not want your children to do the works of the great and mighty one, [then] you are also not to bury your children on the grounds of the great and might one." How bitter the mood grew toward us as a result of this is demonstrated by an incident at the mission. The grandmother of the deceased child had sent for her grandson, who was in our school. He was to participate in the Indian funeral ceremony; we did not want that. So she came herself and mingled with the children, and when I saw her I reproached her about the wrong she had done by leaving her granddaughter to the medicine men. But she did not want to listen to anything of the kind; instead, she suddenly pulled a long knife from under the blanket she was wearing, and as she was motioning to her grandson to walk ahead of her, she made her way through the bystanders with a threatening gesture and the knife swinging. What was I to do? One certainly cannot fight with a woman in an honorable way! So the wiser head gives in, and thus, the pair[d] took off. The old woman wailed all the way home. But now back to my unsuccessful attempt to save the consumptive school boy[d] from the clutches of the medicine man. At least I was able to awaken the acts of faith, hope, love, and contrition, and then I set out to try it elsewhere.

In one of the neighboring huts I found a young woman with a child, a young man, and an old man, the last mentioned lying on the ground wrapped in a blanket. He was ill and therefore was doubly entitled to my pity. Hence I spoke with him of the misfortune of the Dakotas, who have nothing in this world, and then get lost in the other [world]. Finally, I offered to instruct him in the religion, but he told me, very much in the Dakota manner: "I am a weak old man; I want to die like my ancestors. Where they went, I want to go too." I have had to listen to this response a dozen and a dozen more times, and it startled me so that I made a solemn promise to St. Joachim and to St. Anna, if they were to assist me in the conversion of the old. It is bad work and shows more than anything else how strong a hold the wicked enemy and the natural animalism have over these poorest of the poor. Based on my experience with this sort of Indian, one almost has to treat them like underage children. Once they have been taught the most essential truths of our holy religion, and have understood them even to a minimal extent and consented to them, then onward with the baptism and, when death approaches, extreme unction. The long, long life in paganism under the devil's rule, the many sacrifices, the absolute animalism, the apathetic state in which the people pass their lives, and on the part of the missionary, the insufficient language or lack of skill to deal with such creatures, and God knows what else—all of this comes together and lets many of these poor people sink into a second death.

I had just stepped out of the hut and let my gaze wander over the countryside to a distant Indian hut, when I beheld a woman[d] as old as the hills as she was in the process of crawling out of a ravine and disappearing into the hut. True to my resolution to search out old people, I hasten after the old woman and was already in front of the house when I saw another ancient woman crawling toward me on all fours. Now I am opening the door, and behold, I find a third grandmother cowering in a corner. This was a deserving clover leaf, and just to my liking. Thus I am praying in my heart to St. Anna to please help me gain the attention of these poor creatures, and I am starting to speak. But before long one could hear: "What does he want? What is he saying? I am an old woman and understand nothing! I want to die like a Dakota and be buried in the prairie! Do you have tobacco? Give me tobacco! Do you have bread? Give me bread!"—"Yes, granny, you shall have tobacco, but you must also listen to my words! You see, because of you, I drive about like this. You are to go to heaven to the great and mighty one, to your grandchildren who through baptism died as children of God. These you shall see again some day, and so on." But it was all very well for me to talk. One took out her tobacco pouch from underneath old rags, her cutting board, and a long knife, and began chopping up a certain bark and then mixing it with tobacco. Soon after, the long pipe was lit, and my conversion attempt went up in smoke. So, off I go, putting on a good face, and let's remember the place! Perhaps I will yet be successful in saving one of these poor souls at a later time. The sun was already low in the sky, and I needed to look for night quarters. You know what, I said to myself, go to "*alter Zeltpflock*"³¹ and his people. They did not entertain you badly a short while back, and the young lads demonstrated, to the extent that Dakotas do, a fair desire for the prayer of the great and mighty one. No sooner thought than done. As I am approaching, one of his grown sons appears looking friendly, and so I tell him of my decision to stay with him that night and to say holy mass in his hut in the morning. "*Hau, hau, ganz recht, ganz recht*," [all right, all right] was his reply. And now I cared for my horses, took them to the watering place, threw the horse blankets on them, gave them their rations, and tied them to the long lines out on the prairie. Then I entered the hut. But, oh dear! The horror strode ahead of me. A horde of children suddenly scattered into every corner, and only when I put my hand in my pocket and took out bonbons did the fear subside somewhat and moved even two unwashed boys in rags to crawl out from under the bed and receive their share. The old *Zeltpflock* was not at home. Thus I told one of his wives that I wanted to stay with them to teach the children and to deliver the prayer of the great and mighty one here tomorrow. The proposal was not rejected, and so I brought my belongings into a log cabin that had been assigned to me as my night quarters and where I also ate my frugal evening meal: one piece of black bread, a couple of eggs, and one piece of *candy*. Newly invigorated I soon appeared again among the children with my pictures, and although the attention left much to be desired, I was nonetheless satisfied to at least be able to spread some ideas, and thus perhaps be the reason that the young hearers, sometime in the future, will ask for the holy faith and baptism. There were many school-aged children present, and early baptizing presents a serious snag with respect to them. A child like this has to be taught for a more extensive period of time, and that can only happen through repeated visits. But there is often a long delay, and the child is on its own in the midst of pagan customs and influences during the long, intervening period. Moreover, the school-aged child gets worked over in the public schools by Indian Evangelical catechists and by Protestant preachers of the American sectarian propaganda. In like manner, beside us labor Episcopalians as well as Congregationalists (Presbyterians) among the Sioux, and they have substantial funds available to them. In light of this situation, the caution exercised by the missionaries in baptizing maturing youth, at least those who are being raised in the public schools, is understandable.

Having concluded my instruction, I retired to my log cabin, followed by one of the eldest sons of *Zeltpflock*. I wanted to instruct him separately. Already in times past he had expressed a desire to that end, along with several other young people in the camp. Thus we sat down together, and in order to put the pupil into the proper frame of mind, I gave him a piece of black bread with some sugar. While he ate it, I spiced it with relevant and useful comments: How a good Dakota now had to stop dancing, but work instead; become self-sufficient; seek and seize with sincerity and with all his heart the commandment of the great and mighty one—only in doing so could the young people get somewhere in this world. Then I proceeded with the actual instruction and explained to the attentively listening youth the two paths to the other life. I was truly edified, thinking in my heart: "Now this seems to have some effect, and if I return a couple more times, I am perhaps able to achieve something." Finally, my listener also opened his mouth, asking me for a sheet of writing paper. "What do you want with that?"—"Write a letter."—"To whom?" The young lad looked somewhat embarrassed, but then he came out with it and said with the calmest expression in the world: "Friend, I want to get myself a woman. There is a dance tonight and that is where I want to try it!" One can imagine how astonished I was at this revelation and how I now began to doubt whether my instruction had had any effect. Thus I started over, trying to drive this idea out of his head. To what extent I was able to accomplish this for the future, I do not know, but one thing is certain, he stayed at home that night and did not carry out the Dakota wedding. We continued to sit together for some time, and while he once again feasted on my black bread, I sang to him Dakota songs from our prayer book. Then we parted. He slept with his three brothers in one bed, and I retreated to my buffalo [sleeping] bag following the usual evening prayer.

The night was cold and the hut as well. Thus I hurried at daybreak to care for my horses, pray my breviary, and prepare myself for holy mass. Meanwhile, things had begun to stir in the other hut as well, and I hurried to take my effects over and prepare the altar. While going through this preparation, the thought of the stable in Bethlehem often comes to mind. The divine Savior is present; if only the shepherds were present as well!

But, wait. . . . In this hut something happened to me that has never before happened to me during holy mass. Everything was prepared, my pictures hung up, everything around the altar put in order, and the mother admonished to please conduct herself respectfully with her many children. What I was about to do was the most holy prayer that the great and mighty one has given us. So I had said, and in preparation prayed the Dakota prayers while kneeling down. Then I began with the introductory prayer. However, I had not even completed the epistle yet, when the old lady started grinding coffee. I turned around and reprimanded her for that, and she gradually gave it up. Having finished the gospel, I preached, but behold, now the three eldest girls ran out. One can imagine how I felt during the divine offering. I had not expected this.

Following the obligatory breakfast with black bread and eggs, I hitched up my horses and with [both] a sad and happy heart proceeded to the neighboring *camp* school, which had only recently been built for *Zeltpflock* and the Indians living in this area. The teacher received me in a most friendly manner, indeed I was even welcomed as a *quasi auctoritatem habens* [one having authority], and I immediately used this [circumstance] to give a catechistical instruction when school commenced. Because Christmas was near, I explained to the children the life of Jesus Christ, with remarks about His church, His commandments, and sacraments. During the noon meal I learned of a sick schoolgirl, and so I set out after the meal to visit her. The poor thing was suffering from a bout of falling sickness, and only with the greatest effort possible was I able to find out that she was baptized Catholic. She stared into space the entire time, her head almost entirely wrapped in a *shawl*. I consoled her, told her about the dear God, and as I was telling her a few words about contrition and confession, she covered herself completely and went into the hut of her brother, a Protestant, who had just returned home, probably from the nightly dance.

After another unsuccessful attempt and several general comments about the true church, I proceeded from there to another schoolhouse, whose teacher had always received us most kindly and to whose schoolchildren I gave catechistical instructions the next morning. Unfortunately, most of the pupils are already in the hands of the Protestants, who themselves catechize there regularly. The entire schoolroom is covered with pictures of their Bible society. It is exceedingly interesting to observe the mixture of religion and nondenominational instruction in these Indian public schools or government schools. Thus I once had the opportunity to get to know the Yankee sign of the cross in such a school. The children stood at attention in front of their teachers like Prussian soldiers. Now there rung out the word: "Attention!"—"My mind, my words, my heart—to the flag of my fatherland!" and after the children, according to the teacher's example, had touched their foreheads, their mouths, and their chests with their hands, and finally pointed to the Star-Spangled Banner hanging on the wall, they all of a sudden stood there together with their teacher, heads bowed, reciting fully collected and with devotion (?) the Protestant Lord's Prayer! Well, what do you want, you dear Catholic readers! Man must live, and Uncle Sam wants to be a missionary too.

The evening of that very same day found me in Red Leaf's Camp [*Roth-blattcamp*], about 12 miles away, where shortly after my arrival I made the attempt to convert the very ill chief, *Wandelnder Weißer Kranich* [Walking White Crane]. But the man had two wives, and at the same time he spoke so disparagingly of whites that I soon gave up all hope. "What have the whites given me? How have they helped me? They have given me papers, but have not supported me with a cent! I am a Dakota and have faith in my medicine men!" He was firmly under their control; I could tell by the medicine pouches that were fastened to his bed and by the sweat bath tent inside of which they practice their conjuring and whence they hand the magic medicine to the ill. Thus, I merely addressed several general words of consolation to the sick, and then looked for night quarters, which I, in the end, found with an Indian police soldier. He had a pitiful hut. Besides the two beds and the stove there was hardly any room left for my buffalo [sleeping] bag. The husband was in ill humor and was made more agreeable only with a packet of tobacco; his wife, on the other hand, was better, and together with her children listened attentively to the catechism. Excepting the husband, they also conducted themselves rather befittingly during holy mass the next morning. On the evening of my arrival I still toured the surrounding huts on foot and came upon a tent from which the eerie singing of a medicine man emanated. Without hesitation I pulled the tent flap aside and quietly sat down next to the fire. On my right the witch doctor cowered, on my left sat a woman with a child beside her who was suffering from the highest fever, and to which the man was apparently applying his craft. For a while I silently looked into the flickering, smoky fire, then I glanced at the woman and the child, and then also at the doctor, but said nothing. Now he began: "Why are you walking among us? What do you want?" Without looking at him, I replied: "I am walking about to tell the Dakotas not to believe the conjurings of the medicine men. They should only ask for their medicines, and not allow the humbug of singing, drumming, and sucking. The great and mighty one let the medicine grow in the prairie, and he who is knowledgeable of it should give it in exchange for reasonable compensation, but without praying to the devil or performing other frauds. It does not help anyway. The medicine helps only if God wills it. I am walking about to tell this to the Dakotas." The Indian took a deep breath and then uttered our German "Aha!" However, he soon started again: "You should help this woman. The child is not on her billet. If you are a friend of the woman then go to the agent and point this out to him."—"My dear friend," was the reply, "I am a friend of the woman, and because I am her friend, I am coming here from far away, wanting to help her as best I can. I want to teach the woman and baptize the child—I care for her soul; you and the agent, for her body. So, you go to the agent and show yourself as a friend to the woman!" Again, great silence. I used the pause and tried to persuade the woman to let her dying child be baptized. In vain. Then the medicine man started over. "Friend, my arm here is ill, help me and make me well again!"—"But you are a doctor," was the reply, "go ahead and try your medicine on yourself for a change! Suck the illness out of your arm and sing at the same time. But I know, you will not try it. No one gives you a saddle, or a blanket, or a pony for it!" Another "Aha!" and it was again quiet, only the rapid breathing of the child was audible. I again tried to persuade the mother—she also understood English; in times past [she] had attended the government school, had also received the Protestant baptism, but had become fully Dakota again. As I was now thinking about how I could still baptize the child, the medicine man took three coals out of the fire, laid them out in a triangular shape, took a special herb, burned it on top, caught the rising smoke with his hand, and touched the body of the child while constantly blowing and murmuring prayer formulas. It appeared to me as if he wanted to blow the sickness or the devil away. At that moment another small child who was in the tent with us ladled water out of a bucket and drank. I had made up my mind.

"Give me some of that," I said, and having drunk, I turned to the woman and said: "I cannot stay with you for long. Tomorrow I must leave. Promise me only one thing. When your child is about to die, baptize it, and this is how you have to do it." At that moment, I put my hand in the water so that it dripped and [then] let the water fall in drops on the child while I recited the baptismal formula and baptized it. But to her I said: "See, this is the way you have to do it." I was absolutely certain that she would not do it, and she did not do it. Yet the child has died, as I learned later on. The next morning I visited another, consumptive schoolgirl, prayed with her one act of contrition, and then went to the school where I showed the children my pictures. I then set out to return home.

I took my night quarters with an Indian who, although baptized by the Protestants, is still strongly set in the ways of the Dakotas. He has frequently attended catechistical instruction, but there are still no signs of a conversion present. His wife is baptized Catholic and is presently being instructed about receiving the holy sacraments. Next to this Indian, in a pitiful log cabin in which one can hardly stand upright, lives an ancient granny who has been lying on a bed made of rags for who knows how many years, completely paralyzed as a result of having fallen off a wagon. She is my only consolation for miles around. God's joy and the soul's peace are shining from her eyes. How she will look one day, when from her miserable log cabin she enters into the glorious heaven, receiving in place of her old skin, shriveled and covering her thin bones with a thousand wrinkles, a new body resplendent in the glory of resurrection! It is interesting how different the Dakota mothers are! Some are like possessed witches, while others are gentle and soft, and have truly childlike natures! Well, to them belongs the kingdom of heaven.

In another *camp* a great dance was taking place. The longer a missionary lives among the Indians, the more he is revolted by this remnant of heathendom. At seeing the dance for the first time, one has to laugh. The affair looks too comical: the happy faces of the Indians sitting in a round, the untiring beating on the large drum done by a circle of Indians squatting on the ground, while howling their barely changing song by the sweat of their brows, [and] the fantastically decked out figures of the dancers, who with the gravest seriousness hop, spring, and run about within a confined space. In the beginning all of this appears very comical to a person. Going to a second dance, one feels somewhat dreadful and watches in silence. The third time, a deep sense of pity arises; one cries, or would like to cry, and does not go there again. The demoralizing effect of the dance, in my view, does not so much make itself apparent in the dance hall itself, but rather outside around it. Here, you must know, all the young folk of the *camp* not participating in the dance at that moment gather, playing their loose game so that the devil must have real joy with it. How many times in one evening is a good part of our difficult work being destroyed for a long time to come! One must have been present at such a dance to readily understand how the devil is the prince of darkness, catching his prey in the dark. Having made my rounds around the dance house, I went on a nearby hill and, while praying my rosary, looked down on the chaotic scenes, and as I saw the burning fire flaring high and low, illuminating the wild figures of the dancers with its glow, and when I heard the eerie howling and the wild rejoicing, while in the sky the dark snow clouds were forming in a somber and threatening fashion, I could not help but think of the kingdom of the prince of hell and the wicked reception he will give to those Dakotas who so obstinately resist the draw of divine grace. I was long lying in my buffalo [sleeping] bag when the dance ceased and the frolicsome hooting of those returning home awoke me out of my light sleep.

The following day I baptized the youngest child of the chief. During the remainder of my homeward journey the dear God allowed me to admit another little one into His kingdom of grace, and then off it went with a lively trot down into the valley of the little White River and slowly through the sand up on the other side. From there the St. Francis Mission can be seen at a distance, and horses and driver draw ever closer to the dear home in good spirits. So also this time, and I was so much the more joyous given that the now completed tour had been harder and more bitter than usual.

Document 2.15
From: Volume 23 (1895)[32]
News from the missions. North America.

South Dakota. About the execution of the Sioux chief Two Sticks, the Very Reverend Fr. Florentin Digmann, S.J., from Pine Ridge Agency writes:

The execution of the Sioux chief Two Sticks, which ended his life on the gallows on 28 December 1894 in Deadwood, S.D.—as a result of his being charged with participating in the murder of four cowboys at Pine Ridge Reservation—brought to light the most diverse views in the newspapers. Without touching on these, I only want to report what I myself have seen and heard at his preparation for baptism and death, with which the Right Reverend Bishop Martin Marty had charged me.

Some weeks after the death sentence had been passed down, I wrote to Two Sticks and appealed to him to get on friendly terms with the Great Spirit before he had to appear before His seat of judgment. At the same time, I saw Mr. Phil. Wells in Deadwood. The latter brought me word that he [Two Sticks] very much wished to see me. In response to the remark [that] I could not help him gain freedom, [and that] all I was able to do and wanted to do was to prepare him for a blissful death, he replied: the latter was indeed all that he wanted; he wished to be baptized and wished to die like a man.

Shortly after my arrival in Deadwood on December 24, I reported to the sheriff and was given all the liberty to see the prisoner as often and as long as I wanted. Two Sticks was immensely happy to see me. He was permitted to leave his iron cage (cell) and move about freely within the confines of the prison walls. He was constantly watched by an officer, of which he himself was unaware, however.

Above the cells ('*cages*') there was an open, spacious area, whereto we withdrew and were able to speak with each other undisturbed. I soon learned that he had not yet abandoned all hope of receiving another hearing and of clearing himself of the crime with which he was charged. One of his fellow prisoners, a half blood, had communicated everything out of the newspapers to him, which was fostering this hope. Perhaps he and others did so to keep the 63–year-old man in good spirits; however, to me this appeared rather cruel, and in any case, this was not the frame of mind in which I was to expect a GENUINE conversion. For that reason I first went to his advocate, who is a Catholic, and in whom Two Sticks had put the greatest amount of trust, asking him to be honest with the poor man, [and to tell him] that he had no more hope for this world, and that he should take care to die a good death. And so it happened. He completely yielded to this news, and from that point onward listened to the instruction with a great deal of attention.—Because he continually protested his innocence in the murder, I primarily sought to infuse him with the thought of God's omnipresence, omniscience, and righteousness, from whom nothing was hidden, and who forgot nothing. When he nonetheless maintained his assertion, I pointed him to the Savior dying on the cross, who, Himself without guilt, has died for our sins, and whose first prayer had been: "Father, forgive them!" On this occasion, I told him that it was not whites who had delivered him to his death, but his own daughter-in-law and other Dakotas who had given sworn testimony about him. He said these had been great lies, and they would go silent if they were again questioned before him. He nonetheless forgave everyone. "During the war with the Crow Indians," he said, "I killed three men and took their horses, and for that reason I count for a chief among the Dakotas. But I have never taken a shot at a white man. If I wanted to kill whites, there is enough wood here in prison; I could use it as a weapon and slay all the whites here, but I do not want that."—Now and then his desire to live, go home, and end his remaining days in peace as an honest man, arose again. Then he did indeed say: "I do not want to die." I then led him to the Savior in the olive garden. "He too had a human heart," I told him, "and asked his father to be spared. But not as I want, but as you want, He added, and that must also be YOUR prayer now." He accepted this and was satisfied again. Entirely of his own accord, he took a small crucifix, which I had placed on the table during the lessons, kissing it affectionately and with reverence. I left it with him Thursday before noon. By the time I returned to him in the afternoon, he had asked someone for a small ribbon[d] and had hung it about his neck. I had no doubts about his good disposition, and in the afternoon of the same day baptized him Johannes Ev. The priest of Deadwood, *Rev.* G. Traynor, and his attorney, *Mr.* Wm. McLaughlin, were both present as witnesses. The confession of faith, the Lord's Prayer, and the responses to the questions, Do you renounce Satan, *etc.*, and, Do you believe in God, the Father, and so on, he recited with a firm voice. On the evening of the same day the telegram arrived from Washington that the president "refused to get involved," that is, to change the verdict. Two Sticks did not know that his attorney had once more interceded in his behalf. I thought it wiser not to tell him anything about it until the next morning, the day of the execution.

On the morning of the 28th, shortly after 8 o'clock, I informed him that he "would have to go today." He accepted this with his usual calm. The execution of the sentence was set for 10 o'clock in the morning. In the meantime I sang to him several of the beautiful songs in the Sioux language, which contained acts of faith, trust, love, and contrition, also praying these acts and other prayers with him, and he was in the best of moods.

Toward 10 o'clock the jurors came and the death sentence was once again read to him and translated to him by an interpreter. He stayed calm until the end. On the question of whether he had something to say, he gave a longer speech to those standing about. Its content, in short, was this:

"My heart is not in a bad state, but in a good state (that is, not sad, but glad). I have not committed this murder, the other four did it. One day the whites will recognize my innocence and will then be ashamed. My people too will be ashamed at receiving word of my death. My heart is good, and I love everyone. The Great Spirit has made the hearts of the people the same, those of the whites as well as of the Indians. I have a heart like the whites. If I was not innocent, I would not have come here so willingly. I do not say this to be freed, I know that I have to die; but I am not afraid to die, because my heart knows my innocence." He raised his hand as if for an oath and began his death song. He had always had a stentorian voice, but this time its sound was really and truly stirring. It was a short prayer to the Great Spirit, to whose house he was about to go, and which he repeated a number of times until I told him it was enough.

Meanwhile the straps with buckles had been brought in to bind him. The interpreter told him he had to allow his hands to be tied. He laughed heartily, and said: "This is not necessary, I will go like this all right." But when I indicated to him that he should remember what I had told him all these day, and should let it be done, he was immediately ready. At this point it became apparent that his right arm was stiff as a result of an old bullet wound and could not be bent backwards. Hence someone went to get a rope. This delay of about two minutes created an embarrassing scene and demonstrated once again that the wicked enemy is not asleep and tries until the very end. A number of straps were lying on a chair. Two Sticks took one of them in his hands as if for play, made a noose, threw it over his head, and tried to strangle himself. Then he took one step toward the iron bars only 2–3 feet away, behind which were two other Indians, Eagle Louse and Turning Hawk, intending to hand the end of the strap through the cross bars and tell them THEY should kill him. It gave the impression that he did not want to be killed by whites, although he did not voice that. All of this was the work of a few seconds. I extended my hand toward him, and called out to him to cease making another attempt. With the help of those around, the strap was loosened. I pointed out to him the evil of what he had done. He said only ONE word: "*inawachni*," "I wanted to make haste." Having admonished him to repent and having renewed together with him the act of contrition, I gave him absolution, given that he recognized his wrongdoing. Perhaps in the beginning he did not realize the malice of his attempt as such, until I told him that this way he had insulted the Great Spirit and could not enter His house. Now he was again composed and calm. As long as his hands were not tied, he, of his own accord, went to all those standing about and shook hands with them; he particularly pressed the hands of his defender and mine in an affectionate manner, and said: "You, my friends, have stood by me and helped me as much as you could; I will not forget you, and [will] pray for you when I get to the Great Spirit." He calmly let his hands be tied and with a firm step followed the marshal to the scaffold. On the way, he once again invited all those who came near him to shake his hand while laughing good-naturedly. After he had taken his position on the trap door and his legs had been bound, I once more recited to him in prayer the acts of faith, hope, love, [and] contrition, as well as ejaculatory prayers, especially the holy names of Jesus and Mary. As others noticed (I myself did not see it), he nodded by way of approval. Prior to this he had once again sung his Indian death song until I told him it was enough, whereupon he immediately went silent and listed to the prayers until the end. As eyewitnesses said later, the death occurred instantly with the fall, which did not take half of a second. A coffin had been prepared for him. Many came yet to see him. Everyone noticed how peaceful his features were, much more beautiful than he had looked in life. There was no reason to deny him a Christian burial, and so he was laid to rest in the Catholic graveyard on the same afternoon. We may hope that he found a merciful judge in the next world. R. i. p.

Document 2.16

From: Volume 23 (1895)[33]
News from the missions. North America.

South Dakota. The following letter by Fr. Florian Digmann, S.J., from the Holy Rosary Mission at Pine Ridge Agency represents a supplement to the recently published article *"Aus dem Missionsleben von [sic] Süd-Dakota"* [About mission life in South Dakota (doc. 2.14)]:

We are still struggling with the prejudice of the Indians that baptism was killing them, especially the children. It is difficult, frequently impossible, to make them understand that the children, due to their condition, would die regardless, even without baptism, and that this fear was nothing but a trick of that same enemy who deceived our first parents with his, "You will not die,"[34] and who, by contrast, now wants to keep the *Wilden* from the true life with his "baptism kills."

I had a striking case last November. I had visited an 84–year-old sick Indian fairly frequently, had encouraged him to let himself be baptized, had instructed him, had prayed with him, and with his consent, had already set the day for his baptism. When the time came, I once more repeated briefly the principal religious truths, recited to him in prayer the acts of faith, hope, and contrition, and was just about to administer the holy sacrament, when the old man suddenly changed the expression on his face, and said, or rather screamed: "No, I do not want to." When I pointed out to him that he, after all, had said two days earlier he wanted to be baptized, he repeated: "No, I do not want to, and if the Great Spirit, the Father, and His son were sitting here with me, I would tell them, too: I do not want to."

I was as if thunderstruck by this sudden change; one could think to be almost able to grab the evil one with one's hands, and to see him reflected in the features of the old man. "Go home and leave me alone," he repeated several times. I stayed, and after he had calmed down, I learned the reason why he no longer wanted to have anything to do with the baptism. The previous evening a young Indian woman had died, who some years back had been baptized a Protestant. He had learned about it this morning, and with that, the old superstition was reawakened in him. "In that camp," he said, "the children are baptized, and they are all dying off, one after the other; and a white man (!) had told the chief they were dying from having been baptized—the devil had created baptism to kill all the Dakotas." He stuck to that and his mind was not to be changed. "I want to be friends with the GOOD Great Spirit, but not with the one who created baptism in order to destroy us." All of my subsequent attempts remained fruitless as well. The old man simply pulled the blanket over his head and said nothing more than, "No, I do not want to." We, Fr. Bosch and I, could do nothing but pray with him, but he died without baptism.

Frequently, one gets from old Indians, men and women, the reply: "I am too old to have myself baptized." With many this means, as I convinced myself later: "I am too old to reconcile myself to the way of life of the whites," because they think this is part of baptism. With others, however, it is merely an excuse. They just do not want to break with their pagan customs and everything associated with them. When last year a certain Big Rib (*Große Rippe*), who was begging for food, responded to me in this fashion, I asked: "Is heaven only for the young, and not also for you old? Do you really want to go to the house of the devil?" When he answered "Yes," I said: "Good, then go there also for breakfast." That seemed to have put him off, for several days later he came to explain this fatal "Yes." "You whites," he began, "grew up with the plow and with tamed cattle; we with the buffalo hunt. You have entirely different customs than we (he meant the baptism). We pray to the same Great Spirit with the tobacco pipe; you pray in another manner." I: "Say, how many Great Spirits are there?" Big Rib: "One."—"And how many tongues does he have, one or two?"—Big Rib: "No, ONE."—"So, the same Great Spirit who created you and us has also created only ONE prayer (religion) as the sole path to His house, and you do not want to take it?"—Big Rib, pointing to a picture of the Sacred Heart of Jesus in the room: "You whites have killed Him and pushed Him away, not we; we love Him."—I: "It is true, whites have killed Him and many still resist Him today, but you, too, are one of them."

When he denied this vehemently, I reminded him of the Savior's parting words to the first Black Robes prior to His ascension: "Go and teach and baptize ALL nations, therefore also the Dakotas. But you do not want to let yourself be taught and baptized." He knew nothing to say by way of reply. He also had another conflict concerning his parents and several of his children, who had died unbaptized and who he would never see again in the afterworld if he allowed himself to be baptized. I explained to him that if they had lived a good life, and it was due to no fault of their own that they had known nothing about the commandment of baptism, then God would have mercy on them; he, however, could not plead ignorance. Since then, the man has been here frequently, returning to this subject of his own accord, yet so far without having arrived at a decision.

About two weeks ago another Indian, who has children here in school, came and informed me that his last born had died. I expressed my regret about the fact that it had not been baptized. It was only a few weeks old, and when we want to baptize the little ones, they say: "It is still too young." Two days later the Indian again came to the mission [with] one little boy of 3 and another of 5 years by each hand, and said: "You shall baptize these for me; I fear that all of my children are dying, and them, too," he added, pointing to his two wives. "The boys I will baptize right away," I said, "but the women have to be instructed first; besides, according to the law of the Great Spirit you can have only one." It is custom with them that when somebody marries the eldest daughter of a family, he most of the time also takes her younger sister to boot, now and then even two or three of them. This was the first case in nine years that a full blood and heathen brought me his children himself, for fear that they would otherwise die on him.

I have previously reported on another full blood, who is a catechist with the Episcopalians (vol. [22] 1894, p. 118 [doc. 2.12]). He attends our lessons quite frequently. Recently, he came to me alone late in the evening, keeping me until 11 o'clock. He repeated his old objection against the celibacy of the Catholic priests in a new form. "It is true that the Catholic Church was the first, but later on it changed and added some things, for example, that the men of prayer are not allowed to marry." Based on the gospel, it was clear that Peter had been married. I first asked him whether the holy John, Andreas, and Lucas had not been apostles and evangelists or disciples of Jesus as well, and yet had remained celibate. Then:

What, then, had the holy Peter meant by the words: "We have left EVERY-THING," if the wife had not been included in that? He thought, no, everything but her. Thus I directed him to the words of Jesus: "Every one who leaves father and mother, WIFE and children, etc., for my name's sake, will . . ." and to the other word: "Not all men can receive this saying," and asked him whether he believed that even the apostles were part of those who did not understand the saying?[35] It seemed new to him that the wife was also mentioned in this first passage; he wanted to look it up in his Bible at home. This man searches honestly, it seems, and will hopefully arrive yet at the truth and at peace.

Fr. Digmann, furthermore, adds the news of the transfer of the most worthy Bishop M. Marty, O.S.B., to the bishop's see of St. Cloud: "Nothing is known about his successor at this time. The Indians will not be pleased about his leaving."

Document 2.17
From: Volume 24 (1896)[36]
News from the missions. United States of North America.

South Dakota. The 7th [6th][37] **Catholic Indian Congress at Holy Rosary Mission, Pine Ridge Agency.** In previous years we have repeatedly referred to these general congresses of the Catholic Indians of South Dakota. About the course of this year's [congress], which took place on the 17th, 18th, and 19th of July at the Rosary Mission of the German Jesuits, Fr. Aloys Bosch, S.J., the superior of this station, writes as follows:

In more than one respect did the congress proceed in an even more pleasant fashion than the previous ones, as more Catholic life and work manifested itself. Why this was so, I myself cannot say with certainty. It is perhaps a natural development of the seed that was sown during the previous congresses, and besides, the Indians also continue to learn more about how to deal with their sodalities. The happy outcome of this makes me so much the more joyful given that the outlook had been fairly dim. A hungry stomach usually does not listen to the word of God. But it was exactly from this side that there loomed the greatest risk to our congress. Our new agent, you must know, had issued strict instructions to the Indians by which they were not permitted to use young bulls and old cows for the entertainment of their guests. Consequently, the question surrounding the stomach hung like a black storm cloud over the upcoming congress. In the end, there remained no other option but to open the mission purse and purchase the necessary beasts for slaughtering from Nebraska farmers. There were 18 head. The agent, in whom the hungry people had apparently raised somewhat of a concern, gave an additional 12 beautiful bulls, and with that the foundation for higher matters was laid, at least to some extent. Of course, there was the need to open the purse yet another time in order to also procure the necessary sugar, coffee, flour, and other odds and ends; but since the Indians always have this sort of thing available, the outlay was not that enormous. My Brother Baker probably had to feel this the greatest. However, his love for the Indians and the desire to contribute his part to the success of the congress only made him knead the dough harder.

Another point of concern was the manner in which our Pine Ridge people would be able to erect the large tent made of branches in which the meeting was to take place, as well as how my president *Weiße Antilope* [White Antelope] and his staff would execute the entertainment of the guests with justice and righteousness. But here I once again had the opportunity to get to know our Indians' calmness and prudence, and their measured manner. The tent was erected in three days; of course, there was also a good deal of sugar, coffee, and bread spent in the process. Yet *Weiße Antilope* performed the duties of his office with a calmness and prudence that would have been an honor to a German mayor of former days. In the course of the congress several complaints came in, it is true, but I upheld his reputation, and so everything went well.

The third point of concern was: How to receive the right reverend bishop? Not a word of his coming had arrived; concerning the mail, things generally looked hopelessly bad. Thus I received my own letters, which I had written while at St. Francis and in which I had announced my [forthcoming] arrival at Pine Ridge, only after being at the Holy Rosary Mission already for eight days. Could the letter from the right reverend bishop have gotten lost in the same way? If so, then the bishop appears all of the sudden, and the festive reception, a main event at the congress, is impossible! Yet there was an end put to this concern as well. There I was, standing down by the gate, directing several Indians into a schoolroom in order to instruct them, when a very familiar voice reached my ear. I look up, and here stands before me the Right Reverend Bishop Martin Marty, O.S.B., in a light gray duster. That was a surprise! His Lordship had not written me a letter at all, the reason being his weakness. He did not know whether he would have to postpone the trip for one or two days, and so he did not want to and could not settle on a day for his arrival. It goes without saying that we bestowed the best care on our esteemed guest, which was so much the more necessary given that His Lordship felt very much exhausted as a result of his journey. Yet all of that did not deter him from inspecting the entire mission with me that very afternoon, and pay a visit to the agent on the next day. It was on this occasion that he [the agent] delighted us with the present of the twelve bulls.

Meanwhile our Catholic Indians had arrived from the north and east, in a long, seemingly never-ending wagon procession. An imposing sight, but also one that aroused pity. I for one still had to suppress my emotion every time I saw the people and animals tired from their journey, many of whom came marching from over 400 miles away. And when they then meet the Black Robe, they stop, shake his hand simple-heartedly, and rejoice so much that their dark eyes are radiating with sheer joy. The 16th of July, at last, brought to us the dear Benedictine Fathers, Fr. Bernhard and Fr. Franz, along with the Fr. Superior of St. Francis Mission, Fr. Digmann, together with the venerable mother and several sisters (from Heythuizen), and now the congress could begin.

The ceremonial reception of the right reverend bishop was first on the agenda, and it proceeded in a truly uplifting manner. It was a stately, picturesque procession that started moving from the chapel to the arbor tent, with the bishop and the fathers in the center. How cheerfully the banners were fluttering, and how colorful and friendly the Indian men and women looked with their sodality badges! We had pitched the arbor tent near the meeting house; yet at the one end there stood a large square tent inside of which we set up an altar, because the service was to be held there every day. We accompanied the bishop thither. Following a brief and heartfelt address, all of the sodalities, first the men, then the women, came and welcomed their chief shepherd and the fathers. Thereupon the program for the next three days was read aloud, and finally a few practical hints concerning the food distribution were given.

Our itinerary was very simple. For the first few days High Mass was always celebrated at 9 o'clock. Fr. Zahm was the celebrant on the first day, and Fr. Digmann sermonized on the characteristics of faith; on the second day Fr. Digmann celebrated [mass], and Fr. Bernhard, O.S.B., preached on the love of God and charity. The right reverend bishop initially wanted to have high masses *coram Episcopo*, and only upon my persuasion did he yield; I feared with good reason that our chief shepherd could not endure it, and so we had only O N E high mass *coram Episcopo*, and that on the last day of the congress. On that day Communion Mass took place in the oratory at 6 o'clock, where a fairly large number of Indians received the holy sacrament for the first time; then followed a high mass, after which the right reverend bishop preached and administered confirmation, Fr. Digmann being his interpreter. More than one hundred Indians had the good fortune of receiving this holy sacrament, and the bishop spoke so beautifully and apostolically that it warmed the cockles of one's heart. His theme was the church and the workings of the Holy Spirit within the same and among the Lakotas, and, in the end, he recommended to his new converts prayer, work, and humble obedience, which he once more summarized in the rosary prayer, and all of this he most warmly commended to everyone's care. Following confirmation a Lakota *hymnus* was sung, wherein all Lakotas are asked to follow God's calling to the Catholic Church, and with that the 7th [*sic*] general Catholic Indian congress was closed.

However, if one was to think that hearing holy mass in common and receiving the sacraments were the only outstanding features of these congresses, then he would be mistaken. As at the previous ones, our Indians also held meetings at this congress, in the course of which they expressed all their sorrows and joys and plans and hopes. They had such a meeting in front of the bishop in the afternoon of the 17th, and the seriousness and enthusiasm with which the presidents of the individual sodalities spoke did not fail to make the most favorable impression. In addition to this large meeting, there were also many small ones held, and all of them had the one purpose: to promote Catholic life among the Indians. It was truly edifying [to see] how these simple children of nature already early in the morning gathered for the joint morning singing, or how they, in small processions, wearing the badges of their sodalities, visited the sick in the individual camps, to comfort them by way of song and prayer. I had a wonderful opportunity to observe with what intentions such joint proclamations of Christian life are taking place. We had a burial in the course of the congress. The Indians from Standing Rock thus came to me and said: "All of us want to come along to the funeral with all the badges of the sodalities and flying colors; that way your Indians will learn how they should bury [someone]. They do not know anything yet, but we want to show them." The proposal was of course accepted, and the example that was set will surely yield its rewards.

The farewell on Monday, the 20th of July, was extremely beautiful. All the sodalities had lined up down in front of the chapel and were awaiting the bishop. Until he came, they spent the time singing pious songs. His Lordship delivered a heartfelt speech to the gathered multitude, in which he entrusted the foundation of a Christian society, the sacrosanctity of marriage, to their care. Next he conferred the blessing upon everyone. Now the circle dissolved and those from Standing Rock and Cheyenne River, as well as the Lower Brulés and Crow Creeks, passed by my people from Pine Ridge Agency, shaking hands with everyone. And with that they went home, with the dear God and their guardian angels accompanying them safely on their long and arduous return journey.

In closing, I still want to convey three resolutions that the right reverend bishop let be adopted in the course of the large meeting on the first day of the congress. The first one was: Henceforth the general congresses will cease and only local congresses will be held, that is, the individual reservations are to hold their own congress. For next year only, a minor exception was made for the benefit of the Lower Brulés; they are permitted to come to the congress at Rosebud. This way the taxing aspect of these meetings will be avoided. And the Indians living far away will not have to neglect their households.

The second resolution was in opposition to the Kulturkampf [and] the way it has recently manifested itself in the Indian education system. The Indians were asked by the right reverend bishop to stand up for their Catholic schools and to strive for the same liberty that is afforded every citizen of the United States. Every citizen can do with his money as he wishes, yet the Indian money is used by those crammers of culture in the United States in support of nondenominational schools, against the conscience and will of the Catholic Indians. That is what they are to speak out against, and it will happen, no doubt. Whether this is going to have any effect is certainly another matter. In my view, the intent here is compulsory education of the worst kind.

The third resolution, of which I expect much good, concerns our sodalities. At least with us in Pine Ridge, there was not a differentiating mark between actual, functioning members of the sodalities and the candidates. Such was now decided upon, and thus we are in the position to press the rules more forcefully, and to accept only truly eager members into the sodalities. Yet, on the other hand, the door remains open for all the others: they can attend our meetings, look at the model of the good Christians, and should they like it, join as active members. May God give his blessings for these resolutions!

Document 2.18

From: Volume 24 (1896)[38]
News from the missions. North America.

Indian mission in South Dakota. Accomplishments and dangers. We have recently (p. 187)[39] spoken about the dangers facing the Catholic Indian schools from the American government. The following excerpts from a letter by Fr. Florian Digmann, S.J., from St. Francis Mission at Rosebud Agency, contain a few additional contributions. He speaks of the named anti-clerical decrees passed by the Senate, but thinks that "in one year, and with a new government, much could still change. Our faith is and remains in the dear God and the intercession of Mary and Joseph. Human beings cannot be relied on anyhow. The blow that is threatening to come from the government would be so much the more deplorable because the Dakota mission is slowly beginning to reap the harvest of a long and laborious apostolate. During the past ten years we have had 1,330 baptisms and 133 Christian marriages, in addition to the 324 baptisms and 10 marriages that had been recorded by our predecessors. The greatest difficulties with these wild sons of the prairie was created by the [our] demand for Christian marriages: O N E wife, and that in an indissoluble union. 'We are Lakotas,' was the excuse, 'and cannot marry for life.' Only the Catholic Indian congresses brought change regarding this point as well as several others. Their blessing is very visible and encouraging. Anyone who knew these Indians ten years ago and looks at them now is able to see the progress plain as day. 'Father, you civilize these Indians too fast for this government,' an

American (Yankee) told me recently. The gratitude culminates in the most recent law that INTENDS to make our schools impossible. It is evident that our influence with the old comes primarily through the children. But Uncle Sam wants to educate his wards to his own liking—without religion. Here at Rosebud and Pine Ridge, grand government schools are to be raised. Near the one here an artesian well is to be dug. They have gone down 2,100 feet already, and still have no water at the surface. Two million five hundred thousand bricks are contracted for. The brick-baking factory is near the future government school. A single downpour last month ruined 160,000 bricks. [Hot] water heat and electrical lights and all the modern achievements are supposed to make our children of the prairie happy. Well, let's wait and see. The soup is not eaten as hot as it is cooked.[40] In the meantime, we have gained a firm footing, and I do not doubt that our school will stay filled, provided the Indians continue to be able to exercise their free will."

Document 2.19

From: *Volume* 25 (1897)[41]
News from the missions. North America.

The question of the Catholic Indian schools. Petition of the Catholic Sioux of South Dakota to the government. In the previous volume we have repeatedly pointed out the unjust actions taken by the North American government against the Catholic Indian schools (compare, e.g., p. 187 [see note to doc. 2.18]).

This vital question was also one of the main points of discussion at last year's congress of the Catholic Sioux at Holy Rosary Mission, Pine Ridge, South Dakota (compare volume [24] (1896), p. 258 [doc. 2.17]). Prompted by the great Indian apostle, Bishop M. Marty, O.S.B., who in the meantime has passed away in the Lord, it was agreed to submit to Congress a petition to try and perhaps reverse the unjust legislation concerning this matter.

This petition was written by a gifted Indian by the name of John Groß, and reads:

> We Catholics of the Sioux Nation most respectfully and humbly ask & beg of the U.S. Congress now assembled in Washington D.C. that you revise the late law concerning the Religious Schools, commonly called Contract

Schools, according to which (law) these Schools should not receive any support from the U.S. Treasury from the 1st of July 1897.

We so say, because the money that is deposited for us in the U.S. Treasury is _our_ money. For the reason that the money is _ours,_ we are of the opinion, that they should let us have the (choice of) schools as we want & like them, either in our own country or in Cities; Government Schools (Public Schools), or Religious (Contract) Schools.

We do not say so because we oppose Gov't Schools or Schools of a different Creed; but we want you to let us have a School in which our children are taught our religion. Also our friends of other denominations approve of and join in our motion.

We want our children to be taught & brought up in our religion; for that reason we want you to grant our petition.

Please to consider this our statement and our petition; assist us and have pity on us.[42]

(Here follow the signatures of the signatories.)

Now follows the more detailed explanation, which must be called an excellent one in every respect.

This is the wording of the written appeal, the petition of the CATHOLIC SIOUX. They know that the parents have the natural right, as well as the duty revealed to them by God, to provide for the Catholic upbringing of their children, and that no one can deny them this right.

The child belongs first and foremost to the parents; it is the product of the parents and is provided for by them. The soul of the child is the direct gift from God, and to Him it belongs until the very end. The path that leads the child to this final destination is faith in the true religion, keeping the commandments, and use of the sacraments. The parents owe the child its upbringing and teaching. Indeed, one can read about this in the letters of the apostles, Eph.6.4 and 1 Tim.5.8.

No Christian father can shun this duty; he can never again allow that his child attends schools in which it hears nothing about soul and God, and faith and sacraments.

That is why the Catholic Sioux have assumed such a firm stance on this highly important question. Thus they will not leave any lawful means untried to save their Catholic schools, and for that reason they signed the above petition to congress.

In this undertaking they are counting on the support of all the Sioux, baptized as well as unbaptized. Because the Catholic Sioux are part of the Sioux Nation, they also have a claim to part of the Sioux monies and have an absolute and certain right to demand that part of the money is used for the Catholic upbringing of the Catholic children in Catholic schools. . . .

Their thinking is simply and frankly this: "When a Sioux sells a horse to a paleface, then the white man can do with the horse as he pleases; however, the Sioux, in turn, can spend his money on whatever he likes. Now the Sioux have sold the Black Hills and other parts of their land to the United States. They have ownership of the land, thus the others should also have free use of their money, even if it is deposited in the Treasury Department. Not one cent of the education fund of the Sioux represents United States money. Now how do these gentlemen in Congress get off saying that the schools of the Sioux are maintained with money from the United States? . . ."

Thus the Sioux had a right to their Catholic schools, which was also conceded to them in former times, but was now supposed to be taken from them because of sheer hatred against the church.

Along with their religious schools, the Sioux would also lose their faith, and devolve to the American belief system of the state, whose name is "indifference." And the complete decline of this free nation would therewith be sealed.

The author then cites a recent example where the children of two Indians, against the express wish of their fathers, were forcibly removed from the Catholic schools and coerced into attending the government school, because it was [otherwise] unable to continue due to lack of students. In response to a complaint to the commissioner of Indian affairs on this issue came this unbelievable answer: "The Indian parents had no right to choose the school for their children. . . ."

Well, this is compulsory education of the worst kind! And this tyranny is well felt by all those who know the significance of this forced measure.

They now recognize that such a word out of such a mouth is more than an attack on the rights of the Catholic parents, that it is a violation of the family rights of the Indian in general. . . .

Those in favor of the oppression of religious schools, on the other hand, argue thus: "The Indians are charges of the United States. However, a ward has no right to make choices for himself; he must be watched over." Yes, some of these gentlemen even go so far as to assert:

"The Indians have no conscience; they are fools; they have no idea whatever what is good for their children, etc."

Empty and unworthy excuses! The Indians of our days are neither children nor fools. And they were not regarded as such by the government, at least not whenever it came to making treaties with them and imposing laws on them, whose violations were after all subject to punishment.

Moreover, the government schools reportedly cost the Indians disproportionately more than the Catholic *contract* schools.

This truth is wonderfully illustrated by a comparison between the government schools at the Rosebud Reservation and Pine Ridge Reservation, and the two *contract* schools there.

> The construction of the government school on the Rosebud Reservation cost the Indians at least 73,000 dollars.
>
> The salaries of the teachers run to an estimated minimum of 10,000 dollars per year.
>
> For the 200 *boarders* (*Kostschüler*) the Indians must pay at least 33,400 dollars annually.
>
> The Catholic *boarding* school of the reservation, also with 200 *boarders*, receives for 95 pupils per *contract* 108 dollars for each; for the remaining 105 children, the school only receives the allowed rations of meat and other annual allowances to which these children are entitled, even if they do not attend school. The St. Francis Mission, that is the name of this school, thus educates 200 Indian children for **10,260** dollars, while the government school receives for the same number of pupils minimally **43,400** dollars per year.
>
> The Sioux are not so stupid as not to understand the difference between these figures!

A comparison between the Catholic *contract* school and the government school at Holy Rosary Mission is said to yield the same result. Hence the Catholic contract schools were reportedly at least three times less expensive and thus educated three times as many children for the same amount of money.

If nothing else, the financial side of the question should thus deter the government from attempting to destroy the Catholic contract schools.

Moreover, the Indians had a right to have a say in how their monies were spent. The petition closes on these words:[43]

> The Catholic Indians are confidently awaiting a favorable decision on the subject of their just cause.
>
> Should, against all expectations, the recently passed law, which forbids future payments, not be reversed, then the Sioux will nonetheless continue to send their children to the schools of their faith. While they will suffer injustice, they will seek lawful means to continue to do justice to the due welfare of their children.

Document 2.20

From: Volume 25 (1897)[44]
News from the missions. North America.

Indian mission in South Dakota. On page 299 of the last 632 page-long *Jahresbericht des Kommissärs für die Indianer-Angelegenheiten* ([Annual] *Report of the Commissioner of Indians Affairs*) can be found the official report on the status of the Catholic Indian boarding school at St. Francis Mission, Rosebud Agency, which the German Jesuits and sisters oversee. It reads:

> The total enrollment was 177; boys, 74; girls, 103; the average for the whole year being 164. The system of discipline at this school is firm and uniform, yet mild. The pupils are taught to comply with the rules more by a sense of honor and duty than fear of punishment. A good proof of how children felt at home is that we had hardly any runaways throughout the year. Formerly the runaways were encouraged by their own parents. Now even the old Indians, seeing how well their children are taken care of, are anxious to keep them at school. "I have come but seldom to see my boy," said one among others, "not to arouse his homesickness." I want him to become smart."

With the exception of four cases of aggravated scrofula, the health of the pupils has been very good. Though we have two large play halls, these children of the prairie prefer outdoor exercises, and we encourage them in it as much as the season and weather allow. Baseball for the boys and croquet for the girls were the most sought for open-air exercises.

The schoolroom work has been highly satisfactory, both as to the positive knowledge the pupils have acquired and the development of their faculties. The examinations held at the end of each term were a credit to the skillfulness of the teachers as well as to the diligence of most of the pupils. To promote emulation monthly reports have been introduced, the scholarship of each pupil being determined by a previously written examination. Those that attained the highest average were awarded prizes at the public closing exercises.

Bookkeeping was introduced for the more advanced boys and girls, and of these a few liked nothing better in the line of class work. The neatness and correctness of their books was acknowledged by visitors. Letter writing was encouraged and even made obligatory.

Adjoining the play hall there is a reading room. Good and wholesome reading matter has been provided for in the form of magazines and juvenile papers.

There being quite a number of little ones a kindergarten was organized. One of the sisters, being especially qualified and having experience in the work, has made an unexpected success. We hope for good results in that direction the coming year. One great advantage of the kindergarten is that the little ones pick up the language easier and are not so bashful as those of more advanced age.

The closing exercises were largely attended, more so than ever before; in fact, the large hall could not accommodate all. A new feature of this year's commencement was the lately organized brass band, under the direction of Rev. E. M. Perrig, S.J. For the short time they had practiced, their performance was creditable.

The larger boys have been kept busy alternately on the farm, in the garden, and the different shops, as stated in former years.

Tables, bedsteads, cupboards, that went out into the camps, made by our boys under the direction and with the assistance of the brothers, [as well as] mended wagons, implements, tinware, shoes, etc., could not be exhibited like the much and justly admired needle and crochet work of the girls, but surely tended toward civilizing our Indians. For the past ten years the neighboring Indians have freely drawn on the time of our mechanics, carpenters, etc., without being requested to pay a cent for either work or material. Our intention, however, is—and it has been partially executed this last year—to have as much as possible work done for them by their own children, and make them pay for it. This will gradually prepare them for what eventually has to come—to form villages with different handicrafts, not obliging them any more to go to the agency or neighboring whites for everything.

The girls have been particularly diligent in the sewing room, but are encouraged to take hold of every kind of work, so as to fit them for good housekeepers.

J. George Wright, our late agent, whose kindness and interest for St. Francis School we will long remember, had only words of praise and encouragement all these past seven years of his administration, and especially on his parting visit. All inspectors that have seen with their own eyes the work done at this school agree that it is "a good plant and an excellent school." The harmony existing between all the teachers and employees, the mutual attachment of children and teachers made especially this past year a real pleasant one. More than once I heard the remark: "Should this year be our last one, it would be like a beautiful sunset."

With regard to our missionary work I wish only to say that our St. Joseph's and St. Mary's societies, which I mentioned in a former report (1892), are gaining more and more ground and doing excellent work in civilizing and Christianizing these Indians. All of the members have declared their mind to take their allotment, facing boldly and not yielding to a strong opposition on the part of the old-fashioned Indians, who tried hard to pull them back on the old track. For the past ten years we have been breaking prairie. However, the soil begins to yield gratifying fruit. The most necessary thing to help these Indians along on the way of self-support is at present to have wells dug or bored for them, else they can neither settle nor raise cattle on these long tracts of waterless prairie.

So much for this report. It provides us with an idea of what the Catholic mission schools are doing for the benefit of the Indians. They alone are in a position to solve the Indian question in a positive way, for the benefit of this otherwise doomed people, as well as for the benefit of the government and the state.

Document 2.21

From: Volume 25 (1897)[45]
News from the missions. North America.

St. Francis Mission, Rosebud Agency (South Dakota). Sister M. Leopoldine of the Society of Heythuizen sends us the following report about the work of the sisters among the redskins of South Dakota, and about the visit of their new bishop for the purpose of administering confirmation:

> This year there are more than 200 pupils in the house who attend school, which is divided into 4 classes, and who are being instructed in how to work. Although working is a difficult matter for a redskin, things improve with every year that passes. Because the holy sacrament of confirmation had not been administered to our youth since the last visit of the all-admired, unforgettable † Bishop M. Marty, O.S.B., at our request the new right reverend bishop, Thom. O'Gorman, responded to the wishes of many by honoring St. Francis with his visit, as the first of the Indian missions that were entrusted to him. Great was the joy when we finally received a definite word that the right reverend prelate would arrive in Crookston, the station closest to us, on 22 May. Preparations for the reception of our new chief shepherd were made as best as possible, and no effort was spared to give St. Francis Mission a good appearance in every respect. The children prepared for the impending confirmation by means of devotions to the Holy Spirit lasting nine days. Every morning during holy mass, after a hymn had been sung, a special prayer to the Holy Spirit was said.
>
> At long last, the morning of the 22nd of May had dawned. The rising sun as well as the cloudless skies heralded a beautiful, sunny day. One looked out into the prairie probably a hundred times, as far as the eye could see, to spy a horse-drawn vehicle. Then, around 11 o' clock, we saw our wagon rolling in the distance. The alarm was quickly sounded. Some of our Indian boys sped toward the right reverend bishop on their ponies, calling out to him the first "Welcome Bishop" on approaching him. Meanwhile our two large bells were rung, resounding far across the endless

plain. The St. Joseph's men's society and the St. Mary's women's society, as well as the children, fathers, brothers, sisters, and other residents of the mission, moved in procession to meet the right reverend prelate. Our reddish brown women with their light blue veils, which are worn by the society members, must have made a special impression. "It is right and proper," said the old Indians, "that we sing one of our Dakota songs as we are going to meet the bishop." No sooner said than done. Genuine Sioux raised their voices, and the highflown tunes, frequently out of key, filled the air. Now the procession reached the church entrance. On entering, the magnificent double-sided sign, which on the one side carried the words, "*Ecce Sacerdos magnus,*" and on the other, "*Veni, Sancte Spiritus,*" must have been noticeable. It had been made especially for this occasion. Our cathedral, as it is called here, the second largest in his diocese, according to the right reverend bishop, was decked out in its finest decoration. As the right reverend bishop walked up the middle aisle, the choir sang the "*Ecce Sacerdos*" by Rampert in four voices. Next, standing on the high altar, His Lordship, for the first time and in a solemn fashion, conferred his blessings on his flock in attendance. With touching words he expressed his gratitude for the warm reception given to him. From the church it went into the hall, where the children sang a welcoming song, followed by a boy presenting a befitting address, and a girl, a festive greeting. The right reverend bishop again thanked his children in a fatherly manner and once more bestowed on them his blessings, wherein he emphasized that this time they were meant especially for them.

After a three-hour break for the noonday meal and rest, the right reverend bishop was invited to view the various areas, as well as the school and the handiworks of the children. "*Lead on!*" (*Voran!*) was the reply, and now it went from one room into the next, and from one building into the next. It takes a good deal of time, no doubt, to inspect the 16 different structures, yet everything was listened to and viewed with interest. In the evening the residents gathered at their favorite spot, the grotto of the Blessed Virgin Mary, which presented a magnificent sight, illuminated as it was by a hundred candles and by the torches of the boys. When Fr. Perrig, S.J., arrived with his band of Indian musicians, a hymn to the Blessed Virgin Mary was struck up, and the voices rose powerfully to the Queen of Heaven, who doubtlessly looked kindheartedly down upon the flock dedicated to her. Our dear chief shepherd was deeply touched as well. He came out to us and said that this scene reminded him of his visit to Lourdes, where he himself had been witness to three miracles. Then he recounted how he himself had lowered a man, one side of whose body was completely paralyzed, three times into the salubrious bath, and how he [the man] on the third time had emerged from it fully healed, put down his crutches, and had given thanks to the dear Blessed Virgin Mary. In closing, he encouraged all those present to have great faith in the dear Blessed Virgin Mary, for she had the same power here in the vast prairie of Dakota that she had exhibited in France.

Now it had become Sunday. After the solemn high mass and the enrapturing sermon of the most reverend prelate, the holy sacrament of confirmation was administered to 84 children. The adults will be confirmed this coming July, as the right reverend bishop will be returning at this time to attend the Indian congress. In the afternoon, our right reverend bishop, now no longer a stranger to us, was led into a tent especially erected for him, from which he was able to watch the baseball game of the boys. After a short time spent there he went to the meeting hall of the old Indians, where, as usual, speeches were given and this or that matter discussed. Around 5 o' clock everyone was once more assembled in the play hall, where the children, in honor of the high church dignitary, delivered some rather beautiful entertainment. On the following day our good bishop left us again. Surely, he will think back many a time on his first visit to an Indian mission, and we hope to see him in our midst quite often.

Document 2.22
From: *Volume 26 (1897/98)*[46]
News from the missions. United States.

Indian mission among the Sioux of South Dakota. "Since I wrote to you the last time," reports Fr. Florentin Digmann, S.J., from St. Francis Mission (Rosebud Agency), "our Indians have taken another considerable step on the path toward civilization. All the members of our St. Joseph's guild have, without exception, decided to accept their land as proprietors. The opposition on the part of some of the old chiefs and their nonprogressive kin was great, but was not heeded. The former probably felt instinctively that their old patriarchal influence would be broken as soon as communal ownership would cease and everyone would be the master on 'his' piece of land. The previously very limited and blurry sense of justice concerning private property is taking a more distinct shape now, and it is pleasing to see how this awareness pushes them to work to establish a home that they can call 'THEIR OWN.'

"When in the year 1889 General Crook and his commission were here to direct the Indians to take [possession of] their land individually, many chiefs came to me asking for advice as to what they should do. After they had informed me of the government's promises, I said to them: 'Go ahead and pick up the quill as a sign of consent; you will never again receive a better offer.' When the agreement was signed, I encouraged them to soon look for a good location near water, and to settle. 'If someone made you the offer to pick one pony out of a herd to keep as your own, who would wait until all the others have selected the best ones, rather than try to have the first choice?' Some listened to my advice and are now happy about it. Others waited and now have to take what is left. Not all of them can find room along the creeks; but on the waterless prairie they can neither live nor raise cattle if *Uncle Sam* does not have wells dug or drilled for his wards. For this year 1,000 dollars have been earmarked for this purpose. Hopefully they will be successful and continue with this in the coming years.

"The attempt to find an artesian vein has so far been unsuccessful. About 26 miles northeast of our mission the pipes stand 800 m[eters] deep in the gumbo soil and are waiting to be driven even deeper. Approximately 160 m below the surface an inexhaustible stream was struck, but it does not have the force or pressure to rise to the surface. The attempt will nonetheless make a valuable contribution to the geological understanding of this section of the earth's crust, and in the end, will perhaps be crowned with the desired success. In this case, the location would be an excellent choice: at the head of three dry creeks, called Wakpala by the Sioux.

"'Stock raising' is now the issued watchword for our Indians, and given their current stage of civilization, the right means is thus being applied. Our old Indians exhibited an unreserved joy at the fact that their land was declared grazing land and unfit for agriculture by the Great Father in Washington. We, however, encourage them by word and EXAMPLE to cultivate along with the grass, which grows by itself, also produce for their kitchens, as well as oats and grain for their horses.

"The government gave splendid horses to those who took individual pieces of land, but I fear that already in spring, every rib of these poor animals can be counted from 300 paces away. But this is not meant as a general statement. Many care well for their horses, build barns for them, or give them their own log cabins and build better ones for themselves. Progress will no doubt come—patience!

"Their own bill of fare consists of meat (fresh on beef-day, later dried); bread and coffee, with as much sugar in it as possible, for breakfast, the noon, and the evening meal; in summer a couple of corn cobs with it; for a celebration, a dog soup, this also when they run out of beef. I remember that as recent as ten or eleven years ago, when the Indians were begging for food at the mission and were served meat and VEGETABLES, they ate the meat only with bread and coffee, yet left the vegetables on the plate. However, this has long changed. Today they beg for potatoes, turnips,[47] cabbage, and the like. That is always a good opportunity to tell them: 'Grow it yourselves; it grows just as well at your place as at the mission.' Moreover, this spring several came to buy or ask for seed potatoes from us.

"As for the clothing, you no longer see any younger 'Toga-Indians'—the agent and his staff take care of that—and only a few old 'Toga-Indians'; almost everyone wears regular clothing. The same is true for the women. The Indian women belonging to our St. Mary's guild have decided on their own to dress like white women, and are proud of it. The girls who have outgrown school all have strict ordre from the government to dress appropriately.

"Now a word about the school. Our 'mercy contract' for the last year was for 90 pupils; however, we had already at the end of the first month 180 pupils in the house, and the number grew by the end of the year to 207, [with an] average of 195." This means that the government subvention is not enough by far, but it is at least better than nothing.

The father also reports on the obstinacy with which some Sioux hold fast to their old customs, such as their wild and, in part, indecent dances. "A chief, to whom I told the previous summer that he should finally cut off his braid, given that he is otherwise an intelligent person, answered: 'At the great Sunday in the summer (July 4th) I will once more appear in the full glory of Dakotaness and cut my hair the day after.' But he is still wearing his braid. As long as the whites run to their 'shows' (Indian shows), and admire their silliness, and pay with money, the Indians still have an interest in keeping them."

Document 2.23

From: Volume 26 (1897/98)[48]

The Sioux and Their Apostles.

About one century ago, the red man was still the all but absolute lord of the Mississippi and Missouri and of the vast forests and prairies that extended between the[se] two rivers, and farther westward as far as the chain of rocky mountains. Of "free Indians" there are only a few scattered bands existing today; all the remaining Native Americans are crowded into so-called reservations that project like islands above the surrounding flood of civilized America. Yet the Indian did not let himself be displaced from his ancestral dwelling places without resistence. He rebelled in despair against the superior might and cunning of the "paleface," and an endless chain of bloody wars and violent deeds marks the milestones of the advancing culture and colonization. The tribe that in this century has probably led this desperate fight the longest and with the greatest persistence, is that of the Sioux Dakotas. Its history is typical of the Indian policy of North America, and it should be instructive in various respects to briefly sketch it out.

1. The Sioux, now and in former times.

"[T]he [numerous] tribe of Sioux," as G. Catlin,[49] one of the foremost authorities and friends of the North American Indians describes them after his first visit to their country in 1832, "is one of the most numerous in North America, and also one of the most vigorous and warlike tribes to be found, numbering some forty or fifty thousand, and able undoubtedly to muster, if the tribe could be moved simultaneously, at least eight or ten thousand warriors, well mounted and well armed. This tribe take vast numbers of the wild horses on the plains towards the Rocky Mountains, and many of them have been supplied with guns; but the greater part of them hunt with their bows and arrows and long lances, killing their game from their horses' backs while at full speed."

Their ancestral seat at that time, as it had been during the time of Fr. Marquette (†1675), was the entire vast river basin of the Upper Mississippi and Missouri, westward as far as to the foot of the chain of rocky mountains,

northward to Canada, and extending southward to the northern boundary of
Kansas; that is, approximately today's Minnesota, North and South Dakota,
and part of Nebraska. Yet they were nowhere permanently settled, instead
changing their locations frequently, as hunting and war demanded it.

Catlin extols the Sioux—the way he found them back then, still representing the elemental forces of a free hunting people—to be the finest,
most powerful breed of men that he had met on his extensive travels. Their
appearance is exceedingly handsome and imposing, their stature tall and
considerably above the average of most other tribes. "[A]t least one half of
their warriors [are] of six feet or more in height." Their gait and their movements are light and elastic. Their feet and legs acquire an extraordinary
muscular strength due to constant exercise. The facial features are sharply
cut, the noses mostly boldly curved, true eagles' noses, the eyes small, but
sharp. The teeth are even and remain healthy until well into old age. The
life and activities of the Sioux in his wild and free state were focused on
war and hunting, and on the festive games and religious ceremonies that
introduce and conclude them. War was the true element of his life, and
the traditional hostilities among the tribes offered plenty of opportunity
to that end. Hunting was pursued partially for joy and as an exercise of
strength, [and] partially out of need, given that it met the prime demand
for victuals and precious furs. The boundless prairie and the thick, extensive forests at the time still offered an immense wealth in game of the most
diverse kind, and were the inexhaustible larder that the Great Spirit had
given his red children. "There are no parts of the great plains of America,"
writes Catlin, "which are more abundantly stocked with buffaloes and wild
horses (mustangs),[50] nor any people more bold in destroying the one for
food, and appropriating the other to their use."

It would be taking things too far to go into the details of the Sioux form
of government, their religious concepts, [and] their practices and customs
in war and peace; for our purpose it suffices to basically repeat Catlin's
general assessment. The usual, popular description, he says, portrays the
Indian as a beggarly, bloodthirsty scoundrel given to drinking. This was
slander. "I have travelled several years already amongst these people and
I have not had my scalp taken, nor a blow struck me; nor had occasion to
raise my hand against an Indian; nor has my property been stolen, as yet
to my knowledge, to the value of a shilling; and that in a country where no

man is punishable by law for the crime of stealing; still some of them[51] steal, and murder too; and if white men did not do the same, and that in defiance of the laws of God and man, I might take satisfaction in stigmatising the Indian character as thievish and murderous. That the Indians[52] in their *native state* are 'drunken,' is false; for they are the only temperance people, literally speaking, that ever I saw in my travels, or ever expect to see[. . . .] [T]hese people[53] manufacture no spirituous liquor themselves, and know nothing of it until it is brought into their country and tendered to them by Christians. That these people are 'naked' is equally untrue [. . .] [given that their dress is not only quite][54] comfortable for any latitude, but that they also dress with some considerable taste and elegance [as my numerous pictures portrayed from nature prove]. [Finally, it is very much up to question whether people] are entitled to the name 'poor,' who live in a boundless country of [beautiful] green fields, with good horses to ride [through them freely]; where they are all joint tenants of the soil, together; where the 'Great Spirit' has supplied them [in the streams, forests, and prairies] with an abundance of food to eat."

These were roughly the Sioux as Catlin had met them about 70 years ago. No doubt, the Sioux was a true *Wilder*, with all the dark sides of a culturally barbaric state. Bravery and cunning in war, distinction in the games and exercises of physical strength and dexterity, endurance and stoic disdain for pain, [all] shaped his highest aim in life. Cruelty against his enemies, idleness, and abhorrence for work, which according to his view was beneath a man, gross superstition and the like, were the deeply rooted flaws of his race. At the same time, however, he had many noble traits. His religion was mainly sustained by the belief in the one Great Spirit and the immortality of the soul. Hospitality, sincerity, a clear sense of justice, and a certain noble-mindedness were characteristics that he had in common with the other North American Indians to a greater degree than with the Native tribes of South America, and yet, what had the Catholic religion been able to do with those from Paraguay, Chile, and Peru, and so on!

It [the Catholic religion] would have revived the times of the old Huron mission[s] also among the Sioux, who Nicollet calls the ablest of all the North American tribes he had seen, had it not been for a ruthless policy of violence that stepped over them with a crushing foot, rather than elevate the inferior race to its own level. It was clear that such a freedom-loving and bellicose people did not let themselves be readily displaced from their ancestral dwelling places, nor be treated like an underage child. As long as white colonization remained east of the Mississippi, the relationships of the Sioux with the palefaces were the best. According to Nicollet, the officials of the North West Company unanimously confirmed these amicable attitudes. For 35 years the chiefs at their annual great councils had pointed out with pride that they had never soiled their hands with the blood of whites.

But the stream of white settlers pressed westward unchecked. Under President Monroe numerous tribes in the South had been pushed across the Mississippi, partly with fair promises, partly by force, in order to make room. Once settlement had moved into a northwestern direction, the vast tribal lands of the Sioux could not remain untouched for long.

The first treaty made in Prairie du Chien between the Sioux and the United States took place in the year 1830. In 1837 the tribe ceded its entire territory east of the Mississippi in exchange for an annual payment, and in 1851 agreed by a new treaty to also vacate all of Minnesota. How these treaties were made, and how little the Indians understood their implications at the time, we have previously reported on in detail (vol. [4] 1876, p. 133ff.). Until then the relationship had remained a fairly peaceful one. Back then the Sioux no doubt still constituted a force to be reckoned with and one that a smart policy enjoined to provoke. The rift occurred because the government agents did not adhere to the solemn promises made by the treaty of 1851, and disgracefully cheated the Indians out of their annual payments (see loc. cit. 134ff.). In 1854 the wrath of the Sioux flamed up like a prairie fire. One division of government troops suffered a surprise attack and was destroyed. This provided the desired grounds for a bloody campaign of revenge on the part of the North American general Harney. A new agreement put an end to further hostilities. Until 1862 everything remained fairly quiet. Then a new uprising began, brought on by the violence and the illegal advancement of white colonists into Dakota territory. The Indians submitted their complaints, but the investigations that were undertaken did not go anywhere. That is when the Sioux took up their weapons, attacking the nearest settlements of white colonists. More than 1,000 were killed; a great many women and children were carried off. The Sioux had become the enemy of the white man. Woe to the mail or the transport wagon that crossed their path! The ferocious, vengeful riders crisscrossed the country burning, robbing, and murdering, until General Sibley beat them in several battles and pushed them back into the prairies (compare vol. [4] 1876, p. 182ff., 201ff.). The defeated Sioux dispersed, one part migrating to Canada, another withdrawing to what at the time was the still unoccupied Black Hills, the "holy land" of the Sioux; the majority surrendered and even then were confined to reservations. In 1868 it came to a new treaty. By virtue of it the United States awarded the Sioux the entire part of Dakota west of the Missouri as inviolable property. Article 16 read: "The United States hereby agrees and stipulates that the country north of the North Platte River and east of the summits of the Big Horn Mountains shall be held and considered to be unceded Indian territory, and also stipulates and agrees that no white person or persons shall be permitted to settle upon or occupy any portion of the same; or without the consent of the Indians first had and obtained, to pass through the same."[55]

However, at the time the treaty was signed, neither the vast stream of immigrants to Dakota, nor the discovery of gold fields in the territory of the Black Hills, nor lastly, the consequences of the Pacific railway had been foreseen. Thus villages and towns were fast mushrooming around the Indian reservations: Rapid City, Pierre, Mandan, Bismarck, and other centers of commerce and industry. The number of farms increased, the constant influx of new settlers demanded new land and a direct link to Wyoming. The Sioux, for their part, pointed to their just claim and the solemn treaty agreements, and did not want to hear of ceding the Black Hills, their "holy land." The government offer to them of 30 million dollars in exchange for them [the Black Hills], which was supposed to be paid in installments over 15 years, was in vain. The answer of the Sioux remained no, and when asked to name a price themselves, they demanded 250 million so as to forestall any disposition to buy by virtue of the high amount. Massive outrage followed. The land speculators were putting pressure on Washington to respond at once and force the redskins to agree to further cessions. But the Sioux were deadly determined to protect their just claim with weapons in hand. The leading spirit of the resistance was their famous principal chief Sitting Bull (Sitzender Stier), who had also led the previous uprisings. Born in 1837, the son of Jumping Bull (Springender Stier), Sacred Stand (Heiliger Stand), which is what he was called back then, had as a ten-year-old boy already earned himself the name of a "brave" as a daring buffalo hunter; at 14 he took his first scalp and changed his name to Tatanka Yotanka (Sitzender Stier), which stayed with him henceforth. He was unanimously elected principal chief after the death of his father. In him the character traits of his people were personified: courage, attachment to the homeland, [and] hatred against the foreign intruders. At the same time, he was intelligent, calculating, generous to excess, and simply plain with respect to his outward appearance. All of this soon made him an idol to his people. By 1876 his buffalo robe already depicted 23 great heroic deeds in the form of colorful Indian pictographs. That same year a decision was made in Washington to break the resistance of the Sioux by force. General Crook was entrusted with the decisive mission. In response to his appeal to Sitting Bull to surrender peacefully, the same replied proudly: "Come and get me; I am ready." The war was long and bloody. Three columns of the army under General Sheridan simultaneously moved in on three sides against the Indians. On this occasion, on 25 June 1876, the now famous Custer massacre took place. By a pretended retreat Sitting Bull lured the daring cavalry general Custer along with his troops into a narrow, surrounded them during the night, and thus took the enemy into the middle. The entire squadron was destroyed; a single one escaped as a messenger of the terrible defeat (see vol. [4] 1876, p. 199f.). Although almost crushed by the overwhelming force, Sitting Bull nonetheless resisted with great courage for several months. When he saw that a continued resistance was in vain, he fled with a band of his followers into Canadian territory (compare also loc. cit. 201ff.). Asked to return and to move onto the reservations because of a new treaty, he replied: "The government of the United States has already signed 52 treaties with the Sioux, but so far has not adhered to one."[56]

Only in July 1881, with his band having been reduced to 45 men, 67 women, and 73 children as a result of hunger and the hardships suffered, did he deign to sign that particular treaty, which sealed the cession of the Black Hill territory. However, Sitting Bull had reserved the right to keep the weapons.

Yet for the Sioux even their remaining ancestral lands were not inviolable, but were taken from them piece by piece. Their territory no longer formed a continuous tract of land, but consisted now of the four reservations located far apart; Standing Rock and Cheyenne River in the north, Pine Ridge and Rosebud in the south of Dakota, so that the living link to the people was cut as well. As compensation they were promised 70 million francs [sic] and regular distributions of rations. This would sound nice enough if it were not known how little of these sums was actually used for the benefit of the poor redskins.

The government was in a difficult situation, no doubt. On the one hand, the unstoppable flood of white immigrants was pushing, and along with the rapidly advancing colonization the desire for new land purchases and new so-called [land] openings was growing. On the other [hand], there stood the undeniable native right of a [now] weaker race to the ancestral seat of its fathers, and to the promises guaranteed by solemn treaties. In theory, the system of reservations appeared like a tolerable solution; in practice it was and remained an unwarranted expedient, an act of force. It robbed the Indian of his freedom, it forced him without any transition into accepting entirely unfamiliar living conditions, and [it] delivered him fully into the hands of unscrupulous middlemen and agents. The extensive hunting grounds, his source of food until then, were taken from the Sioux, [and] the buffalo herds were exterminated; he also could not and did not want to become a farmer in less than no time, hence there remained only the degrading system of the distribution of rations, which reduced the proud son of the prairie to a hungry beggar. Yet the promised rations were not given to him regularly and as stipulated. (For the disgraceful embezzlements and frauds on the part of the agent see, vol. [4] 1876, p. 135.) "Great Father," wrote the Sioux in 1890 to the president (Evidence before committee of Indian affairs and Indian frauds), "when we ceded the Black Hills you said that we, that is, each one of us, was to receive three pounds of beef every day. But they are not given to us. We are starving and are asking you to keep your promise. We are given one oxen for 30 men, and that for eight days. If you do not want to believe this, send someone to us and summon several of us to you; our chief along with five others will go and tell you how matters stand. If you do not want to do this, at least give us an officer as agent."[57] The investigations that were undertaken found these complaints to be only too justified. Disclosures and warnings to put an end to this indefensible maladministration came from all sides. (Compare, e.g., New York Herald, 24 Dec. 1890.) Distinguished men of the military, such as

General[s] Miles [and] Sheffield, missionaries, and laypersons came forward on behalf of the suffering Indians. The harsh winter of 1890 took the
hardship experienced by the Sioux to the limit. In spite of this, hardly anything happened on the part of the government to mitigate the situation.
Thus the Sioux had no choice but to starve to death, to relinquish another
part of their still remaining land, or to rise up with weapons in their fists.
Several, like the Crows, tried it by selling [land]. On 9 December 1890, they
ceded to the government 750,000 ha of land for 948,000 dollars, a third of
their reservation. The majority, however, and especially the Sioux proper,
were adamantly opposed to a new cession, especially since until then they
had seen little of the payments promised earlier. The watchword was to
fight to the death, and Sitting Bull, who represented them in the main, was
once more called on to lead. The hatred against the palefaces again flared
up with its former might, greatly stirred by strange prophesies about the
impending arrival of a Messiah of the red race who would destroy the
whites, return the open prairies to the Indians, populate them with buffalo
herds, reawaken the deceased fathers, and make the children of the Great
Spirit free and happy. A genuine rage of enthusiasm gripped a large part of
the people. The intention was to break forth in the spring of 1891. (See the
extensive description of the uprising, vol. [19] 1891, p. 44 [doc. 2.5].) But
by that time General Miles was already moving in with his troops to nip it
[the uprising] in the bud, where possible. The best move, it seemed to him,
would be to seize Sitting Bull. Through the *scouts*, Indian reconnoiterers in
government service, he was informed that the old chief along with his selected braves was in the process of moving to the Badlands to unite there
with another tribe. A large division of *scouts*, followed by two cavalry squadrons and one infantry battalion under Captain Drum, were to block the way
of the Sioux. On 15 December 1890, this vanguard came upon the Indians.
The sight of the *scouts*, who the Sioux [Indian] hated above all others as
traitors to his people, inflamed their rage. One volley cut down those in
front, the others fled in retreat. Someone called for the advancing troops to
appear. A fierce battle unfolded. The Sioux stood firm in spite of the horrible artillery fire; the bravest shielded their beloved chief on all sides. Yet
Sitting Bull was surrounded and taken prisoner. At seeing this, the Sioux
summoned their last strength in an attempt to free him. That is when two
bullets hit the old chief, one shattering his shoulder, the other hitting his

heart. With him fell his son Black Bird (*Schwarzvogel*) and the elite of his warriors. (Vol. [19] 1891, p. 64 [doc. 2.6].) The death of Sitting Bull gave the fight a purpose. Some of the Sioux still made a desperate attempt to retrieve the dead body of their leader; the others fled westward, under Big Foot (*Großfuß*). Moreover, the remaining fleeing mass of the Sioux people was to be prevented from emigrating and brought back to the reservations. The troops of General Forsyth closed an arch from the north and south around the fugitives. The march of the Sioux was delayed by 51 heavy wagons carrying their women and children and belongings. It was easy for the *scouts* to track their movements, and on December 21, at Cherry Creek, the Indians found themselves suddenly confronted with an infantry division enforced by a battery of mitrailleuses, while a cavalry regiment caught them in the side. The Sioux realized that any resistance was in vain and surrendered without any other condition but that they be given the rations promised to them. One immediately proceeded to disarm them. Surrounded by the troops and faced by the threatening guns that dominated the hills all around, the Sioux warriors came together in a circle and laid their carabines down in front of them. But when the hated *scouts* stepped out of the soldiers' ranks to receive the weapons, a muffled grumbling arose. In an overpowering fit of furious rage against these traitors to their people and murderers of their chief, the Sioux gathered the weapons they had just laid down and shot at the reconnoiterers. Those in front fell, the others threw themselves flat on their bellies to give the troops a clear shot. Their bullets hit into the tight ball of men, women, and children with a horrible effect. The Sioux, with the courage borne of desperation, nonetheless tried to break through the fire spitting line. This forcible impact caused the troops' ranks to shatter. That is when General Forsyth let the mitrailleuses act their part. From all sides the deadly guns blazed, and yet the Indians continued fighting for more than an hour; they all wanted to die rather than surrender. And die they did, men and women, to the last person. Only six children are said to have survived this horrible blood bath. This cowardly victory cost the troops all of 75 men. The whole country was shocked at this barbaric slaughter. General Forsyth was removed from command and called to account in Washington. A cry of rage and anger went through the other Sioux camps which, in part, had already agreed to surrender. They still numbered about 4,000 warriors. But what could this dispersed, leaderless, half-starved mass of people effect? Thus it was an easy matter to force them into complete surrender following a brief blood-shed. Enclosed by a circle of bayonets and canons, they delivered their weapons on 16 January 1891. From that moment, the fate of the once so powerful and free Sioux people was sealed. "Civilization" had been victori-ous and was now in uncontested possession of the entire continent. A seri-ous resistance on the part of the red race is no longer to be feared. Its pride and strength are broken, and it only has the choice to either die out within a short time, or to create a new future for itself by giving up its national character and by completely absorbing the foreign culture.

In the above, we have briefly described how the government has solved the Indian question in this one case concerning the Sioux people; it now re-mains for us to see how, for its part, the church has defined and attempted to accomplish this task.

The first attempts at missionization among the Sioux extend back to the time of the old Jesuit missions in Canada and on the Great Lakes. The defiant disposition of these "Iroquois of the west," who even back then were described as the terror of all the neighboring tribes, foiled the plan for a Sioux mission, of which Fathers Isaak Jogues, Claudius Allouez, Mar-quette, and Druilletes had dreamed. The first missionary in our century deserving the name of apostle to the Sioux is the noted Belgian Jesuit FR. DESMET.

2. Fr. Desmet and the beginnings of the Sioux mission.

Johann Peter Desmet was born on 31 January 1801 in the small Belgian town of Termonde. At barely twenty he followed his distinguished country-man K. Nerinck to the New World, who had come to Belgium to enlist fresh troops, and there joined the Society of Jesus on 21 October 1821. Appar-ently destined for a different calling in the beginning, he realized in 1838, through a revelation from above, that a mission among the redskins was to be his true life's work. He henceforth dedicated himself to this purpose with heart and soul, until the end of his life. "He was," says the well-known Belgian author and scholar Godefroid Kurth in his wonderful character portrayal (Revue générale XIV [1878], 299ff.), "a born missionary. With a living, passionate faith, God had bestowed on him an unlimited readiness to make sacrifices, and an ardent thirst for souls."[58] His robust, primevally energetic Flemish nature made him equal to the toughest hardships. Added to this was a deeply poetic sentiment marked by a warm appreciation for the beauty of nature and the ability to describe it with unparalleled charm, a happy and childlike disposition, and a most ingratiating appearance and ability to interact with people: all attributes that made him an idol to his red children. What this man has done is absolutely miraculous. In the interest of the mission, he sailed across the Atlantic Ocean seventeen times, three times [on] the Pacific Ocean from Oregon to Mexico; twice he set across the Isthmus of Panama, twice he circumnavigated nearly the entire American continent by way of New York, Rio de Janeiro, Cape Horn, and San Francisco. Several times he crossed France, Italy, the Netherlands, and England on foot, and every year he went on average 2,000 miles through the pathless prairies, forests, and mountains. Kurth calculates that the distances he [Desmet] traveled add up to a good 80,000 miles, that is, several times the circumference of the earth.

This nomadic life was a consequence of his providential commission. Given the very low number of priests in the United States back then, and the enormous demands that the continuous growth in immigration made of them, there was no little danger that in the meantime many of the Native tribes would fall prey to the Protestant sects (compare Kath. Missionen, vol. [21] 1893, p. 49). It was imperative to beat them to it at all cost. The number of missionaries was not sufficient to immediately establish permanent mission posts. Into their place stepped a flying corps that hurried from tribe to tribe to secure the redskins for the true church by connecting to the widespread, still living memories of the Black Robes. Fr. Desmet solved this difficult task brilliantly in concert with a small group of fine comrades from different orders. The ground was so well prepared by them that had the government's unfortunate Indian policy not intervened like a devastating hailstorm, we would probably see in North America today the reductions[59] of Paraguay renewed.

The mission work among the Sioux represented only a single, lesser episode in the life and duties of Fr. Desmet. His principal work was the founding of the formerly, and in part, still beautifully flourishing missions in Oregon among the Plattfüße [Flatfeet], Hängeohren [Hanging Ears], Pfriemenherzen [Awl Hearts], and others.[60] In the summer of 1840 he had laid the foundation for this great enterprise, and in August of that same year hurried back to St. Louis, his headquarters, to procure people and resources. On that occasion, he came upon the Dakotas for the first time. Let us hear how he himself describes this first encounter which, as the great Indian Bishop Martin Marty, O.S.B., says, "shows so very characteristically the general sentiment that the Dakotas since then have always expressed toward the 'Black Robe.'"

"On the ninth day we were in the territory of the Blackfeet Sioux (to be distinguished from the *Schwarzfüße* in Montana). The country undulates and is intersected by innumerable small rivers. As a precaution we took our path through canyons. At about noon a beautiful landscape near a delicious spring appeared to invite us for a brief rest. No sooner had we dismounted when suddenly a dreadful, piercing cry startled us, and from the top of a hill, at whose foot we were encamped, the Blackfeet rushed upon us as swift as lightening. 'Why are you hiding?' the chief asked with a stern voice. 'Are you afraid of us?' Clothed in a priest's robe with a crucifix on my chest—the dress that I always wear in Indian country—I believed myself to be the object of his special attention. He asked the Canadian accompanying me (as interpreter) who I was. The Frenchman said, I was a chief, a Black Robe, a man who spoke with the 'Great Spirit.' He [the chief] immediately shifted to a milder tone, ordered his people to lay down their weapons, and now the handshaking ceremony took place, and the peace pipe was passed round. Next, the chief invited me to accompany them to their village, which was only a short distance away. It comprised approximately one thousand souls. At some distance from it I pitched my tent in a beautiful meadow near the banks of a lovely small river, and invited the chief to share my evening meal with me. When I said my prayer before the meal, he asked the Canadian what this meant. 'He is speaking to the Great Spirit,' was the reply, 'to thank Him for the food that he has given us.' The chief expressed his approval by nodding. Shortly thereafter twelve warriors in full war regalia laid out a large buffalo skin in front of the place where I sat. The chief took my arm and invited me to take a seat on it. I thought this was about smoking a peace pipe. Imagine my surprise when the twelve warriors took the skin, lifted me up and, led by their chief, carried me triumphantly into the village. Inside the dwelling of the great chief I was given the best place, and he then addressed me as follows: 'This is the happiest day of my life. It is the first time that we see in our midst a man who has such a close connection to the Great Spirit. Black Robe, you see here before you the most distinguished warriors of my tribe. I have invited them to this celebration so that they may keep the memory of your arrival for the rest of their lives.' He then asked me to speak to the Great Spirit again. I began: 'In the name of the father, and of the son,' and so on. All those present, along with me, lifted their hands toward heaven, and when I had finished, lowered them all the way down to the ground. I asked the chief about the meaning of this ceremony. 'When we raise our hands,' he explained, 'we make known that all of us are dependent upon the Great Spirit, and that he attends to all of our needs with fatherly care; we touch the earth to show that, before his eyes, we are merely worms and wretched, creeping beings.' He then, in turn, asked me what I had said to the Great Spirit. Unfortunately, my Canadian was but a poor interpreter; I nonetheless tried to explain to them the Lord's Prayer as best I could. The chief paid a great deal of attention to everything I said. He gave his son and two other very intelligent young men orders to accompany me to the fort so that they could thus learn the principals of Christian doctrine and, at the same time, serve as protection against possible hostile Indian attacks."

One can imagine how powerfully these first impressions touched the heart of the apostle. Although at that moment he was not able to stay any longer, he made plans to become active also among this forsaken people as soon as possible. First, however, the Oregon mission required all of his attention. In April 1841 he returned to that place with two fathers (Point and Mengarini) and three brothers, laying the foundation for the Indian reductions[61] St. Maria and St. Ignatius.

"It was a characteristic trait of Fr. Desmet," says Kurth (*loc. cit.* p. 708), never to rest in the enjoyment of what he had accomplished, but to always hurry to new foundings as soon as his work stood on its own feet." This was true here as well. Turning to the most diverse tasks, he continued to keep an eye on the mission to the Sioux. When in 1848 he once again returned from Oregon, he stayed in the Dakota Territory for a longer period of time to closely examine the country and the people, and the conditions for the founding of a mission. He did not, by far, find them as favorable as with the tribes in Kansas and in the distant Northwest. The Sioux were far more wild, almost constantly on the war path. When visiting one of their villages, he was a witness as a group of warriors was just returning from a victorious attack on the Mahas (perhaps Mandans). High on their lances fluttered the bloody scalps of defenseless old people and even of women and children. The warriors were welcomed with a deafening, joyful howling, and in the evening the missionary witnessed the wild scalp dance and the other victory orgies. This notwithstanding, however, Desmet was welcomed here and in other villages with open arms as an envoy of the Great Spirit. There was one celebration after another in his honor. Enormous portions of buffalo flanks and fat dog roasts, [and] roots and fruits were forced upon him, of which "a single one would last him an entire week." But the missionary found that Christianity had in some places already taken root here, being represented by a few hundred baptized half-blood Indians and mixed-bloods. Several hundred baptisms of children and dying older people, among them two ninety-year-olds, were the first fruits that Fr. Desmet harvested here. He told the red warriors about the great chief of the Black Robes, Pius IX, and handed out medals with his image, but he had to cease doing so because they were in no time used as powerful medicine and talismans. One [Indian] placed the coin with his war manitou which had already helped him to receive many a victory and wise counsel. It [his manitou] was a color print of the Russian General Diebitsch on horseback, carefully kept in a small box wrapped in deerskin. By now contact with whites had also introduced the Sioux to vices that were still altogether unknown among the tribes of the chain of rocky mountains. Thus the first impressions were not all too encouraging, especially compared with the exceedingly favorable conditions among the Plattköpfe [Flatheads] of Oregon. Yet Desmet hoped that with longer stays, he could still harvest rewarding fruits here. The number of laborers for this enormous field of work was unfortunately too small to immediately staff Dakota permanently.

Back then the country was still rich in game and buffalo herds, as Desmet points out, yet even then he expresses concern that these would be wiped out within not too long a period of time. Many smaller tribes were already living in great want of food and fell victim to the stronger ones. According to Fr. Desmet's report, during the year 1850 his fellow brother and countryman Fr. Christian Hoecken undertook a journey to the land of the Sioux under inexpressible hardships. Because the cold and heavy snows overtook him, he froze his feet and ears during the nightly encampments out in the open; a severe rheumatism affected both of his knees, and the [his] lame horse[d] was hardly able to continue on. On December 8, the missionary reached Vermillion, more dead than alive, only to press onward to Grand-Siouse[62] and farther after a brief rest. He, too, was received well and was implored to establish permanent mission stations. Everywhere children were brought to him for baptism, and the poor *Wilden* showed a touching devotion to the Black Robe. "Oh, how great and rich is the harvest!" he writes among other things to his provincial, "but alas, it lacks the laborers to bring it in. Thus one truly has to cry out in pain along with the prophet Jeremias: 'The children beg for food, but no one gives to them.'"[63] Indians and half-breeds promised him to assume all the costs if he were to build schools and stations among them. "The *Brülas* [Brulés], Jantons [Yanktons], and other Sioux tribes declared in a council meeting: 'The missionaries are not to die of hunger among us; we want to bring them an abundance of buffalo meat and skins so that they can procure clothing for the children in their care.' For the love of Christ, I implore you, Very Reverend Father, do not postpone the establishment of a mission too long. The good that Fr. Desmet and others have effected here, and the beneficial influence they have exercised on these people during their visits, will be lost if the redskins see that their expectations are frustrated. They measure the character of people only on the scale of loyalty and honesty. He who does not keep a promise is in their eyes guilty, even if the delay is a justified one, or an impossibility gets in the way. Several have their children attend Protestant schools, and there is a risk that this will happen even more if we do not settle among them."

This passionate appeal from the heart of an apostle did not remain unheard, even though the superiors saw themselves unable to respond to it immediately.

Unexpected circumstances worked in favor of the missionaries' plans. The discovery of gold fields in California in 1848 had started a migration westward. Contrary to the provisions of the treaty, the tribal lands of the red man were swarmed through by white adventurers. What did the rights of the Native tribes mean to the Yankee? But they were still powerful and the lords of the prairie. One should not provoke them. A peaceful agreement appeared to be the preferable way to achieve the aim. In a large council meeting, the government wanted to obtain concessions to create public roads across Indian territory and to secure them by forts. The affected tribes were to receive set annual payments and rations over a period of 15 years as compensation. However, because the negotiators did not like risking their necks, the government fixed its eye on Fr. Desmet, who knew the country and people like no other, and who at the time already had an extraordinary influence with the red man. He gladly seized this opportunity, which appeared to be so conducive to his mission plans. He did not suspect how shamefully his services would remain unrewarded and be misused later on.

On 7 June 1852, accompanied by Fr. Hoecken, he set out on his journey into the heart of Dakota Territory. The journey went from St. Louis up the Mississippi, which was extremely swollen because of rain and snow. Numerous enterprisers, adventurers, [and] traders had joined this secure retinue. Then cholera broke out on the steamer. Fr. Desmet was laid up with a vicious bilious fever, and Fr. Hoecken alone dedicated himself with devoted love to the service of the sick and dying. On 18 June Desmet asked for the last sacraments. The loyal fellow brother did not yet see an immediate danger and put him off until the next morning. But during the night Fr. Hoecken himself fell mortally ill and called for help. Fr. Desmet struggled to drag himself to the sickbed. Here the missionaries heard each other's confessions and prepared themselves for death. Fr. Hoecken departed this life toward morning. Fr. Desmet recovered, and in caring for the sick took the place of his faithful companion, whose mortal frame was buried on the banks of the river in the quiet solitude of the forest and later transferred to St. Louis. Having reached Fort Sully, Desmet learned that smallpox was raging among the nearby Yanktons (Santons, Jantons), Mandans, Minitaries, and Arickaras. Still weak himself, he hurried consolingly from *wigwam* to *wigwam*, bearing the blessings of the church. Finally, Fort Union was reached, where the agents of the republic were waiting for the Indian apostle. With them he set out for Fort Laramie, the place of the meeting. The journey took them 800 miles through wild and barely explored country. After six weeks of exertions, Fort Laramie was reached. Ten thousand Indians of different tribes, mainly Sioux, were encamped here, several miles from the fort on a large plain through which the Nebraska flowed. The negotiations lasted 23 days, and the peace pipe passed from hand to hand. A most wonderful order and harmony prevailed among the wild sons of the

prairie. Any national quarrels and tribal feuds were relegated to the background in their understanding that here, as children of the same race, they
were facing the power of the white man in order to demand from him their
collective rights. Fr. Desmet used this unique opportunity to exercise his
apostolate with an equal amount of passion and skill. He had a spacious
tent chapel erected on the meeting ground where he celebrated the holy
sacrifice in the presence of the officials, the attending whites and mesti-
zos, mainly of Canadian origin, and a large number of Indians. Every day
he took turns going from tribe to tribe to preach to the *Wilden* the law of the
true God. He found attentive listeners. "Father," as the chief of the Ogal-
lallas addressed him after a pronouncement of the Ten Commandments,
"we are listening. Until now we did not know the words of the Great Spirit,
and we admit our ignorance. All of us are great liars; we have stolen, we
have murdered, we have done everything that the words of the Great Spirit
forbid us to do, but we did not quite know these beautiful words, and if you
stay among us to teach us, we will try to live a better life in the future." At
the request of the redskins to explain the baptismal ceremonies to them,
which they had observed at the baptism of the mestizo children, Desmet
explained to them the nature and the effects of the sacraments. The result
was that they brought him their children, of whom Desmet baptized several hundred. The sum total of the baptisms on this trip was 1,586.—"One
could be inclined to believe that such singular sermons in front of an audience that was to disperse again the very next day to return to its pagan
customs, had been fruitless," notes Kurth. That was a misapprehension.
The still unspoiled North American redskin had a much deeper and more
introspective disposition than, for example, the light-hearted Negro. The
words of the missionary were akin to the seed kernels[d] airborne by the wind
to which the forests standing in isolated canyons owe their origin. Desmet
often enough came upon Indians who were all filled with the truths of the
faith and for whom baptism was the only element lacking to reach Christianity. How many times did he learn in the responses to his questions that
these men had ONCE in their lives listened to one of his instructions, and
from that moment onward had kept his words as valuable treasure in their
hearts and taken them to be their guiding star for their simple practice of
virtue!

Thanks to the positive frame of mind of the redskins and the influence exercised on them by the Black Robe, the negotiations had a very favorable outcome. Solemn peace was made between the attending tribes and with the whites, [and] the proposals on the part of the government were accepted without objection, as were the ample provisions and presents that the "Great Father" had sent from Washington. The Indians promised to faithfully adhere to their pledges. They were serious about this, for their honest disposition knew nothing of the tricks of American politics. Desmet, too, had great faith in the sincerity of the government. "Now there will be a new era beginning for the redskins," he writes, "one of peace. In the future travelers will be able to cross the wilderness unmolested, and the Indians will no longer have anything to fear from wicked whites." How bitterly were these expectations of a noble heart deceived!

His next task was solved, and Fr. Desmet returned to St. Louis with joyous hopes, accompanied by a group of Indians who, with naive amazement, admired the splendor of civilization. But their greatest joy was the promise of the Fr. Provincial that soon they were to receive a Black Robe to be with them permanently.

The following years found Fr. Desmet in a spirit of restless activity. In 1853 and again in 1856 he had sped to Europe to fetch new laborers and to promote interest in the missions to the Indians, which no one was better equipped to do. From year to year he sent fresh supplies to his establishments. In 1858, at the request of President Buchanan, he accompanied the army on its march against the "Latter-day Saints" (Mormons), and soon after carried for the third time the palm branch of peace among the agitated tribes of the chain of rocky mountains. One of his most extensive circular tours, across and halfway around North America, took place in the midst of the unsettling times of the Sioux uprising of 1862. Because his return trip led him through the territory of the rebels, in St. Louis they thought him lost. But not a hair on his head had been harmed, [he being] the only white man "who did not speak with a forked tongue." When he and his 60 travel companions were encamped in the wilderness on Milk River, they were suddenly attacked by a 600–man-strong band of Sioux. Right away Desmet fearlessly approached the enemy. His keen eye recognized several chiefs he had encountered before. One of them, Rother Fisch [Red Fish], chief of the Ogallala, extended his hand while joyfully exclaiming: "Why, this is the Black Robe who saved my sister." (She had once been stolen by a hostile tribe. Desmet had consoled the distressed chief by promising to return her to him. By a strange coincidence, the girl arrived safe and sound in the camp shortly thereafter, saved by the power of the Black Robe, the *Wilden* thought.) The word of the Ogallala naturally transformed the fierce attackers into friends.

Fr. Desmet was on his sickbed in St. Louis when word from President Lincoln reached him, requesting that he once more assume the role of an angel of peace by escorting the delegates of the "Great Father" safely from Washington into enemy territory. Desmet agreed right away, but subject to the condition that he would not have to travel in the company of the military or the agents, given that all of his influence with the *Wilden* rested on the title of "emissary of the Great Spirit," which they had given him. Otherwise, he explained, his black robe would no longer serve him as a pass. This stipulation, in a temperate form, effectively contained a devastating criticism of government politics.

No sooner was he restored to health than Fr. Desmet set out on this dangerous journey in the summer of 1864. He was indeed successful in appeasing the agitated Sioux. Yet their propositions did not satisfy the peace commission. In the spring of 1865, Fr. Desmet made a second attempt, and during the year 1866 we find him once more in the land of the Sioux, engaged in his work of peace and apostolate. He himself has described the experiences and adventures of these journeys in detail. He had to witness how the poor redskins were driven to the extreme by unscrupulous treatment [on the part of whites]. Shortly before the uprising, the Winebagos had been driven from their dwelling places, partly by lofty promises, partly by force. Two thousand of them had been brought to a "reservation" 3,000 miles away [from their home], simply deposited here in this barren desert devoid of game. "The complaints of the Indians," he writes, "against the whites are very numerous, and the acts of vengeance of the aggrieved are often gruesome and barbaric. Yet it is nonetheless certain that they are less guilty than the whites, and that in nine out of ten cases the provocation proceeds from the latter. . . . God alone is able to extinguish the fury and appease the hearts of the *Wilden* which have been [so] inflamed toward hatred and vengeance." In 1866, on the occasion of the Ascension Day celebration, 200 neutral Sioux had congregated around Fort Sully: *Yanctons, Gros-Ventres, Brûlés, Ogallalas, Sancties* [Santees], *Sioux-Schwarzfüße*

[Blackfeet Sioux]. Desmet shook hands with them as old friends, and they brought before him all of their grievances, told him about the cold winter, the famine that they had suffered, and about the great mortality that prevailed among them. The missionary did what he could to console them and to admonish them to keep the peace. This was no easy matter, for the government, their officials, and the colonists, by their ruthless conduct and breaches of contract, did their utmost to continually tear down what he had built. Fr. Desmet laments this with bitter pain. It was only due to the unlimited trust with which the *Wilden* invested him that his mission was a success. At the same time, he was once again granted the favor to continue the work of evangelizing and to bring his heart's desire, [that is,] to establish a permanent mission, closer to fulfillment. Everywhere he was joyfully received, not as "major," the rank and title the government had given him, but as the great friend of the red man and emissary of the Great Spirit. Among the *Yanctons*, where in the summer of 1866 he built for himself a plain log cabin for the purpose of a longer stay, he found one of the most noble representatives of the red class[64] he had ever encountered: the old Chief Pananniapapi (meaning, the man who beats the rice). It is a truly wonderful character portrait that Desmet sketches of him, showing how far the Indian could have been brought under the blessed influence of Christianity. In 1844 the respected chief had attended one of Fr. Desmet's lessons. God's word had fallen upon good ground and had borne the most beautiful fruits. Although not yet baptized, he had led a truly Christian life ever since, and was an extremely edifying example to his people. After 22 years there was at long last the day that he had so long yearned for, the day of his holy baptism. For hours he sat at the feet of Fr. Desmet during the quiet time of the evening in order to be introduced by him ever more deeply to an understanding of Christian doctrine. Even the whites had to respect the old chief and were amazed to find in a redskin such nobility of the soul, and such warm and deep religiosity.

In 1867 Desmet returned to St. Louis. Within four months he had traveled 2,000 miles in the midst of an average temperature of more than 45° C. He was in urgent need of rest given that his increasing age was already making its effects felt. *Kraeken de beenen, het hert is goed (Krachen auch die Knochen, das Herz ist gut)* [though the bones are creaking, the heart is good], he jokingly wrote on 21 September 1867. "I wish I could stay another two years among the Indians, especially among those who are on hostile terms with the whites. A large number of chiefs are asking me to please make sure to come to them; they appear to be inclined toward peace. But the time of year is already too far advanced, and my declining health requires a postponement until spring." In fact, we find him already in March 1868 back on the trail. The two generals, Sherman and Harney, charged with appeasing the still agitated Sioux, are impatiently awaiting the experienced leader and negotiator in order to resume negotiations in his company. Again, Desmet justifiably resists [joining] this entourage. "The Black Robe in the midst of epaulets will appear strange to the Indians and [will] not make a good impression on them," he writes on 18 December 1867. Thus he wanted to hurry on ahead of the commissioners and prepare for their arrival. But he was not given the time for that. On 31 March he set out on this important journey accompanied by the Generals Sherman, Harney, Sanborn, Terry, Sheridan, and others. It made for a memorable spectacle. Two peoples stood eye to eye across from each other, the powerful republic and a poor but brave nation of warriors, determined to engage in a terrible fight to the death. There was the probability that tides of blood would flow. Thus there steps between the two a venerable old priest in the much reviled robe of a Jesuit who commands—peace. Never had the remarkable power of this famed missionary over the Indians been proven so splendidly real. The majority of the tribes immediately bowed to his word. Only the wildest of them all, the 4,000 to 5,000 warriors strong *Unkpapagas* [Hunkpapas], did not want to hear anything about peace and reconciliation, but had withdrawn into the vast wilderness, resentful and dwelling on revenge, ready to strike a blow. After the successful negotiations at Fort Rice, Desmet volunteered to seek out the hostiles. The Indians themselves asked him to refrain from taking this risk. It would be his sure death. "The little ones," was the beautiful response of the old missionary, "the little ones in their sweet innocence are the darlings, the angels[d] of the Great Spirit on earth. But at home, in front of the image of Mary, the mother of God, the great mother and protectress of all nations, six lights are burning night and day, and thousands of these innocent little ones in St. Louis and in other places pray before these burning lights for the protection of heaven over me and those accompanying me. Thus I can trustingly submit myself and all of my cares into the hands of God." This word of pious faith was met with a loud echo. There were right away 80 redskins who joined as escorts. The Unk-papagas had withdrawn far into the Bad Lands (*Schlechtes Land*). They all were still heathens and knew the Catholic religion only from the reputa-tion that preceded the Black Robe. The difficult journey was a 16-day march, a distance of 100 miles through a desolate plateau, dissected by canyons. On 19 June [*sic*] Desmet and his escorts camped in Yellowstone Valley, and from here sent 4 envoys ahead to request a talk. They were well received and returned with 18 Unkpapagas. The Black Robe, such was their message, was welcome. The chiefs were impatiently awaiting him so as to find out the reason for his coming. But no one besides him was allowed into the camp; any other white person who entered it would be doomed. Desmet set out. On 19 June, 400–500 wild horsemen approached to bid him welcome. "I immediately had my peace flag mounted, which on the one side showed the name of Jesus, on the other side the image of the Vir-gin Mary surrounded by stars. The sight of this puzzled the *Wilden*, [and so] they came to a halt, appearing to take counsel with one another. They had thought this flag to be the American Star-Spangled Banner that they despise so. Four chiefs came charging at full gallop, went around the flag in a circle, and inquired about its meaning. Having learned what was nec-essary, they signaled to the others to approach. The troop of riders formed one long chain. We did likewise and moved toward them, with the flag in front, while from both sides loud shouts of joy were heard. I was moved to tears when I saw what a friendly welcome these still pagan sons of the wil-derness were giving the Black Robe. It was the most beautiful sight that I had ever witnessed." Now followed the indispensable handshaking cere-mony with every single one of the 400 to 500 braves, and the exchange of presents. With this escort Desmet solemnly entered the camp twelve miles distant, consisting probably of around 600 huts. About 5,000 warriors welcomed the arrivals as soon as they entered upon the camp's paths. A pleasant and spacious hut, nearly in the center, was assigned to the Black Robe. He was brought something to eat and, being fatigued, he laid down on his woolen blanket to sleep. Night and day a troop of braves furnished the honor guard in front of the hut. When he awoke, the four principal chiefs, *Vierhorn* [Four Horns], *Schwarzer Mond* [Black Moon], *Mann ohne Hals* [No Neck], and *Sitzender Stier* [Sitting Bull], stood around his bed. "Black Robe," began *Sitzender Stier* with a muffled voice, "the blood of the whites is on my hands. It weighs me down like a great burden. But the whites have started the war. Their injustices, their shameful treatment of our families, the horrible and outrageous massacre of 600 women, children, and old people, all have filled my veins with fire. I rose up, tomahawk in hand, and I have done to the whites any evil I could. Today you are in our midst, and my arms are lying beside me like those of a dead man. I will listen to your words of peace, and I want to become as good toward the palefaces as I have been terrible." The others spoke in kind. Hereupon a large council meeting was called for 21 June, at which the Black Robe was to make his proposals known to all of the people. It was held in an open area. About one-half acre had been fenced off by a high enclosure made of buffalo skins. Inside sat the warriors. Fr. Demet was led by the chiefs into the center, to a place of honor shaded by the flag of peace. First, old *Vierhorn* let the peace pipe be passed around according to the old custom. Next, *Sitzender Stier* permitted the missionary to speak by stating, not without dignity: "Speak, Black Robe, my ears are open so as to hear what you have to say." Standing erect, and raising his hands to heaven, Desmet first addressed a prayer to the Great Spirit for enlightenment and assistance. He then spoke for a full hour, first explaining the reasons that had moved him to come here, pointing out the danger that was threatening the red race from all sides, describing the horror of an unequal bloody war of annihilation, and assuring them that the "Great Father" in Washington wished that all hostility would be forgotten, and that he was extending his hand to them and the means to secure for themselves a better existence through farming, stock raising, trade, and through school and instruction. (It is not superfluous to note that several presidents and other American statesmen had, in fact, truly good intentions with respect to a just solution to the Indian question, condemning the present politics of violence. The statement of President Thomas Jefferson is famous: "Indeed, I tremble for my country when I reflect that God is just." "Our violent actions toward a people that providence has placed under our protection is unworthy of our civilization and rouses to indignation all human sentiment," the secretary of the interior had for his part declared in his report of 1856.[65] At the time, Fr. Desmet was still convinced that the intentions of the government were good.) The speech closed with the suggestion to send four delegates to Fort Rice to negotiate with the peace commissioners. The missionary had been listened to in absolute silence. After holding a brief council, the chiefs arose for a reply. Desmet has conveyed these speeches to us with utmost preciseness. They provide a valuable contribution to the characterization of the red man.

"Schwarzmond, one of the best speakers, was the first to come forward. He stood up and turned, peace pipe in hand, to the gathering: 'Lend your ears to my words.' Thereupon he raised the *calumet* to heaven and lowered it to earth, which in Indian sign language means to call on heaven and earth as witnesses. At his request, I touched the pipe with my lips and, with my right hand resting on the stem, I took several puffs. *Schwarzmond* did likewise, and let the pipe pass around. Then he began with a loud voice: 'The Black Robe has traveled a long way to come to us. His presence in our midst fills me with joy, and I welcome him to our land with all my heart. All the words that the Black Robe has spoken are wise, good, and full of truth. I have carefully retained them in my mind. But our hearts are bleeding, they have suffered deep wounds, and all of these wounds are still open. A brutal conflict has impoverished our country and laid waste to it. The torch of war was not lit by us. The *Sheyennes* [Cheyennes] have sparked it to take revenge for the injustices and cruelties of the whites. We were forced to join them, for we too were victims of the greed and iniquities. When we roam through the prairie today, we find the green in many places stained with blood. These are not traces of sweat from the buffalo and elk that were shot during the chase; no, it is the blood of brothers, or of palefaces who fell victim to our vengeance. Buffalo, elk, pronghorn, bighorn, and deer[66] have left our open plains, and they are found only here and there, far apart, and increasingly rare. Is it perhaps the smell of human blood that drives them away? The whites are cutting through our territory with their big roads of trade and of migration, building fortifications in a number of places, and are planting their thunder (*Geschütze* [guns]) there against our will. They shoot our game, and more than they need; they are cruel to our people, abusing and killing them given only the slightest provocation, even when they are out searching for game and roots to take as food to their women and children. They cut down our forests in spite of our opposition and without offering us compensation. They are completely ruining our land. We oppose their big roads that drive the buffalo out of our territory. It is our soil, and we are fully determined not to give up an inch of it.

Our fathers were born here and they have died here, and our graves shall find room on the same soil. We were forced against our will to hate the palefaces. They shall treat us like brothers, and the war will stop by itself; they shall stay in their settlements, and we will not disturb them there. But the sight of them coming here and erecting their dwellings on our land enrages us, and we are determined to resist this and die. You as a messenger of peace bid us nonetheless to put faith in a better future. Good, be it so! Let us hope, let us spread a blanket over that which has passed, and forget it. I have only one more word to add. Before the whole of the nation I give thanks to you for the good word that you have brought, and for the good advice and fatherly admonitions that you have given us. We accept your tobacco (*Antrag* [proposal]). Several of our warriors will accompany you to Fort Rice to hear the words of the peace commissioners who were sent by the "Great Father." If they are acceptable, then there shall be peace.'"

Sitting Bull spoke in the same manner. A thick blanket shall be laid over the past. He no longer wanted to speak of it. He accepted the message of peace from the east. If the "Great Father" was to leave the Dakotas unmolested in their territory and guarantee them this, then the *tomahawk* would be buried forever. After *Zweibär* [Two Bears] and *Laufendes Zicklein* [Running Kid] had also spoken in a similar fashion, the 2nd of July was set as the day for a meeting with the peace commissioners.

Thus Desmet had been successful in carrying out the apparently impossible work for peace. The chiefs and the people overwhelmed him with demonstrations of love and respect. After the last farewell visit of the chiefs, a large number of children, led by their mothers carrying the *papus* (*Wickelkinder*) [children in swaddling clothes] in their arms, appeared in front of the tent of the Black Robe. "I approached them and they, with an otherwise rare trust exhibited by the Indian youth, crowded around me to extend their little hands to me. The mothers were not satisfied until I had put my hands on the head of their youngest and on all of their little ones."

On 21 June, Desmet set out on his return journey. Eight representatives of the tribe and 30 families joined him. The four principal chiefs along with the core of young warriors escorted him as far as Powder River. Ten days later, Desmet entered Fort Rice. "The arrival of the reverend father," wrote Major-General Stanley to Archbishop Purcell at the time, "gave occasion for a magnificent demonstration of joy by the friendly tribes that were encamped around the fort. They went to get him in a festive procession. The warriors formed a long line and marched with perfect military precision. It was a truly memorable scene, although not really to the taste of the dear father."[67] On 2 July the large meeting convened, in which all of the Dakota tribes participated. About 50,000 redskins came together. Never in the last half century had such a large meeting been seen on the Missouri.

Peace was made. Universal jubilation prevailed in the camp. Gifts were distributed and solemn agreements were made on both sides; it seemed that everything would now have to stay this way. "I am convinced," wrote the aforementioned Major-General Stanley, "that this is the best and most sensible treaty that has so far been made with the redskins." The war that otherwise would have been inevitable would have cost the United States close to 200 million dollars. "We will never forget, and will never stop admiring, Fr. Desmet's selfless readiness to make sacrifices, who, although 68 years of age, nonetheless risked, without hesitation, making the long and dangerous journey through the scorching desert, devoid of tree or bush, in the midst of the summer heat, where he found only unhealthy and tainted water and was in constant danger of being scalped by the Indians. All this without seeking praise or any other reward for himself, but merely with the intention to prevent bloodshed, and where possible, save a few poor *Wilde*.["]

And the generals, who in the name of the government negotiated as war commissioners, did not hesitate to also pay tribute and offer their gratitude to this courageous missionary in writing. This important document is still kept today by the Catholic University of St. Louis.

It reads:

Fort Rice, D. T., July 3, 1868.

Rev. P. J. De Smet, S.J.:

Dear Sir.—We the undersigned, members of the Indian Peace Commission who have been present at the council just terminated at this post, desire to express to you our high appreciation of the great value of the services which you have rendered to us and to the country by your devoted and happily successful efforts to induce the hostile bands to meet us and enter into treaty relations to the Government. We are satisfied that but for your long and painful journey into the heart of the hostile country, and but for the influence over even the most hostile of the tribes which your years of labor among them have given to you, the results which we have reached here could not have been accomplished. We are well aware that our thanks can be but of little worth to you, and that you will find your true reward for your labors and for the dangers and privations which you have encountered in the consciousness that you have done much to promote peace on earth and good will to men; but we should do injustice to our own feelings were we not to render to you our thanks and express our deep sense of the obligations under which you have laid us.

We are, Dear Sir,
With sentiments of the highest respect,
Your Very Obedient Servants,
WM. S. HARNEY
Bvt. Majr.-Gen. & Indian Peace Comr.
JOHN B. SANBORN, Com.
ALFRED H. TERRY,
Bvt. Major-General U.S.A. & Comr.[68]

This man of God did not wait for the congratulations and outpourings of gratitude. Already on July 4, the day after the signing of the peace, he left Fort Rice and returned to St. Louis, everywhere along the way preaching the gospel to the tribes with which he came into contact.

He arrived at his headquarters, St. Louis, much weakened and fatigued from the terrible heat. His hearing also had diminished a great deal, and there were a number of signs that gave rise to the fear that his death was close. But his iron constitution kept him afloat once more. The very same year, 1868, saw the veteran off on a trip to Europe. He broke two ribs during a violent storm. He was thought doomed, but he recovered. After returning, he was, of course, no longer able to go on any extensive journeys, except for a couple of "nice excursions of 2–400 miles." In 1870 he saw his beloved Sioux for the last time, and for the last time did his very familiar voice resound inside the *wigwams* and military posts along the Missouri, consoling, teaching, issuing admonitions for peace. A complete breakdown of his strength finally forced him to return and to rest, something he had not known until then. Only in spirit did he henceforth roam through his beloved forests, mountains, and prairies, and rejoice in the reports of his fellow brothers, who were continuing his work, as well as in the naive letters[d] from his red children of the chain of rocky mountains.

Still more difficult than the afflictions and weaknesses of old age, were the bitter disappointments that were yet to be meted out to him shortly before his death. After all the services that he had rendered the government, the famed Indian apostle surely should have been able to expect that it [the government] would at least apply justice toward the Indians and the Catholic missionaries. The opposite was the case. Not only were the treaties not honored, but General Grant, through a disgraceful act of force, which with bloody irony carries the name *peace policy* (*Friedenspolitik*), took the majority of the Indian missions out of the hands of the Catholic Church which had founded them, and distributed them among the various Protestant sects. In spite of the freedom of religion guarantee under the Constitution, in spite of the protests of the Indians who demanded the Catholic Black Robes and no one else, about 80,000 Catholic Indians were delivered up to the Protestants in one fell swoop (compare among others 1873, p. 93; 1875, p. 26; 1881, p. 162).[69] One can imagine how deeply this forceful measure wounded the heart of an apostle like Fr. Desmet, who thus saw 50 years of arduous work partially destroyed. This preyed on his mind. Half blind, broken as a result of illness and the effects of old age, the venerable old man pulled himself together once more and hurried to Washington in the midst of the harsh winter to issue his protest and demand justice. But the die had been cast, and the gentlemen [there] did not have a mind to listen to the bitter complaints of a Black Robe. The Indians were quiet for the moment. It was believed that one could now dispense with the services of the apostle of peace. It took the last terrible Sioux uprising to open the eyes of those in power.

In 1872, to still be at least somewhat useful to the mission, the old man ventured out on another, his last, passage to Europe. Fifteen times, 17 times according to others, had he thus traveled across the ocean. A stroke in February 1873 reminded him to prepare for the journey to a better homeland. He watched death approach with a childlike calm, resigned to God's will. The thought of the prayers of the numerous little ones, whom he had loved so much and whom he had sent ahead to heaven by the thousands through holy baptism, created a special feeling of consolation during his final hours. In St. Louis, on 23 May 1873, on the eve of the Ascension Day celebration, he softly and peacefully departed this life with the kiss of the Lord.

3. Bishop Martin Marty, O.S.B., and his work.

The unjust measures taken by President Grant,—by which the future missionizing of the Indian agencies would be largely withdrawn from the Catholic Church and [instead] assigned to the "White Robes," that is, the different Protestant sects, against the protest of the redskins who were attached to their "Black Robes"—had at least ONE favorable effect. The Catholic bishops in whose districts Indian missions were located, drew together for a more determined, joint action in order to save what there was left to save. For this purpose the so-called Catholic Bureau for the Indian Missions was created in January 1874, headed by the archbishops of Baltimore, Philadelphia, and later St. Louis, which in Washington, the seat of the government, employed its own commissioner who was to represent the interests of the Catholic Indians in the name and by order of the bishops. At the same time, the bureau was to entice the Catholics of the United States to become actively involved in giving assistance and support to the mission work. By October 1875, the bureau was assisted by an aid organization founded by a number of Catholic women in Washington (*Catholic Indian Missionary Association*) which spread rapidly throughout the various dioceses (compare volume [4] 1876, p. 239) raising not inconsiderable funds. Moreover, it was especially important to add a new and able force to the badly thinned lines of missionaries.

In June 1876 the bureau turned to Reverend Martin Marty, abbot of the young Benedictine monastery of St. Meinrad, with the urgent request to provide missionaries for the most forsaken Sioux tribes of Dakota. "The Benedictines," explained the former director of the *Catholic Indian Missionary Association*, J. B. A. Brouillet, "with the dual purpose of their order, the [principle of] *ora et labora* (*bete und arbeite* [pray and work]), and with their large number of skilled lay brothers, are the right people to take the Christianizing and civilizing of such a populous and important nation as the Sioux into their hands. These fathers have once civilized Europe, and if any one is able to also civilize the Sioux, it is they. It will be their task, while instructing them in the holy religion, to acquaint the Indians with work, and teach them a love and liking for it, making good farmers, cattle breeders, and tradesmen out of them."[70]

The bureau had not been wrong in its expectations. It found in the distinguished abbot of St. Meinrad the man of providence who would finish the work begun by Fr. Desmet, realizing his plan of permanent mission stations among the Sioux.

Martin Marty was born on 12 January 1834 in Schwyz, in the heart of the beautiful Swiss country, a child of good, Christian parents who gave the church and the altar four of their sons. Unusually gifted, Alois, the eldest, began his studies in the then renowned Jesuit college in Freiburg, Switzerland, where the noted Fr. Deharbe, S.J., prepared him for his first Holy Communion, then continuing them in the excellent monastery school of Maria Einsiedeln after the Jesuits had been expelled [from Switzerland]. Fr. Desmet's letters from the missions had early on excited the youngster's heart and mind about the apostolate among the Indians. The sending of the first two Benedictines of Einsiedeln to the United States in 1853 further strengthened these desires. He knocked at the gate of the monastery, was admitted, and on 20 May 1855, he received the robe of St. Benedict and the name Martin. His first sphere of activity included the monastery school, and the pulpit, and the confessional of the heavily attended pilgrimage church.

In 1860 the foresighted Abbot Heinrich once again sent two fathers to the far west, where a new golden age was to begin for the time-honored Benedictine order. These were the young Swiss Fr. Fintan Mundwiller (✝ 14 February of this year in the abbey of St. Meinrad as archabbot of the Helvetian-American Benedictine congregation) and Fr. Martin Marty. At this point we are passing over the unusual merits that Fr. Marty earned—who since 1865 as prior, and since 30 September 1870 as first abbot of St. Meinrad has assumed the leadership of the Helvetian-American Benedictine congregation—by planting the young shoot off the old stock firmly into the new soil, and cultivating it to become an impressive tree. It is solely the apostle to the Sioux whom we want to sketch out here to some extent. For the energetic and still young abbot, the invitation from the Indian Bureau was like a calling from above. The dream of his youth seemed to become reality. He immediately jumped at the offer, and as early as July 1876, we find him, accompanied by a father and brother, on the way to Dakota. He personally wanted to study the new and expansive field of work. The Standing Rock Agency at the upper Missouri, in the heart of Dakota, was to become the foundation and the starting point of the Sioux mission. "Upon my arrival," writes Bishop Marty in a letter of 1 February 1883 to Bishop Chatard of Vincennes, "I found four tribal groups that are part of this agency, the Sihasapi, Unkpapa, Hunpati, and Wicijela, in a state of great excitement as a result of the Custer bloodbath (see April edition, p. 151 [see part 1 of this article]) that had occurred shortly before (June 25), and in which, in large part, their kin had been involved. The military mistrusted them, a station was in the process of being built, six companies of soldiers appeared in September, an army agent took the place of the civil administrator, and in October the cavalry went on a raid through the Indian camps in this and the neighboring Cheyenne Agency, taking the hunting rifles and ponies from the *Wilden*. The missionaries were advised to withdraw, however two rooms in the old log house at the agency were granted them, one serving as a chapel." The bishop is silent on his own efforts to calm the enraged *Wilden* and to effect their peaceful settlement on the reservation. One of the roaming Sioux bands under the leadership of Kill Eagle (*Adler-Tödter*) was causing trouble in the area. Trusting in God's protection and the influence that the black robe had on the Indians, the abbot courageously approached the horde, and he was indeed able to influence the Indians to cease hostilities.

The main threat to a lasting peace, which was absolutely necessary in order to begin the mission work, loomed from the noted principal chief Sitting Bull, who, as we have reported earlier, had together with his braves angrily withdrawn into British territory after having been crushed by the superior American forces. Abbot Marty decided to visit him and to pave the way for mediation. On 18 May 1877 he set out from Standing Rock, accompanied by eight Sioux warriors and an interpreter. The Commissioner's Report of the Bureau of Indian Affairs for 1878 has preserved for us a detailed description of this memorable trip. Bad weather and the ignorance of the guides slowed the journey. For five or six days they passed through an area that still abounded with herds of wild buffalo. On 26 May they approached French Creek, 60 miles north of the American-Canadian border, where Sitting Bull and his people had pitched camp. An Indian outrider announced the arrival of the Black Robe. Right away the great chief along with 100 mounted warriors came two miles to meet him with joyful songs of welcome. The black robe had not yet lost its magic power over the red-skins. Abbot Marty was led into the camp with honors and was assigned a comfortable tent. The entire camp, men, women, and children, came to greet him. "You are coming from America," said Sitting Bull, "but you are a priest, and as such you are welcome. The priest does no one harm; we want to give you food and protection, and listen to your words."

Yet his attempt to convince Sitting Bull to return to American soil was in vain. He liked it better in Canada, was his response. The English left the Indians alone; the Americans could not be trusted.

Marty stayed in the camp for eight days, each day surrounded by the Indians who approached him very trustingly, and who were in the best of spirits on account of the abundance of buffalo meat. The only thing that the abbot accomplished for the moment was the promise of the chief to remain quiet and not to take any action against the whites. Only in 1881 did hardship force Sitting Bull and his people to return to the reservation.

At the end of the year 1877, and in the course of 1878, Abbot Marty visited also two other noted Sioux chiefs: Spotted Tail (*Gefleckter Schwanz*) and Red Cloud (*Rothwolke*), chiefs of the Brulés and Ogalalla tribes, both close to 6,000 strong. Through an embassy to the president, both had once again urgently requested Catholic Black Robes after all of the Sioux chiefs, without exception, had already issued the same demand at the great council meeting at White Clay Creek (17 September 1875). It was the task of the Catholic missionaries to take advantage of the favorable sentiment, and the energetic abbot spared no pains in that regard. "I just now returned from my visit to Spotted Tail and Red Cloud," he writes in a report of 9 October 1878 to the Catholic Bureau. "With the former I had two conferences: during one of them we had a cozy chat, in the course of the second, the head chiefs were present. Spotted Tail opened the meeting with the following speech: 'We now live in an area that we have chosen with the permission of the president. For a number of years the palefaces were obliged to support us; in the future we will have to try to earn our livelihood ourselves. No buffalo and no game are left; hence we will have to draw our food from the soil. The soil of Rosebud (South Dakota) is not the best, that is true, but if you look carefully you will find here and there good plots of land, and you should not heed the distance to the agency, since you have to come here only once a week for the distribution of the rations. We will now need someone to show us what and how we have to do this. Now, this priest who you see before you has promised to come next spring together with other men and women of the church to teach us and our children. The Black Robe is the kind of teacher we want; we do not want others!' Following this address, two chiefs arose, an old one and a young one, to express their joy about my presence and my promise. When I, in turn, spoke to them about Christianity as the source of civil progress and also of material prosperity, they all made their approval known by a repeated, affirmative 'Hau, Hau.' Then I took leave by shaking hands with everyone, and left the tent. On 21 September, Saturday evening, I visited Red Cloud, whose camp of 500 tents or log cabins was at the time located 25 miles north-easterly of Rosebud Agency, on Little White Earth River (*Kleiner weißer Erdfluß*). I met him as he was just returning from a trip to the Missouri. It goes without saying that I was his guest that night. Rarely have I seen a more happy and harmless family circle. Given that Red Cloud and his wife were both already advanced in years, the three daughters prepared and set up the evening meal, having first looked after the wagon[d], horses, and harnesses, and turned over the animals to the care of the stableman. Two boys of 14 and 16 years of age came home at dinnertime. The grandchildren were the object of the most loving attention on the part of all the family members. On my arrival I gave each a medal of the most Blessed Virgin, and half an hour later I saw all of them adorned with it; even the boys wanted to put it on right away. In the morning the chiefs came to tell me how happy they were to see me; I should not leave them again but open a school and return next spring. 'As long as we roamed about,' noted Red Cloud, 'we have only lost time. We now have to follow the example of the whites. The land on which we are to settle appears to me to be better than that which I see around here, and if you come to help us and our children, I hope that we will make a good home of it. You will also remind the president to send us the promised oxen, wagons, plows, and cutting machines.' In the course of our talk I learned a good deal about Red Cloud's life and experiences, and I would not have been able to part from him so soon (the following morning) had I not had a certain expectation to meet him again next spring. My circular tour of the various Dakota or Sioux camps and agencies was herewith concluded. I found the entire nation filled with desire to receive Catholic missionaries, churches, and schools. Had I the necessary people and means, it would be easy to make them into Christians within a short period of time. At each agency there are two to four villages, camps, or settlements. Were there a permanent priest in each, he could guide and regulate their entire lives. The Indians, young and old, would congregate in the chapel each morning and evening; they would, under the direction of the 'man of God' work willingly. Two to three sisters could take over the school, and within a few years Christian faith and Christian life would be firmly rooted in everyone. Sisters for this difficult and laborious life can no doubt be found. Two religious orders are already at work: At Devil's Lake, the Grey Nuns of Montreal, and at Standing Rock, the Benedictine nuns of Ferdinand (Indiana). The Sisters of the Presentation from Ireland have, for the past three years, offered to tend to the education of the poor Sioux children. I cannot in the least describe the privations and hardships of the good sisters, and their efforts, full of blessing, toward all sides."

However, even more necessary were priests and brothers, continued Abbot Marty in laying out his plan. To win them [the Indians] over, instruct and support them, a Benedictine monastery would have to be erected in a suitable location in Sioux country, similarly built and organized like the abbeys that arose a thousand years ago in the wilderness and among the barbaric nations of Europe. Such [an abbey] would, like those in former times, become the focus and a rock of blessings for a new Christian nation. The wild prairie would flourish and resound with songs of joy, of gratitude, and of adoration. What was once possible in Europe could also be realized in Dakota.

One can see how farsighted the plans of this apostolic man were, how passionate and entrepreneurial his heart. Much of this beautiful dream has come true thanks to the energy of this abbot coupled with his zeal for souls, and of the brothers of his order, and assistants, and it is not their but the government's fault that the entire plan could not be realized.

Rev. Fr. Martin Marty had spent fourteen months in Dakota, getting to know the land and its people, had won the hearts of the Indians, and prepared the ground. Then his duties as abbot called him back to St. Meinrad, for the time being. From there he sent new forces into the mission, and under his supervision trained others for this new vocation. Given that this required in particular an intimate knowledge of the Dakota language, he obtained whatever was by then available in terms of dictionaries and the like via the Bureau of Indian Affairs (letter of 14 January 1878). He then went about writing a shorter grammar and a dictionary, translated the catechism, church hymns, and so on, and had the necessary supply produced in the printing office of St. Meinrad. He traveled throughout the east, gave speeches at Catholic meetings, aroused active support for the new work, and negotiated with the government in order to effect a harmonious association of state and church.

Because he could not possibly do justice to his dual position as abbot of a still young monastery and as superior of a large and new mission yet to be founded, Leo XIII, at the suggestion of the American bishops, named him the first apostolic vicar of Dakota on 22 September 1879. Marty resigned from his abbey, had himself ordained titular bishop of Tiberias by Bishop Chatard of Vincennes in February 1880, and transferred his see to Yankton City in the southeast of Dakota. For ten years he dedicated all of his energy to the difficult task of firmly establishing and regulating the ecclesiastical affairs of the new vicariate. Dakota, an area of 390,898 square kilometers, counted at the time about 133,000 white colonists and about 30–40,000 Indians. Almost everything had to be created new here. Posts for ministers had to be established, a *clerus* [clergy] attracted, [and] churches, chapels, and schools erected. But above all, it was his dear Sioux toward whom the bishop directed his care.

Standing Rock increasingly grew into a flourishing center: boarding schools for boys and girls were established, churches built, [and] farming and stock raising introduced under the supervision of able lay brothers so that the Indians of Standing Rock already in 1879 brought in a harvest of 25,000 bushels of grain and 8,000 bushels of potatoes (compare vol. [8] 1880, p. 236). From here there were soon new focuses created at various locations, such as at Fort Totten at the Devil's Lake Agency for the *Sisseton*, *Wahpeton*, and *Cuthead* Dakotas, [as well as] at Fort Yates for the *Schwarzfüße* [Blackfeet], Uncapapa, [and] *Ober-* and *Nieder-Yanktons* [Upper and Lower Yanktons], along with a ring of outposts. Had the government not continuously disturbed and impeded the apostolic work through its previously mentioned unchristian policy, the beautiful dreams of the ardent Indian bishop could all have been realized in time. In 1885 Bishop Marty transferred the mission of South Dakota and the two agencies of Rosebud and Pine Ridge to the German Jesuits, who along with the German Franciscan nuns of Heythuizen have been active there since the beginning of 1886, while the Benedictines retained the North Dakota missions. This paper has repeatedly and in detail reported on the two mission areas (compare among others, vols. 1880, 1886, 1888, 1893, 1894, 1895, 1896, and 1897).[71] Benedictines as well as Jesuits revered Bishop Marty like a father.

In 1889 two new dioceses were formed from the previous Dakota vicariate: Jamestown (later called Fargo), and Sioux Falls, the latter under Bishop Marty's crosier, a measure that had a very positive effect on the ecclesiastical development of the territory. In 1895 Bishop Marty, in need of rest, was transferred to the bishop's see of Saint Cloud, where he served for only about one year, however, given that God prematurely called the brave soldier away for a better life on 19 September 1896.

The highly meritorious prelate, an honor to the American episcopate and his order, deserves a more detailed biography that would provide more information than we are able to furnish here, particularly about his mission work among the Indians. He was justly called the "apostle of the Sioux." With an unshaken determination he kept sight of his goal to save the poor, persecuted nation by securing for it the blessings of the Christian religion and culture. What he accomplished in this regard with the support of fellow brothers of his order and the Jesuits, almost all of them, incidentally, Germans or Swiss, was evidenced, among other things, by the establishment of the general congresses of the Catholic Sioux which were repeated annually starting in 1891, which we described in detail at the time (compare volume [20] 1892, p. 16, 256; [21] 1893, p. 225; [24] 1896, p. 258 [docs. 2.8, 2.9, 2.11, 2.17]). These brilliantly demonstrated how deeply and earnestly the formerly so very unruly warriors had absorbed the Christian ideas and applied them to their lives. This is [also] attested to by the current status of the Sioux mission [as a whole], with its numerous churches, schools, trade schools, with its progress in farming and in stock raising, [as well as] with its two convents[d] of indigenous Indian sisters, in which the wild cuttings of the prairie have transformed themselves into royal flowers of Christian perfection (compare vol. [21] 1893, p. 179; [22] 1894, p. 267). Until his death, "Kamehacha," as he was called by the Sioux, remained the most devoted noble friend and father of his red children, who were attached to him with boundless love. The war of annihilation against the Catholic Indian schools, put into practice by government commissioner Morgan, a former Methodist preacher, was one of the most bitter experiences of the last years of his life, and as the president of the Catholic Bureau of the Indian Missions, he moved heaven and earth to divert this threatening blow, but without striking success.

The profound solemnity of his character, the measured calm and dignity of his appearance, the economical precision of his speech, endeared Bishop Marty most specially to the Indian, who recognized in him familiar traits of his own race. Actually, there was an exceedingly kind and gentle heart beating under the apparently hard shell. "When I once lamented to the unforgettable Bishop Marty about the runaways (in the beginning some of the wild Indian children had a difficult time adjusting to the mission schools)," relates Fr. Digmann, S.J., "he replied in his simple and gentle manner so peculiar to him: 'Make it as easy as possible for the children to feel at home.'"

"This brave, friendly, and popular gentleman," stated the obituary notice in a Protestant newspaper of the Northwest, "earned for himself the respect, the trust, and the love of the Indians by his immaculate life, the noble attributes of his heart and mind, and by his strong Christian character. In this way, he, like no other today, had gained influence both among the tribes that were for as well as those that were against the government. The mission stations founded by him among the Sioux are now forming the most excellent components in the education and cultural elevation of the Sioux Indians, and it is to be hoped that their beneficial influence will be retained with the necessary support and help."[72] The newspaper then tells of another characteristic episode in the life of the bishop. The old chief Red Cloud (see above) also made his appearance at the general Catholic congress at Pine Ridge Agency in 1895. "The stoic chief was hardly any longer able to walk, almost blind and suffering from numerous frailties of old age. But when he was told that Bishop Marty was standing before him, he immediately jumped to his feet, full of joyful surprise, and having recognized him, grabbed his hand, shook it with the greatest intimacy, and said with a trembling voice how happy he was to see and speak with the bishop one more time. A close friendship had existed between the bishop and the two chiefs Red Cloud and Spotted Tail."

"Bishop Marty," so the article closes, "has departed this world, but to the nation that he loved and for which he worked he has left behind the light and the teachings of an immaculate Christian life, marked by a combination of humiliation and unshakable energy."

Is it not immensely sad that the continuation and the successful development of this Sioux mission, which after so many sacrifices and sufferings is now promising such beautiful fruits, is once again called into question by the recent disastrous legislation hostile to Catholics?

Document 2.24

From: Volume 29 (1900/01)[73]
News from the missions. United States.

Mac Kinley's Indian policy. Plight of the Indians in South Dakota. "It was not very long ago that the world renowned Barnum Circus traveled through all the major cities on the European continent to give the inhabitants of the old world an idea of the life of the red man in the far west. Buffalo Bill's Wild West Show attracted large crowds of curious onlookers, and many probably took home with them a rather idealized picture of the free and unconstrained life of the Indians. However, this was only theater, or more precisely, circus performances that stand very much in contrast with reality. Allow me to present today, to the good readers of [Die] katholischen Missionen, the other side, and to give them a rough description of the Indians' actual situation.

"The presidential election with all its bustle and excitement has passed, and with it the hopes harbored by many for a more positive development regarding the Indian question have been buried. Right away in his first address to the senate, the president declared that he saw in his reelection an approval of his policy and intended to stay that course. The poor Indians soon found out what this would mean.

"The delivery of clothing to the Indians had already been suspended on 1 July 1900. At the same time, their rations were severely cut. Previously, they could, with some good will, still manage in some reasonable way. That is over now. These are indeed genuine starvation rations; namely, per head and [per] day: ¾ pound of meat, ⅓ pound of flour, less than half an ounce of coffee beans, less than 1 ounce of sugar, 48 beans of the smallest kind, in addition to that one pinch of salt and baking powder. The reader may notice that the poor people have no vegetables, no potatoes, in short, nothing to add to this. But these measures still did not seem harsh enough to these gentlemen in Washington. The elections had apparently given them courage. Thus, less than one month later, the *Commissioner of Indian Affairs* introduced a motion that, in the future, only schoolchildren and the decrepit should receive rations. All the others should get something only if they worked. Should this proposal be put into action, it would be synonymous with the complete destruction of the last remnants of the Indians. One does not work just at the drop of a hat. One has to learn how to do it, and, in addition, one has to have the opportunity for useful work. But the Indians have neither.

"Until now they did not have to learn how to work. The government took care of their needs as REQUIRED BY TREATY. All the food, [such as] meat, flour, coffee, spice, and so on, all the clothing, even wagon and harness, in short, everything was delivered to them. (By the way, not for free, but [paid for] out of the million dollar funds consisting of sums granted by sworn treaties in exchange for the vast territories ceded.) They had to worry about nothing. Every ten days or so they drove to the agency with bag and baggage, picked up the rations, and for several days lived off the fat of the land. The rations day was the sole object of their thinking and effort, and to be present on time their only concern. Why work, if the larks fall to you ready roasted anyway! Many a white person would have probably thought so. For a *Wilden*, who only a short time back knew nothing but hunting and warfare, it is not surprising if under such circumstances he gives in to his natural indolence. Thus the blame for all this trouble lies with the very same rationing system that they are now so suddenly trying to eliminate. It has made the Indian into what he currently is: a government beggar.

"It would be certainly unfair to accuse the government of not having wanted to instruct the redskins to work, but all of its attempts in this respect were blunders and have failed miserably. Initially, it was believed that the Indians should be made into farmers. They were given oxen, farming implements, seeds, and so on. But the oxen were not trained, and the farming implements were not available in sufficient numbers. The so-called *boß farmer[s]* who were to oversee and supervise the whole affair, frequently knew little more than nothing. Did not one [of them] once issue the order to sow wheat at the beginning of June. But the greatest obstacle was the land itself. The area here is altogether unsuitable for farming. Excepting all but a few places along creeks and rivers, absolutely nothing grows here save grass. In summer there is frequently no rain for two months, and then everything withers. What the heat might spare by accident, the sand storms, which race across the flat, treeless steppe with unbroken force, will ruin altogether. When I drove from the mission to the agency for the first time, I noticed on both sides of the way stretches of land the size of an acre, on which there was nothing growing at all. I inquired about the reason. 'Here the Indians were obliged to plow in times past,' my travel companion said, '[and] today, not even grass grows there any more.' With such mismanagement most whites, too, would have surely given up farming. To toil year after year by the sweat of one's brow without seeing any success whatsoever, requires a certain degree of heroism and a great deal of love and joy for work, which, from a rational point of view, may not be presumed of a *Wilden*.

"Finally, the government also came to its better senses and tried it with stock raising. Now this was a step in the right direction, no doubt. But on 640 *acres* of arid prairie soil, one cannot raise enough cattle to feed a family. Thus there is also no salvation to be expected from this, as long as they [the Indians] are unable to engage in stock raising on a larger scale.

"As is abundantly evident by the aforementioned statements, the Indians cannot get any work, much as they would like. Where there is no industry and no farming, there is also no need for wage laborers. The government itself does nothing to supply them with earnings. Although it would not only be useful, but even most necessary, to repair the bad roads, create irrigation systems, provide for the growth of young wood, [and] build bridges—all of which are tasks for which the Indians could render some good assistance and could earn a decent amount of money—yet, whether intentionally or unintentionally, nothing is happening. Thus, no matter where the poor redskins turn, they are faced with poverty and misery everywhere. Even if they wanted to work—and they want to, necessity forces them—they cannot find work anywhere. They come to the mission in droves, asking for permission to fetch freight, but what is that for so many? Dozens of them loiter about our house every day, begging for the leftovers from the meals. It is a very sad sight to see these haggard, starved figures. A slow death from starvation is their certain destiny. They sell off their horses and their other livestock for a trifling sum, just to manage to live; but there probably will be no peace until even the last remnants of this once so proud nation have disappeared.

"And how do the Indians take all of this? An experienced missionary recently wrote: 'I would not be surprised if the Indians, driven to desperation by hunger, would soon go on the warpath again, as they did ten years ago.' This agitation and general dissatisfaction is not recent. Already in August 1899 the agent of Standing Rock Agency wrote the following in his official report to the Indian commissioner:[74]

"'The Indians are most dissatisfied about their rations having been cut last year, and clouds are gathering. The Indians complain that their treaties with the government are not being abided by. They are holding meetings and are discussing the matter, are recalling old times and customs, and are longing for their return. One cannot find fault with the Indians on account of this dissatisfaction. A couple of days ago, one of the chiefs remarked that it was merely a matter of time, and the sooner they would strike, the better, for they could just as well let themselves be struck dead as allow themselves to be starved to death. He was told not to speak in such a way again, yet I cannot give them a reason for why they are not receiving their full rations.' So much for this Indian agent.

"When in January of last year the Indian agents were meeting in Washington, there were several chiefs who wanted to go there as well. A benevolent friend of the Indians advised one of the chiefs against it: 'You were not summoned and you will not be granted a hearing.' 'We know by now,' he said by way of reply, 'that the "Great Father" wants to see us only when he needs land from us. We will now go at our own expense; if he does not look upon us, we will be ashamed.' 'You want to go on the warpath again? That would probably be the last time; this time the whites would no longer have pity on you, as they did the last time.' 'Just as well. It would be better for us to rest in the grave than to prolong this miserable life.'

"One can tell, the situation is very serious. Already at the beginning of the fall the Sioux Indians held a meeting at which they resolved to sue the government for breach of contract. However, the *Commissioner of Indian Affairs* denied them permission to retain legal counsel. At the end of January of this year they held another meeting at White River. Because of the fear of smallpox, which was just then raging at the border of the reservation, several reservations were not represented, and so there was a no quorum.

"Just as I am writing these lines, the following news is circulating in the papers:[5]

"'The Sioux Indians are dissatisfied with their situation and are threatening an uprising should the "Great Father in Washington" not listen to their demands. The various tribes are meeting in councils, and the Ogallalla Sioux insist on calling the "great council" to decide on war or peace. The Indian commissioner has roused the red wards to anger by the recent order that the distribution to the Sioux of food and goods for everyday use is to be reduced. One of the chiefs has openly declared that the Sioux would go on the warpath if the federal government would not soon guarantee full pots of meat again.'

"Well, whatever the outcome of all of this may be, it is surely not owing to the government if it does not come to a bloody uprising. It [the government] is then only indebted to the influence of the missionaries and the most despised mission schools.

"One more word on this subject. As it is known to the readers from previous reports, the government has withdrawn all support from the mission schools. They are in a position of in loco parentis, as the official term reads, that is, they receive for their pupils only the starvation rations that the children would receive at home with their parents. Yet nothing is taken away from those who attend the nondenominational government school; they receive the full rations as before and, in addition, are being dressed well at government expense. The very same government that two decades ago invited the various mission societies to establish schools and missions among the Indians, promising them government support, is now indulging in this flagrant injustice. They could take court action against the government for breach of contract, as one Protestant mission organization has already done with success. But the Catholic missionary cannot be satisfied with a sum paid in settlement of all claims and then move on. His concern is for the salvation of the immortal souls, and not for earthly gain. He would think of himself as a miserable procurer of souls if he lowered himself to such an action. No, the missionaries are determined more than ever to persevere at their posts as long as it pleases God and the Catholic love and charity bestows on them what is most essential for those in their care. The Indians themselves can hardly manage to live, let alone support the mission. Thus, in their name, the missionaries turn to their brothers in faith with the words of the patient Job: 'Have pity on me, have pity on me, O you my friends, for the hand of God is heavy upon me!'[76] In spite of all the enticing prospects at the government schools, the redskins prefer to send their children to the school of the Black Robe. The number of pupils this year is the same as in times past. We could get many more pupils—the superior of St. Francis Mission, for example, received no fewer than 80 new registrations—but lack of space and the superintendence of Uncle Sam allowed him only 22. One's heart truly bleeds at the thought of having to refuse admittance to so many children, who then grow up in the government schools without God and without Christianity, and who later, in their misery, also have to do without the comfort of religion."

To this statement of a young missionary, Mr. Wilh. Kratz, S.J., we add some words from the mission superior Fr. J. Rockliff, S.J. "Unless Catholic charity comes to our aid," he writes, "and provides a substitute for the former government grants, we will probably have to close the schools sooner or later. If this happens, the Catholic Church will lose its footing among the Indian population. This dying race can only be won by way of their children, and for them there is no salvation except through Catholic schools."

Members of the Orders Who Served at the St. Francis and Holy Rosary Missions

Listed below are the names of all the missionaries who served the two missions from 1886 to about 1900, including each person's place and year of birth. Variations in the spelling of some of the names are in parentheses; the place-names are written as they appear in the sources. Question marks are inserted in those instances where doubts about the names or places of birth exist due to incomplete or inconsistent information contained in the sources. The information on the Jesuits is from the personnel catalogues of the German Province. Brother Markus Pillat, S.J. (Köln), collected the biographical information. The register of the Franciscan nuns is drawn from sources located at Stella Niagara, New York, specifically one register compiled by Mary Serbacki, O.S.F. and supplemented with information provided by Sister Hildegardis Schäfer, O.S.F. (Nonnenwerth). The first names listed here are those assumed by the sisters upon entering the order; they included male names.

1. Jesuits

Fathers
Bosch, Alois, b. 1852 in Augsburg
Digmann (Digman), Florentin, b. 1846 in Heiligenstadt
Eberschweiler, Karl, b. 1841 in Waxweiler
Jutz, Johann, b. 1838 in Frastanz, Vorarlberg
Lindebner, Joseph, b. 1845 in Mainz
Perrig, Emil, b. 1846 in Brig

Brothers
Aufenberg, Joseph, b. 1862 in Reydt
Axt, Anton, b. 1862 in Petersburg, Hessen-Nassau
Berclaz, Vinzenz, b. 1855 in Darnona, Vallais
Bickel, Joseph, b. 1848 in Sonntag, Vorarlberg
Billing, Heinrich, b. 1861 in Malgarten, Hannover
Bous (Bues, Bons), Joseph, b. 1840 in Niedermendig, Rheinland
Brand, Franz Xav., b. 1849 in Bensen, Westfalen
Deutsch, Joseph, b. 1853 in Trier

Figel, Michael, b. 1845 in Hundersingen, Württemberg

Frey, Karl, b. 1860 in Sulz, Bayern

Ganster, Jakob, b. 1850 in Pries, Schleswig-Holstein

Giehl, Johann, b. 1867 in Hochspeyer, Bayern

Graf, Heinrich, b. 1855 in Aachen

Graß (Gras), Karl, b. 1847 in Salzig, Rheinland

Hinderhofer, Bernhard, b. 1860 in Mendelbenien

Klemmer, Hermann, b. 1852 in Köln

Kohls, Joseph, b. 1844 in Varnes

Lehmann, Karl, b. 1844 in Temin

Michalowsky, Franz, b. 1866 in Dalwin, Westpreußen

Müller, Matthias, b. 1858 in Gey, Rheinland

Nunlist, Ursus, b. 1847 in Erlinsbad, Aargau

Pankau, August, b. 1846 in Virchau, Kulm Diocese, Poland (?)

Ritter, Lorenz, b. 1862 in Speyer

Rupp, Heinrich, b. 1859 in Kirchen, Trier Diocese (?)

Schilling, Johann, b. 1856 in Westfalen (?)

Splinter (Splinters), Heinrich, b. 1853 in Brandlecht, Hannover

Stamen, Joseph, b. 1859 in Bremen, Westfalen

Ständer, Georg, b. 1839 in Geismar, Frankenberg/Sachsen

Surich, Heinrich, b. 1828 in Bochum

Tholl, Joseph, b. 1851 in Laubach

Vollmayer, Adam, b. 1856 in Toledo, Ohio

Volz, Joseph, b. 1861 in Mankato, Minnesota

Wissing, Heinrich, b. 1843 in Schermbeck, Westfalen

Scholastics

Van Acken, Johann Bapt., b. 1869 in Lingen, Hannover

Kiefer, Johann, b. 1865 in Ittersdorf

Korte, Heinrich, b. 1865 in Lüchtringen, Westfalen

Visiting scholastics, who published accounts in Die katholischen Missionen

Hillig, Friedrich, b. 1866 in Rengsdorf, Rheinland

Kratz, Wilhelm, b. 1874 in Katzenelnbogen

2. Franciscan Nuns

Albrecht, Gabriele (Gabriel), b. 1860 in Meive, Preußen

Albrecht, Tharsilla, b. 1867 in Buffalo, New York

Becker, Vincentia (Vincent), b. 1859 in Siegburg, Rheinland

Benson, Renata, b. 1869 in Columbus, Ohio

Bernhardt, Bonaventura, b. 1852 in Borklum, Württemberg

Brecker, Perpetua, b. 1867 in Buffalo, New York

Burlinghoff, Estella, b. 1872 in Baden

Clous, Gertrude, b. 1874 in Columbus, Ohio

Diehl [?], Canisia, b. 1864 in Buffalo, New York

Dippold, Barbara, b. 1859 in Oberleinleitern, Bayern

Dreckmann, Adelheid, b. 1840 in Recklinghausen

Edelbrock, Euphrasia, b. 1843 in Havixbeck

Enders, Petra, b. 1865 in Wiesau, Bayern

Esser, Conradine, b. 1844 in Stolzheim

Fallon, Alcantara, b. 1860 in Columbus (Worthington?), Ohio

Fickers, Romana, b. 1877 in Lingen/Ems, Hannover

Frank, Raphaele (Raphael), b. 1860 in Buffalo, New York

Friol, Antonine, b. 1862 in Buffalo, New York

Fritz, Laurentia, b. 1860 in Buffalo, New York

Gangloff (Ganghoff), Sylvester, b. 1870 in Buffalo, New York

Geisenhof, Virginia, b. 1868 in Buffalo, New York

Geuting (Genting), Hilaria, b. 1862 in Anholt, Westfalen

Gülker, Cypriana, b. 1849 in Raesfeld, Westfalen

Haas, Michaela (Michaele), b. 1868 in Buffalo, New York

Hardy, Hildegard (Hildegarde), b. 1858 in Buffalo, New York

Harter, Fidelis, b. 1860 in Hamburg, New York

Hartmann, Walburga, b. 1863 in Sharpsburgh, Pennsylvania

Hemmert, Baptista, b. 1866 in Rimlingen, Elsaß

Hemmert, Johanna, b. 1864 in Rimlingen

Hofmayr [?], Sabina (Sabine), b. 1876 in Buffalo, New York

Homey, Humilis, b. 1881 in Thulenbrock near Bottrop

Howard, Norberta, b. 1868 in Buffalo, New York

Kealy (Koely), Bonifacia (Bonifatia), b. 1864 in Carlton, Ireland

Kessler, Ludovica, b. 1860 in Logan (Lancaster?), Ohio

Leczkowski (Leozkowski, Leozkowsky), Ida, b. 1855 in Rosenberg, Preußen

Lorenz, Odilia, b. 1874 in Irschenbach, Bayern

Lutz, Innocentia, b. 1879 in Lancaster, New York

McGovern (Govern), Alexia, b. 1869 in Fulda (East Union?), Ohio

McMullen, Agatha, b. 1869 in Ireland (?) (Glasgow, Scotland?)

Metzger, Catharina (Katharina, Catherine), b. 1862 in Junction City, Ohio

Miller, Aquina, b. 1864 in Carrollton, Kentucky

Mühlen, Martha, b. 1845 in Mönchen-Gladbach

Müller (Mueller), Francisca (Franziska), b. 1879 in Buffalo, New York

Nienhaus, Adelgonde (Adelgonda), b. 1867 in Buffalo, New York
Niner, Ludgardis, b. 1863 in Jackson, Ohio
Paessens, Pudentiana, b. 1842 in Keppeln (Capellen?)
Phimmes (Thimmes), Angelica (Angelika), b. 1876 in Lancaster, Ohio
Preis, Elisabeth (Elizabeth), b. 1857 in Gebhartsreutz (Gebardsreuth?), Bayern
Ruff, Martina, b. 1861 in Stundweiler, Elsaß
Scheu, Valencia (Valentia), b. 1866 in Krefeld
Schlaghecken (Schlaghecker), Kostka, b. 1850 in Bienen-Haldern near Rees
Schmidt (Schmitt), Salesia, b. 1859 in Quincy, Illinois
Schulte, Rosalia, b. 1858 in Olfen, Westfalen
Serries, Leopoldine, b. 1845 in Diestedde, Westfalen
Shea, Lioba, b. 1869 in Columbus, Ohio
Stabell, Fabiana, b. 1866 in Buehl, Unter-Elsaß
Stockmann, Lucy (Lucie), 1852 in Mettingen, Westfalen
Sturtzer (Stürtzer), Mercedes, b. 1879 in Buffalo, New York
Terheggen, Ludgera, b. 1874 in Buffalo, New York
Uilheim (Nehlein), Desideria, b. 1865 in Grossheubach
Wagner, Genevieve, b. 1864 in Buffalo, New York
Walter, Bruno, b. 1873 in Phillipsburg, Baden
Wessels, Modesta, b. 1877 in Eversum near Olfen
Witzel, Crescentia, b. 1861 in Buffalo, New York

Notes

1. The Founding of the Mission Schools and the Early Years, 1886–1890

1. Enochs (1995), 22. In 1879 Red Cloud, along with other principal chiefs, repeated this demand to the Indian agent: Olson (1965), 268.

2. Archives of the German Jesuit Province, Munich, *Missionarsbriefe*, America septentr. 1, Leßmann.

3. Archives of the German Jesuit Province, Munich, *Missionarsbriefe*, America septentr. 1, Leßmann.

4. Stella Niagara Archives, Mason manuscript, ch. 14, 3.

5. Pers. comm. Hildegardis Schäfer, O.S.F., 26 May 2003; cf. Carroll (2000), especially 70–79.

6. Pers. comm., Fr. Klaus Schatz, S.J., 15 April 2002.

7. Digmann (1909–1911), 99–102. Archives of the German Jesuit Province, Munich, *Missionarsbriefe*, America septentr. 1, Leßmann.

8. Marquette Archives, SFM Records, microfilm reel 2, Provincial's Visitation Book.

9. Until the 1920s: Ostermann (1991), 5.

10. Marquette Archives, BCIM Records, microfilm reel 20.

11. Archives of the German Jesuit Province, Munich, *Missionarsbriefe*, America septentr. 1, Leßmann.

12. Archives of the German Jesuit Province, Munich, *Hist. dom.* 1885–1888, *Historia Domus et Missionis St. Francisci* 1886–1887.

13. Archives of the German Jesuit Province, Munich, *Missionarsbriefe*, America septentr. 2, Van Rossum. In general: McKevitt (1993).

14. Pers. comm., C. F. Feest, 26 Nov. 1998; see also Feest (1999).

2. Ghost Dance, Wounded Knee, and the Aftermath, 1890–1891

1. Marquette Archives, SFM Jesuit Papers, microfilm reel 5, Perrig diary, 26 Sept. 1890. For reference to Christ, see also Mooney (1991), 820.

2. Perrig diary, 23 Nov. 1890.

3. Perrig diary, 3 Dec., 5 Dec. 1890.

4. Marquette Archives, HRM Jesuit Papers, microfilm reel 12, Digmann, History of St. Francis Mission, 24; Perrig diary, 4 Dec. 1890.

5. Stella Niagara Archives, Mason manuscript, ch. 14, 24 (emphasis in the original).

6. Utley (1963) 231–37. The following details are from Perrig diary, 29 Dec., 30 Dec. 1890. Black Elk, the later catechist, furnished his author Neihardt with a detailed description of the gunfight and his role in it: DeMallie (1984), 276–81, Neihardt (1988), 263–69.

7. Quote from Paula (1911), 130–33. The following sisters and Jesuits were at Holy Rosary at this time: Kostka Schlaghecken, Alcantara Fallon, Elisabeth Preis, Walburga Hartmann, Crescentia Witzel, Laurentia Fritz, Katharina Metzger, Hilaria Geuting, Vincent Becker, Salesia Schmidt (Stella Niagara Archives, Mason manuscript, ch. 14, insert at pg. 28), Fr. Johann Jutz, Fr. Emil Perrig, and Brs. Georg Ständer, Lorenz Ritter, Michael Figel, Ursus Nunlist, Hermann Klemmer, and Heinrich Splinter, or Joseph Deutsch (Archive SJ, Munich, *Catalogus Provinciae Germaniae Societatis Jesu*, 1891).

8. Stella Niagara Archives, Mason manuscript, ch. 14, 26–27.

9. Mason (1935), 369–70; Stella Niagara Archives, Mason manuscript, ch. 14, 28–29.

10. Perrig diary, 31 Dec. 1890, 2 Jan. 1891. There were altogether 38 wounded Indians housed in the Episcopal church, and 13 in the military hospital, among them 4 men: Utley (1963), 235.

11. Perrig diary, 4 Jan. 1891.

12. Perrig diary, 9 Jan., 10 Jan. 1891. For a period of time, a rescued baby was cared for by the sisters and the wife of a scout at Holy Rosary: Flood (1995), 60–61; cf. Carroll (2000), 92–93.

13. Stella Niagara Archives, Mason manuscript, ch. 14, 26–27.

14. The following description of the events according to Perrig diary, 30 Dec. 1890 to 31 Jan. 1891.

15. Perrig diary, 31 Jan. 1891.

16. The letter to the editor is printed in Foley (2002), 96–99, with Craft's response; Stella Niagara Archives, Mason manuscript, ch. 14, 32–35, with letter of reply by Jutz of 2 Feb. 1891.

17. The following according to Perrig diary, 12 Dec. to 24 Dec. 1890.

3. Catholic Community Structures versus Government Policies, 1891–1900

No notes.

4. Outlook into the Twentieth Century

1. Archive SJ, Munich, *Missionarsbriefe*, America septentr. 2, Lindebner.

2. For a compilation of Buechel's letters and articles from the mission, as well as descriptions of his life and work, see Kreis (2004).

3. Büchel (1930), slightly revised, reprinted as Büchel (1955); cf. Markowitz (1987), 124–26.

4. See the sharp criticism that has also been issued outside of the United States by, for example, Tim A. Giago in Bolz (1986, 179), Rostkowski (1998, 211), and, for additional reproaches, Vecsey (1999), 68–69.

5. See the interviews in Archambault (1995). Bucko (1988), for example, reports on the incorporation of traditional elements in parish festivities.

6. Vecsey (1999), 43. For Black Elk, see especially Steltenkamp (1996), Archambault (1998). On inculturation, see the inculturation project of the Catholic diocese of Rapid City, founded in 1990: http://www.rapidcitydiocese.org/Ministries/Inculturation.htm.

Section 1: From the Chronicles of the Missions and from the Annual Reports of the Sisters of St. Francis of Penance and Christian Charity

1. This document is a copy of the house chronicle that the individual mothers superior were required to keep. In the nineteenth century the following general principles governed the keeping of the chronicles: missteps and disputes were not to be recorded, given that the texts could "fall into the hands of strangers or find their way into public archives"; in addition, "extensive reflections and ascetical considerations" could "have an unfavorable effect." By contrast, the following were to be recorded: special events with respect to religious life, changes in the number of personnel, and statistical information about the activities of the order. All of this was to be done faithfully and by providing precise dates and names. ("Anleitung zur Führung der Hauschronik," Nonnenwerth Archives). The chronicles were copied for the head of the order (subsequently also for the publication of excerpts in the general annual chronicles). This document is one such copy, here produced for the head of the European province, ending with a brief reference to the Ghost Dance troubles in 1891. This copy probably dates from that year.

2. The introductory section is part of a general overview that, however, was not expanded on, at least not in this version. What follows on the subsequent pages of the document is an assembly of a variety of texts: extracts from a report about the school, edifying stories about illness and dying, references to "heathenish" manners and customs, and an account of church events leading up to the year 1897, accompanied by a final note that suggests that the entire document was produced for readers outside the mission. Mother General Camilla Schweden's visit took place in 1893 (see doc. 1.7).

3. *Affenliebe*, a colloquial expression to refer to the exaggerated love displayed by

some parents toward their children, also to signify a nonviolent upbringing. The presumably blind adoration and doting love exhibited by adult apes toward their offspring became symbolic of this form of child rearing.—Trans.

4. This part of the house chronicle, which covers the initial years of the mission, is a copy of the original kept at Holy Rosary. It illustrates the kinds of changes that were made even when such copies were produced. For example, the description of the Ghost Dance in the copied version does not contain all the details provided in the original with respect to the dancers. Conversely, the subsequent years of the original house chronicle, until 1895, present only spare information regarding personnel, organization of the mission, and edifying events among the community of sisters, in contrast to the more comprehensive accounts related here. From 1896 to 1900 the chronicles were evidently not kept at all. Consequently, in this part of the collection of documents Holy Rosary is only represented with this chronicle.

5. The handwritten original does not contain the following sentence beginning with "These jerkins." Instead, it continues with: "The self-made substances for these ridiculously superstitious hieroglyphs, figures of animals, or paintings, are rather radiant, dried paints mixed with grease. With this precious mixture the figures of these artificial products were applied [to the shirts] so generously, in keeping with their taste, that their outlines were clearly visible even from a distance of more than one hundred [feet?]. There could be seen powerful . . . ." (Marquette Archives, HRM Series 2/1).

6. This version of the house chronicle covers the period from the beginning of the school year in 1894 until the year 1905, here reprinted to 1900. With respect to volume, content, and style, it follows the pattern of the chronicles of the later years. The example of the visit of the bishop in 1897 allows for a comparison between differing accounts about the same event, that is, between the printed annual report (doc. 1.5) and the letter printed in *Die katholischen Missionen* (doc. 2.21).

7. An old German Marian hymn.—Trans.

8. That year a printed annual report appeared for the first time. For the visit of the bishop at St. Francis see doc. 1.5, endnote 6. *Jahresbericht 1897 der Genossenschaft der Schwestern vom hl. Franziskus zu Heythuizen*, Druck Gebrüder Habbel, Regensburg, 24–25.

9. In addition to the excerpts or summaries from the house chronicles, the annual reports frequently contained letters written to the head of the order. M. Ludmilla Birckman was mother general and Fr. Digmann, superior at St. Francis Mission. *Jahresbericht 1898 der Genossenschaft der Schwestern vom hl. Franziskus zu Heythuizen*, Druck Gebrüder Habbel, Regensburg, 4–6.

10. This is a slight variation on a German idiom, connoting that nothing is as serious as it first seems.—Trans.

11. *Jahresbericht 1899 der Genossenschaft der Schwestern vom hl. Franziskus zu Heythuizen,* Druck Gebrüder Habbel, Regensburg, 4–8. According to the introductory comment of the author of this document, the addressee and head of the order, Mother General Ludmilla Birckman, had visited St. Francis Mission along with her predecessor M. Camilla Schweden in 1893.

12. The implication is that by being a heathen, Six Hands' soul is considered to be blind, and so, apparently, are his eyes.—Trans.

13. Leopoldine Serries, mother superior.

14. See note 13.

15. Here reference is made to a German Christmas tradition, where treats are first hung on the tree for decoration and then taken off later to be distributed as gifts.—Trans.

16. Probably a reference to Jesus appearing among his disciples. "Jesus . . . stood among them" (Lk. 24.36, Jn. 20.19).—Trans.

17. Probably Sr. Norberta Howard.

18. The addressee is Mother General Ludmilla Birckman. *Jahresbericht 1900 der Genossenschaft der Schwestern vom hl. Franziskus zu Heythuizen,* Druck Gebrüder Habbel, Regensburg, 5–7.

19. After Mt. 6.33: "But seek first his kingdom and his righteousness, and all these things shall be yours as well."—Trans.

20. "Rejoice, when many make false claims about you on my account." Probably after Mt. 5.11.—Trans.

21. *Jahresbericht 1900 der Genossenschaft der Schwestern vom hl. Franziskus zu Heythuizen,* Druck Gebrüder Habbel, Regensburg, 38–42. This annual report includes excerpts from letters whose authors and addressees remain unnamed.

22. *Jahresbericht 1901 der Genossenschaft der Schwestern vom hl. Franziskus zu Heythuizen,* Druck Gebrüder Habbel, Regensburg, 38–23. This report describes, as does doc. 2.24, the situation at the missions toward the end of the year 1900, at a time when federal financing in accordance with the contract school model had ceased and the subsequent agreement of financing the missions with revenues from the tribal funds had not yet been negotiated. Hence this text was included as the last document for this phase of the mission schools.

23. *Klingelbeutel,* a bag with a bell, attached to a stick, with which a sacristan collected contributions from the churchgoers.—Trans.

Section 2: News and Reports taken from the Journal *Die katholischen Missionen*

1. *Die katholischen Missionen,* vol. 14 (1886), 197–200. The names of the three founding sisters, Kostka Schlaghecken, Rosalia Schulte, and Alcantara Fallon, are

referred to in doc. 1.1. The author of this letter is most likely their mother superior, Sr. Kostka Schlaghecken; the addressee is the mother general, M. Alphonsa Houben.

2. Here and elsewhere the German *Hütte* and *Hütten* are translated as "hut" and "huts," respectively, indicating an unspecified dwelling with one floor.—Trans.

3. *Zwieback*, literally, "twice baked."—Trans.

4. *Die katholischen Missionen*, vol. 15 (1887), 19–22. The introduction by the editors of the journal mentions two letters, but in the printed version they appear as one, again addressed to M. Alphonsa Houben.

5. *Rennthierheerden*, "reindeer herds," most probably a reference to elk.—Trans.

6. *Iltis*, "polecat."—Trans.

7. *Die katholischen Missionen*, vol. 15 (1887), 66–67. Superior Fr. Perrig provides additional details about the founding of St. Francis (compare docs. 1.1, 2.1). There is nothing known about the author and addressee of the second letter. It was probably also written by Sr. Kostka Schlaghecken to M. Alphonsa Houben.

8. *Die katholischen Missionen*, vol. 16 (1888), 258.

9. *Die katholischen Missionen*, vol. 19 (1891), 44–47. For this article, which appeared in the February edition of 1891, the editors of *Die katholischen Missionen* assembled a number of sources: at least one letter by the superior of St. Francis, Fr. Digmann; one report by the American press, without indication of the source, about the negotiation attempt on the part of Fr. Jutz, superior of Holy Rosary, at the beginning of December 1890; an editorial about this topic in the newspaper *Express*; an extensive review of the role of negotiator played by Jesuit Fr. de Smet in the year 1868; a quote from *Christliche Woche* of Buffalo, N.Y.; and telegraph reports about a massacre and an alleged uprising. The original of Fr. Digmann's letter of 4 Nov. 1890 has been preserved, which is rather atypical. A side-by-side comparison with the published version reveals that the editors made only stylistic changes (Archive SJ, Munich, *Missionarsbriefe*, O III 58).

10. *Büffel, Hirsche und Böcke*, "buffalo, elk, and pronghorns."—Trans.

11. The following quotes are translated from the German.—Trans.

12. Instead of retranslating this passage into English, here the original is quoted as published in Hiram M. Chittenden and Alfred T. Richardson, eds., *Life, Letters and Travels of Father Pierre-Jean de Smet, S. J., 1801–1873 . . . . with sketches of the country from St. Louis to Puget Sound and the Altrabasca*, vol. 3 (New York, 1905), 921. We are grateful to John Waide, university archivist at Catholic University of St. Louis, for providing us with a copy of this letter. See also note 68.—Trans.

13. *Die katholischen Missionen*, vol. 19 (1891), 64–67. This article, published in March 1891, draws on the following sources: a characterization of Chief Sitting Bull by Bishop Marty, the founder of the two missions in South Dakota; a descrip-

tion of the Wounded Knee massacre based on American newspaper reports; accounts of the role and the fate of Fr. Craft in the course of the events surrounding Wounded Knee; and a description by Fr. Jutz of the massacre and the subsequent unrest at Pine Ridge written for the German language newspaper *Milwaukee Columbia*. On 31 December 1890, Fr. Jutz wrote a letter in German to Fr. Stephan, the head of the Bureau of Catholic Indian Missions in Washington, in which he—probably for the first time in writing—describes his experiences immediately following the massacre (Marquette Archives and Special Collections, Microfilms, BCIM roll 20, published in: K. M. Kreis, "*Alles ist im vollsten Kriegstumult*").

14. Quote is translated from the German.—Trans.

15. Bracketed comment in the original.

16. Quote is translated from the German.—Trans.

17. *Die katholischen Missionen*, vol. 19 (1891), 157–59, 186–91. The subheadings were added by this editor. The description of the visit to the dance ground for the Ghost Dance is probably that of a sister already referred to in doc. 1.3. Jutz describes his negotiation attempt in greater detail in this document than in doc. 2.6. In 1918 Jutz published several articles about his recollections of these events and their causes, such as in the German language publication *Central Blatt and Social Justice*, in *Canisius Monthly*, the journal of the Jesuit college at Buffalo, N.Y., where he spent the last years of his life, and in *Woodstock Letters*, the journal of the American Jesuits. The report presented here was written a few months after the events (published in August 1891) and is more detailed than those published later.

18. Although the events are in the main known—as a result of our previous communication—our readers nonetheless will be interested in learning about them in context and in greater detail through this report, which was especially composed for them by an eyewitness. [Note in the original.]

19. Possibly a reference to one of the government's beef camps.

20. See note 19.

21. *Die katholischen Missionen*, vol. 20 (1892), 16–19. The year of this congress is 1891. Although the first congress took place on Standing Rock Reservation, Fr. Digmann and Fr. Perrig, along with the Lakota delegations from their missions, were nonetheless actively involved in the events. This article is based on accounts by both superiors.

22. *Die katholischen Missionen*, vol. 20 (1892), 256–57. This report about the second congress, which took place on the Cheyenne River Reservation, was included because it contains the history behind the first large congress held at St. Francis (doc. 2.11).

23. *Die katholischen Missionen*, vol. 21 (1893), 132–33.

24. *Die katholischen Missionen*, vol. 21 (1893), 225–30. Mr. Hillig, a Jesuit scholastic from Cleveland, Ohio, accompanied the bishop on this journey to the congress (see also doc. 2.13).

25. A reference to a dog by that name featured in the fable *"Der Hund"* by the eighteenth-century German poet Christian Fürchtegott Gellert.—Trans.

26. *Die katholischen Missionen*, vol. 22 (1894), 118–19.

27. *Die katholischen Missionen*, vol. 22 (1894), 212–13. The visit took place at the beginning of July 1898, in connection with the congress, about which also Mr. Hillig reported (doc. 2.11).

28. *Die katholischen Missionen*, vol. 23 (1895), 49–55.

29. We have repeatedly published quite delightful news about St. Francis Mission at the Rosebud Agency in South Dakota. The main activity, which even on its own justifies holding out good hopes for the future, concerns the schools; and that it is certainly worth the effort to instruct the poor Indians in the faith, is manifested through our articles about the congresses of the Catholic Sioux (compare vol. [20] 1892 and [21] 1893). But mission work among the pagan Indians and those educated in the government schools is almost hopeless. Yet the missionaries try there as well to save at least individual souls. The difficulties that are associated with this are illustrated by the following, true-to-life description of such a missionary excursion, in which case one has to wonder, however, how the missionary amidst these disconsolate experiences retained such good humor. [Note in the original.]

30. A picture bible. *Bilder-Bibel*, first published by Verlag Herder in 1861, with various reprints until 1927. It consisted of 40 loose pages of lithographed and colored representations of events relating to both the Old and New Testament by Joseph Heinemann, with a short biblical history by Dr. I. Schuster. Through time, they were available either as loose pages, loose-leaf collections in linen folders, laminated, or mounted in oak frames. Pers. comm., Burkhard Zimmermann, Verlag Herder, 15 March 2005.—Trans.

31. Literally, "Old Tent Peg." Here and elsewhere a reference to the Oglala Sioux Picket Pin. See P. Digmann, St. Francis Mission, 10 May 1898, in *Mittheilungen aus der Deutschen Provinz*, vol. 1 (1897–1899), 348–52.

32. *Die katholischen Missionen*, vol. 23 (1895), 112–14.

33. *Die katholischen Missionen*, vol. 23 (1895), 163–64.

34. After Gen. 3.4.—Trans.

35. After Mt. 19.27, Mt. 19.29, and Mt. 19.11, respectively.—Trans.

36. *Die katholischen Missionen*, vol. 24 (1896), 258–59.

37. Reference is made to the 6th congress.

38. *Die katholischen Missionen*, vol. 24 (1896), 279.

39. The article referred to, which is not included in this collection of documents, carries the headline "*Die Gefahr der katholischen Indianerschulen: Protestantische Unduldsamkeit*" (The danger facing the Catholic Indian schools: Protestant intolerance) and expresses the fear that the federal government was determined to "make" Indian schools "impossible through the withdrawal of annual subsidies granted up to this point, and to convert the so-called free nondenominational *contract* schools to nonreligious state schools *(Public Schools)*. . . . Here we already have the first signs of a culture war, in which also the North American Church will not be spared." Additional signs of this "Kulturkampf" are cited (vol. 24 [1896], 187).

40. A slight variation on a German idiom, connoting that nothing is as serious as it first seems.—Trans.

41. *Die katholischen Missionen*, vol. 25 (1897), 115–17.

42. The petition quoted here in English, rather than retranslated from the German, is dated 16 September 1896, Standing Rock (parentheses in the original). It was circulated among several of the reservations, receiving some minor modifications along the way as well as several hundred signatures. In March 1897, John Grass (not "Groß") presented the petition plus signatures to J. A. Stephan, the director of the Bureau of Catholic Indian Missions (Marquette University Archives, Special Collections and Archives, Microfilm, BCIM rolls 25 and 26).

43. This section of the petition is translated from the German, as it is not contained in any of the available versions. (See previous note.)

44. *Die katholischen Missionen*, vol. 25 (1897), 230–31. The original article quotes virtually the entire text from the "Report of Superintendent of St. Francis School, Rosebud Reservation," by Fr. Florentine Digmann, S.J., in *Annual Report of the Commissioner of Indian Affairs, 1896* (Washington DC 1896), 299–300, in German translation. Digmann's account pertains to the year 1895. Rather than retranslate the text from the German, the original English-language report is offered here. The article continues, in general, with a discussion of the current problems related to the financing of the Catholic Indian schools. It laments that the government, "pressed and persuaded by an extremist anti-clerical party, in-so-far as it is dependent on it, was engaging in the complete oppression of the Catholic Indian schools." In support of the Catholic position, a speech by Senator Vest, a Protestant, is reprinted (although not here), in which he lauds the Indian schools managed by the Jesuits (vol. 25 [1897], 231).

45. *Die katholischen Missionen*, vol. 25 (1897), 275–76. Compare docs. 1.4 and 1.5.

46. *Die katholischen Missionen*, vol. 26 (1897/98), 91–92.

47. *Rüben*, "turnips."—Trans.

48. *Die katholischen Missionen*, vol. 26 (1897/98), 150–54, 177–80, 199–203, 220–23. This series of articles summarizes the reporting from previous years and refers to contributions to the journal about neighboring missions, supplements them with literature on the subject, and defines the self-image of the missionaries. This piece focuses on the "apostles" Fr. Desmet (Jean-Pierre de Smet) and Bishop Martin Marty (d. 1896), who are seen as continuing the tradition of the earlier Jesuit missionaries in North and South America.

49. Rather than retranslate the excerpts from Catlin's work that follow, the original English text is quoted instead. George Catlin, *North American Indians, Being Letters and Notes on Their Manners, Customs, and Conditions, Written during Eight Years' Travel amongst the Wildest Tribes of Indians in North America, 1832–1839*, 2 vols. (Edinburgh, 1926), 1:233–36. The bracketed word "numerous" in this sentence was omitted by the editors of *Die katholischen Missionen*.—Trans.

50. Parenthetical word added by the editors of *Missionen*.—Trans.

51. The editors of *Missionen* substituted "the Indians" for "them."—Trans.

52. The editors of *Missionen* substituted "*Rothäute*" (redskins) for "Indians."—Trans.

53. The editors of *Missionen* substituted "the tribes" for "these people."—Trans.

54. Text contained in this bracket and those that follow in this paragraph was added by the editors of *Missionen*.—Trans.

55. The German translation in *Missionen* differs slightly from the original. Here the excerpt quoted is from the English original. Charles J. Kappler, comp., *Indian Affairs: Laws and Treaties*, vol. 2, *Treaties* (Washington DC, 1904), 1002–3.—Trans.

56. Quote is translated from the German.—Trans.

57. Quote is translated from the German.—Trans.

58. This and the following quotes from Kurth are translated from the German.—Trans.

59. A settlement or colony of South American Indians converted and governed by the Jesuits. Implicit in the term "reduction" is the idea of having "reduced" the natives to Christianity by their preaching.—Trans.

60. References to the Flathead Indians, the Pend D'Oreilles, and Coeurs D'Alène, respectively.

61. See note 59.

62. We were unable to positively identify this geographic designation. Possibly a reference to Big Sioux River.

63. Lam. 4.4.—Trans.

64. Written is "*Klasse*," rather than *Rasse* (race).—Trans.

65. Quote is translated from the German.—Trans.

66. "*Büffel, Hirsch, Bock, Großhorn und Reh.*"—Trans.

67. Quoted passages from the correspondence between Major-General Stanley and Archbishop Purcell are translated from the German.—Trans.

68. Instead of retranslating this passage into English, here the original is quoted as published in Hiram M. Chittenden and Alfred T. Richardson, eds., *Life, Letters and Travels of Father Pierre-Jean de Smet, S. J., 1801–1873 . . . . with sketches of the country from St. Louis to Puget Sound and the Altrabasca*, vol. 3 (New York, 1905), 921. The German translation in *Die katholischen Missionen* differs slightly from the original text.—Trans. See also note 12.

69. References are to vols. 1, 3, and 9, respectively.

70. Quote translated from the German.—Trans.

71. The corresponding volumes for the years stated are 8, 14, 15, and 21 through 25, respectively.

72. This and the following quote from the newspaper are translated from the German.—Trans.

73. *Die katholischen Missionen*, vol. 29 (1900/01), 207–10. The author, Mr. Wilhelm Kratz, worked as prefect in the school at St. Francis from June 1900 until May 1902.

74. Quote is translated from the German.—Trans.

75. Quote is translated from the German.—Trans.

76. A modified version of Job 19.21.—Trans.

Bibliography

Sources, Archived Material

Provinzarchiv der Franziskanerinnen von der Buße und der christlichen Liebe, Mutterhaus, Rheininsel Nonnenwerth, Remagen:

Chroniken (Dok. 1.1–1.4).

Jahresberichte 1897–1901 der Genossenschaft der Schwestern vom hl. Franziskus zu Heythuizen. Regensburg: Druck Gebr. Habbel (Dok. 1.5–1.10).

Institut für Missionswissenschaft, Westfälische Wilhelms-Universität Münster:

Die katholischen Missionen, Jg. 1886–1900/1901 (Dok. 2.1–2.24).

Special Collections and University Archives, Marquette University, Milwaukee, Wisconsin:

Digmann, P. Florentine. "History of St. Francis Mission, 1886–1922." Ca. 1922 (Typescript, 1985). HRM Series 7/1.

Perrig, Aemilius. "Diary, 1886–1894." HRM Series 7 (Original), 7/1 (Typescript).

"Chronik der Holy Rosary Mission." HRM Series 2/1 (Photocopy of original).

Catalogus Provinciae Germaniae, 1887–1901.

Archives of the Sisters of St. Francis of Holy Name Province, Inc., Stella Niagara NY:

Mason, S. Liguori. "History of the American Foundation, 1874–1924." Part 4, "Among the Sioux Indians" (Unpublished manuscript).

Secondary Literature

Ackermans, Gian. 1997. The History of the Congregation in the Nineteenth Century. In Ackermans, Gian, Ostermann, Ursula, Serbacki, Mary, eds., *Called by God's Goodness: A History of the Sisters of St. Francis of Penance and Christian Charity in the Twentieth Century.* Stella Niagara NY: Sisters of St. Francis of Penance and Christian Charity, pp. 1–13.

Adams, David Wallace. 1995. *Education for Extinction: American Indians and the Boarding School Experience, 1875–1928.* Lawrence: University Press of Kansas.

Archambault, Marie Therese. 1995. "'Back to Back': Roman Catholicism among the Brulé at St. Francis Mission, South Dakota." M.A. thesis. Department of Religious Studies, University of Colorado.

———. 1998. *A Retreat with Black Elk: Living in the Sacred Hoop*. Cincinnati OH: St. Anthony Messenger Press.

Barry, Colman J. 1953. *The Catholic Church and German Americans*. Milwaukee: Bruce.

Black Elk DeSersa, Esther, et al. 2000. *Black Elk Lives: Conversations with the Black Elk Family*. Lincoln: University of Nebraska Press.

Bolz, Peter. 1986. *Ethnische Identität und kultureller Widerstand: Die Oglala-Sioux der Pine-Ridge-Reservation in South Dakota*. Frankfurt/Main, New York: Campus.

Bosch, Aloysius. 1893. Indians in Council. *Sacred Heart Messenger*, pp. 876–86.

Brady, Charles A. 1969. *The First Hundred Years: Canisius College, 1870–1970*. Buffalo NY: Canisius College.

Buechel, Eugene. 1930. The Lazy Indian—A Myth. *Calumet*, February, p. 2.

———. 1955. Give Him Time. *Calumet* 32, no. 1 (February): 14–15.

Bucko, Raymond A. 1988. The St. Francis Community New Year's Dance. *European Review of Native American Studies* 2, no. 2: 25–34.

Bunse, F. J. Erinnerungen, and P. Johannes Jutz. 1924–26. *Mitteilungen aus den Deutschen Provinzen* 10: 57–60, 86–92.

———. Father John Jutz. 1924. *Woodstock Letters* 53, no. 3: 391–402.

Carroll, James T. 2000. *Seeds of Faith: Catholic Indian Boarding Schools*. New York: Garland.

Deloria, Vine, Jr. 1970. *Custer Died for Your Sins: An Indian Manifesto*. New York: Avon.

DeMallie, Raymond J. 1984. *The Sixth Grandfather: Black Elk's Teachings Given to John G. Neihardt*. Lincoln: University of Nebraska Press.

Dolan, Jay P. 1992. *The American Catholic Experience: A History from Colonial Times to the Present*. Notre Dame IN: Notre Dame University Press.

Duratschek, Mary Claudia. 1947. *Crusading along Sioux Trails: A History of the Catholic Indian Missions of South Dakota*. Yankton SD: Grail.

Eberschweiler, Carl. 1900–1902. Brief vom 24. Febr. 1900. *Mitteilungen aus der Deutschen Provinz* 2: 140–41.

Enochs, Ross Alexander. 1995. *The Jesuit Mission to the Lakota Sioux: Pastoral Theology and Ministry, 1886–1945*. Kansas City: Sheed and Ward.

Feest, Christian F. 1990. Die unfreiwilligen Amerikaner. In Helga Lomosits and Paul Herbaugh, *Lakol Wokiksuye: Zur Geschichte der Plains von Little Bighorn bis Wounded Knee*. Wien: Jugend und Volk. (7 unpaginated pages)

———. 1998. *Beseelte Welten: Die Religionen der Indianer Nordamerikas*. Freiburg: Herder.

———. 1999. Männerwelt (Jagd, Krieg, Bünde). In Hessisches Landesmuseum Darmstadt, *Sitting Bull "Der letzte Indianer,"* pp. 50–54. Darmstadt.

Fitzgerald, Mary Clement. 1940. Bishop Marty and His Sioux Missions, 1876–1896. *South Dakota Historical Collections* 20: 523–58.

Flood, Renée Sansom. 1995. *Lost Bird of Wounded Knee: Spirit of the Lakota*. New York: Scribner.

Foley, Thomas W. 2002. *Father Francis M. Craft: Missionary to the Sioux*. Lincoln: University of Nebraska Press.

Galler, Robert W. 1994. A History of Red Cloud Indian School. M.A. thesis, University of South Dakota, Dept. of History.

———. 1998. A Triad of Alliances: The Roots of Holy Rosary Indian Mission. *South Dakota History* 28, no. 3: 144–60.

Goodale Eastman, Elaine. 1985. *Sister to the Sioux: The Memoirs, 1885–91*. Lincoln: University of Nebraska Press.

Green, Adriana Greci. 1992. German Missionary Participation during the Ghost Dance of 1890. *European Review of Native American Studies* 6, no. 1: 31–34.

Green, Jerry, ed. 1996. *After Wounded Knee: Correspondence of Major and Surgeon John Vance Lauderdale While Serving with the Army Occupying the Pine Ridge Indian Reservation, 1890–1891*. East Lansing: Michigan State University Press.

Grimm, Jacob, and Wilhelm Grimm, *Deutsches Wörterbuch*. 33 vols. Munich: Deutscher Taschenbuch Verlag, 1991.

Hilbert, Robert. 1987. Contemporary Catholic Mission Work among the Sioux. In Raymond DeMallie and Douglas R. Parks. *Sioux Indian Religion: Tradition and Innovation*, pp. 139–47. Norman: University of Oklahoma Press.

Hinderhofer, Bernhard. 1900–1902. Brief vom 29. Juni 1900 aus St. Francis Mission. *Mitteilungen aus der deutschen Provinz* 2: 225–26.

Hoxie, Frederick E. 2001. *A Final Promise: The Campaign to Assimilate the Indians, 1880–1920*. Lincoln: University of Nebraska Press.

Jensen, Richard E., R. Eli Paul, and John E. Carter. 1991. *Eyewitness at Wounded Knee*. Lincoln: University of Nebraska Press.

Jutz, John. 1918. Historic Data on the Causes of the Dissatisfaction among the Sioux Indians in 1890. *Woodstock Letters* 47: 313–27.

———. 1918–1919. Recollections of an Old Indian Missionary. *Canisius Monthly* 5: 16–24, 63–68, 143–49, 212–18, 263–67, 306–10.

Kreis, Karl Markus. 1998. Indianische Spiritualität und christlicher Glaube: Der Seher und Katechet Black Elk. *Orientierung* 62, no. 18: 196–200.

———. 2002. Indians Playing, Indians Praying: German Reports on Native Americans in Wild West Shows and Catholic Missions. In Colin G. Calloway, Gerd Germüunden, and Susanne Zantop, eds., *Germans and Indians: Fantasies, Encounters, Projections*, pp. 195–212. Lincoln: University of Nebraska Press, 2002.

———, ed. 2004. *Ein deutscher Missionar bei den Sioux-Indianern: Der Sprachforscher, Ethnologe und Sammler Eugen Büchel / Eugene Buechel (1874–1954)*. Dortmund: Fachhochschule.

Markowitz, Harvey. 1987. The Catholic Mission and the Sioux: A Crisis in the Early Paradigm. In Raymond DeMallie and Douglas R. Parks, *Sioux Indian Religion: Tradition and Innovation*, 113–37. Norman: University of Oklahoma Press.

———. 1992. "But Great Father, You Promised Us Blackrobes": The Origin Narrative of Saint Francis Mission. In *The Artist and the Missionary: A Native-American and Euro-American Cultural Exchange*, 11–21. Proceedings of the 1992 Plains Indian Seminar. Cody WY: Buffalo Bill Historical Center.

Mason, M. Liguori. 1935. *Mother Magdalen Daemen and Her Congregation*. Stella Niagara NY: Sisters of St. Francis of Penance and Christian Charity.

McKevitt, Gerald. 1993. "Faith Enters by the Ear": Missionary Linguistics in the Pacific Northwest. In Christopher Chapple, ed., *The Jesuit Tradition in Education and Missions*, pp. 242–53. Scranton PA: University of Scranton Press.

Mohr, Klaus H. 1999. Unmögliche Mission? Das Christentum, Sitting Bull und die Lakota. In Hessisches Landesmuseum Darmstadt, *Sitting Bull "Der letzte Indianer,"* pp. 62–65. Darmstadt.

Mooney, James. 1991. The Ghost-Dance Religion and the Sioux Outbreak of 1890. J. W. Powell, director, *Fourteenth Annual Report of the Bureau of Ethnology to the Secretary of the Smithsonian Institution, 1892–93*. Part 2. Washington: Government Printing Office; reprint, Lincoln: University of Nebraska Press.

Münster, M. Paula. 1964. *Mother Aloysia Lenders, 1859–1876: Fourth Superior General of the Sisters of Saint Francis of Penance and Christian Charity*. Heythuysen-Nonnenwerth, 1938; reprint, Stella Niagara NY: Sisters of St. Francis of Penance and Christian Charity.

Neihardt, John G. 1988. *Black Elk Speaks: Being the Life Story of a Holy Man of the Oglala Sioux*. Lincoln: University of Nebraska Press.

Olson, James C. 1965. *Red Cloud and the Sioux Problem*. Lincoln: University of Nebraska Press.

Ostermann, Ursula. 1991. *Mother Valesca Kluxen (1869–1952): Fragments of a Biography Based on Documents and Chronicles of the Congregation*. Lüdinghausen: Sisters of St. Francis of Penance and Christian Charity, Christ the King Province.

Paula, Maria. 1911. *In Nordamerika: Die Missionen der Franziskanerinnen von der Buße und christlichen Liebe (Heythuizen–Nonnenwerth)*. Trier: Paulinus.

Peterson, Susan C. 1983. "Holy Women" and Housekeepers: Women Teachers on South Dakota Reservations, 1885–1910. *South Dakota History* 13, no. 3: 245–60.

———. 1984. Challenging the Stereotypes: The Adaptation of the Sisters of St. Francis to South Dakota Indian Missions, 1885–1910. *Upper Midwest History* 4: 1–10.

———. 1985. A Widening Horizon: Catholic Sisterhoods on the Northern Plains, 1874–1910. *Great Plains Quarterly* 5: 125–32.

Powers, W. K. 1977. *Oglala Religion.* Lincoln: University of Nebraska Press.

Prucha, Francis Paul. 1979. *The Churches and the Indian Schools, 1888–1912.* Lincoln: University of Nebraska Press.

Reiß, Barbara. 1999. Sitting Bulls letzter Tag. In Hessisches Landesmuseum Darmstadt, *Sitting Bull "Der letzte Indianer,"* 103–7. Darmstadt.

Rosebud Educational Society. 1976. *Photo Album: St. Francis Mission, School and Community, 1886–1976.* St. Francis Mission SD.

Rostkowski, Joëlle. 1998. *La conversion inachevée: Les Indiens et le christianisme.* Paris: A. Michel.

Sialm, Placidus. 1921–23. P. Joseph Lindebner. *Mitteilungen aus der Deutschen Provinz* 9: 256–59.

Spack, Ruth. 2002. *America's Second Tongue: American Indian Education and the Ownership of English, 1860–1900.* Lincoln: University of Nebraska Press.

Steinmetz, Paul B. 1998. *Pipe, Bible, and Peyote among the Oglala Lakota: A Study in Religious Identity.* Syracuse NY: Syracuse University Press.

Steltenkamp, Michael F. 1993. *Black Elk: Holy Man of the Oglala.* Norman: University of Oklahoma Press.

———. 1996. Contemporary American Indian Religious Thinking and Its Relationship to the Christianity of Black Elk, Holy Man of the Oglala. In Sandra Yocum Mize and William L. Portier, eds., *American Catholic Traditions: Resources for Renewal,* pp. 29–52. Maryknoll NY: Orbis Books.

Stolzman, William. 1992. *The Pipe and Christ.* 4th ed. Chamberlain: Tipi Press.

Thiel, Mark. 1998. Catholic Sodalities among the Sioux, 1882–1910. *U.S. Catholic Historian* 16, no. 2: 56–77.

Thorpe, Cleata B. 1972. Education in South Dakota: Its First Hundred Years, 1861–1961. *South Dakota Historical Collections* 36: 205–444.

Tinker, George E. 1993. *Missionary Conquest: The Gospel and Native American Cultural Genocide.* Minneapolis: Fortress.

Utley, Robert M. 1963. *The Last Days of the Sioux Nation.* New Haven: Yale University Press.

Vecsey, Christopher. 1999. *Where the Two Roads Meet.* Notre Dame IN: University of Notre Dame Press.

Zens, M. Serena. 1940. The Educational Work of the Catholic Church among the Indians of South Dakota from the Beginning to 1935. *South Dakota Historical Collections* 20: 299–356.

Index of Persons